Where Is God?

WHERE IS GOD?

DIVINE ABSENCE IN THE HEBREW BIBLE

JOEL S. BURNETT

Fortress Press
Minneapolis

To Jamie, Hannah, and Wilson

WHERE IS GOD?
Divine Absence in the Hebrew Bible

Cover image: *Job*, Photo by Brian S. Utesch, Ph.D., Raleigh, N.C., www.brianuteschphotography.com
Cover design: Laurie Ingram
Book design: Douglas Schmitz

Library of Congress Cataloging-in-Publication Data
Burnett, Joel S., 1968-
  Where is God? : divine absence in the Hebrew Bible / Joel S. Burnett.
     p. cm.
  Includes bibliographical references and index.
  ISBN 978-0-8006-6297-4 (alk. paper)
  1. Bible. O.T.—Criticism, interpretation, etc. 2. Hidden God—Biblical teaching.
I. Title.
  BS1171.3.B87 2010
  231.7—dc22
                                        2009044520

The paper used in this publication meets the minimum requirements of American National Standard for Information Sciences—Permanence of Paper for Printed Library Materials, ANSI Z329.48-1984.

Manufactured in the U.S.A.

14 13 12 11 10   1 2 3 4 5 6 7 8 9 10

Contents

PREFACE

THE HEBREW BIBLE PRESENTS a complex collection of literary traditions attesting to ancient Israel's experience of its God. Reflection on that experience of the divine comes in various forms in the combination of narrative, poetic, and legal texts. Through those texts, the memory of past experience is shaped with implications for Israel's ongoing identity and for the continued understanding of Israel's God. In manifold perspective, the Hebrew Bible gives witness to a God whom human beings encounter in life in this world. Although God is the central and unifying figure of the Bible, God's presence in the Bible's pages is scarcely forced on human beings but is more often encountered or sought. Scenes of theophany or deliverance, while vivid and pivotal in their importance, are the exception in the Bible. God takes center stage only rarely. Often God seems absent and not always in a way that is troubling. Though celebrating divine presence, the Bible does not take it for granted.

Capturing the Hebrew Bible's balance of perspective in this regard is the aim of this book. The Bible declares Israel to be a people called into existence through God's appearance and involvement in human life. But most of the time in the biblical portrayal, Israel waits for God to act again, wonders whether God will appear, or simply goes about life with God at an apparent distance. Attention to the biblical status quo of God's silence and absence brings greater clarity to instances of God's vivid appearance in Scripture. It also sharpens the Bible's frequent depiction of the acute and painful experience of God's absence. This dark side of human experience, though integral to the Bible's depiction of the divine, often lacks the attention it merits.

My primary intention in writing this book is to give due attention to this neglected aspect of the biblical portrayal. In doing so, I hope to engage constructively the intellectual and cultural underpinnings of the biblical theme of God's absence. What ideas and assumptions lie behind this way of thinking about the divine? A lifelong fascination with belief in God and a curiosity about where people get their ideas about God form the autobiographical basis for this book. My assumption is that this curiosity holds for many others whose occupational demands do not allow time or opportunity for immersion into the relevant technical scholarship, let alone for mastering the linguistic and historical tools that facilitate answering such questions. Thus, I have written with the intent of making the relevant scholarship accessible to an educated general readership and have tried to confine to the notes most discussion of technical matters or current debate of interest to specialists (however, the discussion of personal names in chapter 2 becomes unavoidably technical at points).

I write as a participant in my academic field at a specific time in its development. As fellow participants recognize, recent decades have seen a resurgence of interest in the history of ideas and practices of ancient Israel's religion but also an accompanying separation of the history of Israelite religion as an area of study from theology both as a distinct discipline and an area of emphasis within biblical studies. Following a century in which modern biblical scholarship was dominated by the historical-critical method's exclusive attention to philological and historical aspects of the text, biblical studies during the last three decades has come to include a variety of literary, ideological, and social-scientific methods with the salutary effect of answering questions and exploring aspects of the biblical text long neglected by earlier studies. While this development has resulted in increased methodological specialization, and often necessarily so, it has also brought about a continued maturing of the field, in which historical interests merge with attention to social, ideological, and rhetorical dimensions of biblical texts as expressions of various interests and not only as records of past events. This maturation of the field also brings a perspective on the collection of documents and voices gathered in the Bible as a whole, or as the canon.

From out of this scholarly context, my operative assumption is that, given the Bible's nature as a complexity of documents produced in ancient times in languages other than our own, the more one knows about the languages, history, and culture that gave rise to the Bible, the better one is able to understand it and to relate to it in the terms of one's own day and circumstances. An important job of specialists in biblical studies, who have been given the leisure of devoting their professional lives to such pursuits, is to place into the hands of other readers of the Bible the insights and perspectives that emerge from current scholarly discussion and study of the biblical text. What I hope to offer in this book is a discussion of the biblical theme of God's absence that is based on a careful consideration of the Bible's language, history, and culture and that encourages further study, including theological reflection.

The O.T. sees God as active in space.

In writing this book, I have focused on facets of the topic that require attention, especially the basic ideas of divine–human relationships and how God is perceived to be present in the world in the Hebrew Bible's creation, wisdom, worship, prophetic, and narrative literature. I have chosen not to recapitulate the well-rehearsed scholarly observations regarding God's absence as a theme routinely covered in the study of much of the prophetic literature, apocalyptic, and briefer works of court narrative like the Joseph cycle in Genesis, Daniel 1–6, or the book of Esther.[1] Instead, I have focused on the most obvious aspect of the biblical motif, namely, its inherently spatial conception of divine–human relationships. Accordingly, after examining the basis of divine–human relationships in the Hebrew Bible, I focus on portions of the canon in which this spatial aspect of relationships to God serves as a basic idea.

While I occasionally use the confessional designations *Tanakh* (from Judaism) and Old Testament (from Christianity), I usually—having a broad audience in view—opt for the scholarly convention "Hebrew Bible," an academic construct that refers to literature common to both arrangements of Scripture. In keeping with the publisher's guidelines, when quoting the English translation of the biblical text, I cite the versification and translation of the New Revised Standard Version (NRSV) unless the context of discussion warrants my own rendering of the Hebrew into English—for example, in instances in which the divine name Yahweh is historically relevant and thus preferable to "the LORD," the standard translation in English Bibles.

ACKNOWLEDGMENTS

OVER THE COURSE OF developing the shape and contents of this book, I have benefited from many helpful conversations, both brief and lengthy. I especially wish to thank Christopher A. Rollston for provoking early thought about the book and its concept. I also thank Ryan Byrne, James Crenshaw, Terence E. Fretheim, Patrick D. Miller, and Samuel E. Balentine for feedback and suggestions of varying scope but all important and helpful. I owe particular thanks to Mark S. Smith for his very generous gift of time in helping me talk through and think through ideas for the book and its writing, for reading earlier drafts of what are now chapters 1, 3, and 4, and for offering extensive feedback that has improved the book significantly. Of course, any remaining errors or weaknesses are my own.

Thanks are due to my home institution, Baylor University and its College of Arts and Sciences and Department of Religion, for supporting my work on a daily basis and for a semester research leave and two summer sabbaticals that have made possible the completion of this book. I am grateful to my department colleagues for a congenial and supportive work environment, for the invitation to present the Department of Religion Annual Lecture (April 2004) on what has become this book's topic, and for their helpful feedback at that point and at many others along the way. I wish to express thanks to my graduate assistant, David Melvin, for various clerical and research tasks and to the excellent staff of the Baylor University Libraries, especially Janet Jasek, whose expertise and attention ensured the availability of resources beyond the extensive holdings of Baylor's libraries.

I also wish to express my appreciation to Seventh and James Baptist Church and St. Alban's Episcopal Church in Waco, Texas, for opportunities to speak on topics related to the book. These talks and the feedback received helped me think through how to communicate the subject matter beyond the language of specialization.

Chapter 2 is an edited version of an article, "Divine Absence in Biblical Personal Names," to appear in *These Are the Names: Studies in Jewish Onomastics* 5, ed. Aaron Demsky (Ramat Gan: Bar-Ilan University Press, forthcoming). Parts of another article, "The Question of Divine Absence in Israelite and West Semitic Religion," *Catholic Biblical Quarterly* 67 (2005): 215–35, have been incorporated into several chapters. Thanks to these publishers for granting permission for that material to appear here.

Last and most important, I thank my family for their cheerful support and inspiration while I have completed this work. My children, Hannah and Wilson, have been willing to share their dad with the writing of a book. My wife, Jamie, carefully proofread portions of the manuscript. As throughout our marriage, she has been a steady presence of encouragement and strength. I am grateful to my family for allowing me to integrate my scholarly pursuits into the life we share together. They have happily lived with me and the book during its writing, so I am glad to be able to dedicate it to them.

ABBREVIATIONS

AB	Anchor Bible
ABD	*The Anchor Bible Dictionary.* Edited by David Noel Freedman. 6 vols. New York: Doubleday, 1992
AEL	*Ancient Egyptian Literature.* M. Lichtheim. 3 vols. Berkeley, 1971–80
AION	*Annali dell'Istituto Orientale di Napoli*
AJSL	*American Journal of Semitic Languages and Literature*
AnBib	Analecta biblica
ANEP	*The Ancient Near East in Pictures Relating to the Old Testament.* Edited by J. B. Pritchard. Princeton, 1969
ANET	*Ancient Near Eastern Texts Relating to the Old Testament.* Edited by J. B. Pritchard. 3rd ed. Princeton, 1969
AnOr	Analecta orientalia
AOAT	Alter Orient und Altes Testament
AS	Assyriological Studies
ASTI	*Annual of the Swedish Theological Institute*
AuOr	*Aula orientalis*
BA	*Biblical Archaeologist*
BASOR	*Bulletin of the American Schools of Oriental Research*
BDB	Brown, F., S. R. Driver, and C. A. Briggs. *A Hebrew and English Lexicon of the Old Testament.* Oxford, 1907
BEATAJ	Beiträge zur Erforschung des Alten Testaments und des Antiken Judentums
BH	Biblical Hebrew
Bib	*Biblica*
BJRL	*Bulletin of the John Rylands University Library of Manchester*
BJS	Brandeis Judaic Studies
BTB	*Biblical Theology Bulletin*
BWANT	Beiträge zur Wissenschaft vom Alten und Neuen Testament

BWL	*Babylonian Wisdom Literature.* W. G. Lambert. Oxford, 1960; repr. Winona Lake, Ind.: Eisenbrauns, 1996
BZAW	Beihefte zur Zeitschrift für die alttestamentliche Wissenschaft
CAD	*The Assyrian Dictionary of the Oriental Institute of the University of Chicago.* Chicago, 1956–.
CAI	*A Corpus of Ammonite Inscriptions.* Walter E. Aufrecht. Lewston, 1989
CANE	*Civilizations of the Ancient Near East.* Edited by J. Sasson. 4 vols. New York, 1995
CBQ	*Catholic Biblical Quarterly*
CBQMS	Catholic Biblical Quarterly Monograph Series
CHANE	Culture and History of the Ancient Near East
CIS	*Corpus inscriptionum semiticarum*
ConBOT	Coniectanea biblica: Old Testament Series
COS	*The Context of Scripture.* Edited by W. W. Hallo and K. L. Younger. 3 vols. Leiden, 1997–2002
CurBS	*Currents in Research: Biblical Studies*
DDD	*Dictionary of Deities and Demons in the Bible.* Edited by K. van der Toorn, B. Becking, and P. W. van der Horst. 2nd ed. Leiden, 1999
DH	The Deuteronomistic History
DJD	Discoveries in the Judaean Desert
EDB	*Eerdmans Dictionary of the Bible.* Edited by D. N. Freedman. Grand Rapids, 2000.
EH	El-Hofra inscriptions. According to the edition, *Le sanctuaire punique d'El-Hofra à Constantine.* A. Berthier and R. Charlier. Paris, 1955
EN	Ezra-Nehemiah
ErIsr	*Eretz-Israel*
FAT	Forschungen zum Alten Testament
FOTL	Forms of the Old Testament Literature
FRLANT	Forschungen zur Religion und Literatur des Alten und Neuen Testaments
GKC	*Gesenius' Hebrew Grammar.* Edited by E. Kautzsch. Translated by A. E. Cowley. 2nd ed. Oxford, 1910
HDR	Harvard Dissertations in Religion
HO	Handbuch der Orientalistik
HSM	Harvard Semitic Monographs
HSS	Harvard Semitic Studies
HUCA	*Hebrew Union College Annual*
ICC	International Critical Commentary

IDB	*Interpreter's Dictionary of the Bible*. Edited by G. A. Buttrick. 4 vols. Nashville, 1962
IDBSup	*Interpreter's Dictionary of the Bible: Supplementary Volume*. Edited by K. Crim. Nashville, 1976
IEJ	*Israel Exploration Journal*
Int	*Interpretation*
JAOS	*Journal of the American Oriental Society*
JBL	*Journal of Biblical Literature*
JBR	*Journal of Bible and Religion*
JCS	*Journal of Cuneiform Studies*
JESHO	*Journal of the Economic and Social History of the Orient*
JHNES	Johns Hopkins Near Eastern Studies
JNES	*Journal of Near Eastern Studies*
JPOS	*Journal of the Palestine Oriental Society*
JSOT	*Journal for the Study of the Old Testament*
JSOTSup	Journal for the Study of the Old Testament, Supplement Series
KAI	*Kanaanäische und aramäische Inschriften*. H. Donner and W. Röllig. 2nd ed. Wiesbaden, 1966–69
KJV	King James Version
KTU²	*The Cuneiform Alphabetic Texts from Ugarit, Ras Ibn Hani, and Other Places*. Edited by M. Dietrich, O. Loretz, and J. Sanmartín. Münster, 1995
LHBOTS	Library of Hebrew Bible/Old Testament Studies
LXX	Septuagint
MT	Masoretic Text
NEA	*Near Eastern Archaeology*
NIB	*The New Interpreter's Bible*. Edited by L. Keck. 12 vols. Nashville: Abingdon, 1994–2004
NIDB	*The New Interpreter's Dictionary of the Bible*. Edited by K. D. Sakenfeld. 5 vols. Nashville: Abingdon, 2006–2009
NJPS	New Jewish Publication Society Version
NRSV	New Revised Standard Version
OBT	Overtures to Biblical Theology
OIP	Oriental Institute Publications
OLA	Orientalia lovaniensia analecta
OTL	Old Testament Library
PEQ	*Palestine Exploration Quarterly*
PH	Primeval History
RA	*Revue d'assyriologie et d'archéologie orientale*

RevExp	*Review and Expositor*
RlA	*Reallexikon der Assyriologie.* Edited by Erich Ebeling et al. Berlin, 1928–.
SAA	State Archives of Assyria
SBLDS	Society of Biblical Literature Dissertation Series
SBLMS	Society of Biblical Literature Monograph Series
SBLWAW	Society of Biblical Literature Writings from the Ancient World
SHCANE	Studies in the History and Culture of the Ancient Near East
SJOT	*Scandinavian Journal of the Old Testament*
SJT	*Scottish Journal of Theology*
TCS	Texts from Cuneiform Sources
TDOT	*Theological Dictionary of the Old Testament.* Edited by G. J. Botterweck, H. Ringgren, and H.-J. Fabry. Translated by J. T. Willis, G. W. Bromiley, D. E. Green, and D. W. Stott. 15 vols. Grand Rapids, 1974–
TH 1–42	The Collection of Sumerian Temple Hymns
TUAT	*Texte aus der Umwelt des Alten Testaments.* Edited by Otto Kaiser. Gütersloh, 1984–.
UF	*Ugarit-Forschungen*
VT	*Vetus Testamentum*
VTSup	Supplements to *Vetus Testamentum*
WBC	Word Biblical Commentary
WMANT	Wissenschaftliche Monographien zum Alten und Neuen Testament
WO	*Die Welt des Orients*
ZA	*Zeitschrift für Assyriologie*
ZAH	*Zeitschrift für Althebräistik*
ZAW	*Zeitschrift für die alttestamentliche Wissenschaft*
ZDPV	*Zeitschrift des deutschen Palästina-Vereins*

Divine Absence
and the Spatial Conception
of Divine–Human Relationships

THE HEBREW BIBLE PORTRAYS a God who is known in this world and in the experiences of human life. In creation, the world itself comes into form through God's active, creating presence (Genesis 1–3; Job 38:4-11; Pss 74:12-17; 89:5-18; Prov 8:22-31). In Genesis, God appears to Israel's ancestors, speaks to them, guides them in their journeys, and promises to "be with" them (Gen 21:22; 26:3, 28; 28:20; and so forth; cf. 21:20; 31:42). Pervading the Hebrew Bible is the memory of the exodus, God's deliverance of Israel from slavery in Egypt (for example, Exodus 1–15; 20:2; Deut 4:45; 5:6, 15; Josh 2:10; Judg 9:9; 1 Sam 4:8; 1 Kings 8:21 = 2 Chr 6:11; Isa 11:16; Hos 2:15; 11:1; Mic 7:15; Ps 78:12-14). God appears and speaks directly to human beings in terrifying theophany (Exodus 19; Job 38–42). The historical narratives and prophetic texts portray God's involvement in Israel's political and military history—choosing its kings (1 Samuel 10–11; 16), fighting its battles (for example, Joshua 1–11; Judges 5), and confronting the people and their rulers for violating the divine will (for example, 1 Kings 21; Amos 1:1—3:2). However, this multifaceted and often dramatic portrayal of God's presence in the world implies the need for such an affirmation. The biblical text itself balances the portrayal of divine presence with an acknowledgment that its clear appearance is somewhat unusual.

In the pages of the Hebrew Bible, the notion of divine absence comes to expression in a variety of forms. In the book of Job, an innocent sufferer challenges the integrity of an absent God. In the account of

1

Sennacherib's siege of Jerusalem, the Assyrian Rab-Shakeh delivers a terrifying speech of propaganda before the city walls, a speech that crescendos with the question "Where are the gods of Hamath and Arpad?" (2 Kings 18:34 = Isa 36:19 NRSV). The motif is one that appears in a range of contexts, from prophetic threat of punishment (for example, Isa 6:11-12; Hos 10:5-8; Ezekiel 10–11), to abandonment of the individual (for example, Psalm 22), to God's working "behind the scenes" in the narratives of Joseph and Esther. Attention to God's apparent absence is nowhere more poignant in the Old Testament than in connection with the Babylonian destruction and exile (for example, Ps 74:1-23; Isa 63:11-19; Lam 5:1-22). And then there is the less ominous, everyday silence of the divine. Including the initial call to "Go from your country and your kindred and your father's house to the land that I will show you" (Gen 12:1 NRSV), God speaks to Abraham only occasionally during his reported 175 years (Gen 12:1-3, 7; 13:14-17; 15:1-21; 17:1-22; 18:1-33; 21:12-13; 22:1-19). Though later interpreted as a metaphor for divine–human relationship, the love poetry of Song of Songs (also known as Song of Solomon) explores one of human life's most intense experiences in the joy and passion of romantic love but with no mention of the divine.[1]

For some time now, scholarship on the Hebrew Bible has given attention to this side of the biblical portrayal of the divine.[2] An especially noteworthy contribution was that of Samuel Terrien, a monograph published three decades ago titled *The Elusive Presence*. In it, he emphasized the positive side of divine absence in the Hebrew Bible as an expression of divine freedom and mystery.[3] Terrien's monograph won a favorable reception by giving due balance to the constructive side of the Bible's portrayal of Israel's Deity as *deus absconditus*, "a hidden god." As Terrien himself would note, the Hebrew language of the biblical text behind this expression is better rendered actively, "a God who hides himself" (*ʾēl mistattēr*; Isa 45:15). Reflecting on the crisis of the Babylonian exile, this passage indicates that the mystery and hiddenness of Israel's God is largely a matter of God's own doing. There is a definite downside to God's elusiveness that poses a challenge to divine–human relationships. Particular aspects of this dark side of divine absence have included Samuel E. Balentine's lexical and thematic study of the "hiding the face" of God in the Old Testament and the recent lexical study by Brian L. Webster, which brings further precision to considering notions of God's absence, silence, aloofness, withdrawal, and abandonment.[4]

Another positive contribution of Terrien's monograph was his effort to locate this idea of the divine within ancient Israel's broader historical and cultural milieu. In so doing, Terrien argued that the absence and elusiveness of Israel's God was unique in the ancient world and that it set apart the Israelite understanding of the divine. Continuing study of texts from the ancient Near East has shown the prevalence of this divine elusiveness among the gods of ancient Israel's neighbors and predeces- sors.[5] Terrien's study reflects a weakness of the biblical theology move- ment of the mid-twentieth century, in that it projects the uniqueness of the Hebrew Bible as a surviving literary source into the past as a coher- ent religious viewpoint that existed in antiquity. The result is an essen- tialist understanding of Israelite religion as belief—specifically, belief in a God who is transcendent through elusiveness—an idea that Terrien characterizes as unique in the ancient Near East. More recent scholar- ship on the Hebrew Bible has sought to avoid this way of confusing historical and theological tasks and this way of equating ancient Israel's religion with the literary outcome of the Hebrew Bible. Nonetheless, the basic goals of integrating theology with history and understanding the Bible in view of what we know about Israel's religion, as Terrien seeks to do, remain laudable. The efforts and achievements represented by Terrien's work deserve an updated approach to ancient Israel's Near Eastern environment. Such an approach could account for beliefs and practices in historical reconstructions of ancient religion, allowing the results of historical investigation to inform contemporary theological interpretation of the biblical text.

As attested in a range of extrabiblical textual sources, the religious motif of divine absence occurs prominently in the Hebrew Bible's Near Eastern background. A cursory overview would include the Egyptian god Amun (literally, "the Hidden One"), Mesopotamian city laments, the motif of divine abandonment in war propaganda, the spoliation of defeated enemies' cult images, Hittite vanishing deities like Telepinush, and dying deities like Dumuzi/Tammuz and Baal.[6] Ancient Near Eastern wisdom texts have shown that the consideration of theodicy in terms of divine absence in biblical wisdom literature belongs to a common inter- national perspective.[7]

The perception of the deity's absence is an experience that ancient Israel clearly shared with its Near Eastern neighbors and forebears. The address of divine absence in the Hebrew Bible thus represents a biblical response to a common concern within ancient Israel's broader cultural environment. The idea of divine elusiveness was not unique to ancient Israel but rather marks Israel's continuity and commonality with its ancient Near Eastern neighbors. Accordingly, in the examination of texts of divine absence, this study will account for the larger cultural background of this biblical theme but with an eye on the distinct expres- sions of divine absence in the Hebrew Bible. As the following discussion

seeks to demonstrate, the true uniqueness of the biblical portrayal of
the divine comes through in considering both ancient Israel's own cultural and social setting and the extent and complexity of the library of
traditions edited, reedited, and shaped ultimately to form the Hebrew
Scriptures.

The Hebrew Bible captures the theme of divine absence most poignantly in the question "Where is God?"[8] Covering a range of circumstances, this expression appears both in the supplications of worshipers
and in the taunts of enemies. From this question arise three vital observations. First, the biblical problem is never stated neutrally but always
according to the pattern "Where is *your* God?" "Where is *my* God?"
"Where is *their* God?" "Where is Yahweh?" Or, as Isa 63:11-12 asks,

> Where is the one who brought them up out of the sea . . .
> who divided the waters before them to make for himself an
>   everlasting name,
> who led them through the depths? (NRSV)

The question of divine absence is always raised in explicit relationship
with the individual, group, or, in the case of the national divine name,
the particular people or nation associated with the deity—namely, Israel.
The inherently relational nature of this concern in the Hebrew Bible
comes through in the question form. One might think of divine absence
as a problem of unfulfilled expectations of divine benevolence or faithfulness; in short, it expresses a crisis in the divine–human relationship.

Second, and as noted, the problem of divine absence was not peculiar to ancient Israelites but also preoccupied their neighbors and forebears. This concern is registered in connection with the Hebrew Bible's
top villainess, the hated Jezebel, whose Phoenician name as accurately
understood means, "Where is the Prince?"[9] This invocation of a favored
epithet for the Canaanite storm god Baal-Haddu has a textual parallel
in the Ugaritic Baal Cycle, where the storm god is mourned with the
exclamation:

> ʾiy ʾalʾiyn bʿl ʾiy zbl bʿl ʾars
> Where is Mighty Baal? Where is the Prince, the Lord
>   of the Earth?
>   (KTU[2] 1.6 IV:4–5, 15–16).[10]

Related to this rhetorical seeking of the deity, the question of divine
absence occurs in reference to numerous other deities in West Semitic
and Akkadian personal names of the same type as Jezebel from the

second and first millennia B.C.E. (names that will be discussed in chapter 2). This dark side of theism, far from being peculiar to biblical mono-theism, belongs to the common religious heritage of the ancient Near East.

Third, this particular form of expression of divine absence shows how divine–human relationships are conceived in spatial terms. The question form is constructed by the common Semitic interrogative particle *ʾay-, which occurs in Biblical Hebrew with the spatial sense "where?"[11] In pursuing relationships to the divine, human beings inquire about God's whereabouts in the world around them. The God of the Bible is a God who is known and sought in life in this world. This study of human seeking of the divine in the Hebrew Bible proceeds with special attention to this spatial dimension of divine–human relationships.

The first section of this book (part I, "Relational Worlds") gives thorough consideration to the basic structures of human relationships to the divine in the Hebrew Bible. In chapter 1, "Knowing God in the Hebrew Bible," I consider patron deities in the ancient Near East and the basis of ancient Israel's relationship to its God in ancient Israel's kin-based social structure. Chapter 2 examines Israelite and other West Semitic personal names as a form of religious evidence in its most personal form. This evidence category includes a particular name type built on the previously described question of divine absence. In considering various biblical traditions of the origins of Israel's relationship to its God, chapter 3 shows how accounts of relational beginnings include the prospect of disruption as well as renewal. Throughout the Hebrew Bible, Israel's identity is intimately bound with the memory of its first encounters with its God and an understanding of various relational foundations for continuing divine presence.

With attention to divine absence as a theme based on the spatial conception of divine–human relationships, part II considers various biblical notions of "Boundaries of Divine Presence and Absence in the World." Chapter 4 examines divine presence and absence in cosmological perspective and considers whether biblical texts suggest God to be most readily present and perhaps absent in particular parts of the earth. Rooted in creation theology, the wisdom literature of the Hebrew Bible gives special attention to a couple of aspects of divine presence in human life in the world—namely, the hidden quality of God's presence in daily life and the problem of evil. Chapter 5 discusses these aspects of biblical divine absence. Chapter 6 explores another group of biblical texts vitally concerned with locating God's presence in spatial existence—namely, the worship literature of the Hebrew Bible, including both ritual texts and psalmody. These texts present an ordered search for the divine through actions and words that attend to boundaries of divine presence and absence in recognized places of divine–human interaction, especially in the temple in Jerusalem. The sacred city marks the central focus of divine presence on earth for most of the Hebrew Bible, as treated in part III, particularly in historical narrative and in certain prophetic texts reflecting on the crisis of the exile. As chapter 7 shows, Jerusalem occupies a central place in the sacred geography of the Hebrew Bible's major historical works—namely, the Deuteronomistic History (Deuteronomy through 2 Kings), Chronicles, and Ezra-Nehemiah. These books provide a narrative context for much of the prophetic reflection on threatened or realized divine absence. Certain prophetic texts complement the narrative literature by showing the center of divine presence in Jerusalem to be the center of divine absence during the Babylonian exile.

By giving focused attention to the spatial conception of divine–human relationships as communicated by this consistent biblical theme, this study attempts to bring a particular perspective to the Hebrew Bible's emphasis on these relationships as lasting bonds formed in this world through the circumstances of human life.

PART I

RELATIONAL WORLDS

His Elusive Presence p2

"The Dark Side of God" His hiddenness, absence absence.
Because of the divine-human relationship. deus absconditus p2
The Presence His absence silence. p2 hidden
aloofness, withdrawal, abandonment. "Why unique to Israel World" p4
Job challenges God absence absence when he needed Him.
The question: where is your God? The Taunt by the p. 1ce.
"   "   of Ana: faith claim   The Test by the People
reliability reliability

In Israel God is perceived perceived in Creation, wisdom,
IX   worship, prophetic: narration

CHAPTER I

Knowing God
in the Hebrew Bible

THIS STUDY OF DIVINE absence in the Hebrew Bible takes as its point of departure three salient aspects of the topic raised in the introduction: first, the relational nature of divine absence; second, its appearance in extrabiblical texts as a common concern in ancient Israel's broader cultural environment; and third, the spatial ramifications of this biblical theme. As a foundation for considering the spatial dimensions of biblical divine absence, the three chapters in this first section of the book consider relational aspects of divine absence in common ancient Near Eastern perspective. This chapter offers as a starting point the basic understanding of deities and of divine–human relationships in ancient Israel and more broadly in the ancient Near East.

DESCRIBING THE DIVINE: WHAT IS GOD LIKE?

In ancient Near Eastern tradition, to know something about humankind is to know something about the gods. In Mesopotamian mythic tradition, the human race began with seven males and seven females created from a mixture of clay and the blood of a slain god with the result "that god and man may be thoroughly mixed in the clay."[1] This mytheme compares with that of Yahweh breathing "the breath of life" into a clay-formed Adam in Genesis 2 or Elohim's creation of humankind "in the image of God" in Genesis 1. These texts reflect a kinship of ideas that the biblical writers shared with their Mesopotamian counterparts when it came to divine–human relationships. Human beings

9

and deities relate in an essential way and bear a mutual resemblance.[2]
This divine–human correspondence is reflected conversely in the craft-
ing of the anthropomorphic divine images and artistic representations
throughout the ancient Near East.[3] Thus, it comes as no surprise that,
beginning in the earliest written and artistic sources, the divine are consistently portrayed in the image of humankind, that is, in highly anthropomorphic terms.[4]

According to that shared understanding, deities are personal; they
speak; they are gendered and can be described or portrayed with
human body imagery; they form relationships with one another; and
they compete and cooperate in pursuit of their own interests.[5] Gods
and goddesses relate to one another in bonds of kinship and descent,
as represented, for example, by "the clan structure of the pantheon"
of ancient Sumer,[6] the Ennead in the Egyptian Heliopolitan theogony,[7]
and the usual reference to the Ugaritic pantheon as "the sons of El"
(bn ʾil) and to its leading members as "the seventy sons of Athirat,"
El's wife (KTU[2] 1.4 VI 46).[8] Nevertheless, as indicated by iconographic
depictions, especially in symbolic and composite imagery for the divine,
deities are not exactly like human beings.[9] Most significantly, they are
much more powerful than mortals and are given credit for providing
and securing what human beings need for survival and prosperity.[10]

Being anthropomorphic, deities have interests of their own and thus
want something in return from their human beneficiaries. Sometimes
they want a great deal in return. According to the ancient Mesopotamian tradition that appears in works like Atrahasis and Enuma Elish
and elsewhere in Babylonian myth, the purpose for creating humans
is so that they might perform the work of the gods—digging canals,
engaging in agriculture, building temples and cities—in short, making
life on earth run so that the gods might have rest.[11]

Something else the gods want from human beings is food and drink.
In cultic expression, the logic of reciprocity understood to exist between
the gods and humanity is captured by the formula do ut des, "I give in
order that you might give." This exchange of worship for well-being and
prosperity, which Leo Oppenheim has called "the care and feeding of
the gods," is often cited as the basis for theistic religion and binds both
human and divine parties in relationships of mutual dependence.[12] In
Atrahasis, the gods mourn the destruction of humanity mainly because of
the resulting loss of food offerings (III iii 30–iv 25). Later in the text, the
gods are drawn to the aroma of the food offering "like flies" (v. 30–35),
a description that corresponds ironically to the earlier description of

mass destruction in the flood, which is said to leave human beings dead "like flies" (III iii 44). Anthropomorphism has its limits—for deities and humans alike! Even still, these texts intimate a relational reciprocity that is grounded in a basic correspondence between the human and the divine.

What is due to the gods in the form of human action extends to ethical behavior toward other human beings, which is needed for harmony on earth. This emphasis is central to the international wisdom tradition.[13] These human deeds of upright cultic and moral behavior issue from a proper disposition toward the divine noted in common ancient Near Eastern parlance as the "fear of god."[14]

At the reciprocal basis of the relationship, human toil, service in worship, and dutiful behavior in the community were offered to deities in exchange for life, security, health, and protection from harmful forces.[15] As typically described by historians of ancient Mesopotamian religion, this relationship was one of mutual dependence and devotion but little warmth.[16] In fact, deities were as much a potential threat to human well-being as a necessary means of ensuring it. In *Atrahasis*, even after the gods create human beings to serve them, they nearly end human existence through the flood.[17] The implication, in Thorkild Jacobsen's words, is that "man's existence is precarious, his usefulness to the gods will not protect him unless he takes care not to become a nuisance to them, however innocently."[18] While the divine–human relationship may be described as mutually beneficial, for human beings it is one that is potentially hazardous and that requires caution. In the ancient Near East, gods, like human beings, were often unpredictable.

The problem of divine absence thus involves the most basic terms of divine–human relationships. Because the deities are like us in many ways and have needs as we do, they are understood to form reciprocal relationships with human beings. Within this framework of divine–human reciprocity, human experiences of hardship, misfortune, and disaster are interpreted as disruptions of the divine–human relationship, as expressions of divine punishment, or perhaps as divine negligence and an unjustified withdrawal of divine protection. In any case, the experience of apparent divine absence requires a repairing of the relational breech.

What is the basis for restoring divine–human relationships? What hope do human beings have in seeking an ostensibly absent god? What is it about these relationships that makes reconciliation possible, and what gives shape to them in the first place?

KNOWING GOD IN THE ANCIENT NEAR EAST: PATRON DEITIES

Just as gods and goddesses were variously conceived in anthropomorphic terms in ancient Israel's broader cultural environment, so were they understood to relate to human beings in personal associations. As ties between parties of related interests but unequal power and status, divine–human relationships took the form of relations between superior and inferior, ruler and ruled. Deities thus related in special ways to individuals and groups of human beings, at various levels of social and political complexity. The recognition of bonds between human subjects and divine patrons was a constant feature of religion in the ancient Near East.

This basic notion of divine patronage is found, for example, in the identification of gods and goddesses of individuals and their households (as identified, for instance, in Old Babylonian cylinder seals and letters).[19] It also includes professions (for example, craftsmen gods as patrons of human artisans: Ugaritic Kothar-wa-Hasis; Mesopotamian Ea as god of crafts generally; Nunurra, god of the potter; Ninagal, god of the smith; Guškinbanda, the goldsmith's god; Egyptian Ptah as patron of those who create handicrafts and work with metal or stone).[20] Localities and cities also had patron gods (especially in Mesopotamia—for example, Enki of Eridu, Inanna of Uruk, and Enlil of Nippur—but also Amun of Thebes, Ra of Heliopolis, Ptah of Memphis, Osiris of Abydos, and Phoenician Baalat, "The Lady of Byblos").[21] In Akkadian texts from the Old Babylonian period, the personal god of the individual is sometimes denoted as the "god of the head" (*ili rēšīya*), as in the case of Yarim-Lim, king of Aleppo, who swears an oath "by Adad the god of my city, and by Sin the god of my head."[22] As this last example illustrates, the same individual, even the king himself, may worship one god as patron deity of the city and another as his own personal and ancestral god.[23]

From the patron deities of cities and regions emerged national pantheons in the case of the Mesopotamian, Hittite, and Egyptian empires[24] and, extending into the first millennium B.C.E., national or "state" deities like Assyrian Assur and Babylonian Marduk.[25] This pattern of a national deity embodying the identity of the "state" becomes definitive for the Iron Age kingdoms of the Levant—for example, Hadad-Ramman of Aram-Damascus (biblical Hadad-Rimmon; 2 Kings 5:18; Zech 12:11), Chemosh of Moab, Qaus of Edom, and Yahweh of Israel and Judah.[26] Closely related is the identification of patron deities of ruling dynasties. A notable example is the god Rakab-El, whom Kulamuwa and later Bar-

Rakib, kings of Sam'al-Ya'udi (modern Zenjirli in southeastern Turkey), designate as "the Lord of the Dynasty" (literally, "house"; *b'l bt*, *KAI* 24.16; *b'l byt*, *KAI* 215.22).[27]

As these various instances illustrate, the notion of a deity's special relationship to specific individuals, groups, and territories is at work throughout the ancient Near East, at various social and political levels beginning with that of the individual or household. By virtue of this close association with a particular person, social group, or place, the patron deity was understood to act as its divine representative and to advance its welfare.

As noted earlier in this chapter, divine–human relationships involve mutual self-interests and responsibilities. Accordingly, divine patronage expresses itself not only in the god's identification with a specific people but conversely in the people's and territory's identification in relationship to the deity. This dynamic is particularly evident among Iron Age kingdoms east and west of the Jordan. Hence, throughout the Hebrew Bible, including some of the earliest traditions it preserves, Israel is identified as "the people of Yahweh" (*'am yhwh*; Num 11:29; 17:6; Judg 5:11; 20:2; 1 Sam 2:24; 2 Sam 1:12; 6:21; 14:13; 2 Kings 9:6; Ezek 36:20; Zeph 2:10). Likewise, the Moabites are known as the "people of Chemosh" (*'am kěmôš*; Num 21:29; Jer 48:46), and the Mesha inscription makes reference to Moab as the land of Chemosh (Mesha lines 5–6). This understanding by which the other nations are identified with their gods is reflected in the Hebrew Bible, for example in Mic 4:5:

> For all the peoples walk
>   each in the name of its god,
> but we will walk in the name of Yahweh our God
>   forever and ever. (adapted from the NRSV)

The language for identification between people and deities indicates relational reciprocity between the divine and human parties. In the Hebrew Bible, which is concerned chiefly with the relationship between Israel and its God, that notion of reciprocity is expressed in statements like "I will be their God, and they shall be my people" (Jer 31:33; see also Exod 6:7; Lev 26:12; Jer 7:23; 11:4; 30:22; Ezek 36:28; Hos 1:9; 2:23). This pattern of expression, known in German-language scholarship as the *Bundesformel* or "relational formula," represents one important way in which the Hebrew Bible emphasizes the God–Israel relationship in terms of covenant (more discussion, later in this chapter).[28] This biblical understanding is a specific form of the common ancient Near Eastern notion of human relationships to the divine and the attendant concepts of personal loyalty and reciprocity. In keeping with the basic ancient Near Eastern view of deities as super-powerful beings on whom human welfare depends, divine–human relationships typically follow this basic pattern of personal relational bonds between divine superiors and human inferiors—simply put, relationships of divine patronage.

That understanding of identity and reciprocity involved in people's relationships to their deities helps explain the expressions of acute dismay and despair that often accompany the experience of divine absence. It also provides a rationale for seeking an ostensibly absent deity in hopes of moving divine–human relationships beyond such experiences of disruption. Having brought into focus the essentially relational nature of this theme in light of a common ancient Near Eastern understanding of divine patronage, one might consider the divine–human relationship at the focus of the Hebrew Scriptures, that between Israel and its God. The nature of divine absence as a crisis of relationship gains greater clarity in view of the basis for relationships among human beings and their patron deities in the social world of ancient Israel.

KNOWING GOD AND HUMANS IN ANCIENT ISRAEL: PATRIMONIAL SOCIETY

Divine and Human Patrons

In keeping with the anthropomorphic portrayal of deities in ancient Israel's cultural context, relationships to the divine took their frame of reference from human social bonds. As described in the previous section, divine patron relationships resembled human associations between parties of related interests but unequal power and status—between superior and inferior, ruler and ruled. In the social order that prevailed in ancient Israel, such relationships were defined not along class lines, but rather as Lawrence Stager explains by mention of the relevant Hebrew terminology:

> The vertical, dyadic relationships of superior to inferior were of a different order and were far more variegated than class concepts allow. For example, the term ʿebed, commonly translated "slave," has a variety of meanings that extend from the highest rung of the social ladder to the lowest. At its lowest level, ʿebed can mean slave, and at its highest, the right-hand man of the king, as in ʿebed hammelek.[29]

In the social context of ancient Israel, these bonds of loyalty and mutual dependence served to join parties of different standing and separate kin affiliation.

Thus, in the Hebrew Bible, an *ebed* might be a slave "bought with money" (Gen 17:12). A young David is referred to as "the servant [*ebed*] of King Saul of Israel" (1 Sam 29:3). Along with other royal officials including "the priest Hilkiah" and "Shaphan the secretary," 2 Kings 22:12 lists Asaiah, "the king's servant" (*ebed hammelek*). A stamp seal excavated from ancient Megiddo names its owner, most likely a royal official, as "Shema, the servant of Jeroboam" (*šm' 'bd yrb'm*).[30] This system of patriarchy and patronage by which males relate to one another variously in hierarchical relationships was basic for Israelite society.[31]

This way of relating superior to inferior in various "master–servant" relationships provided the basic relational model for divine–human relationships in ancient Israel and in the Hebrew Bible. Important figures and leaders, including Abraham, Isaac, and Jacob (for example, Exod 32:13), Caleb (Num 14:24), Moses (for example, Exod 14:24; Deut 34:5), Joshua (Josh 24:29; Judg 2:8), and David (1 Kings 8:66) can be called Yahweh's "servant." As a group, "the prophets" are referred to as God's "servants" (Jer 7:5; 2 Kings 9:7; Ezek 38:17; Zech 1:6), as are individual prophets such as Ahijah (1 Kings 14:18; 15:29), Elijah (2 Kings 10:10), Isaiah (Isa 20:2), and Jonah (2 Kings 14:25). In Haggai, Zerubbabel is called Yahweh's "servant" (Hag 2:23). In Second Isaiah (Isa 40–55), God's people Israel collectively are designated Yahweh's "servant" (41:8-9; 44:1-2, 21; 45:4; 48:20), and the related servant songs celebrate a nameless servant of Yahweh (Isa 42:1-4; 49:1-6; 50:4-11; 52:13—53:12).

As these biblical references show, in ancient Israel and in biblical texts, relationships to the divine were modeled on human "servant–master" or patronage relationships. Knowing God in the Hebrew Bible entails further structural aspects of Israelite society that flowed from this emphasis on male superior–inferior relationships.

The "House of the Father" and Its God

The basic unit of social life in ancient Israel and its broader cultural setting was the patrimonial household, known in the Hebrew Bible as the "house of the father" (Heb. *bêt 'āb*).[32] The patrimonial household could extend up to three generations, consisting of the senior male, his wives, their children, the adult sons' wives and children, and any unmarried paternal siblings.[33] In addition to these family members within the lineage of the patriarch, various servants and clients not having a genealogical tie to the family unit would have been incorporated into it through bonds of patronage, that is, "servant–master" relationships as just described.[34] To cite a well-known instance from the Hebrew Bible, before the birth of Isaac, Abram complains that, rather than his own offspring, a slave born in his household (*ben bêtî*; literally, "the son of my house") stands to inherit his property (Gen 15:3). Through the "house of the father," kinship provided the basic organizational structure for all significant social relationships.

The patrimonial household accordingly played an important role in divine–human relationships in ancient Israel. This role is reflected in the Hebrew Bible, particularly in the ancestral narratives of Genesis 12–50, which present the God of Israel as the patron deity of the patrimonial household.

For example, when Abraham seeks a wife for his son Isaac, he sends "his servant, the oldest of his house, who had charge of all that he had" and binds him with an oath by the household god, Yahweh (Gen 24:2-4). In carrying out the task, the servant prays for help and upon success offers a blessing to "Yahweh, God of my master Abraham" (vv. 12, 27, 42, 48). Just as the narrative reports that Yahweh "had blessed Abraham in all things" (v. 1), his servant, who comes to Laban's house bearing gifts of costly jewelry of silver and gold (vv. 22, 30, 47, 53), is greeted as "blessed of Yahweh" (v. 31). As this narrative illustrates, just as the household exists for the sake of and because of its leader, so does the patriarch's god become the chief deity of the household's members.

Worship of the household patron god was typically passed from one generation to the next through the family lineage.[35] Thus, in the Hebrew Bible, Joseph's brothers speak with him, referring to themselves as "the servants of the God of your father" (Gen 50:17). Though based on relationships centering on the family patriarch, devotion to the patrimonial god reached beyond the individual household unit through bifurcating lines of family descent.

God, Society, and Kingdom in Ancient Israel

Drawing on Max Weber's sociological theory of ancient societies, Lawrence Stager and his students have argued that "the house of the father" gave order to ancient Israelite society on a larger scale as a hierarchy of nested households.[36] With reference to Weber's theoretical model, Daniel M. Master explains, "Weber refers to the level above the household by the term *oikos*, a group of households organized on the model of a single household. Just as in the single household, the entire productive capacity of the *oikos* is mobilized for the material maintenance of its leader, with the leader reciprocally responsible for the material provision and protection of all members of the *oikos*."[37]

This pattern was replicated on levels of increasing social complexity. Ancient patrimonial society was thus construed as an interconnected nesting of households in which the society as a whole functioned as one great household, whose leadership was determined by the relative strength of a given lineage.

Depending on the size and circumstances of the patrimonial society in question, this structure would allow for varying, even oscillating, degrees of centralization, resulting in some cases in a patrimonial state.[38] As Master explains, "the ruler of this state-form, like the head of the household, would have responsibilities and limitations dictated by tradition, and, within these limits, the primary function of the population would be the material maintenance of the ruler."[39] The societal structure supporting the ruling household and lineage would consist of other lineages interrelated to form larger societal units, that is, clans and tribes.[40]

The patrimonial model comports well with ethnographic, historical, and archaeological evidence for tribal identity as an enduring basis for social organization throughout the history of the Levant and the broader Near East, from the Bronze Age even into modern times.[41] By contrast, a prevailing theoretical model in recent decades of scholarship on the history and archaeology of the southern Levant posits an evolutionary development from tribe, to chiefdom, to state—a schema in which mature statehood leaves behind kin-based social structures.[42] The related notion of kingship's incompatibility with kin-based tribal society is reflected in earlier historical reconstructions that suggested the rise of the Israelite monarchy radically diminished kin-based identity and authority.[43] Based on this same framework, others have argued that the "tribalization" of ancient Israel was a relatively late (sixth-century) development.[44]

The evolutionary framework of state formation, however regularly assumed, is at pains to account for the persistence and flexibility of tribes in the modern Middle East—sometimes coexisting alongside territorial state administration, sometimes forming part of it, sometimes developing into tribal states, and even developing from a state form to a less centralized organizational form.[45] In the case of ancient Israel, the biblical twelve-tribe lists, even if representing later literary formulation, are ostensibly rooted in the time of the early monarchy (see, for example, Gen 49:1-28).[46] As Master explains, degrees of centralization vary and oscillate within ancient and modern tribal societies, but the kin-based structure remains a constant.[47]

Stager has demonstrated how the patrimonial basis of ancient Israel's social and political organization is borne out by various forms of archaeological, epigraphic, and biblical evidence. For example, household architectural remains and settlement layouts from Iron Age I reflect the makeup of society in interconnected patrimonial units.[48] In biblical texts, terminology for adult males (especially, the Hebrew word na'ar, "lad, youth, servant") often relates to status in relationship to the patrimonial household.[49] The eighth-century Samaria ostraca show that, well into the time of the monarchy, tribal and clan structures were operative in the allocation of resources supporting the central national administration.[50] The kingdoms of Israel and Judah are characterized as patrimonial states by their neighbors, who refer to them, respectively, as the "House of Omri" (Bīt Ḥumri in Assyrian royal texts) and "the House of David" (byt dwd in the Tel Dan stela of an Aramean king and in the Moabite inscription of Mesha).[51] These titles parallel the names of other Iron Age states of western Asia mentioned in Assyrian sources: Bīt Adini in the upper Euphrates region, Bīt Agusi (Arpad) in northern Syria, Bīt Ḥazaʾili for Damascus.[52] The biblical, epigraphic, and material evidence reflects the patrimonial basis for the kingdoms and societies of ancient Israel and its neighbors in Iron Age Syria-Palestine.

J. David Schloen's ambitious study of the "house of the father" has likewise substantiated this patrimonial social order for Bronze Age urban society, especially as represented by the kingdom of Ugarit on the north Syrian coast.[53] Well noted in scholarship is the degree to which international political discourse as attested in the Amarna Letters and other documents of this period characteristically drew on the language and concepts of family and kinship.[54] Alliances among major powers— such as Egypt, Babylon, and the Hittite kingdom—and between Egypt and local vassal kings of Syria-Palestine are described in these texts as relations among fathers, sons, and brothers, and are regularly sealed by diplomatic marriages. These kingdoms are thus regarded, at least symbolically, as the households and extended domains of their respective rulers and their dynasties. This way of framing relationships on the international political level corresponds to what Schloen understands to have been the kin-based, patrimonial social order that defined the Near East during this period. As Schloen demonstrates, that Bronze Age pattern continued to be the defining social framework for Iron Age Syria-Palestine, one that was, in his words, a "ubiquitous native conception of the social order as a collection of households held together by the great household of the ruler, and ultimately of his god."[55]

Divine Patrimony

For ancient Israel, the apex of authority in this conception of divine and human society is occupied by Yahweh, who in Stager's words "reigns as supreme patrimonial lord, the ultimate authority over the king and the 'children of Israel.'"[56] While individual households might have various gods, for the people as a whole, all other deities would have been subordinate to the leading deity, the God of Israel. Yahweh's role as supreme deity would have been secured by virtue of his role as the patron deity of the leading patrimonial lineage at a critical point in Israel's history.[57]

Royal lineage was intertwined with national and religious identity among Israel's Iron Age neighbors, who were likewise identified in kin-based terms. Just as the Hebrew Bible frequently designates the Israelites as "the children of Israel" (běnê yiśrāʾēl), a seventh-century inscription of an Ammonite king refers to the population over whom he and his ancestors have ruled as "the children of Ammon" (bn ʿmn), Ammon itself meaning "the kinsman."[58] That inscription, the bronze bottle inscription from Tel Siran (CAI 78), enumerates several generations of dynastic succession, placing royal lineage in the context of kin-based identity on a national scale: "Amminadab king of the Ammonites, the son of Hissalil king of the Ammonites, the son of Amminadab king of the Ammonites."[59] Kingship's compatibility with kin-based social definition is encapsulated in the repeated royal title "king of the children of Ammon" (mlk bn ʿmn). The name of the Ammonite chief god, Milcom, as related in the Hebrew Bible (BH milkōm) and in fragmentary form in the late-ninth-century Amman Citadel Inscription ([m]lkm; CAI 59:1), suggests royal connotations of the leading god's status (compare BH melek, "king").[60]

The inscription of the Moabite king Mesha from the ninth century B.C.E. mentions Israel's rule by Omri and "his son" (lines 5–7) and makes reference to King Mesha's own succession from his father as king of Moab (lines 1–3).[61] The Mesha inscription goes on to describe conflicts between the Moabite and Israelite kingdoms over disputed territories, with the claim that his god Chemosh granted Mesha dominion and jurisdiction over the lands that he rules (lines 4, 9, 14–16, 32–33). The connection linking national patron god, human monarch, and land as divine patrimony is thus underscored in this text, which mentions the god Yahweh in close association with "the king of Israel" and Israelite territorial claims (line 18). Accordingly, Moab's past subjugation to Israel is attributed to the fact that "Chemosh was angry with his land" (lines 5–6).

The longstanding association of deity, ruling lineage, and territory making up the divine patrimony is illustrated by a text from Bronze Age Mari (text A. 1121 + A. 2731).[62] In an oracle for King Zimri-Lim, the god Adad reminds the king that the deity has placed Zimri-Lim "on the throne of his father's house" and that the king's "heritage" (Akkadian *niḫlatum*) of land, throne, and capital ultimately belong to Adad, who may revoke it as he sees fit. The deity, who is here identified by his association with a specific and obscure place name, "Adad, lord of Kallassu," nonetheless promises increasing rewards and expanding jurisdiction in return for the king's faithfulness: "throne upon throne, house upon house, territory upon territory, city upon city . . . the land from the rising of the sun to its setting."[63] Though doubtless reflecting some degree of rhetorical hyperbole, this language is consistent with the notion of a segmented society and kingdom having the potential for increasing complexity on a patrimonial basis. Thus, textual evidence reaching back to the Middle Bronze Age attests to the understanding of the political kingdom as divine patrimony governed by a ruling human lineage.

This notion of the chief deity's ultimate rule over a distinct people and territory belongs to the kin-based social order that was foundational for Israel and its neighbors in Syria-Palestine during the Iron Age. As constituents of a nested hierarchy, individual households may worship various patrimonial gods but ultimately acknowledged the supremacy of the leading god.[64] Thus, at various levels, divine patrimony was integral to that kin-based framework, giving coherence to society and giving shape to divine–human relationships.

From the level of the household to that of national identity, kinship provided the basis for all social relationships and all relationships to the divine in ancient Israel. Though based on the notion of biological descent, kinship was adaptable and could be "manipulated in order to admit new members to the group or to make permanent or temporary alliances."[65] Within ancient Israel's kin-based societal framework, kinship bonds were extended through an important social mechanism still to be considered—namely, covenant.

COVENANT

Underlying covenant's place in biblical portrayals of divine–human relationships is a deeply complex background in ancient social, legal, and political life. The main word for covenant in the Hebrew Bible, *bĕrît*,[66] relates to a range of various types of relationships and agreements.[67]

Nearly a hundred years of intense scholarly attention to the topic reached its culmination in what is aptly described as a "covenant centrality" position that prevailed in much of Old Testament studies during the latter half of the twentieth century.[68] In the approach of biblical theology, this position found its fullest expression in Walther Eichrodt's *Theology of the Old Testament*.[69] In religious-historical terms, the suggestion that covenant, rather than being a purely literary phenomenon (as Julius Wellhausen had argued),[70] had a basis in ancient Israel's early institutional life received confirmation from the striking parallels between biblical texts and ancient Near Eastern treaties elucidated by a number of scholars.[71]

In addition to the vassal treaties attested in the Hittite, Assyrian, and Aramean texts, Moshe Weinfeld identified a second political and legal institution as being relevant to the discussion of biblical covenant— namely, the royal land grant.[72] From Late Bronze Age Hittite and Syrian texts, Neo-Assyrian legal and political texts, and most importantly, Babylonian *kudurru* documents, Weinfeld determined that the land grant followed a structure very similar to what George Mendenhall, D. J. McCarthy, and Weinfeld himself had identified variously in the vassal treaties: historical introduction, border delineations, stipulations, witnesses, blessings, and curses.[73] Accordingly, Weinfeld identified two types of covenant in the Bible and the ancient Near East: "obligatory" covenants, as represented by the Mosaic traditions and the vassal treaties, and "promissory" covenants, as represented by the land grants, which Weinfeld understood to be the institutional basis for the covenants of Abraham and David. In both cases, scholars recognized covenant as a political and legal institution that was appropriated secondarily in biblical literature as a model for divine–human relationships.

In arguing for the institutional and textual basis of the promissory type of covenant, Weinfeld invoked extensive similarities in language between the biblical and comparative texts: terminology of truth, loyalty, obedience, integrity of "heart," walking or standing "before" the sovereign, toil and suffering, and description of an unconditional gift of land and "house" to the subordinate party and to his descendants.[74] According to Weinfeld, these similarities of language, along with parallels of structure and content, show Abrahamic and Davidic traditions to have emerged from the same institutional frame of reference as the royal grant texts.

In illustrating this common institutional framework, Weinfeld invoked the language of adoption and sonship, where, in parallel with language relating to the Davidic covenant in the Hebrew Bible (Ps 2:7-8), Mattiwaza of Mittanni recalls the Hittite king Shupilluliumash's words to him: "I shall not reject you, I shall make you my son." According to Weinfeld, this language represents a "forensic metaphor" that "is taken from the familial sphere."[75] For Weinfeld, the legal-political institution of the land grant covenant, though not originating in family life as such, borrows the relational language and concepts of family.

Although Weinfeld views the family language of the land grant as figurative, the promissory grant texts that he cites include many that have their own setting fully in the context of family relations. For example, Weinfeld invokes a text from Susa describing the gift from a husband to his wife and, from Elephantine, the grant of part of a household estate to a daughter, the latter including a motive clause, "since she took care of me . . . when I was old in years and unable to care for myself."[76] Aside from the explicit mention of faithfulness, these texts in their substance are not far removed from the example of a will from Nuzi, cited by Weinfeld, in which a man leaves land and property to his wife and sons.[77] Weinfeld's own examples would suggest that the covenant of grant does not represent a legal or political institution that borrows the language of family relationships, but rather that it has its own origin and meaning squarely within the realm of familial relations.

In connection with the Davidic covenant, Gary Knoppers similarly levels a detailed critique of Weinfeld's covenant typology.[78] Knoppers points to instances like those just mentioned, in which the parallels of language, structure, and content that Weinfeld adduces are drawn from texts representing a number of different genres and settings. Knoppers shows that the Davidic texts themselves represent different settings and literary structures and that the language and concepts shared by the biblical and comparative texts are not unique to land grants.

However, what Weinfeld's comparisons indicate is a situation in which legal-political matters relate to kinship not as a distinct and separate sphere but as part of a unified cultural matrix dominated by the language and concepts of kinship. As previously noted, a recurring insight in various studies has been the prominence of family and kinship language in international political discourse. The approach of much of this scholarship has been to regard the language of "love," "fatherhood," "brotherhood," and "loyalty" as covenant terminology. As Frank Cross and earlier Paul Kalluveettil have recognized, such an approach turns the matter on its head.[79] Rather than originating as a political institution into which family metaphors were imported, covenant itself seems to have emerged from the context of kin relations. Covenant established kinship bonds across lines of biological descent to create what Cross calls "kinship-in-law." Specific kinds of covenant thus include marriage (Ezek 16:8; Mal 2:14; Prov 2:17), adoption (1 Sam 7:14; Ps 2:7; Isa

9:5), and other bonds between individuals and groups. As Kalluveettil emphasizes, covenants do not only establish new relationships between parties but sometimes also reinforce or renew existing ones.[80]

A marquee example from the Hebrew Bible that shows the kin-based nature of covenant is the relationship between David and Jonathan. As Mendenhall conceded, this instance of covenant does not readily lend itself to an understanding of covenant according to primarily legal or political forms or categories.[81] The language of kinship and mutual obligation among kin in the description of David and Jonathan's covenant shows a relationship rooted in kin-based categories: *hesed* ("faithfulness"), "love," loving the other "as himself," enduring loyalty among their offspring, and "brother" (1 Sam 18:1-4; 20:5-8, 14-20; 2 Sam 1:26).[82] In short, through covenant, David and Jonathan establish bonds of brotherhood.

An example of covenant between groups would be the agreement between the sons of Jacob and the people of Shechem (Genesis 34). Though the word *bĕrît* ("covenant") is not used, the anticipated outcome is that the two groups will be joined "as one people" (*lĕʿam ʾeḥād*; vv. 16, 22).[83] By agreeing to undergo circumcision, the people of Shechem join with the people of Jacob in a bond of kinship that would allow for sharing livestock and holdings of land, and for exchanging their daughters in marriage (vv. 9-10, 15-16, 21-23). Kinship-in-law thus becomes kinship-in-flesh.

Through covenant, bonds of family faithfulness—the ultimate bonds of loyalty in the world of ancient Israel—were established not only through circumstances of descent but also by choice. Given the dominance of kin-based categories in the social reality of Bronze Age and Iron Age Syria-Palestine, covenant easily lent itself to being invoked as a model for establishing reliable bonds in various alliances, commitments, and obligations in the realms of patronage and politics. Again, David provides an illustration of covenant's relevance to this overlap of political and family spheres in the Hebrew Bible. In the narrative of David's rise to kingship, David makes a covenant with "all the tribes of Israel," who say, "We are your bone and flesh" (2 Sam 5:1-3). As Cross explains, this is the language of kinship.[84]

Treaty relationships were nearly universal for the ancient Mediterranean world, and in ancient Israel and more broadly in Syria-Palestine during the second and first millennia, those types of political arrangements were formed in accordance with the kind of kin-based categories involved in covenant.[85] Political relationships tended to involve the activities of family faithfulness invoked by political treaties and grants themselves—forging social bonds, giving land, establishing households, and making reliable commitments. Again, as Kalluveettil and Cross have demonstrated, for ancient Israel, covenant is not so much a political institution that borrows kinship forms but is itself a kin-based mechanism that is invoked as a model for various political alliances, commitments, and obligations. These kin-based categories were primary for early Israel. The biblical covenants of Sinai and Deuteronomy, as well as those of David and Abraham, thus show how biblical authors drew on various particular institutional forms in the continuing reinterpretation of ancient Israel's understanding of its relationship to its God as one based in covenant.[86]

Biblical texts do not just speak of covenant as a metaphor for divine–human relationships. They also describe covenants enacted between God and human beings. Parallels from the ancient Near East are rare, but Theodore Lewis has gathered several examples that scholars have understood to refer to divine covenants with human rulers, including that between Urukagina, ruler of Lagash (ca. 2375 B.C.E.), and the god Ningirsu in a Sumerian text; the Marduk "prophecy" (twelfth century B.C.E.), in which the god refers to a covenant with a human prince; and a Neo-Assyrian text (Tablet K. 2401) mentioning a covenant between the god Ashur and King Esarhaddon.[87]

Evidence closer to home for ancient Israel is a seventh-century incantation text from Arslan Tash, Syria (*KAI* 27).[88] Two small limestone plaques display drawings of deities and mythical creatures along with inscriptions, one of which includes the following declaration:

> Ashur has made an eternal covenant with us. He has made (a covenant) with us, along with all the sons of *'El* and the leaders of the council of all the Holy Ones, with a covenant of the Heavens and Eternal Earth, with an oath of *Ba'l*, Lord of Earth, with an oath of Hawran, whose mouth is true, and his seven consorts, and the eight wives of *Ba'l* Qudsh.[89]

While the other extrabiblical examples involve a god's covenant with an individual ruler, the Arslan Tash text might be understood to describe Ashur's covenant with a group of human beings ("with us"), a covenant that is to be recognized by other deities as well.

Finally, the possibility of a divine covenant with a human group comes into view in a Hurrian text from Ugarit mentioning a god called *'il brt*, which may be interpreted to mean "El of the Covenant" (*KTU*[2] 1.128.14–15).[90] Accordingly, the divine epithet would match the book of Judges' references to a deity worshiped at Shechem, who is called alternately El Berit ("El of the Covenant") and Baal Berit ("Lord of the Covenant"; *'ēl běrît*, 9:46; *ba'al běrît*, Judg 8:33; 9:4). As Lewis and others have argued, the deity in Judges was likely understood as a covenant partner with his people.[91]

The biblical and extrabiblical evidence indicates that within the kin-based social world that prevailed among ancient Israel's neighbors, covenant was a mechanism for individuals and groups to seal relationships to the divine. Through the institution of covenant, bonds of family faithfulness—the ultimate bonds of loyalty in the world of ancient Israel—were established not through circumstances of descent but through choice. The discussion will return to covenant's importance for divine–human relationships in the Hebrew Bible. For now, it bears noting that covenant provided a basis for moving beyond the human experience of divine absence, as well as explaining the degree of dismay that accompanied that perception.

Conclusion: Israel as the "People of Yahweh"

As noted in the introduction, divine absence in the Hebrew Bible is first and foremost a relational crisis and one that ancient Israelites shared with their Near Eastern neighbors and forebears. In ancient Israel, as in its broader cultural environment, divine–human relationships were personal, reciprocal, and structured in accordance with human social organization. By considering the patrimonial basis of ancient Israelite society, one understands how relationships to the divine were not only patterned after human social bonds but were also integral to the societal and political order. In short, the God of the Hebrew Bible is known within its pages as the divine patron of the household, clan, tribe, and nation. Knowing God involves established bonds of relationship and identity at these distinct and interrelated levels of social organization.

Being based in kinship, these divine–human ties represent the strongest bonds of faithfulness and loyalty imaginable. As a mechanism for extending kinship bonds, covenant allows for the establishment of such bonds not through birth but through choice. Biblical and extrabiblical evidence for divine–human covenants in ancient Israel's cultural world illustrates the high degree of reciprocity and mutual loyalty integral to these relationships.

The language of family loyalty thus served to describe a people's relationship to its deity not only as divine sovereign but also as divine kinsman, hence the kin-based identification of Moab as "the people of Chemosh" (ʿam Kĕmôš; Num 21:29; Jer 48:46), of Ammon as "the people of Milcom" (ʿam Milkōm; Jer 49:1),[92] and of Israel as "the people of Yahweh" (ʿam Yahweh; for example, Judg 5:11; 1 Sam 2:24; 2 Sam

1:12).[93] To be sure, kin-based identity and authority would have suffered with Israel and Judah's integration into an international economic and political system under first Assyrian and then Babylonian hegemony, not to mention the massive deportations carried out by those empires in 722, 701, 597, and 586 B.C.E. (2 Kings 17; 24–25; Jer 52:28-30).[94] Nonetheless, the persistent witness of textual evidence suggests a kin-based definition of Israel as a "people"—from the earliest extrabiblical reference to "Israel," in the Merneptah stele, to the depiction of Israel as a "people" throughout the national literary traditions preserved in the Hebrew Bible.[95]

Divine–human relationships in the Hebrew Bible thus find their frame of reference in this family-based web of relationships. The experience of divine absence poses a threat to these structures of identity and well-being, which in turn provide a basis for moving beyond the disruption of the relationship.

It still remains to consider how the God of Israel is also recognized as the God of the world in the Hebrew Bible. Before moving in that direction, the next chapter remains in the realm of kin-based relations and considers a special form of religious evidence that applies to the individual: human personal names.

CHAPTER 2

Known by God
in Biblical Personal Names

CHAPTER 1 EXAMINED BASIC structures of the Hebrew Bible's presentation of divine–human relationships in terms of ancient Israelite society and the broader ancient Near East. As discussed, social relationships of household and extended kinship provided avenues for relating to the divine and specifically to Israel's God. Perceived disruptions to these relational bonds give rise to the biblical concern over divine absence. The Hebrew Bible preserves within its pages a distinct form of expression regarding divine–human relationships: personal names.

This chapter will examine a set of biblical personal names that poignantly express the idea of divine absence. Before focusing on these divine-absence names, the discussion will begin by considering anthroponyms as religious expressions in the Hebrew Bible and in ancient Israel.

BIBLICAL NAME GIVING

More than a century of scholarship has recognized the special value of personal names as evidence for Israelite religion.[1] In short, anthroponyms are useful as religious evidence because West Semitic names typically consist of a sentence, word, or phrase that speakers of the language understood, and those expressions often say something about the divine.[2] Scholarship has repeatedly confirmed the generic nature of the religious expressions that West Semitic theophoric names tend to convey.[3] In other words, the names typically do not reference the

specific cult, myth, or theology of a particular god or goddess but rather
convey very basic expressions of trust, hope, thanksgiving, and praise
that could apply to various deities. While personal names mention specific deities, the kinds of divine actions or qualities voiced in the names
are so general as to be appropriate for most any god or goddess. For this
reason André Caquot has spoken of a general "religiosité sémitique"
(ancient Semitic religiosity) made accessible by anthroponyms as a category of religious evidence.[4] Examples from the names of ancient Israel
and its closest neighbors would include the Hebrew *'ēlîyāhû*, meaning
"my god is Yah(weh)" (that is, Elijah; 1 Kings 17:1); Ammonite *mlkm'wr*,
meaning "Milkom is light" (*CAI* 129); Moabite **kamōšnadbi*, meaning
"Chemosh is (a/my) noble" (rendered *Kammusunadbi* in Sennacherib's
Annals);[5] and Edomite *qwsbrk*, meaning "Qos has blessed" (Tel Beer-
sheba, Ostracon 33.4).[6]

As numerous biblical narratives illustrate, parents named children
shortly after birth, and the names often made reference to the divine.[7]
The explanations of names provided by the narratives frequently express
something about the parents' perceived experience of the deity, usually
in connection with the birth of the child:

> "God has appointed for me another child instead of Abel, because
> Cain killed him."   (Gen 4:25 NRSV)

> "Out of the ground that the LORD has cursed this one shall bring
> us relief from our work and from the toil of our hands."
>   (Gen 5:29 NRSV)

> In due time Hannah conceived and bore a son. She named him
> Samuel, for she said, "I have asked him of the LORD."
>   (1 Sam 1:20 NRSV).[8]

In the case of Solomon, after receiving his birth name from David,
he receives a second name: "Yahweh loved him and sent a message by
the prophet Nathan; so he named him Jedidiah [meaning 'Beloved of
Yah(weh)'], because of Yahweh" (2 Sam 12:24-25).

As these examples indicate, personal names were regarded in ancient
Israel as verbal witnesses to God's direct attention, action, and involvement in the lives of individuals, especially in connection with the event
of childbirth. For those so named, the implication is that the divine
protection and guidance that the names signal began from the individual's birth or even beforehand. The basic idea is one encountered in
the prophetic call motif in Jeremiah and the second of the Servant Songs
of Isaiah:

Before I formed you in the womb I knew you,
And before you were born I consecrated you;
I appointed you a prophet to the nations.

(Jer 1:5 NRSV)

The LORD called me before I was born,
  while I was in my mother's womb he named me.
He made my mouth like a sharp sword,
  in the shadow of his hand he hid me.

(Isa 49:1b-2a NRSV)

Similarly, personal names in the Hebrew Bible often signal recognition of divine attention and direction of the name givers' and name bearers' lives even before birth. In the case of theophoric names, this notion is made all the more explicit in the names themselves. As the biblical names and name giving suggest, before an individual is even old enough to know God, one might be known by God.

DIVINE ABSENCE IN BIBLICAL PERSONAL NAMES

As noted in the introduction, the theme of divine absence appears most poignantly in the Hebrew Bible in the question "Where is God?" One group of biblical names stands out in posing this very question; this group of names includes some noteworthy characters in the Hebrew Bible: Ichabod (*'îkābôd*), Ehud (*'ēhûd*), Jezebel (*'îzebel*), Iezer (*'î 'ezer*), Job (*'iyyôb*), and Ithamar (*'îtāmār*).[9] As the following discussion will show, this group of names expresses a concern over the efficacious presence of a given deity, thus meriting the designation divine-absence names.

Given that Hebrew theophoric names, like West Semitic theophoric names more generally, tend to express faith, honor, and trust of the deity, how might one understand these divine-absence names? Do they express a sentiment that is an aberration among biblical names, or do they also ultimately represent expressions of trust and hope in the divine? These questions, as well as what remains a general lack of recognition of this group of names in the scholarly literature, warrant a closer look at these divine-absence names.[10]

The discussion that follows will begin by placing these biblical names into grammatical and historical context of a widely attested West Semitic name type that asks the question "Where?" in connection with the divine. Next will follow an examination of each of the biblical names in question, considering their meanings as divine-absence names and taking into account other explanations offered in the scholarly literature. Finally, the type of religious experience associated with these names will receive further attention.

A WEST SEMITIC NAME TYPE

The recognition in the scholarly literature of West Semitic "Where?" names in connection with biblical names began with William F. Albright, an eminent scholar of the Bible and the ancient Near East.[11] The key to understanding these biblical names is recognizing the more broadly attested name type to which they belong. An overview of the West Semitic "Where?" names sheds considerable light on our biblical divine-absence names. These West Semitic names appear in a variety of ancient Near Eastern sources from the early second millennium through most of the first millennium B.C.E. The evidence reviewed here documents a West Semitic name type that persisted over that considerable span of time.

Second-Millennium Names

These West Semitic question names from the second and first millennia B.C.E. are formulated by a verbless construction with the common Semitic interrogative particle ʾay-.[12] The significance of West Semitic "Where?" names during the second millennium is indicated by their occurrence in a range of Bronze Age sources: the Egyptian Execration texts; cuneiform documents in Akkadian from Mari, Alalakh, Amarna, Ugarit, and Emar; and alphabetic cuneiform texts from Ugarit.[13] With reference to the nominal elements that occur with the interrogative particle, those names can be grouped according to three kinds:

1. Names containing kinship terms, most likely as theophorous elements:[14] ʾAyyaʾabum, ʾAyyâbī, ʾAyyaʾabī ("Where is the Father?"); ʾAyya-ʾabni-ilu ("Where is my Father, the God?"); ʾAyyâḫu, ʾAyya-ʾaḫī ("Where is the Brother?"); ʾAyya-ʾaḫḫī ("Where are the Brothers?"); ʾAyya-dādu(m), ʾAyya-ʿammu, ʾAyya-ḫālu ("Where is the Kinsman?"); ʾAyya-ʾimmī, ʾAyya-ʾummī ("Where is my Mother?").

2. Names containing other terms that may serve as divine elements: ʾAyyâbī-šarrī ("Where is the King?"); ʾAyya-sumu, ʾAyya-lā-sumu ("Where is the Name?"); ʾAyya-sumu-ʾabim ("Where is the Name of the Father?").[15]

3. Names containing clearly theophorous designations: *'Ayya-ma-'ilu* ("Where is God/El?"); *'iyb'l* ("Where is Baal?"); *'iytlm* ("Where is tlm?");[16] *'iydm* ("Where is Damu?"); *'iytr* ("Where is the Bull?").[17]

Short forms also occur, such as *'Ayya* and *'Ayyan*. The continuing use of this name type through the Late Bronze–Iron I transition is represented by the clearly theophoric *'y'l* ("Where is El/the God?") from Qubūr-el-Walaydah in the Western Negeb.[18]

Akkadian names containing the interrogative element *ali* ("where?") and corresponding in meaning and structure to those West Semitic "Where?" names are also well attested for the second millennium.[19] These Akkadian names show the same distribution as observed in the West Semitic "Where?" names:

1. Names containing kinship terms: *Ali-abī* ("Where is my Father?"), *Ali-aḫu* ("Where is the Brother?"), *Ali-aḫḫū* ("Where are the Brothers?"), *Ali-ummī* ("Where is my Mother?").

2. Names containing other terms that may serve as divine elements: *Ali-bēli* ("Where is the Lord?"), *Ali-mālik* ("Where is the King?"), *Ali-ṭābum* ("Where is the Sweet One?"), *Ali-šūnu* ("Where are They?").

3. Names containing clearly theophorous designations: *Ali-ᵈŠamšī* ("Where is the Sun God?"), *Ali-iltī* ("Where is the Goddess?").

As part of what appears to have been a broader Semitic name type, the West Semitic "Where?" names are well attested throughout the second millennium. The occurrence of clearly theophoric elements among the names of this type in West Semitic as in Akkadian shows that these Bronze Age "Where?" names regularly if not always refer to deities, sometimes by a specific divine name but more often by divine titles, epithets, or emblems. Further consideration of the meaning of the names and their name elements will be informed by the following discussion of data from the first millennium. At this point, one may recognize that the question posed by these names suggests concern over the possible absence of the deity in question. [handwritten: Where is God is still asked]

The First-Millennium Names

West Semitic "Where?" names continue into the first millennium, which is represented by names of this type in alphabetic inscriptions: Phoenician and Punic *'y b'l*, *'b'l*, *y b'lym* ("Where is Baal?");[20] *'b'lšm* ("Where is Baal Shamem," with a shortened form of the divine epithet);[21] ʾyspn ("Where is Zaphon?");[22] Ammonite ʾyndb ("Where is the Noble One?");[23] and Hebrew ʾydh ("Where is the [divine] Assembly?"; cf. ʾelʿādâ in 1 Chron 7:20).[24]

The first-millennium attestations of the name type, like those from the second millennium, also include numerous cuneiform transcriptions of West Semitic names, such as the following names from Neo-Assyrian, Neo-Babylonian, and Late Babylonian texts:[25] ʾAyya-ʾabu; ʾAyya-ʾaḫu; ʾAyya-ʿammu; ʾAyya-Būlu ("Where is Bul?");[26] ʾAyya-ḫālu; ʾAyya-dādu; ʾAyya-ṭāb ("Where is the Sweet One?"); ʾAyya-ʾilī, ʾAyya-(ʾi)lūnu ("Where is our god?"); ʾAyya-Milkī ("Where is Milki?"); ʾAyya-Mitūnu ("Where is Miton?");[27] ʾAyya-Nēri ("Where is Neri?"); ʾAyya-Sammu ("Where is Sammu?");[28] ʾAyya-ṣurī ("Where is my Rock?"); ʾAyya-šumu ("Where is the Name?"); ʾAyya-Meri, ("Where is Mer?");[29] ʾAyya-Gašu ("Where is [the deity] Gaš?");[30] ʾAyya-Qīšu ("Where is [the deity] Qīš?").[31]

In many of these first-millennium names in cuneiform, it is not clear whether the initial name element (spelled a-a-, a-i-, a-a-i-, a-ia-, ia-, and so forth) is the interrogative particle ʾayya- found in our name type or a divine element in nominal sentence names.[32] The latter is quite clearly the case in many names that include the Akkadian divine determinative (DINGIR), for example, ᵈa-a-bēl (-EN; "ᵈa-a- is Lord"), ᵐᵈa-a-ṣi-id-qi ("ᵈa-a- is Rightness"), ᵐᵈa-a-ṭu-ri ("ᵈa-a- is a Rock").[33] The deity so named is not likely to be the Mesopotamian goddess Aya, consort of the sun god Shamash, since this divine element appears in anthroponyms only with masculine grammatical forms and never with feminine ones.[34] The divine element in question might well be a syllabic writing of the name of the Mesopotamian god Ea, whose name is also written logographically ᵈÉ.A.[35] In a few instances, names of this kind belong to prominent persons in regions where Ea would not be expected to have had significant influence, namely, ᴵᵈA-a-ram-mu (ʾAyya-ram; "Where is the Exalted One?") king of Edom,[36] ᴵᵈA-a-ka-ba-ru (ʾAyya-kabaru; "Where is the Great One?"),[37] and ᴵᵈA-a-nu-r[i] (ʾAyya-nūr; "Where is the Light?") of the land of Tabeel.[38] For these and other possible "Where?" names, it is reasonable to consider that Assyrian scribes, being accustomed to hearing and writing initial ʾayya-/ʾaya- as a theophoric element in personal names, might misconstrue the West Semitic "Where?" names or deliberately write them in the form of the names with which they were familiar, as a rebus.[39]

Like the second-millennium "Where?" names, those from the first millennium occur with the following distribution according to nominal elements contained:

1. Names containing kinship terms: *ʾAyya-ʾabu, ʾAyya-ʾaḫu, ʾAyya-ʿammu; ʾAyya-ḫālu; ʾAyya-dādu.*

2. Names containing other terms that may serve as divine elements: *ʾAyya-ṭāb, ʾAyya-šumu, ʾyndb, ʾydh, ʾAyya-Milki, ʾAyya-Nēri, ʾAyya-ṣurī,* and possibly *ʾAyya-ram* and *ʾAyya-nūr.*

3. Names containing clearly theophorous designations: *ʾy bʿl, ʾbʿl, y bʿlym, ʾbʿlšm, ʾyspn; ʾAyya-ʾilī, ʾAyya-(ʾi)lūnu, ʾAyya-Mitūnu, ʾAyya-Sammu, ʾAyya-Meri, ʾAyya-Gašu, ʾAyya-Qīšu.*

This breakdown of the names shows the same distribution as observed in the second-millennium names previously reviewed. As this comparison illustrates, the "Where?" names continue into the first millennium with the same structure and the same basic range of meanings. What is clear is a name pattern in which the question "Where?" is posed in reference to the divine. Still requiring further explanation is the meaning of kinship terms in names of this type.

Kinship Terms in "Where?" Names

The meaning of the kinship terms in these and other anthroponyms remains a matter of debate. Johann Jakob Stamm classified the "Where?" names containing kinship terms as *Ersatznamen,* a broader category of names that designate the child so named as a substitute for a deceased relative.[40] Stamm's explanation is problematic in that the notion of *Ersatznamen* does not account for the undeniably theophoric "Where?" names reviewed here.

A second possibility was proposed more recently by Karel van der Toorn, who contends that kinship terms as personal name elements refer to divinized deceased ancestors.[41] In view of the strong case to be made for the cult of the dead in the West Semitic world, this suggestion remains a possibility.[42]

A third and much older explanation is that the kinship terms in our "Where?" names refer to deities. This was the position taken by Gray and by Noth in connection with Hebrew names more generally.[43] Supporting this view are Hebrew names like biblical *yô-ʾāb* (Joab; "Yahweh is Father") and *ʾăḥî-yāh* (Ahijah; "My Brother is Yahweh") and comparisons like the following: *yĕhô-nādāb* (Jehonadab; "Yahweh is a Noble One") and *ʾēl-nādāb* (Elnadab; "God/El is a Noble One") alongside names like *ʾăbînādāb* (Abinadab; "My Father is a Noble One"), *ʾăḥînādāb* ("My Brother is a Noble One"), and *ʿamminādāb* ("My Kinsman is a Noble One"). Here the kinship terms stand in the same place as clearly

Our Father — a kind kinship name ? : Mo'

theophorous name elements. Acknowledging this kind of evidence, van der Toorn argues against this position by observing, "Outside the hypothetical possibility of personal names, gods are never referred to as 'brother' or 'uncle' in relation to humans."[44] Van der Toorn's objection involves the explanation of a specific genre category (personal names) by recourse to information from other genre types (other texts). While this procedure is perfectly valid in support of positive arguments, it is fundamentally problematic in the service of negative arguments from silence involving two separate genres of religious evidence. It is fair to say that the question of kinship terms as elements in Semitic personal names broadly is one that requires further investigation based on data beyond the scope of the "Where?" names specifically.

With respect to this collection of names, their regular occurrence with theophorous elements suggests that the kinship terms likewise refer to deities. Alternatively, if van der Toorn is correct that the kinship terms reference "divinized" ancestors, then the "Where?" names show the same role or roles being filled by deceased ancestors and proper deities alike. Like the question regarding the kinship terms themselves, the implied roles ascribed to their referents by this name type require further consideration.

For the purposes of the present discussion, it suffices to say that the range of extrabiblical evidence adduced here demonstrates a longstanding West Semitic name type in Syria-Palestine that persisted from the second millennium well into the first. On the basis of that evidence, one can affirm that the "Where?" names occur regularly with clearly theophoric elements in West Semitic (as in Akkadian), and thus that these "Where?" names regularly if not always referred to deities. The question posed by these names is one invoked in connection with the divine, suggesting some concern over the possible absence of the deity. The understanding of the precise meaning and religious implications of those names will be informed by the following discussion of the biblical names of this type.

THE BIBLICAL NAMES

The group of biblical names under examination—Ichabod (*'îkābôd*), Jezebel (*'îzebel*), Iezer (*'î'ezer*), Ehud (*'ēhûd*), Job (*'iyyôb*), and Ithamar (*'îtāmār*)—lend themselves to being understood according to the pattern of the West Semitic "Where?" names, as does an additional biblical name that the second-millennium evidence suggests to be of similar form, Ayyah (*'ayyah*). The consistency with which they bear out this pattern indicates that those biblical names do in fact belong to this well-attested West Semitic name category. At the same time, other explanations for some of the biblical names in question have been offered. To evaluate the possible interpretations of the biblical names, it will be useful to examine each name individually.

Ichabod (*ʾîkābôd*)

The case of Ichabod (spelled consonantally, *ʾy kbwd*) is a fortuitous example of a biblical name that appears along with a narrative explanation (1 Sam 4:19-22). While biblical "folk etymologies," rather than offering etymologically correct explanations of the meanings of names, typically involve an ironic wordplay on the name related to some aspect of the narrative, they also occasionally provide some glimpse into the name's historical and philological meaning as it would have been recognized by a contemporary audience.[45] In the narrative about Ichabod's birth, the name is connected not only with the mother's personal tragedy but more poignantly with the Philistines' capture of the ark and the departure of the deity's glorious presence associated with this worship symbol, as signified by the word *kābôd* ("glory"; vv. 21-22).

A lament over the deity's absence in the loss of the ark is consistent with the understanding of the initial name element *ʾy* as the negative particle *ʾî*, with the name thus being understood to mean "no glory" or "inglorious"—a tradition that goes back at least to Josephus and that finds philological support in Phoenician and Ethiopic negative particles.[46] At the same time, it is questionable whether the name element *ʾy* is in fact a negative particle in Hebrew names, as the negative particle *ʾî* is attested in Biblical Hebrew only in Job 22:30 in the expression *ʾî-nāqî* ("not innocent"; see also with the meaning "alas" or "woe" in Qoh 4:10; 10:16). Furthermore, aside from symbolic names like *lōʾ ʿammî* ("Not My People") and *lōʾ ruḥāmâ* ("Not Pitied") in the biblical prophetic books (Hos 1:6, 8; 2:23), the onomastic inventory of West Semitic otherwise lacks names constructed with this or any other negative particle.[47] Equally fitting to the narrative context is the name's correspondence to the well attested West Semitic name type, thus with the meaning "Where is the Glory?"—a meaning that accords with the departure of the ark in the story.[48]

Jezebel (*ʾîzebel*)

Jezebel (spelled consonantally, *ʾyzbl*), the daughter of "Ethbaal (*ʾetbaʿal*) king of the Sidonians," is remembered grudgingly in biblical tradition

as an ardent devotee of the cult of Phoenician "Baal" (1 Kings 16:31-
32; 18–19). The MT vocalization of her name (*'îzebel*) likely preserves a
polemical distortion, in which *zebel* ("dung") occurs for *zĕbûl* (<*zabūlu;
"prince,") an epithet by which Baal-Haddu is named in Ugaritic myth.[49]
The biblical reference to *ba'al zebûb* ("Lord of the Flies") is obviously
a parody of a divine honorific **Ba'l Zabūl* (2 Kings 1:2, 3, 6, 16). In
the Ugaritic Baal cycle, the deity is mourned with the exclamation *'iy
'al'iyn b'l 'iy zbl b'l 'arṣ* ("Where is Mighty Baal, Where is the Prince, the
Lord of the Earth?"; *KTU*² 1.6 IV:4–5, 15–16).[50] Thus bearing a literal
correspondence with this line,[51] the name *'yzbl* ("Where is the prince?")
also bears a formal and semantic correspondence with Ugaritic *'iyb'l* and
Phoenician *'yb'l*, indicating that it belongs to the "Where?" name type
so well known from Ugarit and elsewhere.

Nonetheless, other explanations for the name have been offered.
According to one of those, the initial element of the name is a contraction of *'ḥy* ("my brother"), from a hypothetical full name form *'ḥyzbl*.[52]
Alternatively, it has been suggested that the name as whole is a contraction of a reconstructed locution *'y zh b'l* ("Where is the one who is
Baal?").[53] Due to the nature of the evidence for such contraction names,
their existence is ultimately not subject to verification or falsification;[54]
however, the evidence for such names does allow for a different explanation (see below, the discussion of Iezer (*'î'ezer*). In this case, though,
neither of the suggested longer name forms is even attested.

Another explanation involving hypothetical name forms was offered
by Nahman Avigad.[55] Noting the compatibility of the name *yzbl* on a
stamp seal with the LXX spelling of Jezebel's name (Gk. *Iezabel*), Avigad
tentatively suggested that MT *'yzbl* be understood as a variant of a name
having the alternative forms *yš zbl and **'š zbl*, both meaning "Zebul
exists."[56] While the proposal is an ingenious one, a simpler explanation
for the name on the seal is that it derives from a prefixed verb form.[57] In
view of the morphological and semantic parallels to the name *'iyb'l*, *'yb'l*,
and so forth in Ugaritic and Phoenician and to the lament from the Baal
epic as previously discussed, the understanding of Jezebel as belonging
to the widely attested "Where?" name type has a much firmer basis in
the available evidence.[58]

Iezer (*'î'ezer*)

Another name that has been explained as a contracted name form is
Iezer (spelled consonantally, *'y'zr*; Num 26:30).[59] Outside the Hebrew
Bible, this name is attested, possibly as an Aramaic name, on an unprov-
enanced inscribed seal that Bordreuil and Lemaire date paleographically

to the late-seventh or sixth century B.C.E.[60] The noun *ʿezer* appears regularly as a theophoric element in Hebrew personal names.[61] Iezer appears in Num 26:30 as the eponymous ancestor of the Iezrite clan of Manasseh in Gilead (*mišpaḥat hāʾîʿezrî*). Readings of this passage reflected in the LXX and Peshitta indicate that the name might have been understood as a variant of Ahiezer (*ʾăḥîʿezer*; "My Brother is a help"). However, comparisons with Josh 17:2 and 1 Chr 7:17-19 suggest the name Iezer to be an alternate name for Abiezer (*ʾăbîʿezer*; "My Father is a help"; v. 18).[62]

An alternate name, though, need not be a contracted name. In fact, alternate names in the Hebrew Bible tend rather to involve a variation of elements between name forms that are etymologically related or that are both phonologically similar and semantically compatible. For example, the tendency of *ʿezer* names to occur with name variants is well illustrated by Eleazar (*ʾelʿāzār*) in 1 Sam 7:1, who elsewhere is called Uzzah (*ʿuzzāʾ* = *ʿuzzâ*; 2 Sam 6:3-8; 1 Chr 13:7-11). Similarly, different biblical sources refer to the same Judean king as Azariah (*ʿăzaryâ* = *ʿăzaryāhû*; 2 Kings 15:1-7) and Uzziah (*ʿuzzîyâ* and *ʿuzzîyāhû*; Isa 1:1; 6:1; 2 Chr 26:1-23). In these instances, the alternating name forms lend themselves to being construed not as contractions but rather as variant names involving an alternation of *ʿzr* ("help") with *ʿōz*, ("might") as onomastic elements.[63] The general pattern illustrated here for variant names involves not contracted and fuller forms of the same name, but rather lexically related yet genuinely different names for the same individual. Whether or not the understanding of *ʾîʿezer* as a "Where?" name had at some point become faded, its resemblance to *ʾăbîʿezer* and *ʾăḥîʿezer* constituted a suitable basis for name variation.

Ehud (*ʾēhûd*)

Similar in meaning is the name Ehud, which contains a form of the noun *hôd* ("splendor"; "majesty"). This term occurs in reference to the divine in other Hebrew personal names: see biblical *hwdyh*, *ʿmyhwd*, *ʾbyhwd*, *ḥyhwd*.[64] While the latter two names might suggest that *ʾhwd* is a contracted form,[65] the same deficiencies of this explanation in regard to names previously discussed also apply in this case. Furthermore and in keeping with the MT vocalization, *ʾēhûd* makes more sense as the usual contracted form of the interrogative particle (*ʾay* > *ʾê*)—though with defective spelling, that is, with the omission of the dipthongized *y*, as in Phoenician names like *ʾbʿl*.[66] The name is thus easily understood as an example of the name type in question, meaning "Where is the (Divine) Splendor?"[67] No other explanation for *ʾēhûd* is forthcoming.

Job (ʾiyyôb)

The name Job (ʾywb, vocalized ʾiyyôb) is presumably an altered form of the well-attested second-millennium name ʾAyya-ʾabu, with contraction of the aleph and the change of the resulting long ā to long ō through the "Canaanite shift."[68] The resulting form reflects a possible reanalyzing of the name in accordance with a passive formation on analogy with yillôd or šikkôr. Accordingly, ʾiyyôb would mean "the one attacked, or hated."[69] Perhaps with intended ambiguity, the name could also be construed according to the active construction as in gibbôr, with ʾiyyôb meaning "the hater." Such meanings for the name would be symbolic, in keeping with the literary and theological dimensions of the biblical book.[70] Nonetheless, a most fitting name for a protagonist who questions divine justice and demands an appearance from God would be the original meaning of the name, "Where is the Father?" that is, the divine father. Thus, it is possible that this original meaning of the name would have been recognized in association with the Job tradition early on but then became obscured over time.

Ithamar (ʾîtāmār)

Although Albright declined to include Ithamar (spelled consonantally, ʾytmr; Exod 6:23) among "Where?" names, several scholars have at least considered its categorization as such.[71] Accordingly, this priestly name would mean "Where is the Date-Palm [tāmār]?"—the latter being an emblem of divine presence as abundantly attested in iconographic evidence and in biblical descriptions of Solomon's temple (1 Kings 6:29; Ezek 40:16, 22) and perhaps in the name of David's daughter, Tamar (tāmār).[72]

Other explanations have been offered as well. The suggestion that the name means "island/coastland of palms" admits to no clear rationale.[73] Also, the name ʾîtîʾēl, itself not well understood, has been invoked as suggesting a possible explanation.[74] The comparative philological evidence that William H. Propp marshals in favor of his explanation of the name as a Gt form of the root *ʾmr, meaning "He appeared/saw" or "He obeyed," does not sufficiently cohere so as to suggest an origin for the name either within the development of Hebrew or as an imported name.[75] That is, the understanding of the name as a Gt perfect (with prosthetic ʾalep) leaves the y unexplained, the same obstacle faced by Albright in advancing a similar explanation of the name.[76] Thus, the understanding of ʾîtāmār as a "Where?" name is the only explanation without difficulties.

Ayyah (*'ayyah*)

In addition to the biblical names considered, a Yahwistic name might possibly be represented by biblical Ayyah (spelled consonantally, *'yh*; Gen 36:24; 2 Sam 3:7; 1 Chr 1:40)—thus, "Where is Yah?"—though this conclusion is certainly debatable and would be difficult to confirm.[77] More likely, in view of the Bronze Age short forms *'Ayya* and *'Ayyan* (see above, in the discussion of second-millennium names), the whole of the name is the question particle, though one might expect its vocalization in that case to follow the usual pointing of the word, *'ayyē(h)*. Alternatively *'ayyah*, which also appears in Biblical Hebrew as a common noun meaning "hawk, falcon, or kite," is to be explained as an animal name.[78]

This review of the biblical names under examination can be summarized as follows. In terms of form and structure, all of the biblical names described here conform to the West Semitic "Where?" name type so well attested in second- and first-millennium sources. This fact alone is significant in view of the lack of other corresponding name patterns in West Semitic. With the possible exception of *'ayyah*, all of the biblical names considered here are best construed as "Where?" names consisting of the question particle plus the invocation of a divine epithet or manifestation. Where alternative explanations are offered for the names, these explanations do not account for all the other names, and for the names to which they do apply, those explanations tend to pose further problems. Given the existence of the widely attested West Semitic "Where?" name type, the identification of these biblical names as belonging to that onomastic classification is solid. Stated otherwise, these biblical names ask the question "Where is the deity?" by reference to various divine epithets and manifestations of divine presence. They thus merit the designation divine-absence personal names. The more precise significance of this question of divine absence might be considered further.

THE MEANING OF THE DIVINE-ABSENCE NAMES

As noted earlier in the discussion, the "Where?" names mentioning Baal and related epithets (that is, *'iyb'l*, *'y b'l*, *'b'l*, *y b'lym*; *'b'lšm*, and especially, biblical *'yzbl*) bear a striking correspondence to exclamations of mourning for Baal in Ugaritic myth.[79] Based on that correspondence, one might consider whether this name type expresses a reference to ritual mourning for a deity[80] or else alludes to mythic associations of so-called "dying and rising" gods.[81] The mention of Damu, another deity conventionally understood to belong to that category, in the name *'iydm* would be consistent with such an understanding of the name type (see above, the discussion of Jezebel [*'îzebel*]). Also potentially supporting this possibility for the Semitic name type more broadly is the Akkadian name *Ali-*[d]*Šamši* ("Where is the Sun God?"), the sun deity having nether-world associations in ancient Semitic religion.[82] The possibility that the "Where?" names refer to mourning for dying gods would potentially be consistent with understanding the kinship terms in names of this type as "divinized" deceased ancestors, as argued by van der Toorn in the discussion of kinship terms. Accordingly, deceased ancestors and proper deities would be regarded as serving the same roles in these names.

Such a possibility is best considered within the framework of the conventions that pertain to personal names as a category of religious evidence. As noted earlier in this chapter and as repeatedly confirmed in the study of West Semitic personal names, anthroponyms as religious expressions tend to be generic in nature. While personal names often attribute specific roles and activities to deities—saving, acting benefi-cently, protecting, even ruling—these are not special roles limited to a particular deity or smaller circle of gods among those mentioned in personal names. Thus, a special name type referencing a specific mythic category of deities, such as dying ones, would be out of character for ancient Semitic personal names. Furthermore, among these names are those making reference to deities who are not otherwise associated with death—particularly *'iytr* ("Where is the Bull?") and other "Where?" names referring to El/Ilu.

As mentioned, several prominent biblical examples of the divine-absence name type involve individuals described as being of priestly lineage or otherwise by birth and family identity having significant roles of cultic leadership, most notably, Ithamar, Ichabod, and Jezebel. In 1 Samuel 4, Ichabod's name (*'y kbwd*; "Where is the Glory?") is connected poignantly with the disappearance of the Israelites' central worship symbol, the ark of Yahweh. As noted, the priestly name Ithamar (*'ytmr*; Exod 6:23), meaning "Where is the Date-Palm (*tāmār*)?" makes refer-ence to an emblem of divine presence associated with the adornment of worship sanctuaries, including Solomon's temple. In light of this recur-ring association, one might consider whether in Iron Age Israel, if not in the West Semitic sphere more broadly, the name type had special asso-ciations with the priesthood or other family lines involved in religious leadership.

Again, the question of possible cultic or mythic reference in personal names was prompted by attention to literary texts (namely, *KTU*² 1.5 and 1.6). Accordingly, the consideration of other literary evidence sheds further light on the matter. The question "Where is the deity?" occurs in a number of biblical passages reflecting a range of literary and social contexts but consistently with cultic associations: polemic against the worship of other gods (Deut 32:37); prophetic or poetic rhetoric regarding the proper seeking of one's own god by priests and people alike (Jer 2:6, 8; Job 35:10); personal enemies' taunting of an individual cut off from worship (Ps 42:3, 10); communal lament citing the potential disparagement of the nation by its enemies (Joel 2:17; Pss 79:10; 115:2); wartime propaganda by a military invader (2 Kings 18:34 = Isa 36:19); lament among sanctuary ruins (Isa 63:11, 15). The question voices concern over the apparent lack of the deity's efficacious presence consistently with associations to worship.

Again, due to the general nature of the expressions made by theophoric personal names, it would be surprising for the content of these question names to make reference to a particular divine role or cultic tradition. Accordingly, the names under consideration are best understood to express the basic concern over divine absence generally and not as allusions to a particular cultic role or practice such as ritual mourning, let alone to a cultic role of the name bearer. Nonetheless, it is possible that particular "family names" or name elements might have been traditional within a genealogical line and thus might have been considered suitable or conventional in connection with certain roles, such as priestly or other cultic leadership determined by family descent and identity.

To summarize this point, the use of the divine-absence question in personal names seems to have had its origin not in cult but in a basic religious concern that could be voiced in various situations. Among the biblical literary occurrences of the question, a concern for the cult place and its activities is nonetheless consistently close at hand in those various situations. It is possible that during the Iron Age, when this personal name type was no longer as common in general usage as it had been previously, it continued as a conventional name type among priestly and other family lines specially associated with the cult—not as an allusion to cult or cultic roles but as a name type that had become traditional within certain family lines. Though the divine-absence names did not originate in the cult, continued currency of the name type may have possibly been influenced by factors having to do with worship. In any case, this explanation is offered tentatively as a way of accounting for the noteworthy cultic associations of several bearers of these names in biblical texts.

CONCLUSION

As a reflection of family piety, personal names give explicit reference to divine absence as a fundamental concern for ancient West-Semitic religion. A frequent occurrence of this name type among West Semitic personal names during the second millennium and into the first shows the question "Where?" to have been a standard locution expressing this concern. The question posed by the name type—"Where?"—is, after all, one implying absence generally.

As the narrative of 1 Samuel 4 implies and as the very existence of the name type itself indicates, the question is one that might be voiced appropriately in connection with the precarious event of childbirth. In the ancient world, both the stigma of barrenness and the dangers of delivery made childbirth a matter of great anxiety.[83] The question "Where is the deity?" would thus be a fitting expression of the anxiety that surely accompanied childbirth. At the same time, the successful and healthy birth of the child would be perceived as a favorable divine answer to that concern and to the question expressing it. Thus, while Stamm's *Ersatzname* explanation does not suffice for this name category, the logic of that explanation is in part correct. The "Where?" names designated the name bearer as an answer to the question referenced by the name; however, the question pertained not to the absence of a deceased relative but to the possible absence of one's deity, in this case as needed for a successful and healthy birth. In other words, these divine-absence names point to the birth and continuing life of the name bearer as a divine response to the question of despair.

The relative paucity of these names in the Hebrew onomasticon suggests that their basic meaning and religious significance had fallen out of fashion for ancient Israelites and thus had become obscured, perhaps even during the time of the monarchy. Nonetheless, the name type itself suggests that the question of divine absence can lead to an experience of divine presence and thus can be invoked in recollection of such an experience. In personal names, the question of divine absence is thus turned into an affirmation of divine presence.

CHAPTER 3

God and Israel
in the Hebrew Bible:
Origins of the Relationship

As noted from the outset of this discussion, the theme of divine absence in the Hebrew Bible involves a crisis of relationship. Chapter 1 described how divine–human bonds in ancient Israel were grounded in ancient Israel's kin-based social life. The preceding chapter showed how human personal names in ancient Israel and its broader West Semitic context could reflect the experience of divine absence, especially in the context of family life.

Just as institutional forms and mechanisms like patrimony, tribalism, and covenant interrelate in the structures for human social and political relationships, so too do they provide a framework for conceiving Israel's relationship to its God. Accordingly, these social realities provide models for divine–human relationships in various and distinct traditions accounting for the origin of the relationship between Israel and God. Throughout the Hebrew Bible, the consistent focus is on Israel as distinct from other peoples and nations, so all of these ways of presenting Israel's relationship to God ultimately have in view a national and international frame of reference. Relationships to God in the Hebrew Bible begin and end with national religious identity.

The following discussion of these relational loci and their attendant structures is organized not so much chronologically as conceptually. Against the modern expectation of logical coherence, of a systematized and fully unified view of the divine and of divine–world relationships, ancient societies typically allowed more than one explanation

or representation of the world and its workings to stand side by side.[1]
While the complex processes of editing and formation that produced
the Hebrew Bible have brought about considerable harmonization, the
abiding result is nonetheless several distinct ways of construing divine–
human relationships and their origins: traditions centering around primordial divine inheritance, the Davidic king, the god of the fathers, the
divine warrior, Mosaic law and covenant, and creation. This discussion
also speaks conceptually of how the God of Israel is also recognized
as the God of the world. In different ways in the Hebrew Bible, Israel's
identity is bound up with these various relational foundations of divine
presence.

PRIMORDIAL INHERITANCE:
JACOB-ISRAEL AS DIVINE PATRIMONY

As described in chapter 1, in the Hebrew Bible as in other ancient Near
Eastern texts, the basic social institution of the patrimonial household
can be projected onto the divine realm. Such is the case in Deut 32:8-9,
which, with an international frame of reference, portrays the ordering
of the divine family in relationship to ascending levels of social complexity among humankind. Here, the senior head over the next generation of gods is identified by the divine title Elyon ("the Highest").[2] Elyon
divides the peoples of the earth and their territories "according to the
number of the divine beings."[3] The deity thus assigned to Israel as its
divine sovereign is Yahweh, and Israel is Yahweh's assigned patrimony,
"the measured portion of his inheritance" (*hebel nahălātō*; v. 9). This
mytheme thus describes a parceling of both people and land as a divine
patrimonial estate and in so doing employs the terminology of sonship
and property inheritance.[4]

The heavy use of territorial language (*gĕbulot* "boundaries"; *hēleq*
"portion"; *hebel* "measured portion, territory") in this passage indicates
more than just a metaphorical interest in patrimonial holdings. That is,
along with the population of ancient Israel, the land is clearly in view. A
key term in this regard is *nahălā* ("possession, property, inheritance").
The biblical and extrabiblical evidence related to the term *nahălā* indicates that at its basis the term refers to an inalienable estate of land con-
ferred either through inheritance along lines of kinship or as royal land
grant.[5] Elsewhere in the Hebrew Bible, Yahweh's *nahălâ* refers to the
land of Israel (or to the Israelites in that land; see Joel 2:17) as Yahweh's
inalienable possession (see, for example, 1 Sam 26:19; 2 Sam 14:16;
20:19; 21:3).[6]

The expression that appears in Deut 32:9, *ḥebel naḥălâ* ("portion of inherited property"), occurs in Ps 105:11 (= 1 Chr 16:18) in reference to Yahweh's gift of the land to his people:

> *lĕkā ʾettēn ʾet-ʾereṣ -kĕnāʿan ḥebel naḥălatkem*
> To you I have given the land of Canaan as the measured portion of your inheritance.

Here Yahweh's patrimonial inheritance has become the people's inheritance through the deity's benevolence as divine patron. A similar understanding of the relationship binding deity, land, and people is expressed in the Song of the Sea (Exod 15:1-18). With a focus on the sanctuary site as the center of Yahweh's patrimonial holdings—"your holy abode" (*nĕwē(h) qodšekā*; v. 13), "the mountain of your possession" (*har naḥălātĕkā*; v. 17)—Yahweh delivers the people and "plants" them at the place of his dwelling (v. 17).[7] The book of Deuteronomy is imbued with the concept of Yahweh's gift of the land as the people's "inheritance" (*naḥălâ*; see, for example, Deut 4:21; 15:4; 26:1).

These biblical texts reflect an understanding of the people and land of Israel as the inheritance of Yahweh, originally allotted, according to Deut 32:8-9, by the senior god of the pantheon, Elyon. As Mark S. Smith points out, this passage is extraordinary among other Israelite origin traditions in the Hebrew Bible, invoking as it does an older and widely known tradition of the founding of the world reflected later in Philo of Byblos's work, *The Phoenician History*, in which the god Kronos is identified with El and assigns the lands of the world to different gods.[8] Earlier, the tale of Wenamun includes a speech with a similar picture of polytheistic apportioning of lands to various gods: "For Amun makes thunder in the sky ever since he placed Seth beside him! Indeed Amun has founded all the lands. He founded them after having founded the land of Egypt from which you have come."[9]

People and land are thus integrally connected within the patrimonial holding and are bound to their deity in a relationship of mutual loyalty.[10] As the household and estate of Yahweh, the people and land of Israel belong exclusively to Yahweh and owe special allegiance to him. In turn, as divine sovereign over the people and land, Yahweh has the role and prerogative of protecting and nurturing Israel as his patrimonial holding.

This concept of the nation as divine patrimonial household accounts for the expectations of divine support and favorable presence that are so harshly disappointed by the experience of divine absence. It also explains, in the case of the people's disloyalty, that divine absence can result from the disappointment that Israel's God may experience. Such is the case later in the Song of Moses in Deuteronomy 32 (see especially vv. 19-27).

In keeping with the conception of the divine family as found in Deut 32:8-9, Psalm 82 presents Israel's God among the other "sons of Elyon" (v. 6).[11] Mark S. Smith speaks of the viewpoint here as a kind of "world theology" and aptly summarizes what is at issue in this passage: "Each of these sons has a different nation as his ancient patrimony (or family inheritance) and therefore serves as its ruler. Yet verse 6 calls on Yahweh to arrogate to himself the traditional inheritance of all the other gods, thereby making Israel and all the world the inheritance of Israel's God."[12] Thus, the idea of divine patrimony is one basis on which the biblical traditions extend Yahweh's patronage not only to Israel but also to the whole of the earth. This kind of world theology in turn lends itself to royal conceptions of a God–world relationship as expressed in the Zion tradition.

DAVID AND ZION:
THE HUMAN KING OVER THE DIVINE PATRIMONY

In connection with the Davidic monarchy in Jerusalem, many biblical texts, especially in the books of Psalms and Isaiah, espouse what scholars have identified as the Zion tradition, the basic elements of which are Yahweh's rule as divine king and his choice of Jerusalem as his place of dwelling.[13] For example, Psalms 47, 93, and 95–99 have long been recognized as a distinct group of poems celebrating Yahweh's enthronement as "great king over all the earth" (47:3).[14] In these psalms, the earthly seat of Yahweh's rule over the other nations (96:7, 10; 99:1) and their gods (95:3; 96:4-5; 97:7, 9) is Jerusalem (97:8; 99:2). Also to be noted are the close thematic and verbal correspondences of Psalm 47 with Psalms 46 and 48, which extol Zion as "the city of God" (46:5; 48:2, 9) and which refer to Yahweh not only as "the God of Jacob" (ʾĕlōhê yaʿăqōb; 46:8, 12; compare gĕʾôn yaʿăqōb in 47:5), but also as Elyon, El's title denoting divine supremacy (46:5; 47:3; also 97:9)[15] and as "Great King" (melek rāb, 48:3; melek gādôl; 47:3), exercising dominion over the other nations (46:7; 47:2-4, 8-10; 48:5-8).[16] According to this tradition of royal ideology, Yahweh's dominion over the rest of the earth extends outward from Zion and is mediated by the Davidic king (Pss 2; 45:7-8).

In the prevailing West Semitic understanding of society as recognized by Stager and Schloen, the royal patrimony is at the apex of a social scaffolding of nested households (see chapter 1). Accordingly, royal ideology amounts to an extension of the traditional social structuring based on the patrimonial house. At the top of the hierarchical social stratification is the king's household. Thus, the ninth-century Tel Dan inscription refers to Judah as the "House of David," acknowledging the ruling household of David's lineage, and similarly Assyrian texts from the same period refer to the northern Israelite kingdom as the "House of Omri" (see chapter 1).

That understanding of society's basis endures in the developing traditions celebrating Jerusalem as a place of pilgrimage.[17] Referencing both patrimonial and tribal aspects of society, Ps 122:4-5 declares:

> To [Jerusalem] the tribes go up,
>   the tribes of Yah . . . .
> For there the thrones for judgment were set up,
>   the thrones of the house of David.

With sociopolitical ramifications, the Zion tradition, as an outgrowth of the notion of divine patrimony, presents divine and royal patrimony as heavenly and earthly expressions of the same reality. The extent of the king's claimed dominion corresponds to that claimed for the king's god.

In Jerusalem, the Davidic ruler is understood to be the earthly regent of the true, divine king Yahweh.[18] The human king reigns by virtue of his declared sonship to Yahweh. The ruler's filial relationship to Yahweh accounts for the divine qualities attributed to the Davidic king in the sequence of throne names in Isa 9:5-6: "Wonderful Counselor, Mighty God, Everlasting Father, Prince of Peace."[19] This relationship is celebrated in Psalm 2:

> Why do the nations conspire,
>   and the peoples plot in vain?
> The kings of the earth set themselves,
>   and the rulers take counsel together,
>   against the LORD and his anointed, saying,
> "Let us burst their bonds asunder,
>   and cast their cords from us."
>
> . . . .
>
> I will tell of the decree of the LORD:
> He said to me, "You are my son;

> today I have begotten you.
> Ask of me, and I will make the nations your heritage,
>   and the ends of the earth your possession.
> You shall break them with a rod of iron,
>   and dash them in pieces like a potter's vessel."
>
>   (vv. 1-3, 7-9 NRSV)

The Davidic royal ideal here expressed is built on the recognition of David's rule over the nation, over which Yahweh is the divine patrimonial head.

As discussed in the previous section, Psalm 82 portrays divine jurisdiction over the other nations as having fallen to Israel's God. Thus, Yahweh's patronage of Israel is extended to the entire world through divine inheritance. This understanding of worldwide divine patrimony is assumed in the articulation of Psalm 2. The "world theology" whereby the other nations become part of Yahweh's patrimony as in Psalm 82 grounds the claim to Yahweh's power and authority over the other nations. Although ancient Israel is one nation among many, this mytheme buttresses Davidic royal claims to at least potential dominance over the other kingdoms of the earth. Through the elevation of Israel's God among the gods of the nations, Yahweh's earthly regent, the Davidic king, secures Israel's place among the nations.

Royal theology means that divine–human relations focus on the king and the place from which he rules. Yet the ideological force of such a notion would have been directed primarily toward the broader Israelite population. According to the theology of David and Zion, the people of Israel worship a God whose authority reached to the rest of the world. Like West Semitic royal ideology more generally (as reflected, for example, at Ugarit; see above, chapter 1), the Zion tradition was constructed in terms of the idea of the divine household and estate, which both centers around and extends from the people and land of Israel. The Zion tradition is an important foundation for Jerusalem's place as the center of divine presence and absence in biblical narrative and prophetic traditions (see chapter 7).

As a complement to this focus on divine patrimony, the next relational locus under examination emphasizes the place of the deity within the structure of *human* patrimony. Accordingly, a different vantage point from which to consider the people's place among the nations comes into view.

THE GOD OF THE FATHERS

Through the identification of Israel as the *běnê Yiśrāʾēl* ("children of Israel") and as a union of tribes descending from eponymous ancestors (see, for example, Gen 49:1-28; Deuteronomy 33; Judges 5), the biblical traditions present the beginnings of the people in terms of ancestral origins. Accordingly, the national God is described in terms of familial descent. This notion is invoked occasionally in the prophetic books, harking back to an ancestral origin for the relationship between the nation and its God. Hosea 12 points to the example of Jacob as one who "strove with God" and who "wept and sought his favor" (vv. 2-4). In a lament disparaging Judah as a people too deceptive for commitment to its God, Jeremiah 9 extends to the people the wordplay in the name etiology of their eponymous ancestor, which suggests his character as a supplanter, literally "heel grabber": *kol-ʾaḥ ʿāqôb yaʿqōb* ("every kinsman grasps the heel"; v. 4; see Gen 25:26). In an exilic context, Isa 51:3 implores, "Look to Abraham your father and to Sarah who bore you; for he was but one when I called him, but I blessed him and made him many."

Related narrative traditions are presented in more elaborate form in the Pentateuch (Genesis 12–50; Exod 2:24-25; 3:6, 13, 15-16; Deut 1:11; and other verses). Here the national God of Israel is associated with the people's eponymous ancestors in the guise of "the god of the fathers."[20] In the classic study of the subject, Albrecht Alt identified what he saw as a distinct phase in Israelite religious history in which nameless ancestral deities of the nomadic Israelites first entering the land were identified with the local deities of the indigenous El-religion of the Canaanite central hills of Palestine.[21] Along with Alt's theory of Israelite settlement, his "god of the fathers" hypothesis has since been rejected, mainly for its reliance on a flawed understanding of nomadism as it relates to Israelite origins.[22] An enduring contribution of Alt's study, though, is that it solidified the recognition of a particular mode of divine–human relationship in connection with family lineage and that the deity thus worshiped—in other words, the god of the particular ancestor—need not be the same as the national deity.[23]

In the ancestral narratives of Genesis 12–50, these two social levels of religion—those of household and nation—are presented as being in concert with one another. That is, the national god is vividly portrayed in terms of personal or family religion. The God of Israel is thus portrayed

colorfully as the patron god of its original ancestral family: "the god
of Abraham" (ĕlōhê ᵓabrāhām; Gen 26:24; 28:13), "the 'fear' of Isaac"
(paḥad yiṣḥāq; 31:42), and the god of Jacob/Israel (Gen 35:3). The presentation of Yahweh as "the god of the fathers," involves a conception
of Israel's God based on the model of religion within the patrimonial
household.

At the most personal level, human relationships to the divine were
structured according to primary social structures of kinship. Thus,
one's personal god was typically determined by patrilineal descent.[24]
In an example from the ancestral narratives, Laban tells Jacob, "It is
in my power to do you harm, but the god of your father spoke to me
last night" (Gen 31:29, emphasis added). As the narrative proceeds,
the two men establish an agreement in which they invoke as witness-
ing deities their respective ancestral gods: "The god of Abraham and
the god of Nahor judge between us" (MT: ᵓĕlōhê ᵓabrāhām wēᵓlōhê nāḥôr
yišpĕṭû bênênû; v. 53).[25] With Laban representing the Aramean peoples,
and Jacob the Israelites, each swears by his own ancestral gods.[26] The
Israelite understanding of the national God thus corresponds to that
of the divine patron of the family or of the individual family member,
as depicted throughout the biblical corpus.

Also for women, human relationships to the divine were structured
according to kin relationships, one's personal god being typically determined by household of origin or by marriage.[27] This concept is illustrated in Naomi's admonition that Ruth, like her sister-in-law, should
return "to her kindred and to her god" (ᵓel-ᶜammāh wēᵓel-ᵓĕlōhêhā; Ruth
1:15) and in Ruth's famous response to Naomi: "Your people shall be
my people and your god, my god" (ᶜammēk ᶜammî wēᵓlōhayik ᵓĕlōhāy;
v. 16). Even with the death of Ruth's husband and thus with the end of
the marriage giving her a place among Naomi's kindred, Ruth opts for
relationship to Naomi's people and her God as a matter of choice.

As discussed in chapter 1, the mechanism for establishing bonds of
kinship-in-law is covenant. This kin-based institution in turn becomes
a basis for patron, political, and legal relationships, these realms of life
being enmeshed into the kin-based society of the West Semitic world.
Thus, it is not surprising that in Genesis 12–50, the bond between the
ancestor and deity is sealed by covenant (Genesis 15; 17).

God's covenant with Abraham focuses on promises of land and
offspring, concerns that are fundamental matters of family obligation
and commitment (Gen 15:2-5; 17:3-9, 15-22). While this fact may be
self-explanatory for land and offspring, it is equally valid for the third
promise in view among the ancestral traditions, that of blessing (Gen
12:2-3). As shown by the patrimonial blessings by Isaac (Gen 27:27-29)

and Jacob (Gen 48:15-16, 20; 49:1-28) and their surrounding narratives, blessing too emerges from ancient Israel's kin-based social order to be extended into other relationships in what moderns might recognize as cultic, legal, and political realms.[28]

The traditions of the Abrahamic covenant provide an explanation for the origin of the divine–human kin relationship implied by titles like "kindred of Yahweh" and "god of Israel." As such, those covenant traditions belong with other manifestations of what Cross calls "sociomorphism" for describing Israel's relationship to its God—adoption, marriage, fealty oaths. At the root of all of these specific relational forms is "kinship-in-law."[29] This basic notion of human–divine kin relations also stands behind other forms of covenant between Israel and its God in the Hebrew Bible that will be discussed later in this chapter. First, though, one may consider another biblical tradition accounting for the origins of the divine–human relationship.

THE EXODUS TRADITION: THE DIVINE WARRIOR AND HIS PEOPLE

No tradition of Israel's national origins is more pervasive throughout the Hebrew Bible than the exodus. Yahweh's deliverance of Israel from Egypt and its armies is invoked repeatedly as the defining event for the people's identity and the basis of its relationship to its God (for example, Exod 20:2; Deut 5:6; 6:21-23; 7:8, 18-19; Judg 6:8, 13; Isa 63:11-13; Ezek 20:5-10; Pss 78:12-53; 106:7-46). The exodus is a distinctly Israelite manifestation of what scholars call the divine-warrior tradition in West Semitic religion.[30]

Frank Moore Cross has identified a mythic pattern of the divine-warrior tradition as it appears in Ugaritic and early Hebrew poetry.[31] That mythic pattern comprises the following basic elements: "(1) the combat of the Divine Warrior and his victory at the Sea, (2) the building of a sanctuary on the 'mount of possession' won in battle, and (3) the god's manifestation of 'eternal' kingship."

Regarding the second of those elements, the site of the sanctuary in Ugaritic poetry is called *ǵr nḥlty* ("the mountain of my inheritance"; *KTU*[2] 1.3. III 30; 1.3 IV 20). Similarly, in the Song of the Sea (Exod 15:1-18), the most ancient and extensive poetic text connected with the exodus, the sanctuary site is called *har naḥălātĕkā* ("the mountain of your inheritance"; v. 17). The mountainous aspect of the deity's dwelling is emphasized in accordance with the West Semitic understanding of the deity's sanctuary as a local manifestation of the "cosmic" mountain of

the deity's dwelling.[32] Nonetheless, matters are framed in terms of patrimonial domain. That is, the sanctuary site—the deity's earthly dwelling
place—serves as the focal point of the larger patrimonial domain, the
divine warrior's reward for victory in combat.[33]

A dimension of the Song of the Sea that goes beyond the divine-
warrior tradition is that the deity shares his triumph and rewards with
the people under his patronage. Through his victory at the sea, Yahweh
"ransoms" his people (v. 13). In establishing his "mountain of inheritance" as his dwelling, he not only takes up residence there himself but
also "plants" his people in that place (v. 17). As divine warrior, Yahweh
exercises these acts of benevolence at the expense of the other nations,
beginning with Egypt and then with the enemies surrounding Israel,
who are summarily cowed by Yahweh's might so that his people might
"pass by" unharmed (v. 16). The privileging of Yahweh's special people
is thus couched within the framework of the old mythic pattern, in
which the divine warrior takes possession of his dwelling place through
victory in battle. Thus, as in Deuteronomy 32, both land and people are
linked in the conception of the divine patrimonial estate (see the discussion of primordial inheritance, earlier in this chapter). The description
of the national deity in terms of this kin-based model of divine patronage makes it possible to connect the exodus tradition with that of "the
god of Abraham, Isaac, and Jacob" (Exod 3:16).

COVENANT AND LAW

In the Pentateuchal narratives, the exodus tradition is intimately linked
with the covenant and giving of the law at Sinai/Horeb (see, for example,
Exod 20:1-3; Deut 5:1-7; 6:21-25). The ancient Near Eastern tradition
of the law's divine origin is depicted most famously in the Hammu-
rabi stele, which includes a relief showing the sun god Shamash imparting the law to the Babylonian king.[34] Similarly, in the Sinai pericope in
Exodus 19–Numbers 10 and as recalled in Deuteronomy (for example,
Deut 1:5, 19; 4:10, 15; compare Deut 33:2), after leading the Israelites
out of Egypt, Moses serves as the people's leader and their mediator
before God in receiving the divine law.

The giving of the law at Sinai/Horeb, which is reinforced in Moses'
commands to a new generation of Israelites in Deuteronomy, has its
institutional context within a covenant that Yahweh establishes with
Israel at Sinai/Horeb (Exod 19:3-8a; 2:21b—24:8) and that Moses reiterates on the plains of Moab (Deut 4:10-14; 4:44—5:3; 9:8—10:13). As
discussed, covenant establishes the strongest possible bonds of human

loyalty. In the Deuteronomic formulation of Torah tradition, that notion of ultimate loyalty to the divine is stated concisely in Deut 6:4-5: "Hear, O Israel: The LORD is our God, the LORD alone. You shall love the LORD your God with all your heart, and with all your soul, and with all your might." As Norbert Lohfink has discussed, Deuteronomy 6 represents a kind of commentary on 6:4-5.[35] Taking Lohfink as his point of departure, Mark S. Smith suggests that the surrounding context in chapter 6 reinterprets an earlier statement of Yahweh's incomparability in verse 4.[36] Smith suggests that Deut 6:4 "may belong to the larger effort of Deuteronomy to express its reaction against the neo-Assyrian empire 'one-god' worldviews. The expression may literally mean that Yahweh (and thus not Assyria, its ruler and its god) is for Israel the one god deserving and requiring Israel's [covenantal] obedience and allegiance, what Eckart Otto calls 'ungeteilte Loyalität'" (undivided loyalty).[37] The expression to "love the LORD your God with all your heart" might thus be understood from this original context.

The surrounding literary context further reinterprets the expression. As this text goes on to elaborate, "Keep these words that I am commanding you today in your heart. Recite them to your children and talk about them when you are at home and when you are away, when you lie down and when you rise. Bind them as a sign on your hand, fix them as an emblem on your forehead, and write them on the doorpost of your house and on your gates" (Deut 6:6-9 NRSV). Thus, God's people are to live out a covenant relationship with Yahweh by being ever mindful and observant of divine commands.

In Deuteronomic formulation, covenant law is intimately bound with the exodus tradition: "When your children ask you in time to come, 'What is the meaning of the decrees and the statutes and the ordinances that the LORD our God has commanded you?' then you shall say to your children, 'We were Pharaoh's slaves in Egypt, but the LORD brought us out of Egypt with a mighty hand'" (Deut 6:20-21 NRSV). Around the figure of Moses, what may well have originated as separate traditions—the exodus and the giving of the law—are joined in the concept of covenant.[38]

CREATION

Like the exodus, creation in biblical literature draws on the divine-warrior tradition.[39] Yahweh's identification with the Canaanite deity El early in Israel's history is reflected in the frequent designation of Israel's God as (hā) 'ēl, often written with the definite article in Hebrew, meaning "(the) God," and in imagery and language that characterizes El in extrabiblical texts.[40] El's impact on Israelite notions of divine creation is evident in the biblical reference to *'ēl 'elyôn qōnē(h) šāmayim wā'āreṣ* ("El Elyon, Creator of Heaven and Earth"; Gen 14:19), a variant on a divine epithet for El attested in Phoenician, Punic, and other epigraphic contexts: *'l qn 'rṣ* ("El, Creator of the Earth").[41] This divine epithet occurs in Melchizedek's blessing of Abraham:

> "Blessed be Abram by *'ēl 'elyôn*,
>   creator of heaven and earth;
> and blessed be *'ēl 'elyôn*,
>   who has delivered your enemies into your hand!"
>
> (Gen 14:19-20)

The pairing of epithets in this blessing ("creator of heaven and earth"; "who has delivered your enemies into your hand") suggests that the roles of creator and divine warrior might have been related for West Semitic El.[42]

The West Semitic tradition of a cosmogonic battle between the creator god and the sea is attested within the broader cultural currents represented by the Babylonian creation epic, *Enuma Elish.*[43] Just as Marduk establishes the cosmos through his defeat of Tiamat ("Sea") in Babylonian tradition, so does Yahweh bring about the created order of the world by defeating the sea monster, called alternatively Rahab and Leviathan in biblical poetic texts (Pss 74:12-17; 89:9-12).[44] In both the biblical and the earlier Babylonian tradition, creation through conflict partakes of the general ancient Near Eastern understanding that creation consists of an order imposed on chaos. In this case, the divine warrior established order by defeating chaos as represented by the sea. In *Enuma Elish,* the resulting cosmic order centers on the political order of the Babylonian empire, as embodied by Marduk himself and as dramatized in the epic's culmination in the establishment of Babylon and Marduk's sanctuary Esagil (Tablet 6, lines 48–79).[45] The biblical poetic allusions similarly invoke this motif in connection with the political and temple establishment of Jerusalem but specifically in connection with its overthrow and with hopes for its restoration (Pss 74:1-11; 89:38-51). The most elaborate example of the divine-warrior tradition among surviving West Semitic texts is Baal's defeat of Yamm ("Sea") in the Ugaritic Baal cycle (*KTU*[2] 1.1–1.2).[46] While this text does not describe Baal's victory in terms of cosmogony of the natural world, nonetheless and in keeping with the divine-warrior mythic pattern, the building of Baal's house has cosmological and political implications congruent to those of the building of Marduk's house, Esagil.[47] Baal's role as creator

of the cosmos is not mentioned at Ugarit, but neither is El's.[48] In its lack
of interest in cosmogony, the Ugaritic texts might just as well represent
the exception as the norm for West Semitic tradition.[49]

The integral connection between ideas of creation and deliverance
in the divine-warrior tradition is evident where both are present in the
exilic-period reference in Isa 51:9-10:

> Awake, awake, put on strength,
>   O arm of the LORD!
> Awake, as in days of old,
>   the generations of long ago!
> Was it not you who cut Rahab in pieces,
>   who pierced the dragon?
> Was it not you who dried up the sea,
>   the waters of the great deep;
> who made the depths of the sea a way
>   for the redeemed to cross over? (NRSV)

This biblical formulation of the divine-warrior tradition equates Yahweh's power over chaos in creation and in deliverance.[50]

In the most extensive and, by virtue of their canonical location, dominant creation traditions of Genesis 1–3, conflict recedes from having
any role in creation. Instead, the element these passages share with the
divine-warrior pattern of creation is that of the landed estate. The "J"
account of Genesis 2–3 presents Yahweh as a landowner who plants a
garden and enjoys leisurely strolls through his property "in the breeze
of the day" (3:8). In this way, the Eden narrative represents an extension
of Yahweh's patrimonial domain, depicting Israel's God as creator of a
world that centers on the divine garden.[51]

In the "Priestly" tradition of the Pentateuch, divine patronage is cast
in terms of covenant, a covenant extended to the entire world—"to
every living creature of all flesh that is on the earth" (Gen 9:16).[52] In
covenant as in divine patrimony, God's role as creator makes possible
the extension of divine patronage to the whole world (Gen 1:1–2:4a).
In the Noachic covenant, creation theology and covenant theology thus
mesh. The interrelatedness of these two forms of divine agency is likewise evident in the collocation of creation and covenant language in
poetic depictions of God's creation by conflict as described earlier in
this chapter—for example, in Psalm 89, which mentions God's covenant
loyalty (ḥesed weʾĕmet; "steadfast love and faithfulness"; v. 14) in association with the statement in verse 11:[53]

The heavens are yours, the earth also is yours;
> the world and all that is in it—you have founded them.

Rooted in creation theology are a number of biblical perspectives that take seriously the matter of divine absence—those of wisdom, ritual, and psalmody (see chapters 5 and 6). Creation and cosmology in the Hebrew Bible are at the focus of the following chapter. These various types of biblical literature, along with others, will give shape to the discussion of divine absence that follows.

CONCLUSION

As a concern that ancient Israelites shared with their Near Eastern counterparts, the biblical theme of divine absence is cast, first and foremost, as a relational crisis. In the Hebrew Bible, divine–human relationships are centered on the God of Israel and on that Deity's special bonds with the people. Israel's identity is inextricably tied to its God and relates to a number of ways of describing the origins of that relationship. These major origin traditions account for the foundations of God's relationships to Israel and to the whole of the world, as described in the Hebrew Bible. They are also foundational to various ideas of divine absence that arise in biblical texts and provide a basis for continuing or restoring relationships disrupted, threatened, and disappointed by the perception of divine absence. Having examined the relational basis of this biblical theme, the remaining chapters of this book will examine portions of the Hebrew Bible that engage the spatial dimensions of divine–human relationships that are basic to its portrayal of divine absence.

But Ah Preestn is ever a present
God within Vchich's absence

PART II

BOUNDARIES OF DIVINE PRESENCE
AND ABSENCE IN THE WORLD

The "Valley of the Shadow of Death" is Death Valley Vall̶e̶y̶

Typically to be avoided by tourists —

Hope to see you soon ... when you can.

Dad

CHAPTER 4

Cosmic and Terrestrial Realms of Divine Presence and Absence

As noted in the introduction and in the discussion of personal names in chapter 2, one way in which the biblical idea of divine absence comes to expression in the most direct form is in the question "Where is God?" (ʾayye(h) ʾĕlōhêkā; "Where is your God?" and so forth).[1] Corresponding to this divine-absence interrogative is the first question encountered in the Bible, Yahweh's question to the first human being, "Where are you?" (ʾayyekkâ; Gen 3:9). Just as human beings struggle with the perception of divine absence throughout the Hebrew Bible, so does God in the biblical portrayal seek an evasive humanity. The question "Where?" frames matters of divine–human relationships and God's involvement in the world in terms of spatial existence.[2] Questions of where God is in the world, how the world is put together, and how human beings relate to the Divine within the world are all matters relating to cosmology and creation in the Hebrew Bible.

As discussed in chapter 3, certain biblical traditions of the world's origins, or cosmogony, draw on the divine-warrior tradition and accordingly describe creation in terms of the divine patronage extending to the entire world. Thus, the beginnings and ongoing ordering of creation are cast in relational perspective, in terms of a relationship between Israel's God as creator and humankind as those who have been incorporated into God's extended patrimony in creation. The biblical phenomenon of divine absence within that created world involves further examination of creation and cosmology.

How does the human perception of divine absence relate to the biblical view of the world's structure? In biblical literature, is divine absence a matter of failure in the divine–human relationship or an inherent part of the created order? Is divine absence in any way inherent to the basic terms of the divine–human relationships in this world? In seeking to answer these questions, this chapter will consider cosmology in biblical and broader ancient Near Eastern perspective. Related to that discussion is the place of divine absence in the Primeval History (Genesis 1–11), the most prominent biblical account of the world's ordering and of the basic conditions of human life. A good place to begin, though, is with a recent scholarly suggestion of a conceptual framework for considering divine presence and absence in the world in biblical perspective.

"Structural Divine Presence"

Terence Fretheim describes what he sees as the biblical portrayal of "structural divine presence" in terms of varying degrees of intensifica-tion.[3] As Fretheim explains, one may think of these varying degrees as existing on a continuum. At the extreme of greatest intensity is theo-phanic presence, for example, the Israelites at Sinai or Job before the whirlwind. On the other end of the continuum is God's accompanying presence, as when the Lord tells Jacob in Genesis 28, "I am with you and will keep you wherever you go . . . and will not leave you until I have done what I have promised you" (v. 15 NRSV). In between are God's tabernacling presence as experienced in worship and other forms at intermediate points. Undergirding all of these various degrees of inten-sification—from accompanying presence to theophany—is God's general or structural presence in the world, by virtue of God's role as creator.

Certain biblical texts are key to Fretheim's schema—for example, Ps 139:7-10:

> Where can I go from your spirit?
>   Or where can I flee from your presence?
> If I ascend to heaven, you are there;
>   if I make my bed in Sheol, you are there.
> If I take the wings of the morning
>   and settle at the farthest limits of the sea,
> even there your hand shall lead me,
>   and your right hand shall hold me fast. (NRSV)

For Fretheim, the implication of such statements for the whole of the Old Testament is that God is ultimately always present, even in the face of God's apparent absence.[4] Thus, within the Old Testament as a whole, even apparent divine absence involves God's presence. According to this canonically based theological view, God's absence is always a relative matter of lesser intensification of divine presence, which ultimately is a constant.

While such an inference may be available to the modern reader standing before the whole of the Hebrew Bible, it is contradicted at numerous points within the canon. To take one of the most obvious instances, which Fretheim himself discusses, Ezek 10:1-22; 11:22-25 describes a vision of the departure of the divine presence from the Jerusalem temple. According to Fretheim, the passage "does not mean that God is now absent from the temple (see 11:16)."[5] The latter verse, while referring to God's presence to the exiles abroad, in no way mitigates the clear picture of God's abandonment and absence from the Jerusalem sanctuary, which is, after all, the whole point of the passage.[6]

In Psalm 22, according to Fretheim, "the psalmist prays to a God who has forsaken him but is believed to be present enough to hear."[7] It is only in the psalm's conclusion, after the crisis has passed, that the speaker can claim such assurance (vv. 21b-31). The very premise of the psalm is the sufferer's example of trust in God, calling out to God, even while God gives no sign of being present.

Numerous other examples of divine absence come forward in the Hebrew Scriptures. Even while declaiming any wrongdoing, the speaker in Psalm 69 complains,

> I sink in deep mire,
> > where there is no foothold;
> I have come into deep waters,
> > and the flood sweeps over me.
> I am weary with my crying;
> > my throat is parched.
> My eyes grow dim
> > with waiting for my God. (vv. 2-3 NRSV)

Though the book of Habakkuk assures that "the LORD is in his holy temple" (2:20), all the while outside its doors, the prophet pleads:

> O LORD, how long shall I cry for help,
> > and you will not listen?
> Or cry to you "Violence!"
> > and you will not save?
> Why do you make me see wrong-doing
> > and look at trouble?

Destruction and violence are before me;
    strife and contention arise.
So the law becomes slack
    and justice never prevails.
The wicked surround the righteous—
    Therefore judgment comes forth perverted.
                           (1:2-4 NRSV)

As described in the book of Lamentations, "Jerusalem sinned griev-
ously" (1:8) and thus suffers punishment from God, who leaves even the
most sacred space of the sanctuary vulnerable to invading armies:

Enemies have stretched out their hands
    over all her precious things;
she has even seen the nations
    invade her sanctuary,
those whom you forbade
    to enter your congregation. (1:10 NRSV)

Just though the punishment may be, it is described in terms both of
God's wrathful presence and of divine abandonment: (Not always?)

He has cut down in fierce anger
    all the might of Israel;
he has withdrawn his right hand from them
    in the face of the enemy. (2:3a NRSV)

The speaker in Psalm 88 contends not only, "My soul is full of troubles, / and my life draws near to Sheol" (v. 3 NRSV), but also that it is
God who has placed him in death's power:

You have put me in the depths of the Pit,
    in the regions dark and deep.
Your wrath lies heavy upon me,
    and you overwhelm me with all your waves.
                           (vv. 6-7 NRSV)

The remainder of this psalm presents the sufferer's downward spiral
into hopelessness, with the question to God, "Why have you hidden
your face from me?"—a frequent motif for divine absence in the book of
Psalms and elsewhere in the Hebrew Bible[8]—and concludes ominously
with the word "darkness" (v. 18).

In view of such texts, Fretheim's schema of "structural divine presence" as a constant in creation raises a number of questions. If such a conception is to take into account the whole of the canon, how does one take seriously texts like these that attest to the experience of unmitigated divine absence, be it deserved or not? If the framework of structural divine presence is not just as an inference to which modern readers are privy but can be ascribed meaning for those portrayed in the biblical text itself, why do human beings and communities "within the text" so frequently entertain as a realistic scenario the possibility of God's absence? If, as Fretheim's schema implies, divine absence is largely a matter of limited human understanding, then as humans experience it, is there any difference between divine absence and the perception thereof? When this possibility becomes an apparent certainty, what are the grounds for seeking an ostensibly absent God? Even if divine presence is taken for granted as a constant in creation, what hope do suppliants have in seeking more efficacious forms of God's presence? That is, on what grounds do suppliants bother to seek? What is the rationale for seeking God in the face of apparent divine absence? Is God in any way constrained eventually to respond?

The assumption of "structural divine presence" fully explains neither the human experience of divine absence nor the human appeal to God, even in the most desperate of circumstances. Such a realization compels consideration of the basis of divine–human relationships as examined in the previous chapters in part I. It also warrants another look at divine presence and absence as they relate to creation throughout the whole of the canon. To lend a certain depth perspective to the canonical picture, the following discussion views the biblical notions of divine presence in the world in relationship to ideas of cosmology in the broader ancient Near East. As the contrasting views in texts like Psalms 88 and 139:8 suggest, among the relevant questions is whether and in what sense biblical texts portray God's presence in the realm of death.

WHERE GOD IS AND WHERE GOD IS NOT: "STRUCTURAL" DIVINE ABSENCE

The Hebrew Bible frequently makes reference to the whole of creation by the merism "heaven and earth" (e.g., Gen 1:1; 2:1, 4; 14:19; Pss 50:4; 73:25). This bipartite formulation, far from being "merely poetic," is consistent with iconographic representations of the cosmos as dually composite in ancient Near Eastern iconography, as abundantly illustrated by Othmar Keel.[9]

Less often in biblical cosmology, a third element comes into view with the mention of the netherworld or of the subterranean waters or seas (Exod 20:4; Ps 135:6; Jonah 1:9). As the region of the dead, the netherworld is referred to as Sheol, a shadowy realm bereft of life's joys. Whereas the Hebrew Bible as a whole leaves little doubt as to God's claim on the first two realms, this third element of the cosmos can be regarded at times as being integrated into the ordered world (Ps 148:1-7) or at other times as distinct from it (Ps 115:16-17), even as a threat to the created order, especially in connection with the sea or rivers (for example, Pss 74:13-14; 89:9-10; 104:7, 9; Hab 3:3, 8). Thus, the status of this third realm as a genuine part of creation and its relationship to the presence of Israel's God are somewhat ambiguous.

In connection with this third realm of the world and as suggested in biblical texts like Psalms 69 and 88, is a degree of divine absence integral to the cosmos? Along with Fretheim's view of "structural divine presence," might one also speak of "structural divine absence"? In keeping with such considerations, is God's presence or absence in the world purely a matter of divine choice or a function of the boundaries of the creation? These questions come into focus when we bring biblical cosmology into relationship with views from the broader ancient Near East.

By comparison to the biblical view of the netherworld, among ancient Israel's Near Eastern neighbors and predecessors the place of death's realm in the gods' maintenance of the universe appears more straightforward. A similar third realm appears as a distinct component of the ancient Egyptian cosmology. In addition to earth and sky, what the Egyptians called the *Duat* is described as a place of darkness, sometimes said to be located within the body of the sky goddess Nut (that is, somehow within the sky) and sometimes described as lying beneath the earth.[10] As part of the daily cycle of life and death in the cosmos, the sun makes its nightly journey through the Duat before being born anew just below the horizon each morning. For ancient Egyptians, the Duat was "a place where gods live along with human beings who have died."[11] The realm of the dead thus played a vital role in this daily rhythm of death and rejuvenation and in the gods' oversight of creation.

The integral place of death's realm in the cosmos had implications for the governance of human life on earth, as addressed in Egyptian royal theology. As Leonard H. Lesko summarizes in connection with the Pyramid Texts, "The principal objective of the king in the afterlife was to join the sun-god Re in his heavenly voyage."[12] Egyptian royal theology regarded the Pharaoh himself as divine and accorded death an important role in the cycle of renewal of Egypt's kings. Accordingly, the living Pharaoh was identified with Horus, the son of the Osiris who rules in death's realm. As indicated by the Middle Kingdom Coffin Texts, in time the possibility of an exalted celestial existence in the afterlife was open to nonroyal persons as well.[13]

As described and illustrated in chapter 125 of "The Book of Going Forth by Day" (also known as "The Book of the Dead"), the deceased individual's entry into the afterlife was occasioned by a scene of judgment before Osiris and a divine tribunal.[14] Identification with both Horus and Osiris was essential not only for human kings but also for nonroyal persons. In a favorable verdict, as Lesko explains, "The deceased thus acquired both an identity as Osiris, guaranteeing resurrection with Osiris in his Underworld, and the quality of Horus, as 'true-of-voice.'"[15] In some texts and illustrations, the number of judging deities, like the number of offenses declaimed in the negative confession recited by the deceased, is forty-two, a symbolic number of potential curse or blessing in the ancient Near East.[16] Some Egyptologists have seen in the number of judging deities a possible correspondence to the number of nomes or provinces of ancient Egypt.[17] Accordingly, this detail would indicate a territorial correspondence between the realm of earthly existence and the abode of death. In sum, central to ancient Egyptian ideas about the afterlife was not only the involvement of the gods but also a hopeful view that favorable aspects of the present life continue into the next.[18]

Though sometimes elaborated to as many as six distinct realms, the Mesopotamian cosmology corresponds to the biblical conception of heaven, earth, and a netherworld.[19] As presented in Atrahasis, this conception of the universe is "like a tiered wedding cake," with Anu in heaven, Enlil on earth, and Enki/Ea in the Apsu, the realm of the subterranean waters.[20] Like biblical Sheol, the netherworld in Mesopotamian myth is described as a shadowy counterpart to life on the earth above.[21] Accordingly, society in the netherworld was run by a bureaucracy of netherworld deities, whose duties included welcoming deceased spirits and securing a station for them in death's realm. Heading this state structure was a group of gods known collectively as the Annunaki, over whom the divine pair Nergal and Ereshkigal presided.[22]

In the Mesopotamian conception, as in the Egyptian view, the realms of death and life were joined in the daily cycle around which the cosmos was ordered, the sun god Shamash regularly passing through the netherworld on his nightly circuit.[23] To settle peacefully into the afterlife, the dead depended on offerings from living descendants in a widespread mortuary cult.[24] In turn, the dead were believed capable of bestowing both blessing and trouble on the living. Thus in Mesopotamia, death's realm remains loosely but constantly in contact with the sphere of the living.

Evidence for a mortuary cult in Bronze Age Syria-Palestine includes
mythic and ritual texts from Mari, Ebla, and Ugarit.[25] Through prayers,
offerings, and memorials, the dead were honored as powerful if not
divine and as having the potential from their place in the netherworld to
exert a beneficent influence on the lives of the living. In Ugaritic texts,
these concerns center around the king. For example, KTU^2 1.161 is a
ritual text connecting the accession of Ugarit's last king, Ammurapi III,
with a memorial and invocation of support from deceased members of
the royal line as "the Rephaim of the netherworld" (rp'i 'arṣ; lines 2, 9).[26]
This text thus indicates a connection between the dynasty of the reign-
ing king and the supernatural powers of the netherworld in the ongoing
order of the world and the Ugaritic kingdom. Mythic and ritual texts
from Ugarit celebrate the storm deity Baal as the dynamic leader among
the gods, who enters the netherworld (by being actually swallowed by
Death) and returns to the earth, a motif apparently tied to a seasonal
pattern of drought followed by the return of rain and accompanying
agricultural productivity (KTU^2 1.4.VII:42–1.6.VI; 1.12; 1.17.VI).[27] The
order and governance of the natural and political world require attention to death's powers. The gods' limited involvement in death's realm
is necessary.

With some correspondence to notions about the dead in Mesopotamian and Ugaritic sources, at least one biblical text suggests that the dead
have powers and can be summoned by the living on earth—namely, the
account of Saul's invoking the deceased Samuel by the medium of Endor
(1 Sam 28:3–25). Though scholars who argue for a cult of the dead among
ancient Israelites make reference to biblical and extrabiblical evidence
alike, the prevailing viewpoint among biblical texts eschews Yahweh's
association with the abode and powers of the dead (see Lev 20:27; 1 Sam
28:3, 9; 2 Kings 23:24; 1 Chr 10:13).[28] Certain biblical texts, including Ps
139:8-10, cited earlier in the chapter, suggest God's access to and jurisdiction over this third realm. Additionally, one might cite Amos 9:2:

> Though they dig into Sheol,
>   from there shall my hand take them;
> though they climb up to heaven,
>   from there I will bring them down. (NRSV)

But the rhetorical force of such instances lies in the idea being exceptional and contrary to expectation.

Indeed, much more persistent in the Hebrew Bible is the recognition
of separation from God in this third realm. As Ps 115:16-17 states,

The heavens are the LORD's heavens,
> but the earth he has given to human beings.
The dead do not praise the LORD,
> nor do any that go down into silence. (NRSV)

In death's domain, human beings are said to be cut off from the divine presence, as indicated by Ps 6:4–5:

Turn, O LORD, save my life;
> deliver me for the sake of your steadfast love.
For in death there is no remembrance of you;
> in Sheol who can give you praise? (NRSV)

In Psalm 88, the sufferer likens his own plight to that of the dead, whom "[God remembers] no more, for they are cut off from your hand" (v. 5). The sufferer asks God rhetorically,

Do you work wonders for the dead?
> Do the shades rise up to praise you?
Is your steadfast love declared in the grave,
> or your faithfulness in Abaddon?
Are your wonders known in the darkness,
> or your saving help in the land of forgetfulness?
>> (vv. 10-12 NRSV)

The realm of death, though not completely beyond God's reach, is nonetheless remote from the human experience of God's faithfulness and "steadfast love" (Heb. *ḥesed*). This basis for divine–human relationships in the Hebrew Bible, rooted as it is in Israel's kin-based social ideals, involves a God who works "wonders," "faithfulness," and "saving help" not in death but in the realm of the living. In the Hebrew Bible, the God of Israel is available for relationship in life's sphere of activity. Even if God has access to it, the realm of death is by definition remote from the efficacious presence of the "Living God."[29]

By comparison to the ancient Near Eastern traditions reviewed so far in this chapter, the Hebrew Bible presents the God of Israel as one who normally stands aloof from death and the netherworld. This difference compels reflection about its own implications for biblical notions of divine presence and absence. To begin, one might consider what accounts for that difference between the composite biblical viewpoint and other known traditions from the ancient Near East.

Although representing a variety of distinct geographic areas, cultures, and mythic forms, the ancient Near Eastern cosmological viewpoints in question derive mainly from second-millennium sources and have in common fairly elaborate systems of gods and goddesses involved in the governance of the cosmos. By comparison, the Hebrew Bible reflects a more condensed pantheon centering on a preeminent state deity, a characteristic pattern during the Iron Age, especially for the kingdoms of the southern Levant.[30] As Mark S. Smith has explained, the intervening development from the more elaborate Bronze Age pattern to that of the Iron Age involved processes of "convergence" and "differentiation" in religious identities, practices, and beliefs, including the identities and roles of various deities.[31] For the biblical traditions, that meant both Yahweh's absorption of some roles of other deities—such as Baal, El, and even Asherah—and at the same time distinguishing Yahweh from other divine roles and attributes so as to distinguish Yahweh and Yahwists from the other gods and their worshipers.[32]

Yahweh's curious distance from the realm of death in biblical tradition is one such feature distinguishing him from other known deities, including Baal. Though the precise rationale and historical development of this characteristic of Israel's God may be debated, the Hebrew Bible reflects a thoroughgoing concern to keep Yahweh separate from any association with the powers and realm of death.

As a logical consequence, biblical reflection on this third realm of the cosmos involves a degree of "structural divine absence." God's aloofness from death is a function of the biblical conception of Yahweh in relationship to the Israelite understanding of the cosmos. For biblical Israel, human relationship to God takes place not in death but in this life. The experience of death is by definition excluded from all that Israel's God offers and represents in the Hebrew Bible. In this sense, divine absence is integral to the human experience of death's realm in creation and its reach into the ordered cosmos.

THE CENTER AND PERIPHERY OF THE ORDERED WORLD

The need for saving "wonders" in the inhabited world assumes threats from encroaching chaos even within the ordered realm of human life. This realization appears in the Hebrew Bible and in other West Semitic literature schematically in terms of center and periphery, a rubric that has proved useful now for the last three decades in various discussions in the fields of social anthropology and ancient Near Eastern studies.[33]

Recent studies of Ugaritic society and religion by J. David Schloen and Mark S. Smith give attention to ways in which center–periphery opposition "informs a series of correlations in urban elites' conceptual organization of time and space, between their perception of culture and the cultivated land on the one hand, and uncultured and the uncultivated on the other."[34]

These categories play an important role in mythic depictions of the ordering of the cosmos in ancient Near Eastern literature. As Schloen explains, that conceptual organization applies both to geophysical realities and abstractly to "the order of symbols, of values and beliefs, which govern the society."[35] Taking Schloen's study as a point of departure for examining religious ideas at Ugarit, Smith explains that "at the heart of the center lies the household, which connotes safety and protection as well as familial patrimony and land, the site denoting not only family safety but also domestic conflict."[36] For the kingdom of the Ugarit, the center includes the palace, as the household of the king, and temple cult, that is, the "home" of the beneficent deities of the realm. In spatial terms, the continuation of ordered life moving outward from the capital lies in "the sown" or cultivated land.

Beyond "the sown" lies the periphery in the form of the wilderness, a place of potential danger and threats. Lying as it does at the fringes of the inhabited world, the periphery "stands as a transitional zone between the center and the distant realms of the cosmos lying beyond human experience and control."[37] Thus, the periphery is an intermediate zone between the ordered realm of human life and the "third realm" of death and the netherworld. This spatial opposition has its mythic corollary in terms of the dwelling place of the gods: the center is the dwelling place of the beneficent gods; the periphery of threatening forces is inhabited by monstrous supernatural powers, including Mot, the divine personification of death in Ugaritic texts.[38] Thus, threats encroach upon ordered existence from the symbolically and spatially distant zone bordering death's realm.[39]

This center–periphery opposition is also at work in the depiction of God's relationship to the world in biblical texts. Attention to the periphery as an intermediate zone of certain threat and potential deliverance by Israel's God appears most persistently in the biblical wilderness motif.[40] Representing as it does the encroachment of death's power into the realm of life, the wilderness figures in biblical tradition first and foremost as a place of potential death and disaster.[41] In this connection, the wilderness is fitting as a place of divine judgment, especially in the forty-year wandering as punishment for an unfaithful generation of Israelites in the book of Numbers. By the same token, the wilderness represents

Yahweh's deliverance and provision for his people, as expressed most strongly in the traditions of the exodus and the Sinai covenant. It is with the desire to renew a relationship of dependence on Yahweh that the prophets recall the wilderness experience as relatively favorable in comparison with potential disaster facing God's people because of their unfaithfulness in the prophets' own times (Jer 2:2; Hos 2:14; Ezek 34:25). These traditions demonstrate Yahweh's power to bring deliverance and security, even in the wilderness, at the periphery of ordered existence.

This point is also made in Yahweh's theophany and speeches in the book of Job (38:1—42:6). Behemoth and Leviathan—mythic creatures that embody the powers of chaos—are but Yahweh's playthings (40:15—41:34), much as threatening supernatural powers rank as El's "beloved monsters" in Ugaritic texts.[42] The implication of Yahweh's taming the chaos monsters in Job is similar—namely, Yahweh's power over the forces of chaos. Similarly, the thrust of both speeches directs Job's attention away from the center of human life to the periphery of the natural world, as represented by untamed animals of the wilderness, such as the lion, mountain goat, wild donkey, and ostrich (38:39—39:18). The form of Yahweh's theophany, the storm cloud of desert realms (38:1), identifies Yahweh as a god whose activity in the wilderness is not exceptional but genuine to his character. This form of theophany suggests an unsettling tension between order and disorder in the character of Israel's God.

Early poetic texts in the Hebrew Bible intimate Yahweh's character as a god who comes from the desert region south of Israel—for example, in Deut 33:2:

> Yahweh came from Sinai,
> and dawned from Seir upon us;
> he shone forth from Mount Paran.[43]

Yahweh's theophany in the wilderness is marked by meteorological and geological disruptions, as described in Judg 5:4-5:

> Yahweh, when you went out from Seir,
> when you marched from the region of Edom,
> the earth trembled,
> and the heavens poured,
> the clouds indeed poured water.
> The mountains quaked before Yahweh, the One of Sinai,
> before Yahweh, the God of Israel.

This motif of the convulsion of nature with Yahweh's desert theophany appears in elaborate fashion in Habakkuk 3:

> God came from Teman,
>> the Holy One from Mount Paran.
> His glory covered the heavens,
>> and the earth was full of his praise.
> The brightness was like the sun;
>> rays came forth from his hand,
>> where his power lay hidden.
> Before him went pestilence,
>> and plague followed close behind.
> He stopped and shook the earth;
>> he looked and made the nations tremble.
> The eternal mountains were shattered;
>> along his ancient pathways the everlasting hills sank low.
> I saw the tents of Cushan under affliction;
>> the tent-curtains of the land of Midian trembled.
>
> (vv. 3-7 NRSV)

The verses that follow further develop the scene of nature's roiling and the unsettling of desert peoples in response to Yahweh's advance as divine warrior (vv. 8-14). In the context of the wilderness, representing as it does the ambiguously ordered periphery, Yahweh's reordering presence encompasses forces of destruction and disorder. In view of such traditions of origins, Yahweh might appear to be a God of the desert fringe, a God who shuns the center in favor of the periphery. But such is hardly the case.

The other aspect of center–periphery opposition is clearly at work in the Hebrew Bible's depiction of Israel's God. In keeping with the common ancient Near Eastern conception, the center of earthly existence is marked by the most readily available form of divine presence at the worship sanctuary.[44] As illustrated in the dream theophany to Jacob at Bethel (BH *bêt-'ēl*; "House of El/God") in Gen 28:10-22, the shrine site, even prior to the building of the sanctuary, might be understood as a special portal between terrestrial and heavenly realms and thus a special locus of divine availability.

In the Hebrew Bible and the broader ancient Near East, the joining of cosmic and earthly realms is sometimes depicted as an earthly "garden of God" associated with the temple and royal palace.[45] This motif, which in biblical literature is best known in the Eden narratives of Genesis 2–3, appears in first-millennium Mesopotamian royal inscriptions and palace reliefs, and in the name of the Upper Euphrates kingdom of Bit Adini. Its origins can be traced to West Semitic "cedar forest" traditions connected with the Lebanon and Anti-Lebanon mountain ranges.[46] As the center of favorable divine presence on earth, the divine garden is the place from which the human king receives divine endorsement for his rule. As Yahweh says to the king of Tyre in Ezekiel 28:11-19:

> You were in Eden, the garden of God;
>   every precious stone was your covering.
>
> . . . .
>
> With an anointed cherub as guardian I placed you;
>   you were on the holy mountain of God;
> you walked among the stones of fire. (vv. 13a-14 NRSV)

As described in Ezekiel 28, the divine garden is replete with precious stones, indicating the luxuriant quality of the seat of divine dwelling and earthly rule.

In the more elaborate Eden narratives of Genesis 2–3, the tree and plant imagery of the divine garden is more apparent (2:8-9). Less overt are royal implications, with no direct mention of temple or palace. The original but now lost ideal implied by the outcome of the created order is not the monarchy but humankind generally ($h\bar{a}$ʾ$\bar{a}d\bar{a}m$) exercising oversight as God's earthly regency (2:15, 19-20).

Nonetheless, the narrative description points out that, like the Tigris and the Euphrates, the Gihon finds its ultimate source in Eden (Gen 2:11-14). Yahweh's placement of the cherubim to guard the garden and the tree of life corresponds to the sculpted cherubim that guarded the most sacred space within Solomon's temple and that appeared in reliefs adorning the temple's walls and doors as described in 1 Kings 6:23-35. The palm trees and flowers making up other temple wall decorations and the imagery associated with Solomon's palace (7:2-3) likewise correspond to the general garden imagery in Genesis 2–3.[47] These details belonging to the royal "garden of God" tradition serve within the narrative to foreshadow Jerusalem's eventual place as sacred and administrative capital at the conceptual center of the ordered world.

That center is marked by the unique presence of God on earth, which corresponds to God's heavenly dwelling place, a notion expressed in curious fashion in Solomon's prayer dedicating the Jerusalem temple:

> "But will God indeed dwell on the earth? Even heaven and the highest heaven cannot contain you, much less this house that I

have built! Regard your servant's prayer and his plea, O LORD
my God, heeding the cry and the prayer that your servant prays
to you today; that your eyes may be open night and day toward
this house, the place of which you said, 'My name shall be there,'
that you may heed the prayer that your servant prays toward this
place. Hear the plea of your servant and of your people Israel
when they pray toward this place; O hear in heaven your dwelling
place; heed and forgive."

(1 Kings 8:27-30)

Even in denying that God, who dwells in heaven, is fully present in
the temple, this passage reflects and struggles with the notion that God's
efficacious presence is uniquely available at the sanctuary. This text illustrates the conceptual balance between ideas of divine transcendence and
immanence at the heart of temple theology. In Deuteronomistic terms, it
is not God but God's "name" that is present in the temple.[48]

Intertwined with this struggle to balance divine transcendence and
immanence are questions of God's availability in moments of human
distress. As Solomon's prayer goes on to suggest, the temple site is the
place to turn for God's saving help in the midst of various crises: "When
your people Israel, having sinned against you, are defeated before an
enemy" (1 Kings 8:33); "When heaven is shut up and there is no rain"
(v. 35); "If there is famine in the land, if there is plague, blight, mildew,
locust, or caterpillar; if their enemy besieges . . . whatever prayer, whatever plea there is from any individual or from all your people Israel, all
knowing the afflictions of their own hearts so that they stretch out their
hands toward this house" (vv. 37-38).

Throughout the Hebrew Bible, the temple and the "garden of God,"
as the symbolic and geophysical center, do not represent the full presence
of God, which exists only in heavenly realm. Accordingly, the periphery
of earthly life as embodied by wilderness, threats, and the grave represent not the full power of death, which exists only in the third realm of
the cosmos, but merely its incursion into life's realm.

In the book of Psalms, the center and periphery of the ordered world
are seen to correspond, respectively, to God's presence in the temple
and the encroaching realm of death. For example, in Psalm 18:4-6, the
speaker declares:

> The cords of death encompassed me;
>> the torrents of perdition assailed me;
> the cords of Sheol entangled me;
>> the snares of death confronted me.

In my distress I called upon the LORD;
   to my God I cried for help.
From his temple he heard my voice,
   and my cry to him reached his ears. (NRSV)

These concepts relating to temple theology and worship will receive further attention in the chapter 6 discussion of worship texts engaging divine absence. For now, it suffices to note that, in biblical tradition, God's character as a God who is present and available in this life includes the recognition of a special locus of divine presence on the terrestrial plane—namely, the worship sanctuary. This centrality of the worship sanctuary comes into play in Jerusalem's role in historical narrative and prophecy, as will be discussed in chapter 7.

To conclude and summarize at this point, as divine sovereign over a restricted pantheon, Yahweh governs the universe through both expanded divine rule and selection among divine roles. In defining the identity of Israel's God, the texts of the Hebrew Bible distinguish Yahweh from deities who are involved in death's realm, such as Baal. Yahweh in biblical tradition is celebrated as a God available within the realms of this life, symbolically in temple worship and relationally in human relationships of kin-based faithfulness. Israel's God, though at times described as having entrée to death's realm, normally remains aloof from it. Though Israel's God also proves capable and powerful at the periphery (as represented by the wilderness tradition), God's normative presence in the Hebrew Bible is located at the temple—two ideas rooted in the center–periphery thinking that prevails in ancient Near Eastern texts. Wherever God's people Israel find themselves within the boundaries of life's experience, God is present. Thus, in the Hebrew Bible, it is not the urban center as such but God's presence that defines the center of life's realm and that provides deliverance from death's powers. This notion of God's presence or absence with respect to distinct boundaries of the cosmos raises questions about God's freedom and the moral implications of divine absence, issues that relate to biblical theodicy.

DIVINE FREEDOM AT THE BOUNDARIES:
THEODICY CONSIDERED

Theodicy is a defense of God's goodness and power as an answer to the problem of evil and innocent human suffering.[49] The implied structural boundaries of divine presence in the world bear on an issue central to the problem of theodicy, that of divine freedom. The assumption of God's freedom underlies the problem of theodicy in its classic form—that is, in the questioning of divine justice. Provided a meaningful notion of God's freedom can be substantiated in the biblical portrayal of divine absence, does it qualify as the distinguishing characteristic of divinity, as opposed to power or goodness?

Lothar Perlitt has argued that divine absence is itself an expression of God's freedom and of the uniqueness of the divine character.[50] Fretheim, by contrast, objects to what he sees as overemphasis on the language of divine freedom, preferring to speak of Yahweh's choice to limit his own freedom for the sake of humankind's well-being.[51] Obviously, though, this kind of divine self-limiting is itself an exercise of divine freedom.

At times, divine beneficence might be called into question where God's freedom and power are evident, most notably in the case of Job but also in numerous other instances in the Hebrew Bible, such as the fate of Uzza (2 Sam 6:6-10; 1 Chr 13:9-14) or Yahweh's preference for Abel's offering (Gen 4:1-16). In such instances, as in Psalms 69 and 88, divine presence or absence has destructive consequences that cannot be explained as a response to any human moral offense. In accounting for these apparent lapses of divine justice, an appeal to the prerogatives of divine freedom hardly proves satisfactory. An understanding of God based primarily on freedom only reinforces the dilemma of theodicy.

Taking Qoheleth (Ecclesiastes) as one's cue (see, for example, Eccl 3:11), may one bracket the problems of evil and the experience of divine absence, and attribute them to the limits of human perception? In such instances, are God's total power and freedom really to be assumed? If God's absence from death's realm is a function of the structure of the cosmos, then might other instances of divine absence likewise be inherent to creation? Even if not completely satisfactory, the categories of process theology have proven useful in identifying possible limits on divine freedom and power in the Hebrew Scriptures' presentation of the divine–human relationship.[52]

In the Hebrew Bible, God's presence or absence in the realm of death is presented not so much as a matter of clear-cut divine choice—the Hebrew Bible is fairly mute on this note—as it is Israel's experience of its God. Whether God *can* or *will* enter death's realm is beside the point. In other instances, whether and when God *can* or *will* intervene in human lives is similarly unclear. Even in the exodus, the preeminent tradition of Yahweh's saving activity, God acts only after a full generation of Israelite suffering under the Egyptians has already taken place. Once Yahweh does begin to act, he says to Moses, "I have observed the misery of my people who are in Egypt; I have heard their cry on account of their taskmasters. Indeed, I know their sufferings, and I have come down to deliver them up out of that land" (Exod 3:7-8). In the meantime, was God not *able* to act? Was God not *free* to act? The biblical text neither answers nor asks these questions. It simply affirms that when God does act, God's deliverance is predicated on a relationship of divine patronage, in which Israel is Yahweh's "people" (see chapter 1).

Accordingly, there would seem to be a component of hiddenness to God's self-disclosure that is necessarily inherent to the divine character, at least to the extent that human beings are capable of apprehending it. Divine hiddenness is not only a symptom of limited human perception but, in view of the realization that God is creator of the cosmos and of the human mind, also inherent to the character of God in relationship to humankind. Consider, for example, Ps 8:3-5:

> When I look at your heavens, the work of your fingers,
>   the moon and the stars that you have established;
> what are human beings that you are mindful of them,
>   mortals that you care for them?
> Yet you have made them a little lower than God,
>   and crowned them with glory and honor. (NRSV)

Again, the Hebrew Scriptures do not answer the question of why God creates humankind "a little less than divine" (NJPS; BH *mĕʿaṭ mēʾĕlōhîm*) or whether God even does so as a matter of choice. The Bible simply affirms that God creates and seeks relationship with humankind.

Logically speaking, at the essence of the divine is mystery. This notion of mystery is borne out in the biblical portrayal of God. Ultimately, then, divine absence figures not only as a challenge to the divine character but is itself a kind of defense of the divine, a theodicy. This aspect of divine absence both as a question and an answer of biblical theodicy is rooted in Israel's understanding of its God as creator of the world.

As chapter 1 discusses, biblical ideas of creation grow out of more basic ideas of patrimony, household, and kinship linking people and God in binding relationship. In creation theology, Yahweh's patrimonial claim over his own land and people is extended to the entire world. Thus, some aspects of divine absence are a matter of neither divine punishment nor divine failure but rather are built into creation, at least at the level of human understanding of God. That is, the Hebrew Bible represents a certain degree of "structural divine absence," if not in the world itself, then in the human experience of the world. This structural aspect of divine absence comes through in the Old Testament Wisdom books (see chapter 5). The remainder of the present chapter brings this view of divine presence and absence within creation to the determinative portion of the Hebrew Bible regarding creation: Genesis 1–11.

COSMOLOGY IN CANONICAL SHAPE: GENESIS 1–11 AND DIVINE PRESENCE AND ABSENCE AS GIVEN CONDITIONS OF HUMAN LIFE

The Primeval History (Genesis 1–11, henceforth PH) serves as a kind of preface not only to the rest of the book of Genesis but also to the rest of the Hebrew Bible. For in it, Israel's story is contextualized in relationship to humankind more broadly and within the whole of creation. This brief collection of material thus serves a vital role in foregrounding all that follows it in the Hebrew Bible in an understanding of the relationship of the divine with the world, giving a universal scope to Israel's story and prehistory. PH accomplishes this end in brief and simple fashion, presenting a few narrative episodes joined by genealogical material that in a clear manner lay out the basics of the divine–human relationship. Since virtually all of this material has decisive importance for the biblical depiction of God as a whole and since much of the PH bears on the theme of divine absence, much of its content merits discussion.

Like other ancient Near Eastern stories of cosmic origins, PH offers an account of beginnings as an explanation of the world's present state.[53] As Clifford and Collins observe, in ancient Near Eastern cosmogonies, any distinction between *Weltschöpfung* (the creation of the world) and a separate *Menschenschopfung* (creation of humankind) is artificial.[54] In keeping with this mode of understanding, the account of world origins with which the Pentateuch opens portrays humankind as an integral part of the natural world. Accordingly, humankind is brought into being along with the rest of the world as we know it.

To be sure, efforts to establish the distinctiveness of biblical literature over against its ancient Near Eastern counterparts can be pressed too far.[55] Nonetheless, strong resemblances notwithstanding, one notes a basic difference in interest between creation in Genesis and in surviving Mesopotamian accounts.[56] Whereas the Mesopotamian mythic texts like *Enuma Elish* and *Atrahasis* focus primarily on divine society and relationships among the gods, the Genesis creation narratives focus on humankind and its relationship to the divine. Here, Israel's god Yahweh embodies divine reality, and the other gods recede dimly into the background, represented only indirectly by first person plural speech (1:26; 3:22; 11:7). By contrast, the well-known works from Mesopotamia were created in the setting of larger second-millennium empires, where the deities of numerous locations and urban centers were kept in view (see chapter 1). This heightened emphasis on the national god in the biblical creation accounts reflects the Iron Age background of their composition, one in which local political kingdoms typically identified with a single national god, much in the way that the god Assur had come to represent the divine embodiment of the kingdom of Assyria.[57]

In keeping with source critical analysis of the Pentateuch as a whole, scholarship on PH has included broad agreement over its composite nature, being composed predominately of two types of material, conventionally designated Yahwist (J) and Priestly (P) material.[58] Though the last three decades have brought significant challenges to the classic documentary hypothesis, nonetheless, with respect to PH specifically, those long-standing scholarly rubrics continue to provide a useful convention for the purposes of discussing thematic and theological patterns in the text without implying necessary assumptions of the identification or dating of larger sources of the Pentateuch.[59] Furthermore, irrespective of the dating of the individual source documents, there is widespread agreement that PH took its final form during or after the time of the Babylonian exile.[60] It is from this scholarly vantage point that the remainder of this chapter turns to the theme of divine absence in these pivotal chapters of the biblical literature.

Genesis 1–3: Creation

Scholarship recognizes in the opening chapters of Genesis two distinct cosmoganies, conventionally designated as the Priestly (1:1—2:4a) and Yahwist (2:4b-25) creation narratives, the latter actually continuing into chapter 3. Both the distinct characteristics of each and their combined effect involve aspects of divine presence and absence. The placement of these chapters at the beginning of the biblical corpus establishes these biblical themes as foundational to the rest of the biblical portrayal of the divine.

Genesis 1: The Priestly Creation Narrative

Irrespective of the relative or absolute dating of the composition of each account, the ultimate placement of the Priestly story before the Yahwist account suggests reading the former as a supplement and corrective to the latter. As John J. Collins states, "It is likely . . . that the editor who placed this account at the beginning of Genesis presupposed the Yahwist creation account of Genesis 2–3. The Priestly account is not the whole story. Rather, it supplements the Yahwist account and is meant to forestall a negative interpretation of the human situation, which might be derived from Genesis 3."[61]

With that placement of the Priestly account, the Yahwistic narrative of origins is prefaced by one in which the reliability and sovereignty of Israel's God in creation is more impressive and the order of the world more secure from its origins. As Bernard Batto observes, the main purpose of the Priestly revision was to present to the exiles a more secure picture of their God's hold over the cosmic order.[62] In effect, then, the whole of PH in its finished form is an answer to the sense of divine absence and abandonment brought about by the collective experience of the exile. Indeed, the P creation account of Genesis 1 presupposes a God who in relative transcendence is quite aloof, even remote, from creation. The comfort offered lies in the view that the God who seems so distant is ultimately and supernally in benevolent control of cosmic events. Divine transcendence translates into both apparent absence and inferred presence.

Genesis 2–3: The Yahwist Creation Narrative

The J creation account, too, reflects notions of a distant God. Even while humankind dwells in the garden of Yahweh God, the deity remains distant. In an echo of Mesopotamian myth, Yahweh God, the first gardener, after creating the first human being, assigns him to do what had been the deity's work (2:15). The necessity of providing the man "a helper suitable for him" presupposes that the man has no true companionship with Yahweh God. In the continuing narrative in Genesis 3, Yahweh God is not present to prevent the human encroachment on divine prerogatives, as represented by eating from the forbidden "tree of the knowledge of good and evil." In J, Yahweh's distance from humankind produces problems for himself. In the need to expel "Adam" and Eve from the garden, Yahweh loses the opportunity for divine rest, and thus for complete order in the world.[63] In the view of some commentators, J's Yahweh even comes off as somewhat naive and inept in his own isolation.[64]

Genesis 1–3 Together

The combination of P and J creation narratives results in the portrayal of a deity who, out of the isolation of transcendence, brings forth a creature that shares in the divine likeness and substance ("breath"), a creature of free will to whom God may relate. That story begins in the opening of Genesis 1, creation consisting in God's bringing order and differentiation from out of the primeval formless waters of chaos, tōhû wābōhû (Gen 1:2). According to this view of the world, creation is not preceded by a vacuum—*creatio ex nihilo*—but by formlessness.[65] Something is preceded not by "nothing" but by chaos. Existence is negated not by nonexistence but by disorder.[66] The closest one might come to finding "nothingness" in this view of the world is in this amorphous, barren, meaningless disorder.

In the beginning, God turns from this nothingness to bring about an order that includes the creation of humankind. The original problem, as presented in Genesis, is God's own isolation or absence from anything meaningful. Creation is an answer to this divine problem. This transcendently distant God creates humankind in an effort toward relationship. As an integral part of creation, humankind figures centrally within that created order. Though taken from the ground, humankind is animated by the divine breath (2:7). In the drama of Genesis 2–3, humankind by virtue of its role to tend the garden is at center stage. Other animals are brought to the man as possible companions. At first, the man and the woman are like the animals themselves, naked and unashamed and without anything distinguishing them from the animals.[67] Something changes when they eat from the wisdom tree; they become "like gods" (3:22). Humankind leaves Eden different than when it arrived there. Thus, the centrality of humankind leads to its becoming even closer to God in nature and ability.

Also in Genesis 1, humankind stands apart. Here humanity's distinctiveness from other beings is portrayed as more clearly established from the beginning. Humans are created "in the image of God" (Gen 1:27) and, as in Genesis 2, are given "dominion" to fill the divine roles of oversight on earth. As John J. Collins aptly summarizes regarding this passage,

> In the ancient Near East, images were very important for cult and worship, as the presence of the divinity was made manifest to the worshipers in the statues. . . . Instead, according to the Priestly writer, the presence of God was made manifest in human beings. Moreover, gods in the ancient Near East were often depicted in the form of animals. Such depictions are rejected here. Near Eastern deities were also often depicted in human form. . . . This account of creation, then, attributes great dignity to human beings, both male and female. Moreover, humanity is given dominion over the rest of creation.[68]

In short, Genesis 1 places Genesis 2 in a light more favorable to humanity.

The First Question: "Where Are You?" (Genesis 3–4)

The first question posed in the Bible reflects a breach in the divine–human relationship that is universal in scope. In creating human beings in the divine image, in granting them a role in the maintenance and oversight of creation (1:26-28; 2:15, 19-20), God invites human beings to share in the divine governance of the world. This role for human beings is built into the created order itself. Thus human partnership with the divine is not only invited, it is required for the proper order of creation. In a sense, human agency in the ordering of creation is an extension of the divine presence. The failure of the human response will mean a form of divine absence by which creation will be incomplete.

For the sake of freedom, Yahweh leaves the man and woman alone, to exercise genuine freedom. It is in this situation of being alone, absent from divine guidance, that the exercise of the human will violates the divine intent. The universal human condition portrayed in Genesis 3 involves the freedom to operate in relative isolation from the divine, a freedom that—according to the universal implications of this primeval narrative—inexorably leads to further estrangement from the divine (Gen 3:9-10), from self (v. 10), from each other (vv. 11-12), and from the rest of creation (vv. 16-19). Within the Yahwist narrative in PH, becoming "like gods" represents an encroachment beyond rightful human limits and on divine prerogatives. This threat to the divine is a threat to the relationship. A distancing occurs; humankind is expelled from the abundant ease of the divine garden. In terms of core–periphery conceptions, humankind now finds itself removed from the very center represented by the divine garden, to cultivate the outlying land (vv. 23-24), though the primordial garden and its sources still nourish civilized life (Gen 2:10-14).

The fracturing of relationships resulting in that expulsion continues outward from there, with the story of the first brothers being the story of the first murder (Genesis 4). As in Genesis 3, a case of relative divine absence leads to a tragic exercise of human freedom. For the murder of his brother, Cain is not only condemned to become "a fugitive and wanderer on the earth," but as Yahweh tells him, "Now you are cursed from the ground, which has opened its mouth to receive your brother's blood from your hand. When you till the ground, it will no longer yield to you its strength" (4:13). As Cain recognizes, he is thus cut off from the productivity of the ground and from the protective presence of Yahweh (v. 14).

Cain's banishment develops the center–periphery view of the inhabited world reflected in the expulsion from Eden (3:23-24). Banished from "the sown" area outside of Eden, Cain is a degree further removed from the divine habitation of Eden and faces the threatening prospect of wilderness—a place of minimal human occupation and divine presence. Nonetheless, the threat of divine vengeance communicated by the protective mark of Cain reflects a widespread recognition of God's effective presence extending from the realm of his dwelling in Eden. Cain's establishment of a city further extends the zone of civilized life extending from the inhabited center marked by the recognized divine presence.

Further Fragmentation: Babel

In the story of Babel (Gen 11:1-9), human beings, already united by a common language, seek to reinforce their unity by building "a city, and a tower with its top in the heavens" so as to "make a name" for themselves (v. 4). Implicit and explicit within the story are elements that reflect the center–periphery worldview of ancient urban elites, according to which the city is the seat both of human civilization and earthly divine presence. In keeping with the urban culture of Mesopotamia ("Shinar," v. 2), the ziggurat represents a kind of portal to the divine realm. The passage offers a folk etymology for the name of the city, Babylon, which in Akkadian (*bāb ilim*; "the gate of the divine") likewise suggests a place of earthly access to the gods.

On the contrary, the wordplay in the biblical passage and the narrative show Babylon to be the center of confusion and estrangement from the divine. In this effort, as from the beginning in PH, humankind overreaches, and Yahweh responds by imposing further limitations. In the scattering of the people and the confusion of their speech, the passage shows not only how Yahweh frustrates human efforts to transcend their limitations but also provides an alternative account of the world's variegated peoples and languages in the Table of Nations (Genesis 10).

In the Babel story, the human effort to reach the divine realm represents a threatened intrusion and trespassing of boundaries in the created order. In the Mesopotamian story of *Atrahasis*, the god Enki facilitates human efforts and relations to the divine (III i–iii).[69] By contrast, the enterprise described in Genesis 11 is carried out without the input or involvement of the divine and furthermore without regard for the divine. The city and tower spring from a determined impulse for human unity, fame, and transcendence. As in the Eden narratives, this story portrays a misguided human effort born out of divine absence, one initiated in disregard for the divine and brought to failure by a divine response.

That response is the jealous guarding of divine prerogatives and boundaries within the created order. Ironically, the human desire to go beyond limits without relationship to the divine emerges in a place from which God is absent. Hence Yahweh's admonition, "Come, let us go down" (v. 7).

Divine Speech in PH

Appearing in both J and P contexts in PH is the citation of first-person-plural speech by the divine (Gen 1:26; 3:22; 11:7). This divine plural speech echoes the conventional mythic motif of consultation of the divine assembly, as featured in texts like *Enuma Elish* and *Atrahasis*.[70] The idea of a divine assembly represents more generally the motif of divine royalty; in the same way that human kings address their subordinates by first-person-plural speech, so does Israel's God as divine sovereign address the celestial court, here very much reduced to the background in favor of Yahweh's supremacy.[71]

Such conversation thus ranks as divine self-deliberation. Also noteworthy is that in each case this plural divine speech has humankind as its subject. The reader is thus made privy to divine deliberations about human beings but deliberations that are hidden from human beings. Dynamics for the divine–human relationship are being orchestrated though without the input of the human partner. The progression in these quotations begins with hope for free relationship (Gen 1:26) and moves on to mistrust and a progressing need to set boundaries (Gen 3:22; 11:7).

The initial divine consultation is one of hopeful anticipation for humankind (Gen 1:26). The subsequent instances are in response to collaboration among human beings—first between "Adam" and Eve (Gen 3:22) and then among an increased population at Babel (11:7). The plural speech shows a deliberated divine response to human collaboration that is at odds with the divine will and is a threat to divine prerogatives. Here, the divine deliberates and reacts somewhat in self-defense before the threatening potential of human beings. This dynamic of tension between the divine and human is at home in the well-known Mesopotamian accounts of origins, especially *Atrahasis* and in the flood account in Gilgamesh. As in those instances, the plural divine language in Genesis 1–11 is a dialogue reflecting distance between the divine and humankind. The implication of this account of origins is that such distance is normative for human life and necessarily so.

CONCLUSION

As the first part of this chapter demonstrated, the Hebrew Bible taken as a whole and in relationship to the broader ancient Near East shows aspects of God's apparent absence to result from the structure of the cosmos, at least as human beings experience it and are able to apprehend it. This notion of "structural divine absence" applies especially to the realm of death and its reach into the terrestrial plane of existence. What that means is that certain forms of divine absence are not a result of human sin or divine neglect but rather are a function of the nature of Israel's God as a "living God."

This structural notion of divine absence is reflected in the opening chapters of the Hebrew Bible, in the Primeval History (Genesis 1–11). In the midst of primeval chaos (*tōhû wābōhû*), God's absence from anything meaningful impels the divine ordering of the created world. Essential to that emergent ordering is a free and authentic divine–human relationship. The integrity of that relationship depends on a clear distinction between divine and human identity and prerogatives. Preserving those distinctions requires at times a distancing by Israel's God. That is to say, much of what appears as divine absence results from the cosmic and relational expressions of divine mystery.

165 m/ean 9 th dal
113

�5 p. 13
Cthis
&this
Cthis

CHAPTER 5

Wisdom Literature: P/77
The Search for Divine Presence
in the MUNDANE 9 life see p 11

The structure

DIVINE PRESENCE AND ABSENCE in creation are central to the viewpoint shared by the biblical books of Proverbs, Job, Ecclesiastes (also known as Qoheleth), and certain Psalms, known collectively as the Old Testament Wisdom literature.[1] These writings all posit a natural and moral order grounded in God's creation of the world.[2] With the created order in view, biblical wisdom offers "advice on how to succeed in life as well as reflections on its meanings and problems."[3] Corresponding to these two basic concerns are the two major genres or modes of Wisdom literature: didactic wisdom, which seeks to inculcate the observance of that order, and speculative or critical wisdom, which reexamines and reflects on the "doctrines and values" found in didactic wisdom.[4] Both practical and speculative sides of wisdom engage human existence and the world around it with the conviction that "order derives from divine presence."[5]

Foundational to wisdom's treatment of divine absence are three salient aspects of this portion of Old Testament literature. First, wisdom presents a distinct viewpoint within the Hebrew Bible, centering as it does on the perspective of the individual and on universal concerns of daily life, rather than on national events and crises. Because of wisdom's distinct character, scholarship during the previous century struggled to explain wisdom's theological unity with the rest of the Old Testament.[6] As scholars frequently observe, more than any other portion of the Hebrew Bible, Wisdom literature shows impressive affinities with other ancient Near Eastern texts in its viewpoints and literary forms.[7] This common ground between ancient Israelites and their neighbors and

or For Ec. 7,
Ec. t.

predecessors provides a comparative perspective for considering biblical wisdom's treatment of divine absence.

Second, as the following discussion will show, wisdom trains its focus on the realm of mundane existence, in which divine presence and absence are typically difficult to distinguish. Wisdom confronts the usual hiddenness of God's presence in the world and the need to search for it.[8] From wisdom's perspective, divine presence often appears as divine absence. Wisdom is concerned with discerning the difference between the two.

Third, wisdom thought accentuates the moral implications of divine presence in the created order and in mundane human existence. In this portion of the Hebrew Bible, the theme of divine absence goes hand in hand with the problem of theodicy. As a collection, the Wisdom books offer an acute example of how the biblical treatment of the problem of evil diverges from theodicy's modern philosophical formulation.[9] In wisdom thought, the intellectual problem of innocent suffering is inseparable from its existential dimensions, with theodicy being cast largely in terms of a relational crisis marked by God's absence. In these three respects, Wisdom literature presents important dimensions of divine presence and absence in the Hebrew Bible.

GOD, THE INDIVIDUAL, AND SOCIETY

Even while offering instruction and reflection based on the vantage point of the individual, Wisdom literature nonetheless posits a given social context. As discussed in chapter 1, in the Hebrew Bible and its surrounding environment, relationships to the divine were enmeshed in various social contexts. Recognizing how group identity and context figure into the pronounced individual perspective of Wisdom literature helps the reader understand relationships to the divine and the distinct view of divine absence expressed in Wisdom texts.

By virtue of its place within the literary anthology that is the Hebrew Bible, Wisdom literature ranks as a celebrated part of ancient Israel's national legacy. In addition to their canonical context, the biblical Wisdom books themselves contain details signaling national identity, as do occasionally some wisdom texts from elsewhere in the ancient Near East. For example, in the Akkadian text "I Will Praise the Lord of Wisdom" (*Ludlul bēl nēmeqi*), reflection on the mysteries of human suffering and divine inscrutability gives way to exaltation of the Babylonian national god Marduk.[10] Similarly, the book of Proverbs and the prologue, divine speeches, and epilogue of Job (chapters 1–2, 38–42) prefer the Israelite national divine name Yahweh when speaking of the divine. Solomon's legacy as Israel's premier wise king (1 Kings 3–4) looms large in the introductions of Proverbs and Ecclesiastes.

Beyond its contextual framing as Israelite literature, the focus of biblical wisdom is not so much on particularistic issues of national identity as on the realm of everyday human experience. Its concerns are those of the international wisdom enterprise—namely, the instruction of the young and the reflections of the experienced. Biblical and ancient Near East wisdom literature tends to minimize group concerns in favor of what might be universally observed from the perspective of the individual.[11] As Richard Clifford observes in reference to Egyptian didactic wisdom, "The aim of the instructions is to guide the individual rather than to reform society; readers accepted the world as it was and sought to live according to its rhythms. The instructions advocate not changing the world but helping individuals adapt themselves to it."[12] This observation applies equally to wisdom literature more broadly. Suggesting the distinctiveness of wisdom's viewpoint within the Hebrew Bible, even while betraying a slant against wisdom's place there, Walther Eichrodt observed that "knowledge of Nature, and the moulding of the individual life, formed a bridge between Israel and the pagan world."[13]

Although wisdom plays down the identity of a specific people or nation, essential to its interest is the individual's immediate social setting. Biblical Wisdom literature variously reflects agrarian, urban, and court settings, and this range of circumstance likely corresponds to a variety in its ultimate social origins, from "folk" to royal settings.[14] Along with other evidence, the analogy of Mesopotamian and Egyptian schools affiliated with the palace or temple suggests the likelihood of formal institutional training of scribes in ancient Israel.[15] The Hebrew inscriptions themselves bear formal evidence of systematic scribal training.[16] Like much of Proverbs (especially chapters 1–9), didactic wisdom literature from Egypt and Mesopotamia typically reflects father-to-son instruction in a domestic setting.[17] A court setting in Proverbs is reflected by section headings that refer to kings Solomon (1:1; 10:1; 25:1), Hezekiah (25:1), and Lemuel (31:10); by specific instructions on behavior in the company of the king, especially in 22:17—24:22; and by the extensive parallels between the latter and the Egyptian instructions of Amenemope.[18] For all three major Wisdom books of the Hebrew Bible, various parallels of genre, viewpoint, and subject matter in similar ancient Near Eastern texts indicate, more generally, a self-conscious participation in a broader international wisdom tradition.[19] This cosmopolitan perspective most likely had its institutional context in a royal administrative setting.

Many scholars would see a general correlation between writing and centralized authority in ancient Israel and its environment.[20]

While the wisdom enterprise encompasses this span of historical and social settings, the production of biblical Wisdom literature most likely had its institutional setting in the context of professional scribal activity connected at some level with a centralized state and temple apparatus both before and after the exile.[21] As Michael V. Fox states, "Learned clerks, at least some of them the king's men, were the membrane through which principles, sayings and coinages, folk and otherwise, were filtered."[22] Though the final selection may have rested with the central scribal apparatus, many of these traditions from various levels and spheres of society filtered *up* by way of a more widespread and common basis in Israelite social life.[23]

Wisdom's "House"

As discussed in chapter 1, Israelite society knew an overarching coherence that consisted of a kin-based structure integrating its various levels of complexity. This cohesive social structure was based on the model of the patrimonial household. Kin relationships in the household provided the paradigm for life in the court and academy. In the book of Proverbs, an emphasis on the patrimonial household at different social levels likewise cuts across the various divisions of the book, whether deemed domestic, royal, or otherwise in their orientation and implied settings.[24] In short, the patrimonial basis of Israelite social organization was integral to the transfer of ideals from one social setting to the next, as depicted in biblical Wisdom literature and as most likely involved in its production.

The centrality of the household in ancient Israel belongs to a broader ancient Near Eastern understanding of the world as a hierarchy of households, an idea that figures prominently in wisdom's conceptualization of the relationship between the social and cosmic order. Raymond C. Van Leeuwen has recently shown how texts from ancient Mesopotamia and Israel employ the metaphor of building and filling a house as a wisdom image joining human and divine activity within the cosmic and social order.[25] Acknowledging recent scholarship on the ancient Near Eastern "house of the father" as described in chapter 1, Van Leeuwen explains, "Creation was portrayed as a macrocosmic 'house'—with its fields, waters, and variegated activities—to which temples and ordinary houses with their lands corresponded as microcosms."[26] In this connection, Van Leeuwen cites a statement from the Assyriologist Thorkild

Jacobsen from a few decades earlier: "At home the more important gods were simply manorial lords administering their great temple estates, seeing to it that plowing, sowing, and reaping were done at the right times, and keeping order in the towns and villages that belonged to the manor."[27] It is through these different levels of a single cosmic structure that wisdom serves both divine and human efforts.

This longstanding ancient Near Eastern view of the world appears in Proverbs, as Van Leeuwen illustrates in the pairing of a couple of texts:

> The LORD *by wisdom* founded the earth;
> *by understanding* he *established* the heavens;
> *by his knowledge* the deeps broke open,
> and the clouds drop down the dew.
> (Prov 3:19-20 NRSV)

> *By wisdom* a house is built,
> and *by understanding* it is *established*;
> *by knowledge* the rooms are filled
> with all precious and pleasant riches.
> (Prov 24:3-4 NRSV)

In these two passages, the same terms for divine wisdom and insight appear in the same sequence. As Van Leeuwen explains, "The divine building of the cosmic house by wisdom is the model for human house building; human culture is a form of the *imitatio dei*, especially with reference to God's creation of the cosmos as the house in which all houses are contained."[28] In this comparison, the "house" as architecture and household as social institution are ingrained within the fabric of creation itself.

Accordingly, in Proverbs and in biblical wisdom more generally, divine wisdom is transmitted through this cosmic and social hierarchy of households. As Richard J. Clifford observes, "Heavenly wisdom came to the human race mediated by earthly institutions or authorities: the king, his scribes' literature, and heads of families. In Proverbs, the mediating institutions are the king (Solomon, 1:1; 10:1; 16:10; 20:8; 25:1; and so forth), and the father (and sometimes the mother) in the instructions of chaps. 1–9."[29]

The household figures centrally not only in Proverbs but also in the critical Wisdom books of the Hebrew Bible. This way of framing the individual's place in the world is integral to the premise of each. Job's righteousness is weighed in terms of the sons, daughters, livestock, and servants belonging to his household (Job 1:1-3), and it is largely in those terms that he incurs both personal loss and divine rewards (1:11-22;

42:10-17).[30] The speeches, too, refer to matters of household life and relationships (5:24-25; 18:19; 19:13-19; 29:4-6; 31:9-15). Qoheleth, perhaps reflecting a time of diminished family identity (see the discussion later in this chapter), offers comparatively little reflection on household matters (although see Eccl 4:7-8; 5:14; 6:3-6; 9:9). Nonetheless, the book opens as a fictional royal autobiography and identifies the royal persona of Qoheleth in patrimonial terms: "Qoheleth, the son of David, king in Jerusalem" (1:1), the nation being understood traditionally as the extended household of the king.[31] The scenarios depicted in the biblical Wisdom books reflect the integral role of the household in the social order familiar to ancient Israelites. Even more significantly for the wisdom viewpoint, they reflect the importance of social setting as a given in the perspective of the individual and as an integral part of the cosmic order.

PROVERBS AND THE INDIVIDUAL'S PLACE IN THE WORLD

In Proverbs, the patrimonial view of the world and society stands out profoundly in what has been described as the book's "dominant metaphor of finding a wife, founding a household."[32] Viewing the world from a male's perspective, the book's introduction notes that it is offered for the benefit of "the simple" (BH pĕtā'îm; 1:4) and the "young man, boy" (BH na'ar).[33] As discussed in chapter 1 of this volume, the term na'ar often occurs in the Hebrew Bible in reference not to a child but to a young man who is not yet himself the married head of a household and who, lacking prospects of inheritance from his father's household, might seek status and livelihood in the military, priesthood, or court.[34] This technical sense of the term is consistent with Proverbs' consideration of various settings involving family, society, and court.

In Proverbs, the household is the central frame of reference for the individual's location and activity in these social spheres. Accordingly, throughout the book, certain individuals or groups recur as types representing definitive relationships in the young man's life—relationships to father, mother, slave, friend, neighbor, the king, and women. The metaphor of the household is established in Proverbs 1–9 through instructions from father to son concerning these various relationships. With emphasis on the authority of father and mother, extended instructions and speeches are addressed to "my son," a young man setting out to find a wife and tempted to turn from traditional ways (for example, 1:8-19; 5:1-23; 6:20-35).

As Fox observes regarding similar patrimonial language in Egyptian didactic wisdom, such discourse is typically presented as the actual instructions of real fathers—named kings and powerful officials—to real sons.[35] The same would apply to the Sumerian text titled the Instructions of Shuruppak, a collection of instructions from before 2500 B.C.E. and later translated into Akkadian in copies as late as 1100 B.C.E.[36] Parental authority within the household is paradigmatic for this model of instruction set in primordial times:

> Shuruppak, counseled his son,
> Shuruppak, the son of Uburtutu,
> counseled Ziusudra, his son:

> "My son, I will counsel (you), may my counsel be accepted,
> Ziusudra, a word will I s[ay] to you, may it be heeded! My
> counsel you should not neglect, the word that I have spoken,
> you should not change, the counsel of a father is something
> costly, may your neck be bowed before it." (lines 6–13)[37]

The setting of the family household is apparent in specific instructions of Shuruppak:

> The older brother is actually (like) a father, the older sister is
>   actually (like) a mother!
> May you heed your older brother,
> may you bend your neck to your older sister as you would for
>   your mother. (lines 173–75)

The link between divine and parental authorities through the cosmic–household structure is reflected near the text's conclusion: "The [M]other i[s] (like) Utu [the sun god], she gives birth to human beings, the [F]ather i[s] (like) a God, he makes [. . .] radiant, the [F]ather i[s] (like) a God, his word is reliable, may the counsel of the father be heeded!" (lines 258–61).

The Aramaic Proverbs of Ahiqar, which date from the second quarter of the first millennium B.C.E., regularly address "my son" (for example, sayings 4, 14, 40, and 42).[38] That this language signifies a family relationship is supported by two factors. The first is the setting of household and lineage as reflected in sayings 4–6:

> If I beat you, my son, you will not die;
> but if I leave you alone, [you will not live].
> A blow for a serving-boy, a rebuke for a slave girl,

and for all your servants, discipline!

He who acquires a runaway slave or a thievish maid [. . . and
ruins] the reputation of his father and his progeny by his
own corrupt reputation. [39]

The second factor indicating a family setting is found in the intro-
ductory narrative, which begins "[These are the wor]ds of one Ahiqar,
a wise and skillful scribe, which he taught his son" and then relates
that the childless Ahiqar adopted his nephew Nadin (also Nadan) and
taught him, suggesting that wisdom instruction is properly passed from
father to son. The offering of instructions from father to "son" in Near
Eastern wisdom texts from the third millennium through the second
millennium illustrates the broader cultural understanding in which
Proverbs partakes, one in which the household and its relationships
figure centrally.

The concern for founding a household in Proverbs persists from
chapters 1–9 through its other various collections, with various brief
sayings about domestic happiness running "like a red thread" (15:20;
17:21, 25; 19:13, 26; 23:22-25).[40] In chapters 25–29 ("other proverbs
of Solomon that the officials of King Hezekiah of Judah copied"; 25:1
NRSV), the focus is life in the king's household ("Do not put yourself
forward in the king's presence or stand in the place of the great"; 25:6
NRSV) and relationships to neighbor in the king's realm (27:13-14).
Continuing nonetheless is attention to family and household relationships: treatment of father and mother (28:24), discipline of children
(29:17) and servants (vv. 19, 21), domestic happiness or its opposite
("It is better to live in a corner of the housetop than in a house shared
with a contentious wife"; 25:24 NRSV; see also 27:15-16), and kin-
based household bonds ("Do not forsake your friend or the friend of
your parent; do not go to the house of your kindred in the day of your
calamity. Better is a neighbor who is nearby than kindred who are far
away"; 27:10 NRSV). This section of Proverbs suggests the interrelated
nature of just rule, parental authority, moral and "wise" behavior, and
treatment of neighbors:

When the righteous are in authority, the people rejoice;
but when the wicked rule, the people groan.
A child who loves wisdom makes a parent glad,
but to keep company with prostitutes is to squander
one's substance.
By justice a king gives stability to the land,
but one who makes heavy exactions ruins it.

> Whoever flatters a neighbor
>> is spreading a net for the neighbor's feet. (29:2-5 NRSV)

The moral order of society follows the social order that joins household to household, from the individual to the king.

The numerical sayings in Proverbs 30 touch upon matters of household life—treatment of parents (v. 17) and adultery (v. 20). Again, relationships within the household and the kingdom are interrelated as belonging to the same social order:

> Under three things the earth trembles;
>> under four it cannot bear up:
> a slave when he becomes king,
>> and a fool when glutted with food;
> an unloved woman when she gets a husband,
>> and a maid when she succeeds her mistress.
>> (30:21-23 NRSV)

In its most essential respect, the social order is vitally bound to the natural world, as reflected in this observation on the mystery of conjugal relations:

> Three things are too wonderful for me;
>> four I do not understand:
> the way of an eagle in the sky,
>> the way of a snake on a rock,
> the way of a ship on the high seas,
>> and the way of a man with a girl. (30:18-19 NRSV)

In keeping with the leitmotif of the household and its relationships, Proverbs gives extensive attention to women in the young man's life. Distinct among ancient Near Eastern wisdom texts is Proverbs' personification of Wisdom as a woman (1:20-33; 8; 7:4-5; 9:1-6, 11). At the same time, chapters 1–9 give extensive attention to the adulteress or "strange woman" (ʾiššâ zārâ; 2:16-19; 5:3-14, 20-21; 6:20-35; 7:5-27), strange in the sense of a stranger, having identity outside the legitimate bonds of the household. The adulteress is presented as a foil to the young man's actual or potential wife, "the wife of your youth" (5:15-20), and to Woman Wisdom (7:4-5). Among other things, Woman Wisdom represents legitimate authority and order within the community:

By me kings reign,
>   and rulers decree what is just;
by me rulers rule,
>   and nobles, all who govern rightly. (8:15-16 NRSV)[41]

She speaks openly in public places:

On the heights, beside the way,
>   at the crossroads she takes her stand;
beside the gates in front of the town,
>   at the entrance of the portals she cries out. (8:2-3 NRSV)

Woman Wisdom offers insight and material rewards not just to a select few or to a specific people, but to all human beings (*ʾîšîm, běnê ʾādām;* v. 4). Wisdom bears a universal relationship to humanity, having been present as Yahweh created the world and humankind (vv. 22-31; more discussion later in this chapter). Wisdom thus represents the essential unity between the valid order of the community and the universal and divinely established order of creation.

Herself embodying what society affirms as worthy of celebration, Woman Wisdom holds a public banquet, sending out her "young women" (*naʿărōte(y)hā*) as messengers from her house of seven pillars and calling with an invitation from the most visible places in the city (9:1-6). By contrast, the adulterous woman, who is presented as foolishness personified (*kěsîlût*), calls from the entrance of her house with an invitation to "secret" pleasures (vv. 13-18). Just as the negative female type includes both Dame Folly and the adulterous woman, so does the positive female type include not only Woman Wisdom but also the "wife of one's youth" (5:15-20) and the Excellent Woman described in chapter 31. Like Wisdom, the Excellent Woman is "more precious than jewels" (3:15; 31:10). As part of the overarching metaphor of finding a wife and founding a household, the predominance of female types in Proverbs give vital personal expression to the importance of social context for the individual's engagement of the divine order in the world.

The Individual's Social Setting in Speculative Wisdom

Even while reflecting the importance of family and social context, speculative wisdom in the Hebrew Bible, in its questioning of the traditional wisdom viewpoint, shows occasional tensions between the individual and the community. As noted, in the prologue and epilogue that frame the book of Job, the household defines the parameters of personal loss and divine restitution. Within the poetic speeches of the book, the importance of social context is reflected in the nature of the dialogue among four friends (plus Elihu, Job 32–37). As with the value Proverbs places on "a good name" and on making the right impressions on neighbors and superiors, in the Job dialogue, being in right standing in life is reflected in being held in high esteem within the community (Job 12:4; 16:20; 17:6; 18:17, 20; 19:21-22; 29:7-25; 30:1-15; 34:17-20). At the same time, Job becomes increasingly alienated from his companions as the dialogue proceeds. In the end, Job's part in the debate receives vindication ("You have not spoken about me what is right, as my servant Job has done"; 42:8). For most of the book, the closer Job comes to the truth, the more at odds he becomes with those around him.

Qoheleth, like the Epic of Gilgamesh (Standard Babylonian version), is presented as an autobiographical reflection of a wise king pondering his vast experience as the basis of his wisdom.[42] In Mesopotamian intellectual tradition, kings were an important part of wisdom's line of transmission from its divine origins to the wise among humanity, and as noted, this understanding is reflected in Proverbs.[43] The divine origin of Solomon's wisdom as a gift intended to benefit the nation is depicted in 1 Kings 3:4-15. In Qoheleth, the royal identity of the speaker fades as the book proceeds,[44] and the persona of the reflecting self, often speaking in the first person, persists forcefully. In wisdom generally, observation is an important medium of insight, but the perspective of the individual dominates in Qoheleth. As Clifford has observed, "In no other biblical wisdom book does an author explicitly base all his teaching on his *personal* experience and observation."[45] While the speaker in Qoheleth is thoroughly engaged with his social world, the balance falls on the reflections of this observing individual. As Seow points out,

> In some twenty-six instances, Qoheleth is the explicit or implicit subject of the verb *r'h* "to see." More precisely, Qoheleth observes the happenings in the world (1:14, 7:13, and 8:9), human preoccupations and strivings (3:10, 4:4, 7, 5:1-13, 8:16), divine arbitrariness as reflected in the unequal lots of individuals (2:24, 6:1), society turned upside down (3:16 and 10:7), the prevalence of injustice and oppression (3:16, 4:1, and 8:9), and how the traditional rules are contradicted in reality (7:15, 8:10, and 9:11, 13).[46]

Even while Qoheleth draws on events around him, his perspective as observer places him at something of a distance from both his society and the God standing behind it.

Given the bearing of the individual viewpoint in Qoheleth, it is not surprising that the role of the family household is much less pronounced there than in the Hebrew Bible's other Wisdom books. Qoheleth's language, viewpoint, and themes reflect life under the Persian Empire, when a highly developed but volatile international monetary and commercial economy resulted in pronounced social stratification and abrupt changes in fortune, a time when family relationships and the patrimonial order were likely threatened if not diminished.[47] In Qoheleth, the central metaphor for human life is not the family household but economic dealings, with an emphasis on anxious planning and hard work before the unpredictability of the market. In Clifford's words, "Arbitrary and unquestionable actions of the powerful and of officials mirror the inscrutability of divine governance."[48]

SOCIAL CONTEXT AND RELATIONSHIPS TO THE DIVINE

In addressing contexts where national or household identity is not defined, the didactic wisdom literature of the ancient Near East often refers generically to "the god," that is, the god in question, sometimes paralleled by other generic terms for the divine, such as "the goddess."[49] It is with this general and universal perspective that Qoheleth prefers ʾĕlōhîm ("God") in designating the divine.[50] Similarly, the poetic speeches in Job favor several terms that tend to function interchangeably in Biblical Hebrew as generic designations for God: ʾēl ("God"), ʾĕlōah ("God"), and šadday ("the Almighty"; 5:17; 6:4; 8:3; 13:3; 22:2-3; 27:10; 31:2).[51] The employment of various terms in oblique reference to the divine operates fully in the mode of international wisdom literature. But the persona of a single deity in Job takes on nationalistic implications of one leading God in the context of the prologue's depiction of Yahweh as sovereign over the divine court, the "sons of God" (BH bĕnê hāʾĕlōhîm). Accordingly, the dominion of the national god extends to all peoples of the earth, and Job, though not an Israelite, is nonetheless recognized by Yahweh as a paradigm of human virtue—one who is "blameless and upright, one who feared God and turned away from evil" (1:1, 8; 2:3). Like Noah and Daniel, other international figures legendary for their righteousness and wisdom (Ezek 14:14, 20; 28:3), Job receives special deference from the divine, ranking as Yahweh's favorite and thus being called by Yahweh "my servant" (1:8; 2:3), an appellative that suggests Job's place within the extended divine patrimony over the earth.[52]

Related to the broader social cohesion signaled by the prevalence of the household in Proverbs, national identity is accented in relationships to the divine. In Proverbs, the focus on the Israelite national god as universal divine sovereign is implied in the preference for Yahweh as the divine name throughout the book and in the general principle invoked in the beginning and later in varying forms: "The fear of Yahweh is the beginning of all knowledge" (1:7; cf. 9:10; 15:33; see also Ps 111:10; Job 28:28). Just as *Ludlul bēl nēmeqi* ("I Will Praise the Lord of Wisdom") highlights Marduk's preeminence as leading national god, the books of Proverbs and Job assume an analogous role for Yahweh, emphasizing his functions as creator of the world and guarantor of the natural and moral order. Yahweh's role as creator of the world is explicit both in Proverbs (3:19; 8:22-31) and in Job (38:4-7). Thus, in these books, wisdom's typically generic and universal perspective—as voiced in Qoheleth's consistent reference to God as *'ĕlōhîm* ("God")—is particularized in terms of Israelite national consciousness. By honoring the chief deity in national contexts, Wisdom literature in the Hebrew Bible follows the general wisdom principle of relating favorably to the god in question.[53]

Questions of divine identity require harmonizing wisdom's universal scope with a specific national consciousness. In the common settings of household and court, wisdom literature brings the individual to consider universal concerns of success and suffering. Both practical and speculative modes of wisdom posit divine direction of these dimensions of life experience. Success in life depends on proper behavior in relationship to other human beings and to the divine. Social context is integral to the individual's relationship to the divine through the established order of the world.

GOD'S HIDDEN PRESENCE
IN CREATION AND SOCIETY

In wisdom teaching and reflection, relationships to the divine are mediated through one's involvement in the world. Thus, the key to succeeding in the divinely established order of the world is a correct understanding of reality, as illustrated in the opening verses of the second major section of Proverbs:

A wise child makes a glad father,
    but a foolish child is a mother's grief.
Treasures gained by wickedness do not profit,

but righteousness delivers from death.
The LORD does not let the righteous go hungry,
but he thwarts the craving of the wicked.
(Prov 10:1-3 NRSV)

With reference to this passage, Richard J. Clifford points to a "three-fold" approach to reality that characterizes the wisdom enterprise, one that holds together distinct areas of human life: sapiential ("a way of seeing reality"), ethical ("a way of conducting oneself"), and religious ("a way of relation to the 'order' of God").[54] Accordingly, a proper understanding of the world results in correct behavior, which brings divine rewards. As Clifford notes elsewhere, "So strong is Proverbs' view of human freedom that the book virtually equates knowing the good with doing the good."[55] Thus, recognition of the divine presence in the world is necessary for negotiating it successfully.

From the perspective of biblical wisdom, the divine presence in creation is assured, but it is not obvious. There is a definite hidden quality to God's presence in the world.[56] Wisdom literature stresses not so much divine self-revelation as human seeking. With reference to the royal paradigm of the sage, Proverbs 25:2 asserts, "It is the glory of God to conceal things, but the glory of kings to seek things out" (NRSV).

Perceiving God's presence in the world requires not only observation and reflection but also the correct predisposition toward the divine. A certain rapport with the divine is required in order to perceive the created order and to succeed in the world. As Proverbs states at the outset and repeats in varying forms, "The fear of Yahweh is the beginning of knowledge; fools despise wisdom and instruction" (1:7 NRSV; cf. 9:10; 15:33; see also Ps 111:10; Job 28:28). As Gerhard von Rad noted, the repeated occurrence of this sentence in biblical wisdom literature underscores its importance.[57]

The "fear of God" is a broadly attested expression and concept in the ancient Near East, which suggests a profound reverence toward the divine that translates into appropriate moral and cultic behavior.[58] The basic concept is humanity's rightful place in the universe and awareness of the limits of human prerogatives, power, and understanding in relationship to the divine.[59] As Michael V. Fox points out, "the fear of God" involves both emotions and knowledge that motivate right behavior.[60]

According to Fox, without the repeated affirmation found in Prov 1:7, wisdom has "an ethical question mark over it."[61] In other words, one cannot operate successfully within the world without a proper recognition of humanity's place before the God who has established the order of the world. Wisdom for daily life is no less the domain of God's activity and presence, even if they remain hidden. Fox explains further that Proverbs offers instruction where it is most needed, namely, in areas of activity in which the understanding of right behavior is least apparent: realms of life not governed by law or social sanction, or dealings that are clandestine in nature.[62] It is the limits of human knowledge that both conceal God's presence in these secret and unknown spheres of activity and also require its recognition.

For von Rad, awareness of this human limitation informs the fear of God as an attitude that prepares one to perceive God's presence in the world's order. Even a successful negotiation of the world through divine guidance reinforces a sense of divine mystery and an awareness of the limits of human wisdom. As von Rad explained, "To the extent . . . to which one was aware that God was at work behind the fixed orders, the world, too, which knowledge was endeavoring to control, was drawn into the sphere of the great mystery surrounding God."[63] Von Rad continues, "The fear of God not only enabled a man [sic] to acquire knowledge, but also had a predominantly critical function in that it kept awake in the person acquiring the knowledge the awareness that his intellect was directed towards a world in which mystery predominated."[64]

The discernment of God's hidden presence in the world's order, though disputed among humankind, distinguishes "the wise" from "the fool," the two illustrative types invoked in the overarching principle of Prov 1:7. This typology is invoked in Psalms 14 and 53, which state, "Fools say in their hearts, 'There is no God'" (Psalm 14:1; 53:1 NRSV). Here, the question of God's presence or absence in the world is to be answered in the arena of human events and its moral implications. Psalm 10 similarly illustrates this perspective:

> In the pride of their countenance the wicked say, "God will
>   not seek it out";
>   all their thoughts are, "There is no God."
>
> . . . .
>
> They think in their heart, "God has forgotten,
>   he has hidden his face, he will never see it."
>   (vv. 4, 11 NRSV)

According to wisdom's view of the world, the hidden God of creation is present even in the most secret corners of human social life and holds human beings accountable for their deeds.

Recognizing God's governance of the world is critical to perceiving and living in accordance with the physical and moral order of
creation. The moral and ethical dimensions of life are complex and
cannot be co-opted opportunistically. For example, the "positive correlation between work and wealth" in Prov 24:23-34 constitutes neither
an endorsement of the status quo nor a warrant for mistreating the
needy.[65] In short, the prevailing social order, though under God's direction, does not necessarily equate with the divine order. God's hidden
presence shows through in the divine direction of the moral order of
the universe, which stands independent of human power and expedi-
ency. As Crenshaw explains regarding Prov 22:17—24:22 and its parallels in Egyptian Amenemope:

> Whoever uses false scales provokes God's anger, as do mockers of
> the poor. In ridiculing unfortunate victims of society, one curses
> their maker. . . . The ethical tone of these sayings is distinctive.
> They advise against oppression of the poor who have no defense
> against injury and warn against removing ancient landmarks.
> Widows, orphans, and the poor have the Lord as their redeemer;
> he weighs persons' hearts and keeps watch over their deeds.[66]

Wisdom's portrayal of the human search for God is by no means a
unilateral undertaking. God is ultimately in control, and God deter-
mines how much human beings perceive. In von Rad's way of explaining
the viewpoint reflected in the teachings of the wise, "Yahweh obviously
delegated to creation so much truth, indeed he was present in it in such
a way" that human beings can only find the proper way to proceed in
life by learning to "read" the order of creation and adjust their behavior
in accordance with "the experiences gained."[67] According to von Rad,
humankind "always and everywhere, stands in a hidden partnership
with Yahweh," as reflected in various sayings from Proverbs:

The eyes of the LORD are in every place,
keeping watch on the evil and the good.
                              (Prov 15:3 NRSV)

Sheol and Abaddon lie open before the LORD,
how much more human hearts! (Prov 15:11 NRSV)

The plans of the mind belong to mortals,
but the answer of the tongue is from the LORD.
                              (Prov 16:1 NRSV)

All one's ways may be pure in one's own eyes,
  but the LORD weighs the spirit. (Prov 16:2 NRSV)

All our steps are ordered by the LORD;
  how then can we understand our own ways?
                                    (Prov 20:24 NRSV)

For von Rad, this dialectic between human intentions and divine direction is integral to God's hidden presence in creation and in human events. God's initiative in the divine—human dialectic is presented most favorably in Proverbs 1–9.

WISDOM PERSONIFIED

In Proverbs, the divine–human partnership in creation is mediated by wisdom. As discussed earlier in this chapter, the correspondence between divine and human pursuits in the universe, as represented by the metaphor of house building in Prov 24:3-4, is the implication of Prov 3:19-20:

The LORD by wisdom founded the earth;
  by understanding he established the heavens;
by his knowledge the deeps broke open,
  and the clouds drop down the dew.[68]

Wisdom's value to God is evident from its instrumental role in Yahweh's creation of the world. The divine favor for wisdom and its potential value to humanity in Proverbs might be compared with the following sentiment from Ahiqar:

From heaven the peoples are favored;
Wisdom is of the gods.
Indeed, she is precious to the gods;
her kingdom is et[er]nal.
She has been established by Shamayn;
yea, the Holy Lord has exalted her. (Saying 13)[69]

In this statement, as in Prov 3:19-20, wisdom is clearly of divine origin and is of inestimable value to the divine and to humankind alike.

Wisdom's instruction comes with superior rewards of great value to humankind, as described in Prov 3:13-18:

> Happy are those who find wisdom,
>   and those who get understanding,
> For her income is better than silver,
>   and her revenue better than gold.
> She is more precious than jewels,
>   and nothing you desire can compare with her.
> Long life is in her right hand;
>   in her left hand are riches and honor.
> Her ways are ways of pleasantness,
>   and all her paths are peace.
> She is a tree of life to those who lay hold of her;
>   those who hold her fast are called happy.

Due to its integral role in the divine founding of creation, wisdom holds out to human beings unparalleled value for succeeding in the world.

Though Hebrew grammar allows the translation of wisdom's antecedent pronouns personally as "her," in the texts cited so far, wisdom might be understood strictly in abstract terms. But this foundational quality for divine and human endeavors takes on much more vital dimensions in relationship to wisdom's explicit personification in certain passages in Proverbs 1–9 (1:20-33; 8; 9:1-6, 11). As noted, in this section of Proverbs, wisdom, which in Biblical Hebrew is grammatically feminine (hokmâ), is personified as a woman (1:20-33; 9:1-6, 11) and overlaps the images of human women like the "wife of one's youth" (5:15-20) and the Excellent Wife of chapter 31 as examples of the ideal female type.

Wisdom's instrumental role in creation as noted in Prov 3:19-20 receives elaboration in 8:22-31.[70] In the latter text, Wisdom is personified as a preexistent being who was present with Yahweh at creation. Having enjoyed a uniquely favorable relationship to Yahweh from creation, personified Wisdom stands in a unique position to benefit humanity, in whom Wisdom delights (8:27-31). She calls out in the streets and public places, freely making her instruction available to any who would be willing to learn (1:20-23; 8:1-5), though having no pity for those who suffer the disaster of their own ways after refusing her counsel (1:24-33). As mentioned, Woman Wisdom builds a house and holds a banquet in 9:1-6. Here, Raymond Van Leeuwen's contribution on house building as a motif of cosmic wisdom places this text in full perspective.[71] In keeping with interpreters' suggestion that the seven pillars of verse 1 allude to the pillars of the earth, Wisdom's house represents the whole of the ordered and inhabited world of creation.[72] As this text shows when paired with Prov 14:1, the cosmic order founded in wisdom serves as the archetype for human achievements: "The wise woman builds her house, but the foolish tears it down with her own hands" (NRSV).

Commensurate with this plethora of roles and images, scholarship in recent decades has shown increasing agreement that personified Wisdom in Proverbs is a complex literary figure encompassing various models—including teacher, prophet, desirable woman, wife, artisan, and even goddess.[73] Integral to that literary complexity is the origin of Wisdom's presentation as a preexistent figure in 8:22-31, a question that scholarship continues to debate. Interpreters have compared Woman Wisdom in Proverbs to ancient Near Eastern goddesses, especially Egyptian Maat, the divine principle of justice and order in the cosmos personified as a goddess.[74] A related explanation invokes the category of divine hypostasis.[75] Biblical and epigraphic texts sometimes speak of divine aspects or attributes as reified and almost independent agents of God's presence in worship or in human events—for example, Yahweh's "name," "spirit," "word," or "glory."[76] As scholars have discussed, based on evidence from ancient Israel and its West Semitic neighbors, divine hypostases can be understood to develop into goddesses.[77] Another suggestion of Wisdom's mythological background focuses on the enigmatic Hebrew word ʾāmôn ("master worker" NRSV) in 8:30, which some take to derive ultimately from Akkadian umânnu, the term for the ancient or primordial culture bearers who mediated special knowledge from heaven to humankind in Mesopotamian tradition.[78] The lack of parallels from elsewhere in the Hebrew Bible—either for ʾāmôn meaning "sage" or for Wisdom as a divine hypostasis or goddess—presents an obstacle to these interpretations, though each remains plausible. It is reasonable to consider that all of these figures from postexilic Israel's environment and background serve as models drawn into the multifaceted personification of Wisdom as a symbolic figure representing the divine origins of wisdom teaching.

The figure of Wisdom in Proverbs 1–9 is, if nothing else, a complex literary personification, relating wisdom's more graphically personified depictions such as 8:22-31 to more abstract ones including 3:19-20.[79] Drawing on the older mythological patterns, the wisdom poet(s) behind Proverbs 1–9 found a way to personalize the mediating reality between God and the world without confusing wisdom with either of the two. Woman Wisdom thus appears in Proverbs as a poetic reflex of a hypostatic divine attribute that, at least in the existing form of the text, stops short of deifying wisdom itself.

The book of Proverbs presents wisdom, even in personified form, as a divine attribute whose poetic personification accentuates the notion of God's communication to humanity. As Roland Murphy states, "The call of Lady Wisdom is the voice of the Lord. She is, then, the revelation of God, not merely the self-revelation of creation. She is the divine summons issued in and through creation, sounding through the vast realm of the created world and heard on the level of human experience."[80] The figure of Woman Wisdom functions as a unique representation of communicative divine presence in the Hebrew Scriptures. The reflections of James Crenshaw summarize several of these points: "Although most proverbs subsume divine presence under other categories, the desire to relate God and humanity more directly gave birth to 'mythological' reflection about Wisdom. Through her, God made his presence felt in the lives of his creatures, and in this way made known his great desire to communicate with humankind."[81] Though conceding that she exists on a mediating plane between God and humanity, Fox argues against understanding Wisdom as a mediator, mainly on the basis that Proverbs does not portray God speaking to her.[82] As noted, though, Wisdom is clearly of divine origin (Prov 3:19-20; 8:22), and Wisdom's presence from the world's founding means that she conveys to humankind what God has communicated in the acts of creation. The nature of Wisdom texts precludes human beings from being privileged to direct words from Yahweh, including words to Wisdom.[83]

The persona of Woman Wisdom encourages human pursuit of divine guidance offered in creation. According to this portrayal, wisdom is not obscure and hard to find (compare Job 28), but rather, it seeks out human beings. Wisdom's active seeking enlivens the imagination of what otherwise appears as God's hidden presence in the world. This signal of God's active presence provides a needed hope for human seeking.

The reflection of God's presence through Wisdom remains nonetheless an indirect form of contact with God and a reminder of the limits of human perception and understanding. As Crenshaw remarks, "Awareness of limits imposed upon all knowledge equipped the wise for their biggest struggle of all, the fight to understand divine enmity and indifference."[84] Even armed with this tempered encouragement, one confronts disturbing degrees of God's hiddenness in human life.

THE MORAL CRISIS OF GOD'S ELUSIVE PRESENCE

While the "fear of God" might be the essential prerequisite for recognizing the divine order of the cosmos, it is no guarantee of apprehending the elusive presence of the divine. This realization is explored in the skeptical side of biblical wisdom, as represented occasionally in Proverbs—mainly in the sayings of Agur (30:1-9) and in "rare proverbs like 14:13" ("Even in laughter the heart is sad, and the end of joy is grief")[85]—and more thoroughly by the books of Job and Ecclesiastes. The traditional wisdom view asserts two factors indicating God's presence in the universe: the just governance of the world and the transparency of an orderly cosmos to reverent human observers. The critical Wisdom books of Job and Ecclesiastes presuppose this established view and call into question its twin assertions.

Each of the two books centers on the persona of one who embodies these challenges to the constructive wisdom viewpoint. The critical mode of biblical wisdom thus proceeds from the questioning stance of the individual. As Crenshaw states, "Inasmuch as Israel's wisdom concentrated on the individual, it drew no solace from the age-old belief in corporate solidarity. In time, both the nation and individuals within it nullified the claim that justice inevitably triumphs."[86] Wisdom provides the Bible's most sustained attention to what since the Enlightenment has been called theodicy. In its classic formulation, theodicy seeks to answer the logical dilemma between God's beneficence and God's power in the face of innocent human suffering.[88] By contrast, the Wisdom books approach this moral problem not in philosophical abstraction but existential reflection. In traditional wisdom, the world's moral and natural order provides the chief evidence of God's presence. When that order is no longer reliable or discernible, the unsettling logical conclusion is divine absence in the realm of human life. The writers and speakers of Job and Ecclesiastes engage this notion of divine inscrutability.

The natural world and society being the unified medium of God's discernible presence in wisdom thinking, biblical wisdom is approached in concrete and personal terms. As the following discussion will show, the biblical Wisdom books seek not a logical solution to God's character, but God's presence. The concrete metaphor for this search is wisdom's remoteness as described elaborately in the poem of Job 28. More succinctly, Eccl 3:10-11 describes the vexing irony of humanity's place within the divine order: "I have seen the business that God has given to everyone to be busy with. He has made everything suitable for its time;

. . . moreover he has put a sense of past and future into their minds, yet they cannot find out what God has done from the beginning to the end." In these two books especially, biblical wisdom imputes divine responsibility for human anguish and despair resulting from the ultimate inscrutability of both God and creation. Innocent human suffering and the general human inability to discern God's presence in the order of the world are challenges Job and Ecclesiastes pose to the traditional wisdom view.

In the ancient world, reflection on the problem of evil and unjust suffering did not begin with Israel, nor is it peculiar to monotheism. This speculative mode of wisdom is represented by numerous other ancient Near Eastern texts critical of received tradition.[89] The suggestion of divine responsibility for human suffering is also present in Mesopotamian literature. This notion is voiced in the Epic of Gilgamesh, which like Qoheleth represents the wisdom genre of royal autobiography. The speech of Siduri, the alewife, includes the following admonition:

> Gilgamesh, where do you roam?
> You will not find the eternal life you seek.
> When the gods created mankind,
> They appointed death for mankind,
> Kept eternal life in their own hands.
> So, Gilgamesh, let your stomach be full,
> Day and night enjoy yourself in every way.
> (Old Babylonian version, Tablet X column iii)[90]

The advice to seize the day of enjoyment represents a practical coping with the inevitability of suffering in life. It serves as both a sober reminder of humanity's plight and as a refuge from suffering caused by the knowledge that the full attainment of life remains beyond human reach. Similarly, the Egyptian Harpers' Songs urge readers to enjoy today before an uncertain tomorrow.[91] As in Job, the format of dialogue and recitation represents the appropriate format for wisdom scrutiny in the Tale of the Eloquent Peasant, a confrontation in nine speeches between a peasant and a high official.[92] Other Egyptian texts include the Dispute of a Person with his Ba (that is, vital force), which gives vivid description of life's misfortunes.[93] Using the form of dialogue, the Admonitions of Ipuwer offers a grim recital of the troubles of the land (a common topos in Egyptian skeptical literature), which it ultimately blames on the creator god.[94]

Mesopotamian texts offer numerous examples of wise dialogue that examine divine inscrutability and human suffering. In the "Sumerian Job" (also known as "A Man and His God," attested in a copy dated ca. 1750 B.C.E.), a righteous sufferer who has suffered the loss of health, wealth, and social esteem blames his misfortune on his personal and family deity, who represents his interests before the high gods of the divine assembly.[95] At the advice of the "sages," the righteous man accepts his suffering as the consequence of sin. Upon his confession, his god rewards him, and his suffering gives way to joy. Though deliverance comes through submission to the gods, human suffering itself is presented as the result of divine governance of the world.

The "Babylonian Theodicy," which dates to around 1000 B.C.E., presents a dialogue between a sufferer and a wise friend.[96] Initially, the sage rebukes the sufferer for imputing his misfortune to his god. Nonetheless, the sufferer maintains his point that the gods do not deal equitably with humankind:

Those who neglect the god go the way of prosperity,
While those who pray to the goddess are impoverished and
    dispossessed.
In my youth I sought the will of my god;
With prostration and prayer I followed my goddess.
But I was bearing a profitless corvée as a yoke.
My god decreed instead of wealth destitution. (lines 70–75)

Eventually, the friend admits that the sufferer is right in decrying divine injustice:

Narru, king of the gods, who created mankind,
and majestic Zulummar, who dug their clay,
and mistress Mami, the queen who fashioned them,
gave perverse speech to the human race.
With lies, and not truth, they endowed them forever.

. . . .

They harm a poor man life a thief,
They lavish slander upon him and plot his murder,
Making him suffer every evil like a criminal, because he has
    no protection. Terrifyingly they bring him to his end, and
    extinguish him like a flame. (lines 276–86)

Having won his friend's sympathy, the sufferer acknowledges his kindness and concludes with a prayer: "May the god who has thrown me off give help, May the goddess who has [abandoned me] show mercy" (lines 295–96). No explanation is offered, only the suggestion that the gods are both cause and cure of human ills. One can only hope for mercy from the divine, even after they have brought suffering.

In *Ludlul bēl nēmeqi* ("I Will Praise the Lord of Wisdom," seventh-century copies of what is likely a second-millennium text), an individual experiences a reversal of fortunes and complains of divine abandonment: "I called to my god, but he did not show his face, I prayed to my goddess, but she did not raise her head" (Tablet II lines 4–5).[97] Recognizing divine justice to be incomprehensible ("Who knows the will of the gods in heaven?"; Tablet II line 36), the sufferer turns to his god in praise and ultimately is restored by Marduk (Tablet III). This outcome, in Clifford's words, brings Marduk's "cosmic role into the domain of the individual."[98] With no answer to offer for the intellectual problem of suffering, by the sufferer's example the text commends the praise of the divine. Rather than simply turning praise into "a matter of the heart," as Clifford suggests, the implied message is that human praise can bring the fullness of divine power and presence, as represented by the Babylonian high god, to bear on the suffering, no matter its causes.[99] The notion that the suffering individual has access to the highest levels of divine governance (through priestly mediation; Tablet III lines 40–45) offers tremendous hope, even if not providing a solution to the problem or an explanation of its sources.

Despite the charge of the divine responsibility for unjust suffering, human beings in these ancient Near Eastern texts nonetheless seek the divine from the midst of distress or else seek to enjoy divine gifts while they are available. As in the Hebrew Bible, divine absence "is felt as a real absence" only when human beings believe in the possibility of divine intervention and are surprised by God's silence and inaction.[100] In critical wisdom as in constructive wisdom, outcomes may be divinely engineered, but the onus lies on human seeking.

This ancient Near Eastern tradition of dialogue and recitation on human suffering and divine responsibility includes the biblical book of Job. As discussed in chapter 2, Job's name belongs to the divine-absence name type attested in West Semitic personal names of the second millennium, meaning "Where is the (Divine) Father?" In its origin, the very name of Job voices the concern of divine absence in its most basic form. In its reanalyzed form as vocalized in the Masoretic Text, Job's name may be understood to mean "enemy," a fitting name for one who accuses God of acting as his enemy.

In the dialogue, both Job and his friends assume moral implications of the world's governance. The point of contention is whether the world as it operates gives evidence of God's attentive presence. Job protests his suffering as unjust. He persists in defending his own integrity and accuses God of attacking him as his enemy. As James Crenshaw explains, "Job experiences God's wrath, followed by God's withdrawal and silence; he accuses God hoping to break the divine silence and provoke God into a response."[101] Crenshaw points to Job's circumstances as evidence that God is not only absent and negligent but even actively hostile to Job. As Carol Newsom points out, Job both seeks and dreads a confrontation with God.[102] Though assaulted by God, Job has nowhere else to turn for vindication. In the mode of a human plaintiff seeking a hearing before the divine judge, Job takes an oath of innocence (Job 31).

From his opening speech (Job 3), Job suggests that any moral order in the world is a perverse one. He calls for the undoing of creation, the unleashing of the powers of chaos against what he sees as the perverse order of the world (Job 3:4-10). As Clifford comments, Job in this opening speech "wishes for precreation darkness and inertness . . . . In the narrative plot, Job's reversal of creation, his refusal to accept it and to submit, will be the stuff of God's speech to him in chapters 38–42. Now, however, numbed by his grievous losses, he wishes he were dead, that is, in the darkness of Sheol."[103] Later, in what is usually recognized as a sarcastic parody of Psalm 8, Job suggests that human beings occupy a special place within that perverse order: "What are human beings, that you make so much of them . . . ?" (Job 7:17-18).[104] For Job, whatever order is manifest in the world God governs would be better overthrown. Job assumes the powers of chaos are preferable to any sense of divine presence as represented by the world's order.

A different understanding of chaos, order, and divine presence is offered where the powers of chaos are invoked again in the book's culmination in the theophany and divine speeches (Job 38–42). Appearing in the form of a whirlwind, Yahweh's theophany embodies destructive forces at the boundaries of the ordered world. Yahweh's appearance and the content of the divine speeches defy Job's basic assumption of a moral and orderly universe.[105] Job's assumption is shaped by the traditional center–periphery conception of the universe that was taken for granted in the ancient Near East. The divine speeches' focus on the outlying realms of cosmos, remote from the human center, present an implicit correction to the thoroughly anthropocentric view of the universe.

The first divine speech, which is concerned with the "design" of the world, answers the charge of its unwise governance by God and affirms Yahweh's command over the world's order, even to its remotest parts (Job 38–39). The second divine speech, in answering the charge of God's unjust governance of the world, moves beyond the ordered creation to the powers of disorder as embodied by Behemoth and Leviathan (Job 40–41). As Mark Smith discusses, the motif of the leading deity's "beloved monsters" here as in Ugaritic texts underscores God's ultimate power and control over the powers of chaos and cosmic evil.[106] The motif underscores divine control, even at the threatening periphery of existence. But in connection with theodicy, it displaces an anthropocentric view of the world. As summarized by Clifford:

> The universe in the book of Job has been created by a God, utterly transcendent in wisdom and justice. The universe cannot be analyzed by human beings (chap. 28) and summed up with traditional wisdom, as is shown by the three friends' inability to speak the truth about God (42:7-8). God creates for God; the divine purpose is inscrutable; human beings cannot assume that they are the center of the universe. Traditional creation accounts in the ancient Near East often began with the gods vanquishing evil, which was often personified as a monster. But creation in the book of Job ends with the monsters unvanquished, with God admiring them in splendid poetry! They are, to be sure, on God's leash, but they move in ways that threaten and terrify the human race.[107]

In place of the usual view of creation as the exclusion of chaos, the divine speeches in Job subsume chaos into the order Yahweh exerts over the cosmos even if precariously—note the defensive tone in which Yahweh opens the first speech: "Were you there?" (Job 38:4). As Samuel Balentine points out, in connection with other statements on the meaning of creation—for example, the "tree of the knowledge of good and evil" (Gen 2:9) or Second Isaiah ("I form light and create darkness, I bring prosperity and create disaster (ra⁽: Isa 45:7)—it is hard to escape the notion that "God is ultimately responsible for whatever merits the label 'evil'" (compare Job 2:10).[108] Though posing a constant threat to the created order, these powers of chaos, too, are ultimately under Yahweh's control. As suggested in connection with "structural divine absence" (see chapter 4), God's ability to manage and limit the powers of chaos and death lie not in their divine origins but rather in their exclusion from God's realms of activities. The monsters embody not chaos but the boundaries between chaos and order. The view from the divine speeches of Job impels one to a place of disorienting cosmic and moral liminality. While it is asserted in the form of overwhelming theophany, it is neither explained nor justified.

Yahweh's wager with the satan and test of Job in the prologue, though they do not reappear in the epilogue, nonetheless support affirmation of the divine speeches that the world is theocentric rather than anthropocentric.[109] Over against the speeches of Job's friends, both Job's and Yahweh's speeches emphasize the gulf that lies between God and humankind. In short, the divine speeches affirm the divine transcendence without explaining it.[110]

Nonetheless, the divine speeches and their theocentrism offer a basis for hope. An important factor distinguishing Job from its ancient Near Eastern analogs is God's active presence in Job. As Clifford points out, it is God who "initiates the entire drama in chapters 1–2 and concludes it in chapter 42."[111] As Crenshaw comments,

> The arsenal of rhetorical questions forced Job to concede that he was not the center of things. Indeed, the entire theophanic speech deals with the non-human world, as if God wanted to say that the universe can get along without people. Still, that would be a misreading of the facts, for God does condescend to talk with Job. Even the challenge to play God, if they can, places human beings above every single creature that God paraded before Job. In addition, Job's repentance, however interpreted, signifies a possibility of relationship that conceals wonderful promise.[112]

The book of Job thus answers the concern for divine absence in human suffering with a distinct theodicy of presence. The problem of evil is not solved, but behind this apparent divine absence lies the presence of a God who responds to Job's demands for a hearing.

Job thus takes its place within wisdom's emphasis on the human potential to recognize and choose right response to God's order in the world, even while struggling to apprehend that order.[113] As Crenshaw concludes, in the end "humans must content themselves with the fear of the Lord, which amounts to authentic wisdom."[114] As Newsom points out, the idea of the fear of God "occurs in significant places in the framing of the book of Job, not only in the prose tale but also in the poem that concludes the dialogue between Job and his friends (1:1, 8; 2:3; 28:28)."[115] For Job, what applies to everyday experience often applies to suffering: that is, what might appear to be divine absence is divine presence in less obvious form.

Qoheleth, by contrast, expresses much less confidence in human potential to seek and trust in divine inclination to appear. A single slogan frames the book's contents and encapsulates the message of its reflections: "Vanity of vanities, all is vanity" (Eccl 1:2; 12:8). In Qoheleth, the Hebrew word translated "vanity" (*hebel*, literally a "vapor" or

"breath"; Isa 57:12; Ps 62:9) refers to the utter futility of human existence. As C. L. Seow explains, when Qoheleth says that everything is
hebel, "he does not mean that everything is meaningless or insignifi-
cant, but that everything is beyond human apprehension and compre-
hension. But in thinking about humanity, Qohelet also speaks of God.
People are caught in the situation where everything is hebel—in every
sense of the word. God is transcendent and wholly other, but humanity is 'on earth.'"[116] For Qoheleth, human efforts at apprehending the
divine through the world's order are obscured by what Clifford calls a
basic "misalignment between reality and the mind" (see especially Eccl
3:10-12; see also 1:4-11; 6:10-12; 7:13-14).[117] As Crenshaw explains,
Qoheleth "accused God of concealing vital knowledge about the appropriate time for any single behavior" (see Eccl 3:1-9).[118] In the words of
Clifford, "All moments are in the hands of God, who does them in a
rhythm that is beyond human calculation."[119]

   Although nature reveals an observable order, it is one that forms an
endless cycle of the sun's rising and setting, the circulation of the winds,
and the flowing of waters to the sea through rivers and back to their
source (Eccl 1:3-11). This endless cycle of nature indicates the inconse-
quential nature of human existence. Moving from the realm of nature
to the human social order, all endeavors and achievements, including
the effort to find meaning in life, similarly lead nowhere (1:12-18). The
pursuit of pleasure likewise leads only to death, the inevitable outcome
for humankind (Ecclesiastes 2). As Crenshaw so aptly puts it, "Death
cancels every human achievement" (2:12-17, 26).[120] For Crenshaw, the
finality of death in Qoheleth suggests God's "indifference to the universe for which he was responsible. . . . Qoheleth experienced the religious bankruptcy of life emptied of trust in God."[121]

   Nonetheless, the book offers glimpses of hope. Among the responses
considered by Qoheleth is seizing the day of enjoyment before meeting the common fate of all in death: "So I commend enjoyment, for
there is nothing better for people under the sun than to eat, and drink,
and enjoy themselves, for this will go with them in their toil through
the days of life that God gives them under the sun" (8:15 NRSV; see
also 3:16-22; 6:1-6). In Seow's reading of the book, God thus relates to
humanity, even if mysteriously, and offers to humanity "the possibilities
of each moment."[122] Hence it is up to human beings to accept what happens, whether good or bad, and to respond spontaneously to life, even
in the midst of uncertainties, seeing both the possibilities and limitations of being human.

   Limits on human understanding need not lead to despair but to an
appropriate "fear of God": "I know that whatever God does endures

forever; nothing can be added to it, nor anything taken from it; God
has done this, so that all should stand in awe before him" (Eccl 3:15).
In reference to this verse, Agustino Gianto concludes, "To fear God is
the human capacity to recognize the divine presence despite its incom-
prehensibility."[123] Gianto goes on to say that in 7:18, Qoheleth "suggests that those who fear God know how to deal with both traditional
wisdom teaching and the critical attitude toward it. This is indeed the
key to success."

Having established that the same end in death awaits everyone,
Ecclesiastes in the last section (9:7—12:7) emphasizes the prudence of
facing life with an attitude of joy. Some interpreters thus see this last
section of the book developing an ethical response to the human condition described earlier in the book as "the portion of humankind in
the created world."[124] The ability to enjoy one's work is a gift of God
that provides some lasting enjoyment. As Gianto observes, "Ecclesiastes
believes that what is important now is the time in which one lives, where
toil is no longer the lot of humankind but a gift to be enjoyed."[125] The
certainty of human futility should lead not to despair but to joy and
enjoyment. The word *śmh* ("to rejoice") occurs regularly throughout the
book, both as a verb (2:10, 26; 3:12, 22; 4:16; 5:18; 8:15; 10:19; 11:8,
9) and as a noun (2:12; 5:19; 7:4; 8:15; 9:7, although with a negative
connotation in 7:4).[126]

The final word of Qoheleth ("Fear God, and keep his commandments"; 12:13-14), taken by most as a late editorial addition, commends
reverence and obedience to God. But as interpreters point out, it is also
integral to the book's content, which commends genuine religious devotion, the certainty of divine judgment, and warnings against empty dis-
plays of piety (see especially 3:14; 5:1-7; 8:12-13). With special attention
to divine presence and absence in Qoheleth, Gianto concludes that God
as described in Qoheleth

> is not at the service of people, ready to be called upon when in
> distress. God is sovereign; no one knows when God will act,
> or under what conditions God's intervention can be expected.
> In this respect, Ecclesiastes's view of God is unique. This God
> remains elusive despite being present in all spheres of human life.
> No action secures divine favor and there is [no] way to tell which
> actions will gain favor. Nonetheless, no one should disregard
> God's presence.[127]

Ecclesiastes is not the final word or the only voice in the Hebrew
Scriptures. It serves as a balancing note. It presses the honest admission
of human limits to its logical extension and back to the point of trust in

the divine. The book's sense of divine absence rests on human knowledge of divine presence unfulfilled. The partial understanding it reflects
is based on authentic experience. In this way, Qoheleth presents divine
absence as a necessary complement to divine presence in the cycle and
spectrum of life's experience.

Conclusion

This discussion of the Hebrew Bible's Wisdom literature has shown it
to be an important locus of biblical reflection on divine absence. Fundamental to wisdom's view of the world is the hiddenness of God in the
world and in human life. The constructive wisdom mode as represented
by Proverbs presents optimism concerning the human ability to discern
God's hidden presence and, from that discernment, to succeed in life.
Proverbs presents a confident approach to apparent divine absence in
the world.

However, the skeptical mode of Wisdom literature challenges the
traditional wisdom view. The book of Job questions the sense of God's
justice and God's favorable presence in the world by innocent human
suffering. Without offering an explanation of the problem of evil, the
book nonetheless portrays God's answer to Job's request by appearing
to Job, something unique among critical wisdom texts of the ancient
Near East. In its theodicy of divine presence, the book of Job both dig-
nifies and decenters the real problem of human suffering. In comparison
to Job's portrayal of an inscrutable but present deity, Qoheleth portrays
an utterly elusive God. For Qoheleth, God may be present in the world,
but God's presence and any meaningful order of the world are inexorably beyond human reach. Thus, the immediate joys of life take on new
meaning as gifts from the divine to be grasped and enjoyed while time
allows.

CHAPTER 6

Seeking Divine Presence
in Worship

THE PREVIOUS CHAPTER SHOWED how the biblical wisdom enterprise attends to the hidden presence of the divine in the mundane experience of human life. As another avenue for seeking the divine, worship involves the direct and often explicit engagement of divine presence and absence under set conditions of life for the individual and the community. The cultic engagement of divine absence includes ritual words and acts as presented in an array of biblical texts, including various ritual texts and the poetic words of worshipers in biblical psalmody.[1]

In ancient Israel and its broader cultural world, ritual gave shape to divine–human relationships in time and space. In the praise and lament of biblical psalmody, the theme of divine absence denotes an aspect of a cultic understanding of the world's makeup and of worshipers' experience of it in relationship to the divine. The worship literature brings the boundaries between divine presence and absence into razor-sharp focus and offers some of the most intense expression of this human concern in the Hebrew Bible.

Biblical worship texts represent various modes for locating both the individual's and the community's place in the order of creation, securing blessing in weal and woe in this life, and ordering the present moment in connection with the past through memory. Both ritual and psalmody show various ways of seeking divine presence and contending with divine absence through patterned behavior and speech. The worship literature of the Hebrew Bible presents ordered means of marking the boundaries between divine presence and absence. The following discussion gives attention to these realities in light of cultic concerns for status, time, and space.[2]

115

PRELIMINARY WORDS ABOUT WORSHIP
AND WORSHIP TEXTS

As recent studies have emphasized, biblical ritual texts are neither the full instructions for the performance of worship nor texts that were actually used in worship.[3] Nonetheless, they both reflect this activity among ancient Israelites and represent in textual form this way of relating to the divine. As discussed below, the Priestly literature of the Pentateuch provides the most elaborate presentation of ritual in biblical texts. But the following discussion of ritual and worship literature also includes descriptions and allusions to ritual in a variety of narrative, prophetic, and poetic texts in the Hebrew Bible.

Dimensions of various ritual forms that correlate with divine presence and absence will be noted in the discussion of individual texts. The groundwork is laid for that discussion by first giving attention to a basic aspect of personal ritual status in theoretical perspective. For both the community and the individual, life experiences translate into conventionally recognized emotional and ritual states, thus having implications for cultic relationships to the divine. This aspect of ancient Israel's worship shows social ramifications of the personal experience of divine absence or presence.

Ritual States in Sociological Perspective

As noted in chapter 1, the perception of divine presence or absence in ancient Israel and its broader context often correlated with the human experience of welfare or deprivation and corresponded to emotional states of grief and joy. Studies by Erhard Gerstenberger and Thomas Podella have made important contributions regarding the literary, social, and ritual dimensions of grief as a response to God's perceived absence or withdrawal in the Old Testament.[4] More recently, biblical scholars drawing on social anthropological analysis have examined the way the opposing emotional states of grief and joy come to social expression in ritual activity. Such analysis illuminates the social dimensions of divine presence and absence as addressed in worship.

From this perspective, Gary Anderson's important work examines celebration and lament as opposing ritual states that serve to set "boundaries on the unbounded" in communal life, that is, to limit the chaotic extremes of intense joy and grief.[5] For Anderson, these states represent separate and distinct spheres that nonetheless in their tension complement one another within a "ritual cycle of mourning and joy." Anderson speaks directly to the theological implications of such a balance for understanding divine absence in the Hebrew Bible:

> Lamentation, as outlined here, is not simply an outpouring of grief, but a very intricate ritual sequence that has as its initial goal a descent to Sheol. God commands the Israelite to experience God's absence. Indeed, in the spirituality of the Psalter the joyous sensation of God's presence cannot be appreciated apart from the sharp sting of his absence. For Bible readers of the present era, for whom the feeling that God is absent can be so poignant, it may be of comfort to know that these feelings have their place in the divine economy. To recall Qohelet, for everything there is a time, including even the absence of God.[6]

Stated differently, in the theologizing of human experience, the sense of divine absence is a necessary complement to that of divine presence. The sense of God's absence thus is not always the result of human sin, but can be rather a necessary part of the human relationship to the divine. Worship thus engages the "structural/divine absence" inferred from cosmological perspective (see chapter 4) and perceived in reflection on everyday human experience (see the discussion of wisdom in chapter 5). Ideas of divine absence and presence are the theological correlates of the sorrow and joy inherent to human existence. As the ritual expression of such experience shows, the sense of divine absence is regarded as a normal part of human experience.

Though representing mutually complementing realities, the places and activities of mourning and celebration are, according to Anderson's treatment, completely discrete and separate from one another, as they are rooted ultimately in the dichotomy between life and death. To view the matter in spatial terms, just as the sanctuary is the earthly counterpart to God's celestial place of dwelling, so is the experience of Sheol outside the sanctuary, especially at the grave, the earthly counterpart to the netherworld.[7] Rites of mourning represent identification with the dead and with the realm of death; worship represents identification with the giver and guarantor of life in the realm of God's presence.[8] Worship at the sanctuary is a ritual experience of God's presence; mourning, which renders one unfit for presence in the sanctuary, is a ritual experience of God's absence. To repeat, for Anderson, the larger purpose of this ritual cycle is to maintain the community's life between the extremes of joy and grief. Within that socioreligious economy, the ultimate purpose of mourning is, through an identification with the dead, to enable a movement forward from an experience of death to one of life—that is, in social and ritual terms, from an experience of God's absence to one of divine presence.

According to Anderson's treatment, all mourning, whether for the dead or in connection with some other terrible event, is ultimately an identification with death and is thus wholly incompatible with God's presence in the worship sanctuary. The main obstacle to this understanding is that it fails to account for biblical descriptions of petition or communal mourning at the sanctuary (for example, 1 Sam 1:9-18; 2 Kings 19:1, 14-19; 2 Chr 20:1-19; Ezra 10:6; Neh 8:9).

Taking Anderson as a point of departure, Saul Olyan examines the matter further in his book *Biblical Mourning*. Olyan is in agreement with Anderson that the cultic observance of mourning and celebration represent antithetical ritual states and that death and mourning for the dead are incommensurate with God's presence in the sanctuary;[9] however, the relationship of mourning to death differs in Olyan's analysis. Based on a close reading of the biblical texts, Olyan identifies four principal types of mourning: (1) mourning for the dead; (2) petitionary mourning; (3) nonpenitential mourning at the time of personal or communal calamity; and (4) mourning by the person with skin disease.[10] As Olyan demonstrates, the biblical texts use the same vocabulary and describe the same actions for all four.

According to Olyan, the last three types are patterned after mourning for the dead, but the primary and defining concern linking all four is not death itself but self-abasement.[11] While all four of these forms of mourning are incompatible with behaviors of celebratory worship, only the first and fourth render one unfit for entering the sanctuary. Thus, instances of petitionary and nonpenitential mourning at the sanctuary are explained as not really having to do with death. Olyan points to instances in which celebration and mourning occur simultaneously as sanctioned worship activities but with different worshipers carrying out the two separate modes of ritual. According to Olyan, the key is that the two ritual states of mourning and celebration may not normally coexist within the same individual. The rare instances attesting such (Jer 41:4-5 and Amos 8:3) indicate a severe expression of grief and a conviction that the ritual order is disrupted beyond return. For Olyan, the greater social function of mourning is to provide an opportunity for affirmation or alteration of existing social bonds.

The strength of Olyan's schema is that it corresponds to the biblical presentation of a complex set of relationships among various forms of ritual mourning. Nonetheless, a couple of factors suggest a more thoroughgoing association between mourning and death than Olyan's treatment allows. For one, as Olyan has so impressively demonstrated, the language and actions associated with the other three types of mourning are based on mourning for the dead and even make the mourner resemble the dead, so as Olyan himself asserts, "One can never completely dissociate other mourning types from mourning for the dead."[12] It thus seems strained to remove those other forms of self-abasement from any association with death. Though explicit verbal reference to death might be lacking in these instances, the gestures of mourning for death themselves qualify as explicit symbolic behavioral references to the power of death in some form, even if the actual death of specific individuals might not be the issue. That is, one might consider whether the other types of mourning represent some degree or potential of death's power.

Differing degrees of death's potency in association with mourning are also suggested in connection with the social function Olyan identifies for mourning, namely, social reaffirmation or reorganization. The clearest examples Olyan cites in support of this conclusion apply mainly to mourning for the dead (2 Sam 3:31-37; 15:14—16:13; Jer 41:6). This fact suggests that the opportunity for social reorganization or affirmation Olyan recognizes has more to do with death's removal of the individual from the community's life than with the ritual expressions of mourning. The adjustment of social roles necessitated by the absence of the dead would also apply to those excluded from social life by the impurity of skin disease—for example, in the case of Jotham's regency in place of his "leprous" father Azariah/Uzziah (2 Kings 15:5; 2 Chr 26:21). Of course, these two forms of mourning that require social reorganization—for death and skin disease—are the same two forms associated with physical conditions that necessitate exclusion from the sanctuary. This fact suggests that, though all forms of mourning represent some concern over the realm and powers of death, these two types are associated with a finality of death that requires a stricter observance of boundaries excluding the destructive forces of death from the human and divine spheres of life. Other degrees of death's power are connected with Olyan's examples of other types of mourning that bring social reorganization. In one of those instances, Ezekiel 26, prophetic mourning over the fallen city of Tyre is closely connected with what is described as the city's descent into the abode of the dead:

> [W]hen I bring up the deep over you, and the great waters cover you, then I will thrust you down with those who descend into the Pit, to the people of long ago, and I will make you live in the world below, among the primeval ruins, with those who go down to the Pit, so that you will not be inhabited or have a place in the land of the living. (Ezek 26:19b-20 NRSV)

In the case of mourning over marriages to foreign wives in Ezra 9–10, the language of Ezra's prayer spells out that what is at stake is whether or not the people will survive (see especially 9:8-9). Their disobedience threatens their ability to "stand before" the one who has revived them as a community (vv. 10-15).

Thus, the examples Olyan cites suggest that the potential for death, as confronted in petitionary and nonpenitential mourning, is an ever-present reality in human life and a condition that worshipers can bring before God. Death and skin disease, by contrast, are recognized in ritual and social terms as accomplished results of destructive forces that are wholly outside the realm of divine and human life; therefore, those bearing their contamination are excluded from the realm of God's presence in the sanctuary. The potential opportunity for reorganization or reinforcement of existing social roles and relationships in connection with all four of these forms of mourning can hardly be extricated from an association with death.

The social and ritual dimensions of divine absence show that in the Hebrew Bible, death is recognized as a realm separating human beings from God's presence. Yet as petitionary and nonpenitential mourning illustrate, God does not stand completely aloof from the experience of death. Rather, God is present and available at the sanctuary to engage even the threat of death's powers. A certain degree of ambiguity in the ritual engagement of death's powers corresponds to the overall ambiguity of God's presence or absence in biblical depiction of human life. As Anderson and Olyan agree, the stringent marking of the boundary between mourning and celebration allows for movement from ritual engagement of death to that of life and vice versa. While the movement from joy to lament, from life to death, in social experience is generally forced on human beings by life's circumstances, "the ritual cycle of mourning and joy" (to use Anderson's words) makes possible what would otherwise not be so, namely, a movement from death to life.

The socio-ritual observance of divine absence involves a human effort to move beyond that experience to one of God's presence. This forward progression requires some sense of a divine response in worship (see later in this chapter). This aspect of ritual's attention to boundaries and status illuminates one facet of divine absence in the Hebrew Bible, one in which human suffering and distress are normalized as an inherent part of human life. This insight from the work of Anderson and Olyan is one to which the following discussion will return often in connection with the engagement of divine absence in various biblical worship texts.

Sacred Time:
The Festal Calendar and Memory
of God's Presence

Built into the ritual cycle of the community are recurring events that
mark the boundaries of recurring sacred time in biblical texts. In connection with the annual seasons, these celebratory occasions involve the
community's observance of divine presence and absence in relationship
to the land. The ritual calendar of the Hebrew Bible is oriented around
three annual pilgrimage festivals (ḥaggîm), all linked to ancient Israel's
agricultural cycle: unleavened bread at the beginning of the barley harvest in the spring, "weeks" at the end of the wheat harvest, and "booths"
following the date, grape, and olive harvests "at the end of the year" in
the fall (Exod 23:14-17; 34:22-23; Lev 23:1-44; Deut 16:1-17).[13] The rite
of Passover was celebrated in the spring in connection with the seasonal
movements of pasturage (Exod 12:1-28; Lev 23:5-8).[14]

Ancient Israel's observance of this festival calendar most likely owes
to its common Canaanite heritage.[15] Scholars have identified the observance of a seasonal pattern in mythic and possibly in cultic expression
in texts from Ugarit.[16] Although the presence of this pattern in myth and
ritual remains debated, Ugaritic and biblical texts indicate that natural
and agricultural seasons were understood as expressions of divine blessing in ancient Israel's West Semitic cultural context.

The suggestion of ritual mourning for Baal occurs in the Ugaritic
Baal Cycle, where other deities mourn the storm god with the following
exclamations:

'i 'ap bʿ[l . . .] 'i hd
Where then is Baa[l]? . . . Where is Haddu?
                    (KTU² 1.5 IV: 6-7)

'iy 'al'iyn bʿl 'iy zbl bʿl 'arṣ
Where is Mighty Baal? Where is the Prince, the Lord of the
     Earth?
                    (KTU² 1.6 IV:4-5, 15-16).[17]

The possible ritual observance of Baal's absence is sometimes compared with 1 Kings 18's description of rites performed by priests of
"Baal" in the contest with Elijah on Mount Carmel. Ritual mourning
among Israelites with a possible seasonal component is indicated by
references to mourning for Tammuz and possibly Adonis in Ezek 8:14

and Dan 11:37.[18] In the prophetic book of Joel, an apparent disruption
of agricultural productivity in the form of a locust plague is perceived
as divine warning and punishment.[19] In the typical mode of prophetic
literature, disaster is interpreted as divine judgment and abandonment.
The major festal calendar involved this recognition of divine presence
and absence in the form of the seasonal cycle and the accompanying
productivity and barrenness of the land.

In keeping with the patrimonial basis of ancient Israelite society, the
chief participants in the major agricultural festivals were adult males
(see Exod 10:7-11). The three occasions of pilgrimage require "all your
males" to make pilgrimage to a local or central sanctuary to "appear
before Yahweh" and to present offerings (Exod 23:14-17; 34:22-23;
Deut 16:16-17). As presented in these texts, the cultic experience of
divine presence in the seasonal festal cycle is mediated to the people
through its household heads and other males. By way of its patrimonial structure, society as a whole acknowledges and accordingly offers
thanksgiving for the land's productivity as Yahweh's gift. Deuteronomy
additionally mentions participation by "your sons and your daughters,
your male and female slaves, the Levites resident in your towns, as well
as the strangers, the orphans, and the widows who are among you"
(Deut 16:11, 14).[20] Divine provision in the concrete form of agricultural
harvest, prosperity and well-being, and most basically in the unfailing
provision of life's necessities, constitutes an indication of God's favorable presence in the world. The corresponding expression of thanksgiving to the divine is a means of securing continued blessing.

Though based on the pastoral-agricultural cycle, each of these
festivals comes to be associated with Yahweh's provision and deliverance in specific events of the past.[21] Passover and Matzoth together are
brought into relationship with the exodus from Egypt (Exodus 12; Deut
16:1-8). "Weeks," which followed seven weeks (fifty days) later, comes
into association with the covenant at Sinai (Exod 19:1). "Booths," along
with "New Year's Day" and the Day of Atonement, are connected with
Israel's time in the wilderness (Lev 23:23-43). With reference to Passover, Frank Gorman notes ritual's role in cultivating collective memory:
"The Passover meal provided the occasion for a 'remembering' of Yahweh's saving acts on behalf of the Israelite community. 'Remembering,'
however, gave rise to a 'retelling' of the Exodus story. In this ritualized narration, the Exodus from Egypt was actualized in such a way
that the story of God's actions in the past became a present reality.
Israel recognized the power of ritualized memory and narration."[22] The
joining of ritual and past event as represented by these biblical texts
perpetuates the shared experience of divine presence through recurring

communal observance of worship. In its textual portrayal, ritual is part of an exercise of collective memory that actualizes anew the experience of God's presence in events that define Israelite identity. The repeated performance of worship reinforces shared identity through the recurring exercise of collective memory.

In certain instances, the memory of a past event can imbue a particular location with special status as a place for ongoing worship. This is the function of "cult legends" or etiologies that preserve the shared memory of God's presence at a place—for example, the etiologies of Bethel in Gen 28:10-22 and 35:6-15. Along with recurring divisions of sacred time, biblical worship texts mark divine presence and absence through the boundaries of sacred space.

God in Place: Divine Presence in Sacred Space

A chief concern of biblical worship texts is the localization of divine presence at the worship sanctuary. As emphasized in the work of Menaham Haran, the zoning and gradation of sacred space in Israelite sanctuaries is an important concern of biblical worship texts, especially Priestly ritual texts (discussed later in this chapter).[23] In this connection, Baruch Levine observes, "The demarcation of zones on the basis of graded sanctity . . . not only served to restrict and control human access but to lend a particular character to certain, more sacred areas, those in which the deity (or deities) resided, or sat, when they were present."[24] Biblical and archaeological evidence shows a range and variety of temples, sanctuaries, cultic corners, and worship sites characterized by varying degrees of spatial delineation and dedication to worship activities.[25] Of those various cult places, the one that dominates the biblical presentation of Israel's worship is the Jerusalem temple.

TEMPLE THEOLOGY: SPACE AND STATUS

Temple theology in ancient Israel and its broader cultural world followed two important social and symbolic patterns of the ancient Near East that have figured prominently throughout this study: the patrimonial household and the urban center–periphery continuum. These interrelated aspects of temple theology in Mesopotamian context are well summarized in the quotation from the Assyriologist Thorkild Jacobsen cited in chapter 5: "At home the more important gods were simply manorial lords administering their great temple estates, seeing to it that plowing, sowing, and reaping were done at the right times, and keeping order in the towns and villages that belonged to the manor."[26] Following the same general conception, texts in the Hebrew Bible regularly refer to the Jerusalem temple as the "house of Yahweh." As the patrimonial house of Israel's God, the temple stands as the center of Israelite society and territory. It is also the architectural instantiation of God's dwelling on earth. With the notion of Yahweh's ascendancy over the other nations and their gods (as reflected in Psalm 82), the domain of the national god extends to the rest of creation (see chapter 3). Temple worship as presented in the Hebrew Bible tends to focus on the maintenance of divine presence uniquely available at the central sanctuary.

The most elaborate presentation of instructions for worship at the central sanctuary is found in the Priestly (P) material of the Pentateuch, beginning in Exodus 25 and continuing into the book of Numbers. Though focusing on the portable sanctuary of the Israelite wilderness experience, the Priestly cultic traditions are based on centralized worship in the Jerusalem temple.[27] The discussion later in this chapter will give more attention to the Priestly inversion of a Jerusalem-centered view of the world. For now, it bears considering P as a reflection of temple-based worship.

Within the Priestly presentation, spatial dimensions of worship are built around proximity to the holy as represented by the place of divine presence at the sanctuary. As suggested in the classic cross-cultural analysis by the anthropologist Mary Douglas, ancient Israel's concept of holiness, especially as represented in Leviticus, is defined by notions of completeness and integrity.[28] The Israelite idea of holiness is projected onto concepts of the cosmos and society. An analogy to the human body as an expression of completeness, maintaining physical wholeness in community and worship, and avoiding its opposite, pollution, requires upholding external and internal boundaries of spatial organization.[29] Those boundaries and zones within and around the worship sanctuary correspond to degrees of divine presence.[30] Entrée and access to those demarcated areas of holiness correspond to status in relationship to divine presence. A clear example is the inner sanctum or most sacred place within the Israelite sanctuary—designated in the idiom of Biblical Hebrew as "the holy of holies" (qōdeš haqqŏdāšîm; for example, Exod 26:33, 34)—which only the high priest may enter and only once a year for the sanctuary purification ritual known as the Day of Atonement (Yom Kippur), as described in Leviticus 16. This passage gives vivid illustration of the vital interrelationship of sacred time, place, and status in biblical ideals of worship.

In Leviticus 16, status relates not only to individuals but also to the worship place itself, most basically with respect to the opposition between wholeness and pollution. When the high priest enters the most sacred space of the sanctuary, he places on the cover of the ark, which symbolizes the presence of Israel's God, the blood of a bull and goat ritually slaughtered as a *ḥaṭṭāʾt* ("sin") offering. In Jacob Milgrom's description, blood serves an expiatory function as a "ritual detergent" that removes from the community and its central sanctuary the people's accumulated impurity, which represents death.[31] Securing life's realm in the sanctuary and the community provides for Yahweh's presence. The purifying blood of the ritual secures the status of the sanctuary as a fitting place for God's presence.

Blood can affect status in ritually established human relationships as well. Building on the insights of Zvi Abusch, Theodore Lewis has recently shown that blood figures prominently in the ritual and sacred meal observance accompanying covenant ceremonies, the blood being understood to establish "life" relationships among human participants and between human and divine parties.[32] As Lewis concludes, the role of blood in ritual shows cultic and covenant observance to be related rather than completely distinct. In temple theology, relationships to the divine are mediated primarily through the place of worship, with worshipers finding their place within the "house" of Israel's God.

THE ORDERED WORLD OF RITUAL

In P, the spatial ordering of ritual around the divine presence at the sanctuary relates to the broader social and natural order of the world. The cosmic order is expressed in terms of divisions, classifications, and boundaries recognized in Gen 1:1—2:4a (see chapter 4). Just as God establishes the cosmic order through speech (Gen 1:1—2:4a), so does God bring the cultic order into being through speech in the instructions for building the tabernacle and the cultic apparatus (Exodus 25–31).[33] The cultic system is founded as an integral part of that created order.

Perhaps the most extensive example of ancient Near Eastern cosmogony is one that bears numerous parallels to creation in Genesis, namely, the Babylonian epic *Enuma Elish*.[34] In this text, the founding of the cosmos culminates in the establishment of Marduk's temple, Esagil, in Babylon. In keeping with the center–periphery thinking of ancient Near Eastern urban elites as discussed in chapter 4, *Enuma Elish* presents Babylon and its main temple as the political and cultic center of the world. By contrast, the biblical Priestly traditions fix the tabernacle as a mobile cultic center of the cosmic order, established not at the beginnings of creation but later, in the time of the nation's founding with Moses. This way of grounding ritual within the cosmic order in the Priestly worldview reveals self-conscious attention to Israel's identity at a time when it lacked a clear geographic center—namely, during the Babylonian exile (586–538 B.C.E.).

Priestly tradition locates the cult's foundation and meaning not in cosmic origins but in the origins of the nation, in the exodus event. As Yahweh's words summarize in Exod 29:43-46:

> I will meet with the Israelites there [that is, at the entrance of the tent of meeting], and it shall be sanctified by my glory; I will consecrate the tent of meeting and the altar; Aaron also and his sons I will consecrate, to serve me as priests. I will dwell among the Israelites, and I will be their God. And they shall know that I am the LORD their God, who brought them out of the land of Egypt that I might dwell among them; I am the LORD their God. (NRSV)

In Biblical Hebrew, the other word for the tent sanctuary of the wilderness, tabernacle (BH *miškān*), means literally "dwelling place." As this term indicates, in the central sanctuary, Yahweh is understood to dwell in the midst of the Israelite tribes, whose encampments mark the boundaries of the community. Thus, the sanctuary as the locus of the divine presence marks the center of the societal and cosmic order. As Gorman explains, the cult ensures the maintenance of this order, which "was threatened by the sin of the people and the impurity that arises from that sin and defiles the sanctuary. The sin of the nation threatened Yahweh's continued presence in the midst of the community and brought about the possibility that Yahweh might be driven from their midst."[35]

The Priestly instructions for building the tabernacle and the rest of the worship apparatus in Exodus 25–31 and the execution of those instructions in Exodus 35–40 establish the community's place in the order of creation. With the work of the tabernacle completed, the book of Exodus reaches its conclusion through a vivid description of how God takes residence in the portable sanctuary: "The cloud covered the tent of meeting, and the glory of the LORD filled the tabernacle" (Exod 40:34). Maintaining the community's place in that cosmic and sacred order is the purpose of Priestly cultic traditions included in Leviticus through Numbers 10. The geographic dislocation of community life reflected in the Priestly cultic legislation is also inscribed in its narrative context within the Sinai pericope (Exodus 19–Numbers 10).

THE NARRATIVE CONTEXT OF PRIESTLY RITUAL:
THE CENTRAL SANCTUARY AT THE MARGINS

The location of the sanctuary's legislation and construction at Sinai means a disorientation of the typical center–periphery pattern of temple theology. The sanctuary and worship apparatus are bestowed at the geographic periphery. In the Priestly tradition, the center is defined not by natural geography but by God's presence, which marks the true center of Israel's life. The P traditions give elaborate expression to the delineated order of the world, with the boundaries marking ambiguity and threat. It is fitting that the narrative context of these traditions is Israel's experience in the wilderness. As discussed in chapter 4, the wilderness in traditional ancient Near Eastern thinking symbolically marks the boundary between the ordered center of life and the realm of chaos and threat at the periphery. In the Pentateuchal narrative, the wilderness represents the people's experience at the margins, facing the threat of destruction. It is there that Israel's decisive encounter with God takes place, in the Sinai theophany and in the giving of instructions. Following upon Yahweh's deliverance from Egypt, the decisive moment for Israel's future hinges on whether it will enter into the covenant and law.

Furthermore, several references in Biblical Hebrew poetic texts indicate Yahweh's early associations with the desert regions far to the south of the central hills of Canaan (Judg 5:4-5; Hab 3:3; Ps 68:8; see more discussion later in this chapter). In other words, not only are the biblical wilderness traditions meaningful in the context of the center–periphery worldview of ancient Near Eastern urban elites, but they also express something about the distinct character of Israel's God. Having originated as a desert God, Yahweh is equally "at home" at the center or the periphery. The God of Israel is a God whose presence and power are reliable in times of security or threat, order or chaos.

To summarize at this point, the Priestly cultic traditions are based on centralized worship in the Jerusalem Temple, though retrojected to the portable sanctuary of the Israelite wilderness experience as described in the books of Exodus, Leviticus, and Numbers. The ritual marking of boundaries between divine presence and absence in community life and in creation's sacred order in P transposes the Jerusalem-centered temple theology to the people's formative experience in the wilderness. The Priestly worship instructions are presented at a pivotal time in the people's story, in the context of threatened existence at the margins and as part of the Sinai covenant. The placement of the Priestly ritual legislation within this decisive episode of covenant underscores its importance for Israel's continued existence and identity, an emphasis that would have had special significance during the time of the Babylonian exile (586–538 B.C.E.).

Having considered the location and maintenance of divine presence in the central sanctuary as reflected in P, it remains to consider the basic idea of the deity's presence at the worship place as reflected in P and elsewhere in the Hebrew Bible.

WORSHIP 101:
SUMMONING DIVINE PRESENCE AT THE CULT PLACE

A basic requirement of ritual is the perceived need to attract the deity to the worship place. This point has received emphasis in the work of Baruch A. Levine, who has demonstrated a concern for the deity's location in relationship to worshipers as reflected in the organization of space in worship sanctuaries as represented both in biblical ritual texts and in archaeological remains.[36] For example, the courtyard's function as the place of sacrificial offering, even in open-air sanctuaries like Horvat Qitmit and Tel Dan (as opposed to enclosed temples), indicates the need to summon the deity to the place of interaction with worshipers from the interior of the sanctuary and perhaps from the celestial habitation beyond the earthly cult place.[37] In Levine's analysis of Priestly ritual legislation, the consistent sequence of the *'ōlā(h)* sacrifice (usually translated "whole" or "burnt offering") always preceding the *zebaḥ šĕlāmîm* (NRSV: "sacrifice of well-being") is consistent with the role of the *'ōlā(h)* in summoning the presence of an otherwise absent deity.[38] Complementing this "vertical" dimension of sacrificial ritual's commencement is the "horizontal" one in which the *šĕlāmîm* offering, as developed within Israelite religion, invites the deity to interaction with the assembled worshipers in the sanctuary courtyard.[39]

Levine invokes several biblical narratives depicting ritual that graphically illustrate the function of the *'ōlā(h)* sacrifice to summon the deity's presence in worship (including 1 Kings 18; Judges 6; 13).[40] One of these narratives is the description of a battle between Israel and its neighboring rival Moab in 2 Kings 3:21-27. The Israelites' initial success in the conflict suggests to the Moabites, as it does to the biblical narrator, the absence and inaction of the Moabite god, Chemosh. In desperation, the Moabite king makes an offering *'ōlā(h)* of his firstborn son on the wall of his city, an extreme measure that compels the deity to act, as evidenced by the divine wrath (*qeṣep*) unleashed against the Israelites to the advantage and ultimate success of the Moabites.[41] This narrative shows how both ritual warfare and worship at the sanctuary hold in common a primary concern for summoning the deity's efficacious presence through the appropriate offering.

Other cultic references in narrative and prophetic texts of the Hebrew Bible summon the presence of Israel's God in worship by invoking the memory of a past event, namely, the exodus. In Jer 2:6, 8, the question of divine absence is articulated in a description of cultic matters: "They did not say, 'Where is Yahweh, who brought us up from the land of Egypt?'" (v. 6); "The priests did not say, 'Where is Yahweh?'" (v. 8). These references occur within the broader framework of prophetic accusation against "the House of Jacob . . . all the families of the House of Israel" (v. 4).[42] The charge is that Yahweh's people have "changed gods" (v. 11). In making the case, the prophet singles out the offenses of the people's religious leaders by their respective offices (v. 8). Betrayal of Yahweh is represented by the following specific accusations: "Those who handle instruction (*tōpĕśê hattôrâ*) did not know me; the leaders (literally, "shepherds"; *hārō'îm*) transgressed against me; the prophets (*nĕbî'îm*) prophesied by Baal." The corresponding betrayal by the priests is that "they did not say, 'Where is Yahweh?'" In criticizing the priesthood's performance of certain verbal elements of the cult, Jeremiah, himself of priestly stock (1:1), cites the formula as it is presumably to be recited in the liturgy. The divine-absence question as referenced here would seem to be a kind of invocation of the deity's name and presence in worship.

A more extensive quotation of this interrogative cultic formula is cited in verse 6 in connection with "your ancestors" (*'ăbôtêkem*), suggesting that not only the priests but also the people more broadly shared in its recitation. Here the formula is cited as follows: "They did not say, 'Where is Yahweh who brought us up from the land of Egypt, who led us in the wilderness?'" The question acknowledging perceived divine absence is accompanied by the recollection of God's past acts of deliverance.[43] Such recollection can be a mode for celebrating divine presence in worship, as is well illustrated by Westermann's form-critical category of psalms of declarative praise or thanksgiving (for example, Psalms 30; 107; also Exodus 15; Judges 5), or, alternatively, for challenging the deity to act in the present as in the past, as illustrated in some psalms of lament (for example, Pss 9:4-13; 44:2-9; 71:14-19; 106).[44] The formula in Jeremiah expresses a similar tension, whereby the remembrance of past deeds heightens the sense of divine absence or inactivity in the present. In addition to the deity's name, the worship formula invokes the god's past deeds, specifically those of the exodus tradition, in the seeking of his cultic presence. This recitation of mighty deeds from the past engenders a movement from divine absence—acknowledged by the question "where is Yahweh?"—to anticipated divine presence, the basic progression addressed in Gary Anderson's analysis of the Israelite ritual cycle (as discussed in an earlier section of this chapter).[45]

Such a movement forward in worship requires an answer to the question posed within the liturgy. This kind of cultic question that anticipates a direct and explicit answer is attested in the following examples.

Q: *mî hûʾ zeh melek hakkābôd*	Who is the king of glory?
A: *yhwh ṣĕbāʾôt*	Yahweh Sebaoth—
. . . .	. . . .
hûʾ melek hakkābôd	he is the king of glory. (Ps 24:8, 10b)
Q: *mēʾayin yābōʾ ʿezrî*	From where does my help come?
A: *ʿezrî mēʿim yhwh*	My help comes from Yahweh,
ʿōśēh šāmayim wāʾāreṣ	maker of heaven and earth. (Ps 121:1b-2)[46]

In Biblical Hebrew, *ʾayyē(h)* ("Where?") questions can receive an answer, sometimes with the particle of immanence, *hinnē(h)* ("Here"), as in Gen 18:9.[47] Thus, in terms of its language and formulation, the cultic question of Jer 2:6 could be answered as follows:

Q: *ʾayyē(h) yhwh hammaʿăleh ʾōtānû mēʾereṣ miṣrāyim*
Where is Yahweh, who brought us up from the land of Egypt?
(Jer 2:6)

A: *hinnē(h) ʾĕlōhêkā yiśrāʾēl ʾăšer heʿĕlûkā mēʾereṣ
   miṣrāyim*
Here are your gods, O Israel, who brought you up from the
   land of Egypt!
(1 Kings 12:28)

According to 1 Kings 12, the latter cultic statement was featured prominently in worship at Bethel, as part of the national religious establishment endorsed by Jeroboam I.[48] The compatibility of Jeremiah's *ʾayyē(h)* question of absence to this formula's *hinnē(h)* statement of

immanence also extends to a shared focus on the exodus and in corresponding lexical and syntactic formulation, a relative clause crediting
the divine with "bringing up" the people "from the land of Egypt."[49]
The alternation of pronouns might even suggest a responsive pattern:

> Q: "Where is Yahweh, who brought *us* up from the land of
>   Egypt?"
> A: "Here are *your* gods, who brought *you* up from the land of
>   Egypt."

The one obviously conflicting element between these two passages is
the use of divine designations in each case. The declaration of 1 Kings
12:28 would seem to be formulated as an answer, not to the question
of Jer 2:6—"Where is Yahweh?"—but to the question "Where are your
gods (Elohim)?" a question that does in fact occur later in the chapter
(v. 28).

In the context of Jeremiah's cultic accusation, the prophet reproach-
fully turns the question of divine absence in 2:6 against the people and
its leadership when he asks, "Where are your gods (*'ayyēh 'ĕlōhêkā*),
whom you have made for yourself?" (v. 28). Receiving no answer, the
question stands as a taunt. This semantic contrast is underlined by the
similarities in syntactic structure between the two:

> *'ayyē(h) yhwh hamma'ăleh 'ōtānû mē'ereṣ miṣrāyim*
> Where is Yahweh, who brought us up from the land of Egypt?
> (Jer 2:6)

> *'ayyē(h) 'ĕlōhêkā 'ăšĕr 'āśîtā lāk*
> Where are your gods, whom you have made for yourself?
> (Jer 2:28)

In each case, the interrogative particle is followed by a divine designation that is then modified by a relative clause recalling past acts
involving the divine. In mocking irony, the same formulaic structure is
followed in verse 28 in recalling not divine saving acts but the people's
"making" of the deities in question, that is, their images. Within the
whole of Jeremiah 2, a certain rhetorical force is achieved through the
ironic tension between the cited worship litany and the mocking use of
the same question against the people.

The difference in divine designations further reinforces that tension. For Jeremiah, the correct wording of the cultic question is
"Where is *Yahweh*?" But the wording suitable for those of the religious

establishment—who according to the prophetic indictment have turned the people to other "gods"—is "Where are your gods (Elohim)?" As mentioned, this is the form of the *ʾayyē(h)* question that would match the *hinnē(h)* statement of 1 Kings 12:28. This correspondence between the two, along with the similarities of formulaic structure, language, and content these passages share with the formula of Jer 2:6, 8, indicates that Jer 2:28 is not merely a rhetorical distortion of the latter passage but also draws on genuine cultic language for the divine as reflected in 1 Kings 12:28, most likely in recitation of the exodus tradition. That is to say, the forms of the divine-absence question in Jeremiah 2—with "Yahweh" in verses 6 and 8 and with "Elohim" in verse 28—represent variant formulations of a broader worship tradition relating to cultic observance of the exodus. The examination of other relevant texts might shed further light on the cultic address of divine absence.

The formula of 1 Kings 12, like its variant in the passage about Aaron in Exod 32:4, 8, is depicted as being recited cultically in association with the statue of the bull-calf.[50] The formula declares the immediate availability of the divine presence represented by the cult image. In the narrative context of Exodus 32, the construction and presentation of the bull-calf image with the recitation of the formula are prompted by the people's perception of divine absence during Moses' absence (v. 1). Thus, like the formulae of Jeremiah 2, this narrative depicts cultic measures that address the concern for divine absence; in both instances, these measures include formulaic recitation of the exodus tradition. In either case, the cultic recitation of divine acts affirms the divine presence, answering the basic fear of divine absence.

This sense of divine nearness is conveyed in the variant forms of the recitation by the particle of immanence *hinnē(h)* ("Here") and alternatively by the demonstrative pronoun *ʾēlle(h)* ("these"). Use of the demonstrative pronoun in liturgical language occurs in the formulation of the cultic question as in Psalm 24, discussed earlier in this section, and in the climactic assertion of Psalm 48: *ze(h) ʾĕlōhîm ʾĕlōhênû ʿōlām wāʿed* ("This is Elohim, our God forever and always!"; v. 15). Like the use of *hinnē(h)* in the exodus formula variant, the use of the demonstrative pronoun *ʾēlle(h)* emphasizes the cultic immanence and presence of the deity.

The same is true of the complement to this formula that is found in 1 Sam 4:8b, a passage for which lexical, syntactic, and semantic correspondences to the calf formula indicate a genetic relationship:[51]

ʾēlle(h) hēm hāʾĕlōhîm hammakkîm ʾet-miṣrayim bĕkol-makkâ
ūbĕmō-deber

These are the gods who struck Egypt with every plague and with pestilence![52]

(1 Sam 4:8b)

Here, the deity's near presence is recognized in association with another cult symbol, the ark. The formulaic recollection of plague against the Egyptians is placed on the lips of the Philistines, who sense the immanence of Israel's god or gods with the appearance of the ark of Yahweh in the Israelite camp. It bears noting that this passage, like the other part of the formula cited in Exodus and 1 Kings, mentions (plural) Elohim as the only divine designation. The exodus litany represented by these passages uses the language of "going up" from Egypt by divine assistance in the same way as the cultic formula cited Jer 2:6.[53] These correspondences of phraseology, detail, and general content are matched by an affinity of syntactic structure between the interrogative and declarative formulas, all of which can be observed as follows:

'ayyē(h) yhwh hamma'ăleh 'ōtānû mē'ereṣ miṣrāyim
Where is Yahweh, who brought us up from the land of Egypt?

(Jer 2:6)

'ayyē(h) 'ĕlōhêkā ('ăšer 'āśîtā lāk)
Where are your gods, (whom you have made for yourself)?[54]

(Jer 2:28)

hinnē(h) 'ĕlōhêkā yiśrā'ēl 'ăšer he'ĕlûkā mē'ereṣ miṣrāyim
Here are your gods, O Israel, who brought you up from the land of Egypt!

(1 Kings 12:28)

'ēlle(h) 'ĕlōhêkā yiśrā'ēl 'ăšer he'ĕlûkā mē'ereṣ miṣrāyim
These are your gods, O Israel, who brought you up from the land of Egypt!

(Exod 32:4, 8)

*'ēlle(h) hēm hā'ĕlōhîm hammakkîm 'et-miṣraim bĕkol-makkâ *ûbĕmō-deber*
These are the gods who struck Egypt with every plague and with pestilence!

(1 Sam 4:8b)

These striking convergences indicate a shared pattern of cultic recitation of the exodus tradition in answer to the basic religious concern over divine absence. If the passages under discussion derive from a common, perhaps responsive, litany pattern, the question of divine absence receives a direct answer in the cult, including a recitation of the deity's past deeds. Accordingly, the question would serve as an invocation, the continuing recitation making verbally explicit what is expressed visually and dramatically in other aspects of the cult, such as the iconography of the cult image and symbolic gestures. In this way, the question "Where is our/your/their God?" being answered emphatically in worship is turned from a potential taunt into an affirmation of divine presence.

The biblical passages gathered here attest to the cultic observance of the exodus according to two alternative forms of tradition based on opposing preferences of divine designations, Yahweh and Elohim. Jeremiah's own preference in this regard is made clear in his polemical use of Elohim formulaic language in 2:28. In the context of the prophetic accusation, that form of the question rings as a discordant echo of the preferred version of the worship formula with "Yahweh," as voiced in verses 6 and 8. Thus the liturgical impropriety that Jeremiah regards as a turning to other gods may have involved not simply a neglect of the invocation formula but the use of an *improper form* of it, one compatible with the Elohim tradition witnessed in these other passages. Through the exclusive use of the generic divine title, the Elohim formula avoids the mention of a specific divine name. It is this failure to specify Yahweh explicitly as Israel's God in statement and in behavior that Jeremiah opposes. For Jeremiah, the divine name employed ensures the response of Israel's one, true God, a response that marks the difference between divine presence and absence.

To summarize, a fundamental concern of worship at the sanctuary is summoning the deity's presence. Ritual texts from the Hebrew Bible attest to acts of worship that attend to this need, especially the ʿōlā(h) sacrifice. Other biblical texts give evidence of spoken responsive formulas for invoking the deity's presence in worship. These biblical acts and words of ritual portray how ancient Israelites and their priesthood sought direct encounter with God at the cult place. As Jeremiah 2 shows, with the community's failure to engage its God appropriately in worship, the effects of divine absence can be most disastrous.

Human Words to God in Worship:
The Book of Psalms and the Liturgical Engagement of Divine Presence and Absence

Though precise historical analysis of many aspects of the book of Psalms has proven difficult, there is general agreement among scholars that the psalms derive from ancient Israel's worship life.[55] Though many scholars have argued for origins of some of the psalms in regional or local worship places or in northern Israelite sanctuaries, numerous specific references establish Jerusalem and its temple as the place of worship in the perspective that prevails in the Psalter.[56] The discussion will return to this focus on Jerusalem as the place of worship, but first the basic modes of worship as reflected in the book of Psalms merit attention.

Divine Presence and Absence in Praise and Lament

In a major development of modern study of the Psalter, Claus Westermann recognized two basic categories of psalmody encompassing the various psalm types identified by form-critical scholarship beginning with Gunkel: praise and lament.[57] These two modes of worship represented in the Psalter correspond to the opposing ritual states examined by Gary Anderson and Saul Olyan (see the discussion near the beginning of this chapter) and likewise correspond to human experiences of divine presence and absence. As discussed in the previous section, the recollection of God's past acts of deliverance can be a means of invoking and celebrating divine presence in worship, as is well illustrated by Westermann's specific form-critical category of psalms of declarative praise or thanksgiving (for example, Psalms 30; 107; see also Exodus 15; Judges 5), or, alternatively, for challenging the deity to act in the present as in the past, as illustrated in some psalms of lament (for example, Pss 9:4-13; 44:2-9; 71:14-19; 106).[58]

Of the two basic modes of psalmody recognized by Westermann, the one that more consistently addresses the human experience of divine absence is lament. The lament psalms typically reflect universal situations of danger, isolation, or disaster for the individual and community. As Fredrik Lindström observes, "In Psalms evil is usually existential and victim-oriented. Suffering is not a theoretical problem but an experienced reality."[59] The causes and symptoms of affliction cited in the laments are various and general—physical infirmity, social enemies, and

in communal laments, national enemies.[60] With reference to such afflictions, the lament psalms present some of the most poignant expressions
of divine absence in the Hebrew Bible.

Perhaps the best-known example is Psalm 22, which opens with the
question, "My God, my God, why have you forsaken me?"[61] As Hermann Spieckermann has observed, the theme of divine absence serves
as a leitmotif for the greater part of this psalm.[62] The poem describes
the speaker's affliction in impressionistic fashion, employing an inventory of imagery describing social alienation (vv. 6-8, 16-18), physical
illness (vv. 14-15), and attacking animals (vv. 12-13, 16, 20-21). The
individual's suffering is attributed to God's withdrawal: "O my God, I
cry by day, but you do not answer; and by night, but find no rest" (v. 2).
For the sufferer's enemies, God's absence is a cause for scorn:

> All who see me mock at me;
> > they make mouths at me, they shake their heads;
> "Commit your cause to the LORD; let him deliver—
> > let him rescue the one in whom he delights!" (vv. 7-8)

In the sufferer's pleas, God's absence is cast thoroughly in spatial
terms, with the repeated use of the Hebrew verbal root *rhq* ("to be far,
distant"): "Why are you so far from helping me, from the words of my
groaning?" (v. 2) and the repeated petition "Do not be far [away from
me]" (vv. 11, 19).[63]

While some laments include an admission of guilt on the part of
the speaker (for example, Pss 38:3-5; 40:12; 41:4; 51:1-9), Psalm 22,
like most laments, lacks any such confession. In these psalms, divine
absence, divine retribution, and human sin do not necessarily correlate.
Lindström underscores the role of divine absence in the "irrational and
bewildering" nature of suffering in the psalms, in which God's hiding
has no apparent cause but is itself the cause of human suffering: "The
divine hidden-ness is the basic problem in these psalms, and the descriptions of suffering are concretizations of the absence of YHWH, which
are both consequences of the loss of the presence of God. The characteristic 'Why?'-question is a genuine one."[64] For Lindström, the idea of
divine wrath as part of the problem of human suffering is a function of
God's role as "prima causa of the entire world process."[65] At the same
time, while God's power is not doubted, it is not absolute. Since God
rather than human guilt tends to bear the blame, something more or
other than human repentance is needed to resolve the difficulty. The
natural and social world, and hence natural and moral evil, are not distinguished, and thus evil comes from the realm of death and chaos.[66]

This notion of incompatibility of God's presence with death corresponds to observations made in chapter 4 regarding God's potential access to death's realm but usual aloofness from it. The sufferer's difficulties in the laments arise not so much from a disturbance of relationship to the divine by his deeds as from these threats that are ultimately related to death. Thus, the individual's prayers are typically for deliverance from enemies rather than forgiveness of sin (though exceptions exist—most notably, Psalm 51).

Affliction from enemies is cited in Psalm 42–43, which like Psalm 22 represents the specific category of the lament of the individual, the most frequent type of specific psalm category in the Psalter.[67] In the individual lament psalms, the speaker brings a complaint before the deity and does so typically from within a state of social alienation. Often the sufferer is said to receive from family and from the broader community not support and comfort but scorn and rejection. In similar fashion to Ps 22:8, that state of social alienation is mirrored in the perception of divine absence, as expressed most directly in the taunt "Where is your god?" (Ps 42:3, 10; compare 42:9; 43:2).

The suffering individual longs for restoration to the life of the worshiping community, which he or she knew in times past. In Psalm 42–43, the suffering individual recalls

> how I went with the throng,
>> and led them in procession to the house of God,
> with glad shouts and songs of thanksgiving. (42:4)

As the speaker resolves, "I shall once again praise him" (42:6, 11). But, for the present moment, praise is not a current activity for the sufferer. It is anticipated from the individual's present state of isolation and lament. Return to public praise comes only with restoration to the community of worship. For the suffering individual, absence from the worshiping community means the absence of God.

The movement from divine absence to divine presence relates to a characteristic feature of the individual lament psalms much discussed in form-critical scholarship.[68] From Gunkel onward, scholars have suggested various literary and cultic explanations for the "abrupt change in mood" from complaint to celebration that characterizes these psalms.[69] The shift in tone and structure in these psalms has suggested to scholars following Gunkel a turning point in worship accompanying some cultic act and signaling an assurance of divine hearing. The influential explanation of Joachim Begrich is that an oracle of salvation pronounced by cultic functionary had brought the worshiper an assurance of God's attentive presence and hope for the future.[70] In support of this suggestion, Begrich pointed to parallels in Mesopotamian texts and to texts including Isa 41:8-16 and 44:2-5 as biblical examples of salvation oracles.

A biblical narrative depicting cultic assurance with a similar effect on the worshiper is that of Hannah's experience at the Israelite sanctuary at Shiloh (1 Sam 1:9-18). Suffering the despair and social affliction that came with barrenness in ancient Israelite society, Hannah made a petition and vow to Yahweh at the entrance of the sanctuary (vv. 9-16). The priest Eli offers to this earnest worshiper the following words of assurance: "Go in peace; the God of Israel grant the petition you have made to him" (v. 17). Hannah's response is an abrupt turn from despair to joy and feasting (1 Sam 1:9-18). Whatever specific cultic practice may have been behind the "assurance of hearing" in the lament psalms, these texts relate a decisive movement from divine absence to anticipated or realized divine presence on the part of petitioning worshipers.

As Gary Anderson has discussed, in ancient Israel's ritual worldview, death's power on earth correlates spatially with the grave as the place of ultimate divine absence, and in turn, the worship sanctuary, as the earthly abode of God's presence, represents the center of life in earthly existence.[71] It is not surprising to see the psalms reflect a progression from divine absence to divine presence in the worship sanctuary. This progression in worship is evident not only in lament psalms but in other psalms in which temple theology has a prominent place.

The Temple as the Center of Divine Presence for the Individual in the Book of Psalms

Psalm 73 provides an illustration of the worship sanctuary's importance as the place of divine encounter in the Psalter. Though not classified as a lament, Psalm 73 is concerned with the question of divine justice as reflected in the individual's social circumstances. The speaker begins by recalling an experience of personal despair and doubt about God's goodness due to the prosperity of the wicked and the lack of apparent rewards in return for the speaker's own efforts at pious living (vv. 1-16). A turning point from despair to hope occurs with the mention of the individual's visit to the worship place:

> But when I thought how to understand this,
>   it seemed to me a wearisome task,
> until I went into the sanctuary of God;

> then I perceived their end.
> Truly you set them in slippery places;   *as an elderly per ... fails to step in jail*
>   you make them fall to ruin.
> How they are destroyed in a moment,
>   swept away utterly by terrors!
> They are like a dream when one awakes;
>   on awaking you despise their phantoms.
>   (Ps 73:16-20)

Jo the comfort ... at death? ... ever

The experience in the sanctuary somehow imparts to the troubled individual the prospect of divine punishment that awaits the wicked, a realization that gives the speaker personal comfort and assurance of God's faithfulness and justice. In similar fashion, in Psalm 63 a suffering individual finds comfort in the assurance of his enemies' ultimate doom after a direct encounter with God in the worship place: "I have looked upon you in the sanctuary, / beholding your power and glory" (Ps 63:2; see also vv. 9-10). Rather than the imparting of specific information, it is the direct experience of God's "power and glory" in worship that confirms the divine faithfulness to worshipers. However childish and inordinately self-assured this sentiment may ring to modern ears, it represents an earnest human reflection on the life of faith and a movement to greater trust in God in spite of personal shortcomings.[72] Whatever acts or words of worship might have been involved, the result is a sense of assurance that comes only with a direct encounter with divine presence in the sanctuary. *yes*

The temple is a refuge against threats to the individual in Psalm 27. This psalm uses the specific vocabulary for a temple in Biblical Hebrew (especially *hêkāl*, translated "palace" or "temple," and *bêt yhwh*, "the House of Yahweh," in v. 4). As discussed in chapter 1 and earlier in this chapter, temple theology and the designation of the sanctuary as the deity's "house" draw on the structuring of Israelite society according to household and patrimony. As the individual declares in Ps 27:10, "If my mother and father forsake me, the LORD will take me up." As an alternative or substitute for his own ancestral house, the speaker looks to Yahweh's place of dwelling—that is, the divine sanctuary—as a place of refuge: *yes*

> One thing I asked of the LORD,   *God has a house too —*
>   that will I seek after: *: a family (has father &*
> to live in the house of the LORD (*bêt yhwh*)   *father*
>   all the days of my life,
> to behold the beauty of the LORD,
>   and to inquire in his temple (*hêkāl*).

> For he will hide me in his shelter
> > in the day of trouble;
> he will conceal me under the cover of his tent;
> > he will set me high on a rock. (Ps 27:4-5 NRSV)

Ancient Israel's patrimonial social order provides the social framework for the language for worship: "dwelling" in God's "house" (see
also Pss 23:6; 84:4).

As discussed earlier in chapter 1, in the ideal conception of society
in ancient Israel's broader cultural world, the leading deity stood as the
ultimate ruler over the nation.[73] Accordingly, the language of the Psalms
often elaborates the royal dimensions of Yahweh's "house" and rule as
divine king, as in Psalm 84:

> How lovely is your dwelling place,
> > O LORD of hosts!
> My soul longs, indeed it faints
> > for the courts of the LORD;
> My heart and my flesh sing for joy
> > to the living God.
> Even the sparrow finds a home,
>
> . . . .
>
> at your altars, O LORD of hosts,
> > my King and my God.
> Happy are those who live in your house,
> > ever singing your praise. (Ps 84:1-4 NRSV)

The language for worship in Yahweh's temple equates it with refuge
in the court and palace of the divine king, "the God of gods . . . in
Zion" (v. 7). Within the Israelite social order as discussed, the individual's place in the world is defined by association with one or more
households. That notion is reflected in the book of Psalms, in which
the temple figures as the household at the center of the entire world
and is critical to the individual's search for divine presence. At the
temple, the worshiper can share in a progression from despair to hope,
from fear to assurance, from a sense of divine absence to divine presence. The temple's importance for the individual in the book of Psalms
is based on its role as the central worship place for the nation as a
whole.

The Temple as the Center of Divine Presence for the Community in the Book of Psalms

In the Psalter, Yahweh's rule is claimed not only for Israel but also for the whole of the earth (see, for example, Psalm 2). This perspective comes through in the book of Psalms most clearly in the Zion tradition (see chapter 3).[74] Its basic elements are Yahweh's rule as divine king (through the human agency of the Davidic monarch) and Yahweh's choice of Jerusalem as his place of dwelling.[75] For example, Psalms 47, 93, and 95–99 celebrate Yahweh's enthronement as "great king over all the earth" (47:3).[76] These psalms' emphasis on God's earthly rule as divine king in Jerusalem employs the imagery of temple theology, the temple being the "house" of the divine king in the ancient Near East.

Also reflecting the Zion tradition, the book of Isaiah describes the prophet's vision of Yahweh enthroned in the temple as "the King, Yahweh of hosts" (*yhwh ṣĕbāʾôt*; Isa 6:5; compare v. 3). The title *yhwh ṣĕbāʾôt* denotes Yahweh's rule as a divine warrior who commands armies and appears in intimate association with the ark in 1 Samuel (for example, 1:3, 11), most fully in the (perhaps textually expansive) formula "Yahweh of hosts, who is enthroned on the cherubim" (*yhwh ṣĕbāʾôt yōšēb hakkĕrūbîm*; 1 Sam 4:4; 2 Sam 6:2).[77] The narratives of Samuel and Kings describe David's transport of the ark to Jerusalem (2 Samuel 6) and Solomon's transfer of it from a tent shrine to the completed temple, where it comes to rest beneath the wings of two sculpted cherubim built into the most sacred space (the "holy of holies"; 1 Kings 6:23-28, 32, 38; 8:1-21).

In Psalm 132, the ark's procession expresses Yahweh's own choice of David and Zion and reflects the ark's symbolism as the "footstool" of the invisible deity (vv. 6-8). The cherubim imagery is invoked in association with Jerusalem in the celebration of Yahweh's enthronement in Ps 99:1-2:

> The LORD is king; let the peoples tremble!
>> He sits enthroned upon the cherubim; let the earth quake!
> The LORD is great in Zion;
>> he is exalted over all the peoples. (NRSV)

In accordance with the temple theology of Psalms, the sanctuary is the earthly manifestation of Yahweh's enthronement in heaven:

The LORD is in his holy temple;
>   The LORD's throne is in heaven.
>   His eyes behold, his gaze examines humankind.
>   (Ps 11:4 NRSV)

Within the book of Psalms, the Jerusalem temple is the unique place of divine presence on earth and of human interaction with the divine:[78]

We ponder your steadfast love, O God,
>   in the midst of your temple.
> Your name, O God, like your praise,
>   reaches to the ends of the earth.
> Your right hand is filled with victory.
>   Let Mount Zion be glad,
> let the towns of Judah rejoice
>   because of your judgments.
> Walk about Zion, go all around it,
>   count its towers,
> consider well its ramparts;
>   go through its citadels,
> that you may tell the next generation
>   that this is God,
> our God forever and ever.
>   He will be our guide forever. (Ps 48:9-14 NRSV)

In accordance with the Zion theology, as the central locus of divine presence on earth, the temple is the source of the people's strength and is thus integral to the fortified city as a whole. In Psalm 68, the temple's presence as an architectural manifestation of divine power is related to God's victories over the people's enemies as divine warrior:

Summon your might, O God;
>   show your strength, O God, as you have done for us
>   before.
> Because of your temple at Jerusalem
>   kings bear gifts to you.

. . . .

Awesome is God in his sanctuary,
>   the God of Israel;
>   he gives power and strength to his people.
>   (Ps 68:28-29, 35 NRSV)

The God worshiped in Jerusalem is not confined to the place of earthly abode but is a warrior who "goes out" before the people in battle, as recalled earlier in the same psalm:

> O God, when you went out before your people,
>   when you marched through the wilderness,
> the earth quaked, the heavens poured down rain
>   at the presence of God, the God of Sinai,
>   at the presence of God, the God of Israel. (68:7-8 NRSV)

Employing the imagery of earthquake and storm, the wilderness theophany in this psalm recounts the emergence of Israel's God from Sinai. These verses acknowledge the earlier location of Israel's God not in Jerusalem but in regions to the south (Judg 5:4-5; Hab 3:3).[79] Nonetheless, for the overarching viewpoint that prevails in the book of Psalms, the unique place of Yahweh's presence shall ever be Jerusalem:

> For the LORD has chosen Zion;
>   he has desired it for his habitation:
> "This is my resting place forever;
>   here I will reside, for I have desired it."
>   (Ps 132:13-14 NRSV)

Being forged by the Zion tradition, the book of Psalms is an important foundation for Jerusalem's place as the center of divine presence in the Hebrew Bible.[80] The Psalter also reflects a concern for the temple's destruction and hence its place as the center of divine absence on earth.

The Temple's Destruction and Divine Absence in the Book of Psalms

The one example of direct and extensive reflection on the temple's destruction in the Psalter is the communal lament known as Psalm 74:

> Remember Mount Zion, where you came to dwell.
> Direct your steps to the perpetual ruins;
>   the enemy has destroyed everything in the sanctuary.
> Your foes have roared within your holy place;
>   they set up their emblems there.
> At the upper entrance they hacked
>   the wooden trellis with axes.

And then, with hatchets and hammers,
    they smashed all its carved work.
They set your sanctuary on fire;
    they desecrated the dwelling place of your name,
        bringing it to the ground. (Ps 74:2b-7 NRSV)

This psalm presumably reflects on the 586 B.C.E. destruction of the temple by the Babylonians, who are mentioned only generically as "the enemy" (vv. 3, 18), the "foes" of God's people (vv. 4, 23), and "the impious" (v. 22).

In accordance with a general ancient Near Eastern theology of reward and retribution, the defeat of cities in war is often understood as the result of divine punishment and the destruction of temples as the result of the deity's abandonment of the sanctuary.[81] Sumerian city laments, dating to ca. 2000 B.C.E., mourn the devastation of cities and their temples by their patron deities—for example, "The Lamentation over the Destruction of Sumer and Ur."[82] The poem, one of two laments on Ur's destruction, opens with a description of how the gods and goddesses of the land abandon their temples, leaving the land and people vulnerable to military defeat and destruction:

Nanna has abandoned Ur,
    his sheepfold (became) haunted.
Suen has abandoned the Ekishnugal [a sanctuary in Ur],
    his sheepfold (became) haunted,
    his consort, Ningal, has abandoned it,
    her sheepfold (became) haunted. (lines 13–15)[83]

In Psalm 74, the enemy's destruction of the temple is assumed to be an expression of God's anger and rejection of the people:

O God, why do you cast us off forever?
    Why does your anger smoke against the sheep of your
        pasture? (v. 1 NRSV)

In the historical narrative of 1 and 2 Kings, the Babylonian destruction of Jerusalem and its temple are clearly caused by the people's repeated violation of their covenant with Yahweh under the leadership of their kings (2 Kings 17:19; 24:1—25:26; see more discussion in chapter 7). By contrast, in Psalm 74 not only is it unclear what, if anything, the people have done wrong (Ps 74:1), but the speaker even appeals to

Yahweh's covenant with the people in the hopes of motivating God to act on their behalf and to repay their enemy (vv. 20-21).

Invoking the mythopoeic imagery of Yahweh's defeat of the sea monster Leviathan, Psalm 74 expresses confidence that God will eventually act, as "my King . . . from of old, working salvation in the earth" (vv. 12-17). Yet in the meantime, the speaker and the community wait: "How long, O God, is the foe to scoff? / Is the enemy to revile your name forever?" (v. 10). Even with the hope expressed in verses 12-17, a temple in ruins (v. 3) begs the question of Jerusalem's future and the people's future relationship to God.

In addition to the explicit reflection found in Psalm 74, concern over the temple's destruction also appears in aspects of the Psalter's larger structure and organization. Scholarship refers to Psalms 42–83 as the Elohistic Psalter because of its distinct pattern of divine names. Whereas Yahweh (usually translated in most English Bibles as "the LORD") is the dominant name for God throughout most of the book of Psalms, this section of the book prefers (though not exclusively so) to call God Elohim—in Biblical Hebrew, the general word for "(a) god," plural "gods," or, when referring to the God of Israel, "God." Besides its distinct pattern of divine names, Psalms 42–83 as a group are also set apart by their organization and numbering. As Laura Joffe has pointed out, the number 42 figures centrally in the Elohistic Psalter as a collection of forty-two psalms beginning with Psalm 42.[84]

Both in the Hebrew Bible and in textual and artistic depictions from the broader ancient Near East, the number 42 has a thematic significance as a number representing potential divine blessing or curse. For example, in a series of ancient Egyptian mortuary texts known as the Book of "Going Forth by Day" (better known as "The Book of the Dead") and in associated illustrations, the dead stand in judgment before a jury of forty-two deities waiting to dispense reward or punishment in the afterlife.[85] The epithets of these forty-two judging deities are given for the deceased to pronounce as part of a declination of forty-two deeds that would bring punishment.[86] In the biblical book of Numbers, the prophet Balaam invokes a divine verdict regarding Israel through three occasions of two sacrificial offerings on seven altars, for a total of forty-two sacrifices (Numbers 22–23).[87] Although the Moabite king Balak had secured Balaam's services with hopes of a curse against Israel, the result is emphatic blessing. By contrast, the prophet Elisha curses a group of "little boys" "in the name of Yahweh," causing two bears to emerge and kill exactly forty-two of them (2 Kings 2:23-24).[88] Other biblical references illustrate 42's potential significance as a number of divinely ordained disaster (Judg 12:6; 2 Kings 10:14; 2 Chr 22:2; Dan 7:25; 12:7; Luke 4:25; Jas 5:17; Rev 11:2-3; 12:6; 13:1, 5-6). Throughout the Bible and the broader ancient Near East, the number 42 represents divine punishment and its potential reversal, sometimes with an emphasis on divine names (see also Matt 1:1-17).

One specific application of the number's general thematic significance is its use as an organizational device in Mesopotamian hymn collections and catalogs from at least the Ur III period (that is, around 2000 B.C.E.) to Neo-Babylonian times (roughly 1000–500 B.C.E.).[89] Hymn incipit catalogs, in which compositions are grouped by listing their opening verses, sometimes present groups of forty-two hymns and less frequently twenty-one hymns, the only numberings to occur more than once in the hymn catalogs. Another recurring organizational principle in the hymn catalogs is the grouping of compositions according to the names of the deities honored.

More scholarly attention has gone to a composition known as the Collection of Sumerian Temple Hymns (TH 1–42), a collection of forty-two hymns celebrating the first empire builder, Sargon of Akkad (ca. 2300 B.C.E.).[90] Scholars understand this text to relate to Sargon's restoration of temples destroyed in wars that brought Sumer (southern Mesopotamia) under his rule. Thus, TH 1–42 relates to the ancient Near Eastern theology of divine abandonment, according to which military defeat and the destruction of temples were interpreted as expressions of divine disfavor (as discussed earlier in this section). It celebrates the restoration of worship in these temples following upon Sargon's conquest and unification of those cities of Sumer and Akkad, and it survives "as implicit praise for any given king who was solicitous of the temples."[91] In other words, this temple hymn collection was used and reused subsequent to its original circumstances in an effort, on behalf of the king, to invoke the sympathy or favor of the gods. Its aim was to counter divine wrath associated with the destruction of these temples or resulting from their restoration and continued use within the realm of his rule.

TH 1–42 and the hymn incipit catalogs represent a tradition of Mesopotamian hymn collection in which divine names and the number 42 figured prominently as organizational devices. The ancient Mesopotamian tradition spanned two millennia and persisted into the time of the Neo-Babylonian empire that brought about Jerusalem's destruction and the experience of the exile. The Elohistic Psalter's organization around the number 42 can be understood in light of the number's longstanding significance in Mesopotamian hymn collection and most likely results from the influence of the Mesopotamian tradition on the formative phases of the Psalter's editing during the exile.[92]

While TH 1–42 consists exclusively of hymns celebrating restored sanctuaries, the Elohistic Psalter is composed predominantly of laments, which in some cases make explicit reference to temple ruins (Pss 74:1-8; 79:1).[93] In this respect, the content and tone of the Elohistic Psalter as a collection are more analogous to those of Mesopotamian collections of *balag* and *ershemma* laments, which, like the city laments from which they derived, make constant references to the destroyed temples and thus suggest not the celebration or dedication of restored sanctuaries but the anticipation of their rebuilding.[94] In other words, the Mesopotamian evidence suggests that the Elohistic Psalter was created with a view to the desired rebuilding and restoration of the Jerusalem temple. While this prospect is one that Haggai and Zechariah show to have been attended by a fervent messianism right up to the time of the temple's completion, the book of Ezekiel (especially Ezek 41–44) shows it to have been alive as a hope if not a priestly agenda already in the context of the exile itself (more discussion of this in chapter 7).

As a collection of forty-two psalms privileging the divine designation Elohim, the Elohistic Psalter (Psalms 42–83) is joined by a roughly equivalent number of psalms more typically favoring the name Yahweh and all labeled by their superscriptions as psalms "of David" (Psalms 3–40). These psalms are known as the first Davidic collection and are preceded by the endorsement of the Davidic monarchy in Psalm 2. The Elohistic Psalter comprises sequences of psalms "of Korah" (Psalms 42–49) and "Asaph" (Psalms 50; 73–83) along with the second Davidic collection (Psalms 51–72) and is followed by what Joffe calls the "tail" of the Elohistic Psalter (Psalms 84–89).[95] The Elohistic Psalter is made up of another sequence of Korah psalms (Psalms 84–85; 87–88) with a psalm "of David" in the middle (Psalm 86), followed by a psalm lamenting the end of the Davidic dynasty (Psalm 89). The result is a two-part psalm book dominated by a concern for the Davidic monarchy and divided by divine-name preference—Yahweh psalms in Psalms 3–41, Elohim psalms in Psalms 42–83—with its appendix (Psalms 84–89) displaying a preference for Yahweh but also a variety of divine names.[96] This sequence, Psalms 2–89, makes up the greater part of what the Dead Sea Scrolls attest was in place well before the second century B.C.E. as the first phase of a gradually developing book of Psalms.[97] This shaping evidence indicates that, as an integral component of the two-part Davidic psalm book resulting in Psalms 2–89, a psalm book dominated by laments and culminating in a call for a restoration of the Davidic dynasty (Psalm 89), the Elohistic Psalter was created as a plea to the divine for David and Zion.

Though the Jerusalem temple would eventually be rebuilt (Ezra 6), the Davidic monarchy—the persistent focus of the first three books of the Psalter (Psalms 1–89)—would never be reestablished. Reflecting this political reality is the emphasis of books 4 and 5 of the Psalter on the kingship of Yahweh over any human king. The shift in focus is signaled by the concentration of divine enthronement psalms (Psalms 93; 95–99) closely following the conclusion of book 3 with Psalm 89. Viewed in canonical perspective, the latter psalm's plea for the restoration of David's line (Ps 89:19-51) receives an answer in the repeated proclamation *yhwh mālak* (NRSV: "the LORD is king," or alternatively "Yahweh has become king"; Pss 93:1; 96:10; 97:1; 99:1) and in other forms of emphasis on Yahweh's kingship in these psalms (for example, Pss 95:3, 7; 98:6; 99:4). Scholars who have given attention to the canonical shape of Psalms and its meaning have noted these other ways in which the last two books of the Psalter reflect the kingship of Yahweh as one transcending the failure of the Davidic monarchy.[98] In the structure and progression of the book of Psalms, the failure of human kingship with the exile gives way to a focus on the kingship of God.

As books 4 and 5 of the Psalter make clear, the place of Yahweh's rule on earth remains Jerusalem and its temple. One might consider, for example, Psalm 99:

> The LORD is king; let the peoples tremble!
>> He sits enthroned upon the cherubim; let the earth
>> quake!
> The LORD is great in Zion;
>> He is exalted over all the peoples.
>
> . . . .
>
> Extol the LORD our God,
>> and worship at his holy mountain;
>> for the LORD our God is holy. (Ps 99:1-2, 9 NRSV)

Among the "Songs of Ascents" (Psalms 120–134), a collection of psalms probably related to pilgrimage, one reads expressions like the following:

> I was glad when they said to me,
>> "Let us go to the house of the LORD!"

> Our feet are standing
> > within your gates, O Jerusalem.
>
> . . . .
>
> Pray for the peace of Jerusalem. . . .
>
> . . . .
>
> For the sake of the house of the LORD our God,
> > I will seek your good. (Ps 122:1-2, 6a, 9 NRSV)
>
> May the LORD, maker of heaven and earth,
> > bless you from Zion. (Ps 134:3 NRSV)

Or, in the conclusion to Psalm 135, "Blessed be the LORD from Zion, / he who resides in Jerusalem" (v. 21 NRSV).

Though the final portion of the Psalter contains a third sequence of psalms "of David" (Psalms 138–145) and occasional references suggest continuing hopes for the Davidic ideal (for example, Pss 110; 132:11-12, 17), the weight of emphasis suggests a present reality of Yahweh's rule over the people from the temple rebuilt during the Persian period (538–332 B.C.E., with the completion of the temple's rebuilding dated to 516 or 515 B.C.E.).

Within the Hebrew Bible, the book of Psalms solidifies Jerusalem's place as the terrestrial center of divine presence as experienced in worship. As reflected in the Psalter, an important component of ancient Israel's worship was the engagement of divine absence, especially in the form of individual and communal laments. In the content of some of the psalms and, more subtly, in the shaping of the Psalter as a whole, the book of Psalms reflects on specific experiences of divine absence for the nation in the exile and the temple's destruction and restoration. In all of these respects, the book of Psalms shows how Israel's worship met the need for movement from divine absence to divine presence.

Conclusion

Ritual and psalmody as presented in biblical worship texts give extensive attention to the human experience of divine absence and provide ways to move beyond it to a sense of God's affirming presence. Cultic

texts indicate the importance of invoking divine presence in the sanctuary through acts and words of worship. The narrative context of the
Priestly ritual traditions of the Pentateuch not only shows how, in the
formative experience of the wilderness, Israel encountered its God in
the context of possible divine absence, but also more importantly, God's
ability to appear even where the powers of death threaten. Within the
worship literature of the Hebrew Bible, it is the book of Psalms that
brings Jerusalem into focus as the center of Israel's worship.

Largely a ‡ Psalm.

Part III

The Center of Divine Presence and Absence on Earth

CHAPTER 7

Jerusalem before and after the Exile: Historical Narrative and Prophetic Vision

THE PREVIOUS CHAPTER SHOWED the importance of places and practices of worship in the Hebrew Bible's engagement of divine absence. The worship literature of the Hebrew Bible is focused on the idea of a center of cultic life. The Zion theology expressed in the book of Psalms explicitly identifies Jerusalem as the geographic location of God's unique presence for worship on earth. The major works of historical narrative in the Old Testament bring a different perspective to this focus on the Jerusalem temple as center of history and of Israel's dealings with its God. In these narrative works, it is the loss of Jerusalem in the Babylonian conquest and exile that solidifies Jerusalem's place of centrality in biblical literature. These narratives provide a historical and geographic context within which to understand the prophetic books and Jerusalem's place in those prophetic books that deal directly with the exile.

The following discussion treats Jerusalem's place as the geographic center of divine presence and divine absence in the Hebrew Bible's major works of historical narrative, namely, the Deuteronomistic History (Deuteronomy–2 Kings), 1 and 2 Chronicles, and Ezra-Nehemiah. The narrative framework of Israel's story in these books emphasizes Jerusalem as the center of history and as the earthly center of God's relationship to Israel and to humankind more broadly. With the loss of Jerusalem in the Babylonian destruction and exile, this major locus of divine presence becomes the center of divine absence. The exile stands as the point of reference for the historical sweep covered by the historical narratives of the Hebrew Bible.

Along with the focus on these major historical works, this discussion will give attention to the books of exilic and postexilic prophets in which Jerusalem figures prominently, namely, Jeremiah, Ezekiel, Haggai, and Zechariah 1–8. Before examining Jerusalem's place in the historical books, the chapter considers the theological ramifications of exile in the ancient Near East, especially as it bears on Jerusalem's loss and restoration as portrayed in those prophetic and narrative books.

DIVINE ABANDONMENT AND THE MEANING OF THE EXILE

Chapter 1 discussed the ancient Near Eastern tendency to interpret life's circumstances as expressions of divine favor or punishment. In keeping with that worldview, the motif of divine abandonment appears regularly in the literature of ancient Israel's neighbors and predecessors, particularly in connection with military defeat.[1] As discussed in chapter 6, ancient Near Eastern texts like the Sumerian city laments (ca. 2000 B.C.E.) mourn the devastation of cities and their temples by their patron deities.[2]

The motif plays a central role in the most extensive inscription surviving from Iron Age Palestine, the Moabite Inscription of Mesha from the ninth century B.C.E.[3] Through the speaking voice of the inscription, Mesha frames his own achievements as king of Moab against the background of Israel's previous domination of Moab and control of territories that Mesha now claims for his realm. As Mesha explains, his national god Chemosh allowed Moab to suffer in the past because the deity was "angry with his land" (see more discussion of the inscription in chapter 1). Describing his own defeat of the Israelite city of Ataroth, Mesha mentions that he carried off the city's cultic objects and brought them before "the presence of Chemosh" in that god's sanctuary in Kerioth (lines 10–13). The spoliation of defeated enemies' divine statues or worship symbols is mentioned frequently in royal inscriptions from ancient Mesopotamia.[4] The act of seizing an enemy's cult images has a symbolic meaning, indicating either the defeat of the deity represented or the deity's deliberate abandonment of its people.[5]

This act and its accompanying theology figure prominently in a portion of the books of 1 and 2 Samuel known in scholarship as the Ark Narrative (including portions of 1 Samuel 2; 4; and 2 Samuel 6).[6] Prior to being incorporated into the Deuteronomistic History (discussed later in this chapter), the Ark Narrative existed as an independent document, whose purpose was to explain why Yahweh allowed the Philistines to

defeat the Israelites in battle and seize their divine symbol, the ark. As
the narrative shows, the God of Israel is in full control of events surrounding the ark and its return by the Philistines. God allows the Israelites to suffer defeat and to lose the ark as an act of abandonment
expressing Yahweh's displeasure with his people. In the narrative, the
worship sanctuary at Shiloh, which 1 Sam 1:9 calls the "temple of
Yahweh" (*hêkal yhwh*), houses the chief cult symbol of Yahweh's presence as represented by the ark. In the broader span of the ongoing Deuteronomistic narrative, Shiloh figures as a precursor to Jerusalem as the
Israelite central sanctuary.

Shiloh's anticipation of Jerusalem as the chief worship place of Israel's God figures into the temple sermon of the book of Jeremiah, which
appears in variant forms in the prose sections of the book (Jer 7:1-15;
26:4-6). The narrative depicts Jeremiah standing at the gate of the Jerusalem temple, calling the people of Judah to turn from ethical and cultic
offenses (Jer 7:5-12). As a warning against false confidence in divine
protection through Yahweh's earthly place of dwelling, Jeremiah quotes
with irony what might have been a familiar worship slogan: "Do not
trust in these deceptive words: 'This is the temple of Yahweh, the temple
of Yahweh, the temple of Yahweh'" (Jer 7:4 adapted from the NRSV).
The prophet then delivers an oracle of doom, in which Yahweh threatens retribution for the people's accumulated offenses: "Therefore I will
do to the house that is called by my name, in which you trust, and to the
place that I gave to you and to your ancestors, just what I did to Shiloh.
And I will cast you out of my sight, just as I cast out all your kinsfolk, all
the offspring of Ephraim" (Jer 7:14-15 NRSV). Yahweh's words invoke
the Assyrian destruction of the northern Israelite kingdom, an event
from more than a century prior (722–721 B.C.E.), and even earlier the
destruction of Shiloh. The fall of the earlier sanctuary city is not mentioned in the Ark Narrative in Samuel but is intimated in Ps 78:60-62:

> He abandoned his dwelling at Shiloh,
> > the tent where he dwelt among mortals,
> and delivered his power to captivity,
> > his glory to the hand of the foe.
> He gave his people to the sword,
> > and vented his wrath on his heritage. (NRSV)

In Jeremiah 7's narrative portrayal of prophetic oracle, these earlier
instances of divine abandonment by Israel's God underscore the threat
of Yahweh's abandonment of Jerusalem. What might seem a contradiction of the Zion tradition's emphasis on God's protection of Jerusalem

and its temple (see chapter 6) is a reminder of God's power and ultimate independence from the earthly place of dwelling in the central sanctuary—in short, God's freedom to be absent.

DIVINE ABANDONMENT OF THE TEMPLE IN EZEKIEL

Another prophetic text viewing the Babylonian crisis in terms of divine absence is the book of Ezekiel. The book identifies Ezekiel as a prophetic figure of priestly stock who had been deported to Babylonia in the 597 B.C.E. exile of Johoiachin (Ezek 1:1-3; see also 1 Chr 6:50-53; 24:31). Ezekiel's keen interest in Jerusalem and its temple is reflected in the visions of idolatry taking place at the Jerusalem temple (Ezekiel 8–11) and in the vision of a restored temple (chapters 40–42). After reporting the news of Jerusalem's fall (33:21-22), the book describes a detailed vision of the restored land with an idealized Jerusalem and its temple at the center (chapters 40–48).

As commentators have noted, Ezekiel's ideal sanctuary includes many changes from the temple of Solomon (as described in 1 Kings 6) and reflects an affinity with the Priestly ritual traditions of the Pentateuch.[7] Among those changes, the temple is separated from the royal palace (Ezek 43:7-9). Yahweh explains to Ezekiel the rationale for this feature of the visionary temple:

> He said to me: Mortal, this is the place of my throne and the place for the soles of my feet, where I will reside among the people of Israel forever. The house of Israel shall no more defile my holy name, neither they nor their kings, by their whoring, and by the corpses of their kings at their death. When they placed their threshold by my threshold and their doorposts beside my doorposts, with only a wall between me and them, they were defiling my holy name by their abominations that they committed; therefore I have consumed them in my anger. Now let them put away their idolatry and the corpses of their kings far from me, and I will reside among them forever. (Ezek 43:7-9 NRSV)

In keeping with classic temple theology (see above, chapter 6), Yahweh speaks of the envisioned temple as the place of God's earthly habitation. Traditional mythic elements of the temple are also invoked in this context, including its location on the cosmic mountain (Ezek 40:2) and the source of sacred waters (47:1-12).[8] The oracle in Ezek 43:7-9 condemns the royal temple-palace complex in Solomon's Jerusalem (1 Kings 6–8) as an offense against God's presence. In ancient Near Eastern tradition, temple building is a royal endeavor. In an ironic twist revealing priestly political interests, Ezekiel's vision of the ideal temple views the monarchy as a defilement of God's presence at the central sanctuary. The temple vision confirms the earlier notice that Yahweh will be shepherd over the renewed Israel (Ezek 34:15; though compare 34:23-24; 37:22-25).

In Yahweh's explanation of the vision, as previously quoted, the notion of divine presence figures prominently, with the motif of divine punishment cast in active terms as God's wrathful presence. A more literal depiction of divine abandonment occurs in the vision of divine departure from the temple portrayed in Ezek 10:1-22 and 11:22-25. As a hypostatic form of God's presence in the temple, the divine "glory" (BH *kābôd*) of Yahweh forsakes the temple and departs to the Mount of Olives, "the mountain east of the city" (11:23).[9] With the description of the future temple envisioned in Ezekiel 40–42, the divine "glory" returns to dwell in the earthly central sanctuary (43:1-12). As John F. Kutsko explains, the motif of divine abandonment in Ezekiel shows the exile to be an expression of Yahweh's power in response to the illegitimate portrayal of divine presence by the preexilic royal temple establishment.[10]

The negative attitude toward the monarchic temple establishment in Ezekiel's priestly vision is tempered by the mention of a Davidic "prince," through whom Yahweh will shepherd his restored people (Ezek 34:23-24; 37:22-25). These passages, which indicate the complexity of the book's literary development, stem either from abiding hopes for a restored Davidic monarchy, as were attached to Zerubbabel leading up to the rebuilding of the temple (Hag 2:20-23; Zech 3:8; discussed in connection with Ezra-Nehemiah, later in this chapter), or else from the persistence of the David ideal as the model for leadership of other forms (Zech 6:9-15).[11] In any case, the favorable view toward David in Ezek 34:23-24; 37:22-25 stands out against the more critical attitude toward the monarchy that prevails in most of the book, reflecting questions about the importance of the monarchy to the temple's heritage and its ongoing importance after the exile. These concerns are central to the portrayal of Israel's relationship to its God in the Deuteronomistic History and Chronicles.

Jerusalem and the Path to Exile in the Deuteronomistic History

The biblical story of Israel's life in the land through the end of its monarchy is related in the books of Joshua through 2 Kings, known in the traditional Hebrew canon as the Former Prophets.[12] Following Martin

Noth, scholarship since the mid-twentieth century has generally agreed in viewing this sequence of books as a unified literary work taking Deuteronomy as its preface and theological foundation.[13] The resulting narrative work, which scholars call the Deuteronomistic History (DH), provides a theological explanation for the failure of the Israelite monarchy, culminating in the Babylonian exile and destruction of Jerusalem in 586 B.C.E. The Deuteronomistic narrative of the people's history in the land leading up to that catastrophe is a story of accumulating unfaithfulness to their God. In short, DH presents a classic case of divine abandonment.

The relevant expectations for national obedience to Yahweh are set forth prior to Israel's entry into the land in Deuteronomy and its emphasis on the Mosaic covenant. As discussed in chapter 1, the kinbased social mechanism of covenant in the ancient Near East extends to the realm of international politics, where it becomes the metaphor for vassal treaties as witnessed in Hittite and Neo-Assyrian documents (see chapter 1). Deuteronomy's presentation of law and covenant with Israel's God shows the influence of this institutional and textual form.[14] One of its most impressive parallels in this regard is the resemblance of the ceremonial pronouncement of curses and blessings in Deuteronomy 28 and the Neo-Assyrian treaties such as the Vassal Treaty of Esarhaddon.[15] In Deuteronomy's covenant-centered view of national fortunes, the common ancient Near Eastern tendency to theologize prosperity and disaster reaches full pitch.

Examples of this emphasis on divine reward and retribution as covenantal consequences of obedience and disobedience loom large throughout DH: in Joshua, in the negative and positive examples in the crossing of the Jordan and in the battles of Jericho and Ai (Josh 3:1—8:29); in the Judges cycle of sin, divine punishment, "crying out to Yahweh," and deliverance (especially Judg 3:7—16:31); and in the formulaic evaluations of the kings of Israel and Judah as leading the nation in faithfulness or, more frequently, in disobedience (for example, 1 Kings 22:41-50). In the account of the monarchy, the fall of the northern kingdom (2 Kings 17) and, less explicitly so, that of the southern kingdom (2 Kings 23:31—25:17) result from national disobedience to Yahweh.

The name Deuteronomy derives from the dominant ancient Greek translation of the Hebrew Bible known as the Septuagint, specifically in reference to "the copy of this law" (Gk *to deuteronomion touto*) mentioned in Deut 17:18. As a title for the entire book, the Greek phrase might rightly be understood to mean a "second law," for a distinct legal collection forms the terms of the covenant in Deuteronomy, as compared with the earlier portrayal of the Mosaic covenant and law at Sinai in Exodus, Leviticus, and Numbers. Like the Sinai portrayal of the Mosaic covenant, Deuteronomy has as its main requirement exclusive worship and obedience to Yahweh as Israel's God. This notion of exclusivity is expressed explicitly in both contexts in the introduction and first commandment of the Decalogue or Ten Commandments (Exod 20:1-3; Deut 5:6-7). In Deuteronomy, the demand also comes through in Deut 6:4-5: "Hear, O Israel: The LORD is our God, the LORD alone. You shall love the LORD your God with all your heart, and with all your soul, and with all your might."[16] In Deuteronomy, the terms of the covenant are elaborated in the divine instructions of its law collection (chapters 12–26). In comparison with legal material and worship instructions elsewhere in the Pentateuch, a distinguishing feature of the Deuteronomic legal collection is its explicit requirement of worship centralization.[17] As Deuteronomy 12 states:

> You must demolish completely all the places where the nations whom you are about to dispossess served their gods. . . . But you shall seek *the place that the LORD your God will choose out of all your tribes as his habitation to put his name there.* You shall go there, bringing there your burnt offerings and your sacrifices, your tithes and your donations, your votive gifts, your freewill offerings, and the firstlings of your flocks. (Deut 12:2a, 5-6; italics added)

Similarly, verse 11 speaks of "the place that the LORD your God will choose as a dwelling for his name" (see also verses 12-14, 18). Deuteronomy's requirement of worship centralization comes into focus by comparison to similar language in the altar law of Exod 20:24: "You need make for me only an altar of earth and sacrifice on it your burnt offerings and your offerings of well-being, your sheep and your oxen; in *every place where I cause my name to be remembered* I will come to you and bless you" (italics added).

As discussed in previous chapters, the "name" of Israel's God in these passages refers to a hypostatic form of God's presence in the worship sanctuary.[18] This command occurring near the beginning of the law collection in Exod 20:22–23:19, known by modern scholars as the "book of the covenant" (see Exod 24:7), allows for a plurality of places of worship for Israel's God. By contrast, the Deuteronomic law collection begins with instructions that centralize worship at a single location.[19] The name theology of Deuteronomy and DH balances divine immanence and transcendence, making God's worship presence available at the sanctuary without limiting other forms and possibilities of divine presence on earth.[20] Receiving the land as Yahweh's gift and remaining in it require observing the unique location of divine presence at the central sanctuary.

While Deuteronomy does not specify the location of the central worship place, beginning with Solomon's construction and dedication of the Jerusalem temple (1 Kings 6–8), it figures as the central sanctuary for DH (1 Kings 8:1-66; 12:26-33; 13:1-3; 2 Kings 17:21-22; 23:15-20). In keeping with the role and prerogative of kings as temple builders in the ancient Near East, Solomon figures prominently in this narrative as the temple's royal patron and ceremonial leader of its dedication. Accordingly, the kings of Israel and Judah play an important role in DH's presentation of the national story. In anticipation of the monarchy, another unique feature of the Deuteronomic law collection is the provision for the king's regular reading of the law (Deut 17:14-20). Even while subjugating the king to the law as an expression of divine will for ruling the people, this requirement communicates the vital role of the king within the Deuteronomic vision of the people's life in the land in Deuteronomy and the historical narrative that follows it.

Beginning in 1 and 2 Samuel, DH holds up David as the ideal king of God's own choosing (1 Sam 13:14; 16:12-13; 2 Sam 7:1-29; 1 Kings 3:14; 11:32-39; 2 Kings 18:3; 22:2). Under Yahweh's direction, David secures Jerusalem not only as a political capital (2 Sam 5:6-12; 6:1-23; 7) but also as a religious center, bringing the ark of Yahweh there (2 Samuel 6) and designating the site for the future temple through his own cultic measures (2 Sam 24:18-25). For DH, David is the standard against whom subsequent kings are measured.

In the regnal formulas that evaluate the kings of the northern and southern kingdoms, the only two reviewed without criticism, Hezekiah and Josiah, are compared favorably with David (2 Kings 18:3; 22:2). Both of these kings are credited with carrying out temple-centered reforms (2 Kings 18:4-8; 22:1—23:25). Those reforms included the dismantling of outlying sanctuaries and removing offensive objects and practices from the Jerusalem temple. Josiah's demolition of the rival Bethel sanctuary is even foretold by prophetic oracle (1 Kings 13).[21] In these ways, the Davidic monarchy is integral to DH's temple-centered view of history.

For DH, the fall of the northern and southern kingdoms was largely due to their kings' leadership into accumulated cultic sins of idolatry and violation of Jerusalem's place as the central sanctuary. Just as DH credits specific kings as ideals of faithfulness, so does it single out rulers who bear primary responsibility for divine punishment—namely, Jeroboam I of the northern kingdom for establishing rival national sanctuaries at Dan and Bethel (1 Kings 12:25-33; 2 Kings 17:21-23) and Manasseh of

Judah for reversing his father Hezekiah's temple-centered reform and sponsorship of various excluded practices (2 Kings 21:10-16; 23:26-27). Like Ezekiel, DH places responsibility for the exile on apostate worship practices related to the Jerusalem temple, and the monarchy is singled out for blame. Unlike Ezekiel, DH is not antimonarchic in principle but rather underscores the importance of a monarchy that in practice did not measure up to the Deuteronomic ideal of a king like David, who was faithful to the laws of Yahweh's covenant with the people (1 Kings 3:14). Neither is DH opposed to the Jerusalem temple establishment but rather stresses the importance of right worship at the Jerusalem temple as the national central sanctuary.[22] As Gary N. Knoppers points out, the foreshadowing of the exile in Solomon's prayer of dedication frames the exile not as an indictment of the temple but rather as an event reiterating Jerusalem's continuing place as the focal point for seeking God's presence even for deportees in exile: "If they repent with all their heart and soul in the land of their enemies, who took them captive, and pray to you toward their land . . . the city that you have chosen, and the house that I have built for your name; then hear in heaven your dwelling place their prayer and their plea" (1 Kings 8:48-49).[23]

In the sacred geography of DH, Jerusalem is paramount as the place of the central sanctuary (Deuteronomy 12) and the ruling line of David, who sets the standard as the king obedient to Israel's God (2 Kings 18:3; 22:2). The city, temple, and Davidic king are all integrally related in Jerusalem's legacy as recounted in this historical work. The hope DH holds out for the Davidic monarchy in the scene of Jehoiachin's release from confinement (2 Kings 25:27-30) implicitly bears on hopes for a restored temple.[24]

JERUSALEM AS THE CENTER OF DIVINE PRESENCE IN CHRONICLES

More explicit hope for the temple's restoration comes in the conclusion to the other major historical narrative of the monarchy in Chronicles.[25] Cyrus's decree as portrayed there includes provisions for the Persian Empire's restoration of the Jerusalem temple (2 Chr 36:22-23). The muted word of hope concluding DH (2 Kings 23:27-30) reflected an exilic situation in which Babylonian policy toward Judah included no provisions for a restored temple. The conclusion of Chronicles with Cyrus's decree implies a very different situation of imperial relations. The outcome of the narrative is the temple's explicit role in Israel's future hopes. *Cf Isa 4*

Cyrus's edict appears again at the beginning of the book of Ezra (1:2-4). While this repetition has suggested to some modern interpreters Chronicles' original unity with Ezra-Nehemiah as the product of a single writer, others point to differences of language, style, and interests that suggest Chronicles and Ezra-Nehemiah were created separately by different hands.[26] In any case, their sequence presents a larger narrative that continues Israel's story beyond the exile to restoration. The overarching concern of those books making up the narrative is the centrality of Jerusalem and its temple for the people's relationship to God.

As most scholars agree, Chronicles utilizes material from DH's portrayal of the monarchy in Samuel and Kings.[27] In so doing, it surpasses DH in its thoroughgoing attention to David and his dynasty. Chronicles accentuates positive aspects of David's reign as an ideal king, excluding any mention of adultery with Bathsheba, Absalom's rebellion, David's conflict with Saul, and other suspicious aspects of David's rise to kingship related in Samuel. David becomes king by the decision of Israel's God, who is in full control of events. This view is in keeping with what Sara Japhet describes as Chronicles' presentation of "'theocentric historiography,' in which every sphere of life derives its significance and ultimate reality from its relationship to God."[28] As aptly summarized in the words of Ralph W. Klein, for Chronicles, "kingship is equated with the kingdom of God (1 Chr 28:5; 29:23; 2 Chr 13:8) and is inalienably linked to the Davidic dynasty (1 Chr 17:13)."[29]

The reigns of David (1 Chronicles 11–29) and Solomon (2 Chronicles 1–9) form the central and most significant part of the Chronicler's history, which it treats as "one continuous period."[30] They are tied together by royal speeches, which focus on the building of the temple (1 Chronicles 13; 15; 22; 28; 29; 2 Chronicles 2; 6; 29).[31] Though making it clear that Solomon actually carried out the temple's construction (2 Chr 8:16), Chronicles also presents David himself in the fashion of a temple builder and the founder of the worship establishment. His first act as king is capturing Jerusalem (1 Chr 11:4-9), an achievement completed by bringing the ark into the city (15:25—16:3). David makes arrangements for the ordering of priests and Levites (1 Chr 16:4-7, 37-42; 2 Chr 7:6). At God's direction, David chooses the site for the temple with divine approval being signaled by fire from heaven (1 Chr 21:18—22:1; compare 2 Sam 24:15-25). According to Chronicles, David made extensive preparations for the building of the temple before his death (1 Chr 22:2-5; 28:11-19; 29:2-5). The centrality of the temple shapes the Chronicler's portrayal of David, as reflected in the oft-cited observation by Julius Wellhausen: "See what Chronicles has made out of David! The founder of the kingdoms has become the founder of the temple and the public worship, the king and hero at the head of his companions in arms has become the singer and master of ceremonies at the head of a swarm of priests and Levites."[32] As the founder of the royal dynasty in Jerusalem, David assumes an ideal place in Chronicles' history as the founder of temple worship. Chronicles' depiction of David's rule shows that monarchy and temple go hand in hand.

Chronicles portrays unified support for David's succession by Solomon, even among David's other sons (1 Chr 29:23-25; compare 1 Kings 1–2). Without any mention of Solomon's idolatry as reported in 1 Kings 11, Chronicles presents Solomon as an ideal royal patron of worship, completing David's arrangements for temple and worship personnel. Solomon makes his own preparations for the temple, which he constructs on David's chosen site (2 Chr 2:2-16). Solomon brings the ark into the temple (2 Chr 5:2-14) and installs priests and Levites in their offices (2 Chr 8:14-15). Having shed much blood in war, David is prevented by Yahweh from building the temple, but his son Solomon, being a man of peace, is well suited for the task (1 Chr 22:8-10). Just as Yahweh chose David to found the dynasty, so does God choose Solomon to build the temple (1 Chr 28:10; 29:1).

The Chronicler's recasting of events known from DH communicates an especially intense focus on the temple. For example, Chronicles relates Solomon's sacrifice at the high place of Gibeon and God's appearance to Solomon there (1 Kings 3:4-15) but adds that the tabernacle of the wilderness experience and its bronze altar were located at Gibeon and that David had assigned the priest Zadok and his kindred to officiate "according to all that is written in the law of the LORD" (1 Chr 16:39-42; 2 Chr 1:3-6). Undoubtedly, this added information was prompted by DH's mention that Solomon would later install the tent of meeting, along with the ark and other cultic furnishings, at the temple upon its completion (1 Kings 8:4). In addition, Chronicles mentions groups of Levitical singers and gatekeepers assigned at Gibeon as well as at Jerusalem, where the ark was housed in a tent shrine since David had brought it there (1 Chr 16:38, 41-42; 2 Chr 1:4). The effect is to turn Solomon's private pilgrimage encounter with Yahweh into an event of national celebration consistent with ongoing centralized worship both reaching back to Israel's experience at Sinai and anticipating structures of worship to come in the completed second temple.[33] To this end, Chronicles portrays the decades leading up to the temple's completion as what Gary N. Knoppers aptly describes as a "temporary bifurcation of Israel's national cult," in which the worship of praise and song took place before the ark in Jerusalem and animal sacrifice was carried out at the altar before the tabernacle at Gibeon. In Deuteronomistic

terms, Gibeon qualified during this time as "the place that the LORD
your God shall choose . . . [to bring] your burnt offerings and your
sacrifices (Deut 12:5-6).[34] In Chronicles' presentation, all of these elements of ancient Israel's national worship will converge in the Jerusalem
temple, connecting the second temple of the Chronicler's day both with
Solomon's temple and with the centralized worship at Sinai.

For Chronicles, the temple's centrality carries into the reigns of
Judah's kings following David and Solomon, as emphasized by the
placement of royal speeches and prayers. Just as the prayers of David
bracket the beginning and end of his participation in the building of
the temple (1 Chr 17:16-27; 1 Chr 29:10-19), so is the era of the divided
monarchy enclosed within speeches calling for repentance by Abijah (2
Chr 13:4-12) and by Hezekiah (2 Chr 30:6-9).[35] Both speeches indicate
the Chronicler's encouragement of northern participation in the Jerusalem cult. The north's apostasy consisted mainly in its idolatry in worship at Dan and Bethel and in its rejection of the Jerusalem temple as the
only appropriate worship site (2 Chr 13:4-12). As Klein states, "When
Hezekiah calls for Israel and Judah to repent, he called for a return to
the sanctuary which God had sanctified forever (2 Chr 30:6-8)."[36]

Whereas the account of Hezekiah's reign in DH emphasizes political
matters (2 Kings 18–20) and gives only one verse to Hezekiah's religious
reform (2 Kings 18:3), Chronicles devotes three full chapters to the
reform (2 Chronicles 29–31) and deals with political aspects of his reign
only in "an abbreviated and theologically oriented fashion" (2 Chronicles 32).[37] As Sara Japhet notes, "The space which the Chronicler has
devoted to Hezekiah's story is one way of expressing that Hezekiah is
the greatest Judean monarch after David and Solomon."[38] As a number
of scholars have argued and as H. G. M. Williamson has demonstrated
with thoroughness, Chronicles presents Hezekiah as a kind of "second
Solomon."[39] He leads a national celebration of Passover on a scale not
seen since the time of Solomon (2 Chr 30:26), and its fourteen-day duration (2 Chr 30:23) matches the duration of the temple dedication under
Solomon (2 Chr 7:8-9).[40]

Chronicles' vision of a united twelve tribes of Israel is reflected in
its description of Josiah's centralizing reform, which reaches as far as
the territory of Simeon and Naphtali (2 Chr 34:6-7), far beyond the
geographic extent reported in 2 Kings 22–23. In the Chronicler's portrayal of the monarchic era, the notion of the Jerusalem temple as the
legitimate central sanctuary for all Israel is invoked as the ideal for the
second temple.[41]

Chronicles' focus on the temple and cult also reflects a marked concern for the temple's cultic personnel, which includes both "the priests

and the Levites." The priests are sons of Aaron and descendants of Zadok, with special rights and status over and against the Levites. The Levites consist of minor clergy who appear in a variety of roles as singers, leaders in singing and praise, gatekeepers, bakers, judges, scribes, teachers (especially of legal ordinances), and those having charge of various holy objects, including showbread.[42] For Chronicles, the temple is central to the activities of worship and to the nation's encounter with the unique divine presence in worship.[43]

A distinguishing feature of Chronicles' theologically oriented narrative of history is its emphasis on immediate divine retribution.[44] Comparisons with parallel content in DH point out this emphasis by the Chronicler. For example, DH describes Manasseh as the wickedest of kings to reign in Jerusalem and assigns to him ultimate responsibility for the Babylonian exile and destruction of the temple (2 Kings 21; 23:26-27). Nonetheless, DH reports for Manasseh a reign of fifty-five years (2 Kings 21:1; dated 687–642 B.C.E.). The Chronicler adds the episode in 2 Chr 33:10-13. It describes how, in response to Manasseh's failure to heed Yahweh's warnings, Yahweh allowed the Assyrians to take Manasseh captive to Babylon, where he "entreated the favor of the LORD his God and humbled himself greatly before the God of his ancestors," so that Yahweh restored Manasseh to his throne in Jerusalem, with the result that "then Manasseh knew that the LORD indeed was God" (v. 13). This additional information resolves the apparent contradiction between Manasseh's long reign and a belief in immediate divine punishment for the king's evil.

On the opposite end of the retribution spectrum, the most righteous king for DH, Josiah, presents another challenge to the Chronicler's view of consistent divine retribution. As both Kings and Chronicles report, Josiah dies tragically while going to Megiddo to intercept King Neco of Egypt, who is on his way to the Euphrates (2 Kings 23:29-30; 2 Chr 35:20-27). In Kings, Josiah's untimely death not only disappoints any hopes DH places in his centralizing cultic reform but also contradicts DH's own retribution theology, which views Josiah as an incomparably righteous and faithful king: "Before him there was no king like him, who turned to the LORD with all his heart, with all his soul, and with all his might; according to all the law of Moses; nor did any like him arise after him" (2 Kings 23:25). Chronicles reshapes the episode to show the otherwise righteous Josiah acting in defiance of God by confronting Neco. The text has the Egyptian king himself say to Josiah, "I am not coming against you today, but against the house with which I am at war; and God has commanded me to hurry. Cease opposing God, who is with me, so that he will not destroy you" (2 Chr 35:21).[45] The narration then removes any doubt about the divine origin of Neco's warning: "He did not listen to the words of Neco from the mouth of God" (v. 22). Chronicles clarifies the theologically ambiguous circumstances of the great reformer's death by invoking divine causation in service to a rigid doctrine of divine retribution. It also portrays the speech of a foreign king as a kind of prophetic word.

In Chronicles, the prophets figure importantly in the people's relationship to its God, especially as mediated through its kings (2 Chr 29:25).[46] Nearly equating trust in God with trust in the prophets, King Jehoshaphat says to the people of Judah before engaging in battle against their enemies, "Believe in Yahweh your God, and you will be established; believe his prophets, and you will succeed" (2 Chr 20:20; compare the NRSV). With the Babylonian destruction and exile, the Chronicler makes clear that the catastrophe was the result of divine punishment and only after a failure to heed divine warnings through an abundance of prophets sent by God (2 Chr 36:15-21). The conclusion of Chronicles appeals to prophetic authority in bridging Israel's story before the exile with times that follow (2 Chr 36:21-23). The duration of the exile is spanned by the reference to Jeremiah's oracle of seventy years (Jer 25:11-12; 29:10; see also Zech 1:12; 7:3,5), with 2 Chr 36:21 interpreting the conventional period of divine punishment (see Isa 23:15) in this instance as a time of the land's desolation, allowing repayment both for neglected sabbath years and for general unfaithfulness as articulated in Lev 26:34-35, 43.

The pronouncement marking the end of the exile is Cyrus's decree (2 Chr 36:22-23), which itself is regarded as a fulfillment of Jeremiah's prophetic word. Like the words of Pharaoh Neco cited in 2 Chr 35:21, the Persian emperor's speech communicates the words of Israel's God:

> Yahweh stirred up the spirit of King Cyrus of Persia so that he sent a herald throughout all his kingdom and also declared in a written edict: "Thus says King Cyrus of Persia: Yahweh, the God of heaven, has given me all the kingdoms of the earth, and he has charged me to build him a house at Jerusalem, which is in Judah. Whoever is among you of all his people, may Yahweh his God be with him! Let him go up." (2 Chr 36:22b-23, adapted from the NRSV)

Through Cyrus, Yahweh issues a command to the exiled Judeans to return to Jerusalem for the purpose of rebuilding the temple. The conclusion of Chronicles reiterates the book's view of sacred geography. As the "God of heaven," Israel's God is by no means limited to one earthly location. Nonetheless, the temple in Jerusalem remains the center of divine presence on earth.

To summarize, in the narrative of Chronicles, God relates to Israel and Judah through the arena of historical events.[47] For Chronicles, the temple is critical to those events as the place of God's dwelling on earth and as the institutional center for the divine–human relationship within the history's realm (2 Chr 36:15). The temple's centrality in Chronicles' account is not only geographic but also temporal, incorporating Israel's most important cultic institutions from the times of Moses and David.[48] In minimizing the degree of discontinuity posed by the exile (2 Chr 36:17-23), Chronicles suggests that the worship ideal represented by the first temple extends to the second temple of his own day.[49] For Chronicles, the Jerusalem temple is the institutional bridge between the past ideal and present hopes, and the ongoing center of unique divine presence in human events.

THE CENTRALITY OF JERUSALEM AFTER THE EXILE: EZRA-NEHEMIAH

The reestablishment of temple, city, and community after the exile is portrayed in Ezra-Nehemiah (EN).[50] As Sara Japhet has convincingly demonstrated, the structure of EN presents a historical periodization in two parts, each lasting a generation.[51] The first unit (Ezra 1–6) covers the period from Cyrus's decree to the temple's dedication (538 B.C.E. to 516 B.C.E.) and features two important leaders, Zerubbabel and Jeshua (Ezra 2:2; 3:2). While this first period treated is defined by its central project, the building of the temple, the second unit of EN (Ezra 7–Nehemiah 13) is defined by its two leaders, Ezra and Nehemiah. It begins with Ezra's arrival from Babylonia, continues with Nehemiah's arrival, and concludes with Nehemiah's second tenure in Jerusalem, all of which Japhet understands to fall within the reign of Artaxerxes I as a period of twenty-six years (458 B.C.E. to 432 B.C.E.).[52] As in Chronicles, "the history of Israel" is the arena of God's relationship to humanity in EN. As Japhet explains, in EN God extends grace to Israel through the kings of Persia.[53] In this portrayal, as in that of the Chronicler, the center of earthly divine presence and concern is clearly Jerusalem. Nonetheless, EN's distinct character comes into view through attention to elements distinguishing it from Chronicles.

By comparison with Chronicles, EN is noticeably silent on the heritage and line of David. The Davidic lineage of both Sheshbazzar, who led the initial group of returning exiles after Cyrus's decree (Ezra 1:8-11;

2:68; 5:14-16), and Zerubbabel is muted in EN and must be traced by
reference to 1 Chronicles 3.[54] As Japhet points out, the status of both
Zerubbabel and the other major leader in Ezra 1–6, Jeshua, is left unde-
fined, presumably in keeping with the focus on the temple itself in this
first portion of EN.[55] Jeshua's role as high priest may only be inferred by
the reader indirectly (Ezra 3:2; 10:18; Neh 12:7, 10, 26), but EN never
calls him "the high priest" or even simply "a priest" (compare Hag 1:1,
12, 14; 2:2, 4; Zech 3:1, 8; 6:11). Similarly, Zerubbabel is given no
administrative title, and his leadership role is indicated only indirectly
(Ezra 4:2; 12:47; compare Hag 1:1, 14; 2:2, 21). In the account of the
temple's completion and dedication (Ezra 6), neither Zerubbabel nor
Jeshua appears, and neither is mentioned again in EN. Is the conspicuous absence of these leaders at this point in the narrative a function of
EN's literary structure and emphasis on the temple itself in Ezra 1–6,
or does it indicate their possible removal from leadership before the
temple's dedication?

The likelihood of their removal receives support from a comparison with the focus on the temple's rebuilding in books named after
two prophets mentioned in Ezra (5:1; 6:14), Haggai and Zechariah. As
noted, both of these prophetic books give explicit emphasis to Zerubbabel's status as Davidic scion and Jeshua's as high priest (see the citations
of these books in the preceding paragraph). Haggai presents a call for
the temple's rebuilding in the second year of Darius's reign (Hag 1:1;
520 B.C.E.). The book's prophetic appeal is framed in classic terms of
weal and woe, correlating material prosperity and hardship with divine
presence and absence. Haggai blames the current economic hardships
in Judah on the people's failure to complete the temple's construction
(1:2-11; 2:15-19) and promises wealth, prosperity, and political dominion that will come with the temple's completion (2:6-8, 20-23). For
Haggai, the key to the rebuilding effort is the leadership of Zerubbabel,
"governor of Judah," and Jeshua "the high priest" (1:1, 12, 14; 2:2,
4, 21). The book's concluding oracle (2:20-23) promises Zerubbabel's
ascendancy as much more than a governor under Persian rule and paints
a picture of military defeat in which Yahweh overthrows "the throne of
kingdoms" (v. 22): "On that day, says the LORD of hosts, I will take you,
O Zerubbabel my servant, son of Shealtiel, says the LORD, and make
you like a signet ring; for I have chosen you, says the LORD of hosts"
(v. 23). The oracle's language portrays Zerubbabel in accordance with
the Davidic ideal, as a ruler representing Yahweh's authority on earth.
Reflecting ongoing hopes for a Davidic king who rules from Jerusalem, Haggai's call for the temple's restoration draws on the earlier Zion

tradition, in which the temple is inseparable from a ruling Davidic line (see chapters 3 and 6 of this volume).[56]

Contemporaneously with Haggai, Zechariah 1–8 also promises the transformative effects of a rebuilt temple and on a more cosmic scale in the mode of apocalyptic.[57] Through angelic messengers and elaborate visionary symbolism, Zechariah 1–8 depicts a coming ideal age predicated on the temple's rebuilding. Like Haggai, Zechariah 1–8 shares a keen interest in Zerubbabel's and Jeshua's importance for this endeavor, portraying both of them in messianic terms.[58] Zechariah 4 describes a vision of a lampstand, fed by the oil of two olive trees representing two "anointed ones" (Zech 4:14). Though the Hebrew expression employed is not the usual term for "anointed" on which the word *messiah* is based (*māšî(a)ḥ*), the vision depicts the twin leadership of Zerubbabel and Joshua as royal and priestly leaders inaugurating an ideal age to come with the temple's completion.[59]

These messianic hopes placed on Zerubbabel and Jeshua, as represented by these two prophetic books, reflect ideals that would certainly be at odds with Persian imperial interests. They likely belong to a historical situation of mounting tensions between Persian interests and traditional Judean national heritage leading up to the temple's completion, a situation in which Persian intervention and removal of Zerubbabel and Jeshua (behind the scenes of Ezra-Nehemiah's account) would have been quite conceivable. Since the rebuilding of Jerusalem's temple was predicated on Persian imperial policy toward the province of Judah, the project's completion could go on without those originally assigned to carry it out.[60]

EN's especially muted treatment of these two figures contrasts with its portrayal of Ezra and Nehemiah as diligent and loyal servants of the Persian empire in the second half of its narrative. Given the profile of these two prominently celebrated leaders and the scenario reflected in Haggai and Zechariah 1–8, EN's contrasting treatment of Zerubbabel and Jeshua likely involves both literary artistry and political-historical reality.[61] A focus on the temple's rebuilding does not require minimizing the leadership responsible for it. Conversely, the focus on Ezra and Nehemiah in the second period of EN (Ezra 7–Nehemiah 13) hardly diminishes the prominence of the projects they enact (as discussed in the remainder of this section). In contrast to Chronicles (and to Haggai and Zechariah), EN implies a distinct discontinuity between the past Davidic ideal of the temple and second temple of its own day. Yet both agree on the importance of Jerusalem and its temple in centering divine presence as expressed through events of history.

With the completed temple in place, the second unit of EN (Ezra 7–Nehemiah 13) depicts the rebuilding of the city and community around the temple. In so doing, EN focuses on the two leaders who carry out these measures, Ezra and Nehemiah. As Japhet explains regarding this portrayal, "In the beginning Ezra works by himself (Ezra 7–10), in the end, Nehemiah works by himself (Neh 13:4-31), and in between, Ezra and Nehemiah work in parallel or together."[62]

Ezra 7–10 deals with events surrounding Ezra's arrival in Jerusalem, which take place within a one-year period (Ezra 7:9; 10:17).[63] One of the titles given to Ezra is that of "priest" (Ezra 7:11, 12; see also Neh 8:9; 12:26). He arrives in Jerusalem in "the seventh year of King Artaxerxes" (that is, Artaxerxes I; 458 B.C.E.), accompanied by other priests, singers, gatekeepers, and other temple functionaries from among the exiles (Ezra 7:7, 13) and supplied by the Persian empire with generous funding for temple worship as well as ritual objects to be installed in the temple for worship purposes ("the vessels . . . for the service of the house of your God"; Ezra 7:15-20).

Ezra also bears the title of "scribe" (Ezra 7:11, 12; see also Neh 8:9; 12:26). More specifically, he is called "a scribe of the words of the commandments of Yahweh and his statutes for Israel" (Ezra 7:11) and "the scribe of the law of the God of heaven" (v. 12). Along with the support for temple worship, the Persian king sends Ezra to Jerusalem with a copy of "the law of your God" (Ezra 7:14), which will become the basis for legal and social reforms that Ezra will enact (Ezra 7:10, 25-26). Ezra's law is called "the law of Moses that Yahweh the God of Israel had given" (Ezra 7:6), suggesting that Ezra's *torah* might have been some version or portion of what now exists as the Pentateuch.[64] Artaxerxes' decree depicted in Ezra 7 also refers to "the law of your God and the law of the king" (Ezra 7:25-26), indicating that Ezra's mission situates the Jewish law within Persian imperial policy.[65] Later in the book, Ezra's law will be read in concert with Nehemiah's reforms (Neh 8:1-8; 9:3; 13:1; see later in this section).

Nehemiah's activities of rebuilding Jerusalem's walls, social reform, and repopulating the city form the focus of the remainder of EN.[66] Nehemiah is presented as a Jewish official, specifically the king's "cupbearer" (Neh 1:11), serving in the imperial court at Susa, who is sent to Jerusalem for two terms of administration as governor. Nehemiah is troubled by the news of the destruction of Jerusalem's walls and the dispersal of most of its population (1:1-3). In response, Nehemiah weeps and prays for God to forgive him and his people for their sins that have brought about the disaster and to restore the city and its population (1:4-11). An answer to Nehemiah's prayer comes soon thereafter when the king initiates a conversation with Nehemiah that results in Nehemiah's mission to rebuild Jerusalem (2:1-8). The Persian king commissions Nehemiah to lead a group of returning exiles to rebuild Jerusalem's defenses in "the twentieth year of King Artaxerxes" (445 b.c.e.; Neh 2:1). Despite various obstacles (Neh 4:1—6:14), Nehemiah and the people of Judea complete the walls' construction in fifty-two days (6:15-19).

Though this discussion stresses elements separating EN from Chronicles, an interest in Jerusalem's walls is one that they share in common. In keeping with its content and outlook, Chronicles' interest falls on the initial fortification of Jerusalem during the united monarchy. As Sara Japhet explains, a comparison between Chronicles and DH on this score sheds light not only on Chronicles' theological interests but also on the historical circumstances of its own time.[67] While DH credits Solomon with fortifying the city (1 Kings 3:1; 9:15), Chronicles retrojects this accomplishment to David (1 Chr 11:7-8; compare 2 Sam 5:9), a move in keeping with Chronicles' effort to portray the reigns of David and Solomon as one unified period.[68] What is more, in comparison with Chronicles, DH in depicting the foundation of Jerusalem shows little interest in the physical city and its fortifications.[69] The more extensive attention to the city walls in Chronicles, as in EN, likely reflects regional volatility and concerns for security during the time of these books' composition during the Persian period. As Japhet states, "'Building' is a negligible element in Kings, but it is both historically and theologically significant in Chronicles."[70] Though belonging to the mundane details of political life, attention to Jerusalem's walls is an important part of the theologizing of history that Japhet and others attribute to Chronicles and EN alike.[71]

Like the temple, the city's defensive walls are a traditional symbol of royal power, protection, and authority. In Ezra-Nehemiah, those royal prerogatives have been transferred from the Davidic monarchy in Jerusalem to the Persian Empire on the distant horizon. As Japhet explains, EN depicts Persia's kings as the conduit of God's grace to Israel.[72]

In Nehemiah's request to the king, the city walls are described as part of the temple's gates and fortifications ("the gates of the temple fortress"; Neh 2:8). The endeavor to rebuild the city walls implicitly centers on the temple as the place of God's dwelling among God's people. Fortification of the community surrounding the temple is the focus of Nehemiah's other endeavors, with the book's narrative sequence placing the social reform during the time of the walls' construction (Nehemiah 5) and plans for populating Jerusalem immediately following the completion of construction (Neh 7:4-5).[73]

The following chapters of Nehemiah present a series of both solemn and celebratory observances involving both Ezra and Nehemiah and serving to solidify the structures of temple, community, and city as presented in the larger account (Nehemiah 8–12). This final reiteration begins with the account of Ezra's public reading of "the book of the law of Moses, which the LORD had given to Israel" (Neh 8:1). The response by the assembled people is one of confession and renewed commitment to follow the divine will expressed in the written *torah* (Nehemiah 9–10). A final summary of repopulation and census (11:1—12:26) is followed by the report of a final dedication service (12:27—13:3).

After this period of overlap in the activities of Ezra and Nehemiah, the book concludes with Nehemiah's second term in Jerusalem, when he returns to correct violations regarding temple access and provisions, rights and duties of the Levites, Sabbath observance, and the ban on foreign wives (Neh 13:4-31). This concluding account of Nehemiah's corrective measures suggests the need for ongoing diligence around duties and observances of temple worship.

In the ideal of divine–human relations offered by Ezra-Nehemiah's account, divine presence is known through human events of international history and community life as exemplified in Jerusalem's restoration. At the center of these events stands the second temple. The sacredness of God's earthly dwelling extends to all of Jerusalem as "the holy city" (Neh 11:1).

CONCLUSION

In the Hebrew Bible, the Babylonian exile turns Jerusalem from the terrestrial center of divine presence to a place of acute divine absence. In accordance with the classic ancient Near Eastern motif of divine abandonment, disaster in the form of military defeat and temple destruction can serve a belief in the deity's displeasure and punishment of the people. The temple sermon of Jeremiah 7 and 26 threatens such an exercise of divine freedom despite the presumed inviolability of Jerusalem as expressed in the Zion tradition. In the Bible and in the ancient Near East, the motif of divine abandonment serves as a theological counterweight to presumptions of the temple's importance as monarchic prerogative and symbol.

The prophetic books of Ezekiel, Haggai, and Zechariah 1–8 present both visionary and concrete hopes for the temple's reestablishment. From the perspective of the exile, Ezekiel blames the Babylonian destruction on the defiling influence of the monarchy, as expressed architecturally in the sanctuary's integration into the royal temple-palace complex (Ezek 43:7-9). Ezekiel's ideal temple (Ezekiel 40–42) is one that stands alone, free from the corruption of royal associations. By contrast, both Haggai and Zechariah 1–8 see the restored temple as inextricably tied to its Davidic heritage. These prophetic books provide some insight into various views surrounding the temple's destruction and hopes for its restoration during and after the exile.

The temple's central importance even before the Babylonian crisis is reflected in the Deuteronomistic History (DH). Placing a high value on the monarchy, DH holds the kings of Israel and Judah responsible for leading the people into the accumulated unfaithfulness that brought about the Babylonian exile and destruction. Though not directly entertaining any designs for a new temple, the vague hopes for the Davidic monarchy at the end of the book would entail such a possibility (2 Kings 25:27-30). A retrospective view from after the exile is offered by Chronicles, which implies the second temple to stand in strong continuity with the monarchic-period temple and the ideal of its Davidic origins. In contrast with DH's interest in Jerusalem as the place of Yahweh's choice for the center of worship (Deuteronomy 12), Chronicles is attentive to the physical city, its temple and fortifications, as the concrete result of historical events, through which God is known to Israel.

With a similar perspective, Ezra-Nehemiah (EN) presents an account of the temple's reconstruction as being central for the reestablishment of the city and its population. In distinction to Chronicles, as well as to Haggai and Zechariah, the Davidic ideal is not part of the renewed temple for EN, and any such associations are noticeably downplayed. Highlighting the achievements of its leaders as loyal officials of the Persian Empire, EN presents a blueprint for ongoing life for the "holy city," one that is based on maintaining ethnic distinction as a requirement of divine law. For the community of Jerusalem and the temple, life has moved on without the Davidic monarchy. Though focused on the mundane details of life outside the temple, EN shares with the other biblical books considered here the continued perspective on the temple as the center of God's dealings with Israel in history, as the center of divine presence on earth.

CONCLUSION

Divine Absence
and the Relational God
of This World

Summary

AS A BALANCE TO THE ATTENTION that often goes to the exceptional occasions of divine presence in the Bible, this study has considered the more frequent portrayal of God's absence in Scripture. The effort has been to consider this biblical theme as it occurs in various forms in a variety of texts throughout the Old Testament. Beginning with the nature of divine absence as a relational concern that the Hebrew Bible shares in common with other texts from the ancient Near East, part I of this study examined Israelite conceptions of divine–human relationships from this comparative perspective. The thorough examination of the basis and portrayal of divine–human relationships serves as a foundation for examining divine absence in various portions of the Hebrew Bible. In keeping with the ancient Near Eastern tendency of modeling relationships to the divine on human social structures and relationships, ancient Israel's kin-based social organization provided the basis for conceptualizing relationships to God in the Hebrew Bible. Human relationships to the divine are modeled after hierarchical social relationships, with society being understood both as a hierarchy of households and as one great household ultimately headed by Israel's God.[1]

A form of written religious expression that especially relates to the family-based structure of society and relationships to the divine is that of theophoric personal names. As discussed in chapter 2, anthroponyms in the Hebrew Bible and its broader West Semitic context reflect a concern for divine absence, especially through the divine-absence name

175

type, which asks the basic question of divine absence, "Where is God?" As religious evidence, personal names relate both to the household and to the larger community, which throughout the Hebrew Bible is the people and nation of Israel. Thus, chapter 3 considers a variety of biblical traditions accounting for the origins of Israel's relationship to its God. In invoking collective memory of beginnings, these various origin traditions ground Israel's ongoing identity in the people's relationship to its God. Accordingly, a sense of divine absence poses a disorienting threat to the sense of identity and existence of Israel in the Hebrew Bible. By the same token, the invocation of origins also provides a basis for overcoming threats posed by potential divine absence.

Another aspect of divine absence noted from the outset is that it assumes an inherently spatial conceptualization of divine–human relationships. This aspect of the topic leads to the consideration of particular portions of the Hebrew Bible in parts II and III. Chapter 4 examined boundaries of divine presence and absence in cosmological perspective with reference both to various biblical texts and to the comparative ancient Near Eastern concepts. The Hebrew Bible shares in the common ancient Near Eastern understanding of a three-tiered universe that separates the realm of the dead from terrestrial and heavenly levels of existence (Exod 20:4; Ps 135:6). With a few exceptions that tend to prove the rule (for example, Amos 9:2; Psalm 139), the biblical texts are fairly pronounced in excluding Israel's God from death's abode (Pss 6:5; 30:9; 88:10-12; 115:16-17). Threats and disasters posed by death's incursions into the ordered world of creation do not represent a lack of divine power or will but rather are inherent to the structure of the cosmos and to the nature of Israel's God as a God known in life's realm. This biblical notion of "structural divine absence" in the cosmos offers something of a theodicy, a defense of the "living God" of the Bible. On balance, the biblical view of the cosmos offers something of a theodicy, a defense of the divine. Though God has access to death's realm, it lies outside the normative realm of God's presence in the ordered cosmos.

In establishing its view of human existence in universal perspective, the Primeval History in Genesis 1–11 shows that divine presence in the world allows for human choice. God's ordering of the cosmos is relational in nature; in creation, God brings about relationship to the world in which human beings are active participants in God's ordering of the world but without constraining human freedom. What appears to be divine absence is God's allowance of human freedom even while guarding the boundaries of divine prerogatives. The picture is one of divine–human reciprocity but also a careful guarding of that basic distinction. The relationship is negotiated often in spatial terms: "Where are you?"

(Gen 3:9); "the LORD God sent him forth from the garden of Eden" (3:23); "Enoch walked with God; then he was no longer [there], because God took him" (5:24; compare the NRSV); "Be fruitful and multiply, and fill the earth" (9:1); "I have set my bow in the clouds, and it shall be a sign of the covenant between me and the earth" (9:13); "Come, let us go down, and confuse their language" (11:7).

Proceeding from a basis in creation theology, the wisdom literature of the Hebrew Bible cultivates the recognition and negotiation of the boundaries of divine presence and absence in the world and in everyday life, as discussed in chapter 5. Proverbs, Job, Ecclesiastes (Qoheleth), and certain Psalms alternately reinforce and question a sense of God's hidden presence as mediated through creation. In Job, the limits of human understanding and perception (as highlighted by Job 28) are cited in support of a theodicy of presence. In Qoheleth, human limitations translate into an insurmountable barrier against apprehending a God who remains ultimately elusive. In Qoheleth, divine absence serves as a prompt for embracing the immediate and transient joys of life with acceptance and trust.

Worship traditions of ritual and psalmody constitute another category of biblical texts that engage divine presence through the understanding of an established divine order in the universe. Chapter 6 examined different ways in which these worship texts of the Hebrew Bible attend to the boundaries of divine presence and absence in creation and in human life. Dominating the biblical worship traditions is the recognition of the Jerusalem temple as the center of Israel's worship and thus as the center of God's presence on earth.

Biblical reflection on divine absence reaches perhaps its greatest proportions in consideration of the exile, in which the Babylonian destruction makes Jerusalem and its temple the center of divine absence instead of divine presence. As discussed in chapter 7, the exile stands as the critical point of reference for biblical narrative works and for prophetic books of exile and later (Jeremiah, Ezekiel, Haggai, and Zechariah 1–8). Jerusalem is central to these biblical traditions' consideration of quintessential forms of divine presence and absence on earth in the destruction and restoration of the city and its temple. Consistent throughout these traditions is the understanding of the Babylonian exile in accordance with the common ancient Near Eastern motif of divine abandonment. The historical narratives of the Deuteronomistic History, Chronicles, and Ezra-Nehemiah each present a temple-centered view of history as the arena of God's dealings with Israel.

As anticipated at the outset of this study, divine absence figures in the Hebrew Bible not so much as a problem to be solved but more as an integral part of the biblical portrayal of God. To some degree, this state of affairs as presented is a function of human limitations and divine mystery. Though it is by no means a satisfactory answer to problems of intellectual inquiry, mystery is by definition the essence of the divine character. But in keeping with biblical wisdom's viewpoint and with the biblical depiction of structural divine absence in the cosmos, that sense of mystery also pertains to the world itself, at least as understood by human beings.

In summary, based on the Hebrew Bible's thoroughly relational depiction of God as established in part I of this study, the contours of parts II and III developed around the inherently spatial notion of divine absence as addressed in various biblical traditions dealing with cosmology, wisdom, worship, and geographic dimensions of narrative and prophecy. From these perspectives, the Hebrew Bible presents a variety of ways of relating to God within the spatial dimensions of life in this world. Accordingly, this study has illustrated how the Hebrew Bible through its various depictions of divine absence frames divine–human relationships in accordance with this very human understanding of existence.

In the status quo of various biblical portrayals, God is not obviously present though nonetheless is involved in the circumstances of daily life and in the events of larger history. On occasion, intense manifestations of God's presence occur, in theophany or miraculous deliverance. At times, though, an intense experience of God's absence deserves to be taken seriously. Human suffering and distress cannot be simply swept aside. Though the experience of God's apparent absence often occasions tremendous human pain and suffering, it also involves God's way of indwelling and relating to the world more broadly. In any case, this biblical theme consistently presents a God of mystery. Human relationships to the divine typically correlate with human experiences of weal and woe in life, but not always in predictable fashion. Through the theme of divine absence, the Hebrew Bible portrays a God who freely chooses relationships with humankind, a God whom human beings are free to seek, a God who responds.

NOTES

PREFACE

1. For secondary literature discussing various aspects of the theme of divine absence in these portions of the Hebrew Bible and offering further bibliography, see Gordon Wenham, *Genesis 16–50,* WBC 2 (Dallas: Word, 1994); Terence E. Fretheim, "The Book of Genesis: Introduction, Commentary, and Reflections," *NIB,* 1:320–674; Jon D. Levenson, *Esther: A Commentary,* OTL (Louisville: Westminster John Knox, 1997); Sidnie White Crawford, "The Book of Esther: Introduction, Commentary, and Reflections," *NIB,* 3:853–941; Lawrence M. Wills, *The Jew in the Court of the Foreign King: Ancient Jewish Court Legends,* HDR 26 (Minneapolis: Fortress Press, 1990); John J. Collins, *Daniel: A Commentary on the Book of Daniel,* Hermeneia (Minneapolis: Fortress Press, 1993); David L. Peterson, "Introduction to Prophetic Literature," *NIB,* 6:1–23; and the commentaries on various prophetic books found in the same volume and in *NIB* 7.

INTRODUCTION

1. For an excellent commentary on the book's poetry and a history of the book's interpretation, including additional bibliography, see J. Cheryl Exum, *Song of Songs: A Commentary,* OTL (Louisville: Westminster John Knox, 2005).

2. A sampling of the secondary literature includes Hubert Schrade, *Der Verborgene Gott: Gottesbild und Gottesvorstellung in Israel und im Alten Orient* (Stuttgart: Kohlhammer, 1949); Lothar Perlitt, "Die Verborgenheit Gottes," in *Probleme Biblischer Theologie,* ed. H. W. Wolff, 367–82 (Munich: Kaiser, 1971); Samuel E. Balentine, *The Hidden God: The Hiding of the Face of God in the Old Testament* (Oxford: Oxford University Press, 1983); Terence E. Fretheim, *The Suffering of God: An Old Testament Perspective,* OBT 14 (Philadelphia: Fortress Press, 1984), esp. 60–78; Gary A. Anderson, *A Time to Mourn, a Time to Dance: The Expression of Grief and Joy in Israelite Religion* (University Park: Pennsylvania State University Press, 1991), esp. 108–114; Erhard S. Gerstenberger, "'Where Is God?' The Cry of the Psalmists," in *Where Is God? A Cry of Human Distress,* ed. C. Duquoc and C. Floristan, 11–22, Concilium (London: SCM, 1992); John F. Kutsko, *Between Heaven and Earth: Divine Presence and Absence in the Book of Ezekiel,* Biblical and Judaic Studies 6 (Winona Lake, Ind.: Eisenbrauns, 2000); Steven S. Tuell, "Divine Presence and Absence in Ezekiel's Prophecy," in *The Book of Ezekiel: Theological and Anthropological Perspectives,* ed. Margaret

S. Odell and John T. Strong, 97–116, SBL Symposium Series 9 (Atlanta: Society of Biblical Literature, 2000) and written for a general readership; Richard E. Friedman, *The Disappearance of God: A Divine Mystery* (Boston: Little, Brown, 1995); also published as *The Hidden Face of God* (San Francisco: Harper, 1995, 1997); Amelia Devin Freedman, *God as an Absent Character in Biblical Hebrew Narrative: A Literary-Theoretical Study,* Studies in Biblical Literature 82 (New York: Lang, 2005).

3. Samuel Terrien, *The Elusive Presence: Toward a New Biblical Theology* (San Francisco: Harper & Row, 1978). See also Perlitt, "Die Verborgenheit Gottes," 367–82.

4. Balentine, *The Hidden God*; Brian L. Webster, "Divine Abandonment in the Hebrew Bible" (Ph.D. diss., Hebrew Union College–Jewish Institute of Religion, 2000).

5. A thorough overview of ancient Near Eastern texts illustrating various forms of this motif is provided by Thomas Podella, *Şôm-Fasten: Kollektive Trauer um den verborgenen Gott im Alten Testament,* AOAT 224 (Kevelaer: Butzon & Bercker, 1989), 33–70.

6. On Egyptian Amun, see Erik Hornung, *Conceptions of God in Ancient Egypt: The One and the Many,* trans. John Baines (Ithaca: Cornell University Press, 1982), 66. For a thorough list of cuneiform texts dealing with the pillaging and return of divine statues, see Kutsko, *Between Heaven and Earth,* 157–69. For discussion of various disappearing or dying gods in the ancient Near East, see Tryggve N. D. Mettinger, *The Riddle of the Resurrection: "Dying and Rising Gods" in the Ancient Near East,* ConBOT 50 (Stockholm: Almqvist & Wiksell, 2001).

7. See, e.g., Antti Laato and Johannes C. de Moor, eds., *Theodicy in the Biblical World* (Leiden: Brill, 2003); James L. Crenshaw, *Old Testament Wisdom: An Introduction,* 2nd ed. (Louisville: Westminster John Knox, 1998), 205–226; John G. Gammie and Leo G. Perdue, eds., *The Sage in Israel and the Ancient Near East* (Winona Lake, Ind.; Eisenbrauns, 1990), 1–271.

8. Deut 32:37; 2 Kings 2:14; Isa 63:11, 15; Jer 2:6, 8; Joel 2:17; Ps 42:3, 10; 79:10; 115:2; Job 35:10; consider also Judg 6:13.

9. See, e.g., Gale A. Yee, "Jezebel," *ABD,* 3:848–49. For more discussion and bibliography, see Joel S. Burnett, "Divine Absence in Biblical Personal Names," in *These Are the Names: Studies in Jewish Onomastics 5,* ed. Aaron Demsky (Ramat Gan, Israel: Bar-Ilan University Press, forthcoming), and chapter 2 below.

10. See also, elsewhere in the Baal cycle, the mourning of this deity by the question, *'i 'ap b'[l . . .] 'i hd* ("Where then is Baa[l]? . . . Where is Haddu?"; *KTU²* 1.5 IV: 6–7).

11. On this interrogative adjective/adverb and its grammatical use, see, for example, Edward Lipiński, *Semitic Languages: Outline of a Comparative Grammar,* OLA 80 (Leuven: Peeters, 2001), 336–37 sec. 36.59–60, 463 sec. 47.7. For its use in Biblical Hebrew, specifically, see GKC, 296–97 sec. 100 o 5, 475–76 sec. 150 l; Bruce Waltke and Michael O'Connor, *An Introduction to Biblical Hebrew Syntax* (Winona Lake, Ind.: Eisenbrauns, 1990), 318 par. 18.1f.

I. KNOWING GOD IN THE HEBREW BIBLE

1. See the collation and translation of *Atrahasis* in the standard edition of Wilfred G. Lambert and Alan R. Millard, *Atra-Ḥasis: The Babylonian Story of the Flood*, with Miguel Civil (Oxford: Clarendon, 1969; repr. Winona Lake, Ind.: Eisenbrauns, 1999), 59–63. For a convenient translation and more bibliography, see Benjamin R. Foster in *COS*, 1:450–53.

2. Compare the discussion in Lambert and Millard, *Atra-Ḥasis*, 21–22.

3. See, e.g., *ANEP*, 160–91 and the essays and illustrations collection in Neal H. Walls, ed., *Cult Image and Divine Representation in the Ancient Near East*, American Schools of Oriental Research Book Series 10 (Boston: American Schools of Oriental Research, 2005).

4. For a classic treatment of Mesopotamian religion that emphasizes human-like qualities of gods and goddesses, see Thorkild Jacobsen, *The Treasures of Darkness: A History of Mesopotamian Religion* (New Haven: Yale University Press, 1976), 23–164. For thorough treatment of anthropomorphic depictions of deities in artistic forms before the earliest written sources, see Silvia Schroer and Othmar Keel, *Die Ikonographie Palästinas/Israels und der Alte Orient: Eine Religionsgeschichte in Bildern*, vol. 1, *Vom ausgehenden Mesolithikum bis zur Frühbronzezeit* (Fribourg: Academic Press Fribourg, 2005).

5. See William H. Hallo, "Lamentations and Prayers in Sumer and Akkad," in *CANE*, 3:1871–81, esp. 1875–77; Karel van der Toorn, "God (I) אלהים," in *DDD*, 352–65, esp. 360–61; Mark S. Smith, *The Origins of Biblical Monotheism: Israel's Polytheistic Background and the Ugaritic Texts* (New York: Oxford University Press, 2001), 83–103.

6. As Lambert points out, "It is not a coincidence that most of the major deities of the Sumerians belong within three generations, which is precisely the state of affairs at any given time with a human clan." Wilfred G. Lambert, "The Historical Development of the Mesopotamian Pantheon: A Study in Sophisticated Polytheism," in *Unity and Diversity: Essays in the History, Literature, and Religion of the Ancient Near East*, ed. H. Goedicke and J. J. M. Roberts, 191–200 (Baltimore: Johns Hopkins University Press, 1975), esp. 192, 197.

7. James P. Allen, *Genesis in Egypt: The Philosophy of Ancient Egyptian Creation Accounts*, Yale Egyptological Studies 2 (San Antonio: Van Siclen Books for the Yale Egyptological Seminar, Yale University, 1995), esp. 8–35.

8. Smith, *The Origins of Biblical Monotheism*, 54–66.

9. See, for example, Jeremy Black and Anthony Green, eds., *Gods, Demons and Symbols of Ancient Mesopotamia: An Illustrated Dictionary*, illustrations by Tessa Rickards (Austin: University of Texas Press, 1992). In a careful study of Mesopotamian iconography from the mid-second to the mid-first millennium, Tallay Ornan tracks increasing suppression of anthropomorphic depictions of the divine in favor of depictions in the form of animals, composite creatures, and symbols. Tallay Ornan, *The Triumph of the Symbol: Pictorial Representation of Deities in Mesopotamia and the Biblical Image Ban* (Fribourg: Academic Free Press; Göttingen: Vandenhoeck & Ruprecht, 2005). In ancient Egyptian art, though deities were depicted in anthropomorphic form by the time of the first written sources, anthropomorphic depiction of deities never fully developed, as

deities were portrayed not only in human form but more regularly in theriomor-
phic, hybrid, or symbolic form. See, for example, Richard H. Wilkinson, *The
Complete Gods and Goddesses of Ancient Egypt* (London: Thames & Hudson,
2003), esp. 12–15. See also Stephen Quirke, *Ancient Egyptian Religion* (London,
British Museum Press, 1992), 14–16; and Gay Robins, "Cult Statues in Ancient
Egypt," in *Cult Image and Divine Representation in the Ancient Near East,*
ed. Neil H. Walls, 1–12, American Schools of Oriental Research Book Series 10
(Boston: American Schools of Oriental Research, 2005).

10. On this point, see Smith, *Origins of Biblical Monotheism*, 86–93,
102–103.

11. See the discussion in Lambert and Millard, *Atra-Ḥasis*, 15–25; and Jean
Bottéro, *Religion in Ancient Mesopotamia* (Chicago: University of Chicago
Press, 2001), 98–103. As Bernard Batto points out, in ancient Near Eastern myth,
divine rest represented the correct order of the world. Bernard F. Batto, "The
Sleeping God: An Ancient Near Eastern Motif of Divine Sovereignty," *Bib* 68
(1987): 153–77; and "Creation Theology in Genesis," in *Creation in the Biblical
Traditions,* ed. Richard J. Clifford and John J. Collins, 16–38, CBQMS (Wash-
ington, D.C.: Catholic Biblical Association of America, 1992), 33.

12. A. Leo Oppenheim and Erica Reiner, *Ancient Mesopotamia: Portrait of a
Dead Civilization* (Chicago: University of Chicago Press, 1977), 183–98.

13. See Wilfred G. Lambert, *Babylonian Wisdom Literature* (Oxford: Clar-
endon, 1960; repr. Winona Lake, Ind.: Eisenbrauns, 1996). For a discussion of
Mesopotamian, Syrian, and Egyptian wisdom literature, see the treatment by
James Crenshaw, *Old Testament Wisdom: An Introduction* (Louisville: Westmin-
ster John Knox, 1998), 205–26; and the essays collected in John G. Gammie and
Leo G. Perdue, eds., *The Sage in Israel and the Ancient Near East* (Winona Lake,
Ind.: Eisenbrauns, 1990). For more discussion and bibliography, see chapter 5.

14. Michael Barré, "'Fear of God' and the World View of Wisdom," *BTB* 11
(1981): 41–43.

15. For textual examples illustrating this basic dynamic of the relationship,
see J. J. M. Roberts, "Divine Freedom and Cultic Manipulation in Israel and
Mesopotamia," in *The Bible and the Ancient Near East: Collected Essays*, 72–82
(Winona Lake, Ind.: Eisenbrauns, 2002).

16. F. A. M. Wiggermann, "Theologies, Priests, and Worship in Ancient Mesopotamia" in *CANE*, 3:1857–70, esp. 1859–61; Bottéro, *Religion*, 36–41.

17. *Atrahasis* Tablets II–III. See also *The Epic of Gilgamesh* (Standard Babylonian Version) Tablet XI cols. i–iv. See the edition of Simo Parpola, *The Standard Babylonian Epic of Gilgamesh: Cuneiform Text, Transliteration, Glossary,
Indices and Sign List,* SAA 1 (Helsinki: The Neo-Assyrian Text Corpus Project,
1997). For a convenient translation of Tablet XI and more bibliography, see *COS,*
1:458–60.

18. Jacobsen, *The Treasures of Darkness*, 121.

19 See Karel van der Toorn, *Family Religion in Babylonia, Syria and Israel:
Continuity and Change in the Forms of Religious Life,* SHCANE 7 (Leiden: Brill,
1996), 66–93. Devotion to and identification with the god of the individual was
conventionally passed along patrilineal descent. Van der Toorn, *Family Religion*,
71–78; Hermann Vorländer, *Mein Gott: Die Vorstellungen vom persönlichen
Gott im Alten Orient und im Alten Testament,* AOAT 23 (Kevelaer: Butzon &
Bercker, 1975), 4, 7–8; Rainer Albertz, *Persönliche Frömmigkeit und offizielle*

Religion: Religionsinterner Pluralismus in Israel und Babylon, Calwer theologische Monographien 9 (Stuttgart: Calwer, 1978), 77–81, 88–91; Henri Cazelles,
"Der persönliche Gott Abrahams und der Gott des Volkes Israel," in *Der Weg
zum Menschen: Zur philologischen und theologischen Anthropologie für Alfons
Deissler,* ed. R. Mosis and L. Ruppert, 46–61 (Freiburg: Herder, 1988). A special class of patron deities in Mesopotamian religion are designated in Akkadian
by the terms *lamassu* and *šēdu.* See D. Foxvog, W. Heimpel, and A. D. Kilmer,
"Lamma/Lammassu," in *RlA,* 6:446–53.

20. See Lambert, "Historical Development," 196; Dennis Pardee, "Koshar
כשר," in *DDD,* 490–91; M. Heerma van Voss, "Ptah *פתוח / *פתח," in *DDD,*
668–69.

21. See Lambert, "Historical Development," 191–200, esp. 191–93; Wiggerman, "Theologies, Priests, and Worship," 1860; Sabatino Moscati, *The World of
the Phoenicians,* trans. Alastair Hamilton, Praeger History of Civilizations (New
York: Praeger, 1968), 31–34.

22. Georges Dossin, "Une lettre de Iarîm-Lim, roi d'Alep, à Iašûb-iaḫad, roi de
Dîr," *Syria* 33 (1956): 63–69; quoting 67 lines 27–28.

23. Van der Toorn, *Family Religion,* 76–77.

24. Lambert, "Historical Development," 191–200; Bottéro, *Religion,* 53–55;
Erik Hornung, *Conceptions of God in Ancient Egypt: The One and the Many*
(Ithaca, N.Y.: Cornell University Press, 1982), 223–26; Quirke, *Ancient Egyptian
Religion,* 70–103; Oliver R. Gurney, *Some Aspects of Hittite Religion* (Oxford:
Oxford University Press, 1977), 4–24; Oliver R. Gurney, *The Hittites* (1952;
repr., London: Penguin, 1990), 114–20; Volkert Haas, *Geschichte der hethitischen Religion,* HO Erste Abteilung 15 (Leiden: Brill, 1994), 35–37, 315–81,
616–39; Gregory McMahon, *The Hittite State Cult of the Tutelary Deities,* AS
25 (Chicago: Oriental Institute of the University of Chicago, 1991), esp. 1–6.

25. Both of them began as city gods. See Wiggerman, "Theologies, Priests,
and Worship," 1860; Daniel I. Block, *The Gods of the Nations: Studies in
Ancient Near Eastern National Theology,* 2nd ed. (Grand Rapids: Baker Academic, 2000); Steven W. Holloway, *Assur Is King! Assur Is King! Religion in the
Exercise of Power in the Neo-Assyrian Empire,* CHANE 10 (Leiden: Brill, 2002).

26. See Jonas C. Greenfield, "The Aramean God Rammān/Rimmōn," *IEJ* 26
(1976): 195–98; J. C. Greenfield, "Hadad הדד," in *DDD,* 377–82; Gerald L.
Mattingly, "Moabite Religion," in *Studies in the Mesha Inscription and Moab,*
ed. Andrew Dearman, 213–38, Archaeology and Biblical Studies 2 (Atlanta:
Scholars, 1989); John R. Bartlett, *Edom and the Edomites* (Sheffield: Sheffield
Academic, 1989), 200–207; E. A. Knauf, "Qôs קוש," in *DDD,* 674–77; Jeffrey H.
Tigay, *You Shall Have No Other Gods: Israelite Religion in the Light of Hebrew
Inscriptions,* HSS 31 (Atlanta: Scholars, 1986), 19–20.

27. See *KAI,* 2:34, 225; John C. L. Gibson, *Textbook of Syrian Semitic
Inscriptions,* 3 vols. (Oxford: Clarendon, 1971–82), 2:80–81, 3:34–35. For a
recent English translation of Kulamuwa's inscription, see K. Lawson Younger Jr.
in *COS* 2:147–48; Karel van der Toorn, "Rakib-El," in *DDD,* 686–87.

28. See, e.g., Lothar Perlitt, *Bundestheologie im Alten Testament,* WMANT
36 (Neukirchen-Vluyn: Neukirchener, 1969), esp. 49–54; and the rendering of
the term into English in Dennis J. McCarthy, *Treaty and Covenant: A Study in
Form in the Ancient Oriental Documents and in the Old Testament,* AnBib 21a
(Rome: Pontifical Biblical Institute, 1981), 22 n. 42.

29. Lawrence E. Stager, "The Patrimonial Kingdom of Solomon," in *Symbiosis, Symbolism, and the Power of the Past: Canaan, Ancient Israel, and Their Neighbors from the Late Bronze Age through Roman Palaestina*, ed. William G. Dever and Seymour Gitin, 63–74 (Winona Lake, Ind.: Eisenbrauns, 2003), 69. In Old Babylonian and Iron Age West Semitic name seals, individuals (presumably of high status) identify themselves as "servant" only of gods and kings. See the appendix "The Significance of the Title *'Ebed* in Northwest Semitic Seals and Seal Impressions," in Lawrence J. Mykytiuk, *Identifying Biblical Persons in Northwest Semitic Inscriptions of 1200–539 B.C.E.*, Academia Biblica 12 (Atlanta: Society of Biblical Literature, 2004), 207–10.

30. Nahman Avigad and Benjamin Sass, *Corpus of West Semitic Stamp Seals* (Jerusalem: Israel Academy of Sciences and Humanities; Israel Exploration Society; Institute of Archaeology, Hebrew Union University of Jerusalem, 1997), 49–50 seal no. 2.

31. Carol Meyers suggests the notion of heterarchy not as a denial that hierarchy was a basic dynamic in Israelite society but as a more nuanced conception that accounts for various relationships sometimes cutting across the formal hierarchical structures of Israelite society, including "guilds" and "professional" associations of women. Carol Meyers, "Hierarchy or Heterarchy? Archaeology and the Theorizing of Israelite Society," in *Confronting the Past: Archaeological and Historical Essays on Ancient Israel in Honor of William G. Dever*, ed. William G. Dever, Seymour Gitin, J. Edward Wright, and J. P. Dessel, 245–54 (Winona Lake, Ind.: Eisenbrauns, 2006). In this connection, Meyers criticizes the scholarly characterization of Israelite society by the term *patriarchy*, partly as an overgeneralization and partly as an anachronistic designation that risks importing into an ancient setting modern Western concepts of social organization (see esp. pp. 245–49). While the latter concern at least equally applies to Meyers's own discussion of Israelite women's "guilds" and "professional" associations, both points are well taken. Even so, a broader (rather than absolute) notion of patriarchy seems fitting in reference to the formal structuring of Israelite society around the roles and prerogatives of males, as consistently expressed in texts but also as observed in the archaeological record (see the next two sections for the discussion of evidence Stager adduces for patrimonial social organization in Israelite society). For more on Meyers's point, see also Carol L. Meyers, "Contesting the Notion of Patriarchy: Anthropology and the Theorizing of Gender in Ancient Israel," in *The Question of Sex? Gender and Difference in the Hebrew Bible and Beyond*, ed. Deborah W. Rooke, 83–105, Hebrew Bible Monographs 14 (Sheffield: Sheffield Phoenix, 2007).

32. S. Bendor, *The Social Structure of Ancient Israel: The Institution of the Family (beit 'ab) from the Settlement to the End of the Monarchy* (Jerusalem: Simor, 1996).

33. Bendor, *The Social Structure of Ancient Israel*, 48–53; Philip J. King and Lawrence E. Stager, *Life in Biblical Israel* (Louisville: Westminster John Knox, 2001), 4–5.

34. See Carol Meyers, "Families in Ancient Israel," in *Families in Ancient Israel*, ed. Leo G. Perdue et al., 1–47 (Louisville: Westminster John Knox, 1997), 17, 19; and Joseph Blenkinsopp, "The Family in First Temple Israel," in Perdue, *Families in Ancient Israel*, 48–103, here 52. The anthropologist Gillian Feely-Harnick discusses the ambiguous status of slaves in the Hebrew Bible as

representing the antithesis of kinship yet having the ability to be incorporated into kinship structures. See Gillian Feeley-Harnick, "Is Historical Anthropology Possible? The Case of the Runaway Slave," in *Humanizing America's Iconic Book,* ed. Gene M. Tucker and Douglas A. Knight, 95–126 (Chico, Calif.: Scholars, 1982).

35. See Van der Toorn, *Family Religion in Babylonia, Syria and Israel,* 66–93, 255–57.

36. Lawrence E. Stager, "The Archaeology of the Family in Ancient Israel," *BASOR* 260 (1985): 1–35; Stager, "Patrimonial Kingdom," 70–71.

37. Daniel Master, "State Formation Theory and the Kingdom of Israel," *JNES* 60 (2001): 117–31, here 128–29.

38. Ibid., 128–31.

39. Ibid., 129.

40. King and Stager, *Life in Biblical Israel,* 39–40.

41. See, for example, Eveline J. van der Steen, "Tribes and Power Structures in Palestine and the Transjordan," *NEA* 69, no. 1 (2006): 27–47. See also Piotr Bienkowski and Eveline van der Steen, "Tribes, Trade, and Towns: A New Framework for the Late Iron Age in Southern Jordan and the Negev," *BASOR* 323 (2001): 21–47, esp. 28–29; and for a more extensive study, Eveline J. van der Steen, *Tribes and Territories in Transition,* OLA 130 (Leuven: Peeters, 2004); Øystein LaBianca, "Salient Features of Iron Age Tribal Kingdoms," in *Ancient Ammon,* ed. Burton Macdonald and Randall W. Younker, 19–29 (Leiden: Brill, 1999).

42. See the review of scholarship and viewpoint offered by Israel Finkelstein, "The Emergence of the Monarchy: The Environmental and Socio-Economic Aspects," in *Community, Identity, and Ideology: Social Science Approaches to the Hebrew Bible,* ed. Charles E. Carter and Carol L. Meyers, 377–403 (Winona Lake, Ind.: Eisenbrauns, 1996), esp. 380–81. See also Niels Peter Lemche, "From Patronage Society to Patronage Society," in *Origins of the Ancient Israelite States,* ed. Vokmar Fritz and Philip R. Davies, 106–120 (Sheffield: Sheffield Academic, 1996); Alexander H. Joffe, "The Rise of Secondary States in the Iron Age Levant," *JESHO* 45 (2002): 425–67, esp. 426.

43. Roland de Vaux, *Ancient Israel* (New York: McGraw-Hill, 1961), 133–35; G. Ernest Wright, "The Provinces of Solomon," in *ErIsr* 8 (E. L. Sukenik Volume), ed. N. Avigad et al., 58*–68* (Jerusalem: Israel Exploration Society, 1967). Compare Baruch Halpern, "Sectionalism and the Schism," *JBL* 93 (1974): 519–32, esp. 528–31.

44. See Lester L. Grabbe, *Ancient Israel: What Do We Know and How Do We Know It?* (London: T&T Clark, 2007), 105–107.

45. See Philip S. Khoury and Joseph Kostiner, "Introduction: Tribes and the Complexities of State Formation in the Middle East," in *Tribes and State Formation in the Middle East,* ed. Philip S. Khoury and Joseph Kostiner, 1–22 (Berkeley: University of California Press, 1990), esp. 3–4; Richard Tapper, "Anthropologists, Historians, and Tribespeople on Tribe and State Formation in the Middle East," in Khoury and Kostiner, *Tribes and State Formation,* 48–73, esp. 49–57; Bassam Tibi, "Simultaneity of the Unsimultaneous: Old Tribes and Imposed Nation-States in the Modern Middle East," in Khoury and Kostiner, *Tribes and State Formation,* 127–52; Thomas Barfield, "Tribe and State Relations: The Inner Asian Perspective," in Khoury and Kostiner, *Tribes and State*

Formation, 153–82, esp. 164–75. See also Master's discussion of this literature; Master, "State Formation Theory," 127–28.

46. Zecharia Kallai, "The Twelve-Tribe Systems of Israel," *VT* 47 (1997): 53–90; idem, "A Note on the Twelve-Tribe Systems of Israel," *VT* 49 (1999): 125–27.

47. Master, "State Formation Theory," 127–30.

48. Stager, "The Archaeology of the Family," 11–23.

49. Ibid., 25–27.

50. Ibid., 24–25; idem, "The Patrimonial Kingdom," 68–69.

51. Stager, "The Patrimonial Kingdom," 70.

52. See Paul E. Dion, "Aramaean Tribes and Nations of First-Millennium Western Asia," in *CANE*, 2:1281–94; on this point, 1286.

53. J. David Schloen, *The House of the Father as Fact and Symbol: Patrimonialism in Ugarit and the Ancient Near East,* Studies in the Archaeology and History of the Levant 2 (Winona Lake, Ind.: Eisenbrauns, 2001), 255–316. Although for Schloen the patrimonial household model was foundational for the whole of the Bronze Age Near East, it might not explain all social, political, and economic relations in all locations. See the review and discussion of cuneiform evidence from Mari and Emar by Daniel E. Fleming, "Schloen's Patrimonial Pyramid: Explaining Bronze Age Society," *BASOR* 328 (2002): 73–80.

54. J. M. Munn-Rankin, "Diplomacy in Western Asia in the Early Second Millennium," *Iraq* 18 (1956): 68–110, esp. 76–84; William L. Moran, "The Ancient Near Eastern Background of the Love of God in Deuteronomy," *CBQ* 25 (1963): 77–87; Hayim Tadmor, "Treaty and Oath in the Ancient Near East: A Historian's Approach," in *Humanizing America's Iconic Book,* ed. Gene M. Tucker and Douglas A. Knight, 127–52 (Chico, Calif.: Scholars, 1982), esp. 131–32; Mario Liverani, "The Great Powers' Club," in *Amarna Diplomacy: The Beginnings of International Relations,* ed. Raymond Cohen and Raymond Westbrook, 15–27 (Baltimore: Johns Hopkins University Press, 2000), esp. 18–19; Samuel A. Meier, "Diplomacy and International Marriages," in Cohen and Westbrook, *Amarna Diplomacy,* 165–73; Mark S. Smith, *God in Translation: Deities in Cross-Cultural Discourse in the Biblical World,* FAT 57 (Tübingen: Mohr Siebeck, 2008), 76–81. For the Amarna Letters in English, see William L. Moran, *The Amarna Letters* (Baltimore: Johns Hopkins University Press, 1992).

55. Schloen, *The House of the Father,* 316.

56. Stager, "Patrimonial Kingdom," 71.

57. Karel van der Toorn (*Family Religion,* 266–86) argues that Yahweh became Israel's chief God primarily because of the Yahwistic family lineage of its first king, Saul. Yet the Song of Deborah (Judges 5), regarded as one of the earliest portions of the Hebrew Bible, describes premonarchic Israel already as a group of tribes centered around allegiance to Yahweh, "the God Israel" (vv. 3, 5). See Mark S. Smith, *The Early History of God: Yahweh and the Other Deities in Ancient Israel,* 2nd ed., Biblical Resource Series (Grand Rapids: Eeerdmans; Dearborn, Mich.: Dove, 2002), 184–85.

58. The Hebrew Bible follows suit, almost always referring to the Ammonites as *běnê ʿammôn* (for example, Gen 19:38; Num 21:24). For more discussion of these points, including the name's implications for the kin-based social structure of the Ammonite kingdom, see Paul-Eugene Dion, "The Ammonites: A Historical Sketch," in *Excavations at Tall Jawa, Jordan,* vol. 1, *The Iron Age Town,* ed. P. M. Michèle Daviau, 481–518, CHANE 11/1 (Leiden: Brill, 2003), 481–85.

59. See the translation and further bibliography provided by Walter E. Aufrecht in *COS*, 2:139–40.

60. See E. Puech, "Milcom מלכם," in *DDD*, 575–76.

61. See Kent P. Jackson and J. Andrew Dearman, "The Text of the Mesha᾽ Inscription," in *Studies in the Mesha Inscription and Moab*, ed. J. Andrew Dearman, 93–95 (Atlanta: Scholars, 1989), and the translation and further bibliography provided by K. A. D. Smelik in *COS*, 2:137–38.

62. Martti Nissinen, *Prophets and Prophecy in the Ancient Near East*, with contributions by C. L. Seow and Robert K. Ritner, ed. Peter Machinist, 17–21, SBLWAW 12 (Atlanta: Society of Biblical Literature, 2003). For earlier publication and discussion of the text, see A. Lods and G. Dossin, "Une tablette inédite de Mari, intéressante pour l'histoire ancienne du prophétisme sémitique," in *Studies in Old Testament Prophecy Presented to Professor Theodore H. Robinson*, ed. H. H. Rowley, 103–110 (Edinburgh: T&T Clark, 1957), 103–106; Bertrand Lafont, "Le roi de Mari et les prophètes du dieu Adad," *RA* 78 (1984): 7–18.

63. Nissinen's translation (*Prophets and Prophecy in the Ancient Near East*, 19).

64. For various forms of evidence that Israelites worshiped a plurality of deities, see Ziony Zevit, *The Religions of Ancient Israel: A Synthesis of Parallactic Approaches* (New York: Continuum, 2001).

65. Van der Steen, "Tribes and Power Structures," 28.

66. The etymology of the Hebrew *bĕrît* remains elusive. Of a number of possibilities advanced, the most compelling explanation for the word's derivation is in comparison with Akkadian *birītu* ("clasp," "fetter"), which corresponds in meaning to Akkadian *riksu* and Hittite *išḫiul*, both meaning "bond" and both serving as regular terms for treaty. In Aramaic texts, the term usually understood to refer to treaties and oaths is *ʿdt*. For these points and for other possibilities for the etymology of *bĕrît*, see James Barr, "Some Semantic Notes on the Covenant," in *Beiträge zur alttestamentlichen Theologie: Festschrift für Walther Zimmerli zum 70. Geburtstag*, ed. Herbert Donner, Robert Hanhart, and Rudolf Smend, 23–38 (Göttingen: Vandenhoeck & Ruprecht, 1977); Moshe Weinfeld, "בְּרִית; *berîth*," in *TDOT*, 2:253–79.

67. George E. Mendenhall, "Covenant," in *IDB*, 1:714–23, here 714–15; George E. Mendenhall and Gary A. Herion, "Covenant," in *ABD*, 1:1179–1202, here 1179–80. This aspect of covenant as mentioned in biblical literature was recognized very early on; see Richard Kraetzschmar, *Die Bundesvorstellung im Alten Testament in ihrer geschichtlichen Entwickelung* (Marburg: Elwert, 1896), 29–41. Nicholson discusses the range of English terms that define *covenant* depending on context: "treaty, pact, agreement, solemn promise, obligation, etc." Ernest W. Nicholson, *God and His People: Covenant and Theology in the Old Testament* (New York: Oxford University Press, 1986), 104–105.

68. Robert A. Oden Jr., "The Place of Covenant in the Religion of Israel," in *Ancient Israelite Religion*, ed. Patrick D. Miller, Paul D. Hanson, and S. Dean McBride, 429–49 (Philadelphia: Fortress Press, 1987), 434.

69. Walther Eichrodt, *Theology of the Old Testament*, trans. J. A. Baker, 2 vols. (Philadelphia: Westminster, 1961–67), trans. of *Theologie des Alten Testaments*, 6th Germ. ed. (Stuttgart: Ehrenfried Klotz, 1959; orig. pub. Leipzig: J. C. Hinrichsm, 1933–39).

70. Wellhausen had contended that the Israelite concept of covenant was a relatively late development and that its importance was confined to its place as

a literary phenomenon with no institutional basis in Israel's history. See Julius
Wellhausen, *Prolegomena to the History of Ancient Israel* (New York: Meridian,
1957), 342–419, originally published as *Prolegomena zur Geschichte Israels*
(Berlin: G. Reimer, 1883); similarly, Lothar Perlitt, *Bundestheologie im Alten
Testament*, Wissenschaftliche Monographien zum Alten und Neuen Testament
(Neukirchen-Vluyn: Neukirchener, 1969). Nicholson, who concludes that the
search for an institutional basis for biblical covenant is a dead end, represents
something of a return to Wellhausen's position (*God and His People*, 83–117).
For criticisms of the view of covenant as a late idea in Israelite religion and litera-
ture, see Barr, "Some Semantic Notes on the Covenant," 23–38, esp. 37–38.

71. George E. Mendenhall, "Covenant Forms in Israelite Tradition," *BA* 17
(1954): 50–76; Moshe Weinfeld, "Traces of Treaty Formulae in Deuteronomy,"
Bib 41 (1965): 417–27; Klaus Baltzer, *The Covenant Formulary in Old Testa-
ment, Jewish, and Early Christian Writings* (Philadelphia: Fortress Press, 1971);
Dennis J. McCarthy, *Treaty and Covenant: A Study in Form in the Ancient
Oriental Documents and in the Old Testament*, 2nd ed., AnBib 21a (Rome:
Pontifical Biblical Institute, 1981). The suggestion that covenant was rooted in
early Israel's tribal life was made by William Robertson Smith in *Lectures on the
Religion of the Semites: The Fundamental Institutions*, 3rd ed. (London: A&C
Black, 1927), 318–19 and n. 2. Von Rad, noting the structure of Exodus 19–24,
argued for its origin in an early Israelite covenant renewal ceremony. See Gerhard
von Rad, "The Form-Critical Problem of the Hexateuch," in Gerhard von Rad,
From Genesis to Chronicles: Explorations in Old Testament Theology, ed. K. C.
Hanson, trans. E. W. Trueman Dicken, 1–58 (Minneapolis: Fortress Press, 2005),
16–31, esp. 21.

72. Moshe Weinfeld, "The Covenant of Grant in the Old Testament and in
the Ancient Near East," *JAOS* 90 (1970): 184–203; idem, *Deuteronomy and the
Deuteronomic School* (Winona Lake, Ind.: Eisenbrauns, 1992); idem, "The Loyalty Oath in the Ancient Near East," *UF* 8 (1976): 379–414.

73. Weinfeld, "The Covenant of Grant," 184–85.

74. Ibid., 185–88.

75. Ibid., 192.

76. Ibid., 187, citing, respectively, Vincent Scheil, *Actes juridiques*, Mémoires
de la Mission Archéologique de Perse/Mémoires [de la] Délégation en Perse 24
(Paris: Leroux, 1933), 3:379 lines 7–8; Emil Gottlieb Kraeling, *The Brooklyn
Museum Aramaic Papyri: New Documents of the Fifth Century* B.C. *from the
Jewish Colony at Elephantine* (New Haven: Yale, 1953), 9:16–17.

77. Weinfeld, "The Covenant of Grant," 190, citing Edward Chiera, Robert
H. Pfeiffer, Theophile James Meek, eds., *Excavations at Nuzi*, vol. 1, *Texts of
Varied Contents* (Cambridge: Harvard University Press, 1929), 1:73, lines 1–28.

78. Gary N. Knoppers, "Ancient Near Eastern Royal Grants and the Davidic
Covenant: A Parallel?" *JAOS* 116 (1996): 670–97.

79. Paul Kalluveettil, *Declaration and Covenant: A Comprehensive Review of
Covenant Formulae from the Old Testament and the Ancient Near East*, AnBib
88 (Rome: Pontifical Biblical Institute, 1982), 205, 209–12; Frank Moore Cross,
"Kinship and Covenant in Ancient Israel," in *From Epic to Canon: History and
Literature in Ancient Israel*, 3–21 (Baltimore: Johns Hopkins University Press,
1998), 11; see also Mark S. Smith, "'Your People Shall Be My People': Family and
Covenant in Ruth 1:16-17," *CBQ* 69 (2007): 242–58, here 253–55.

80. Kalluveettil, *Declaration and Covenant*, 6–9.

81. Mendenhall, "Covenant," 717.

82. Cross, "Kinship and Covenant," 9.

83. The notion of two parties declaring themselves "as one," that is, as a single political entity, is one of a variety of treaty-covenant expressions attested in biblical and comparative texts. Kalluveettil, *Declaration and Covenant*, 102–103; Smith, "'Your People Shall Be My People,'" 247–52). As scholars have repeatedly pointed out, the word *běrît* need not be present in order for covenant concepts to be operative in biblical texts. See Delbert R. Hillers, *Covenant: The History of a Biblical Idea*, Seminars in the History of Ideas (Baltimore: Johns Hopkins University Press, 1969), 4–5; Kalluveettil, *Declaration and Covenant*, 3; Steven L. McKenzie, "The Typology of the Davidic Covenant," in *The Land that I Will Show You: Essays on the History and Archaeology of the Ancient Near East in Honour of J. Maxwell Miller*, ed. J. Andrew Dearman and M. Patrick Graham, 152–78, JSOTSup 343 (Sheffield: Sheffield Academic, 2001), 155–56.

84. Cross, "Kinship and Covenant," 3–4.

85. See Mendenhall and Herion, "Covenant," 1180; Smith, *God in Translation*, 51–81.

86. See Hillers, *Covenant: The History of a Biblical Idea*, 6–7.

87. Theodore J. Lewis, "The Identity and Function of El/Baal Berith," *JBL* 115 (1996): 401–23, here 403–10; Theodore J. Lewis, "Covenant and Blood Rituals: Understanding Exodus 24:3-8 in Its Ancient Near Eastern Context," in *Confronting the Past: Archaeological and Historical Essays on Ancient Israel in Honor of William G. Dever*, ed. Seymour Gitin, J. Edward Wright, and J. P. Dessel, 341–50 (Winona Lake, Ind.: Eisenbrauns, 2006), esp. 341. In the latter essay, Lewis discusses ritual and symbolism accompanying human and divine–human covenants.

88. The Arslan Tash amulets were recovered from the antiquities market and lack archeological context, a generally problematic circumstance for ancient evidence. With reference to the objects' material, script, and especially their iconography, Teixidor and Amiet have raised doubts about the amulets' authenticity. Javier Teixidor and P. Amiet, "Les tablettes d'Arslan Tash au Musée d'Alep," *AuOr* 1 (1983): 105–109. However, responses have come from a number of scholars who have not found these arguments convincing, including epigraphers who note the provincial and informal nature of the inscription and accordingly the reasonable consistency of the script with known paleographic sequences. As Cross points out, it is highly unlikely that the knowledge of paleography, language, and contents necessary to produce a forgery of this order would have been available at the time of the inscriptions' discovery in 1933. See Frank Moore Cross and Richard J. Saley, "Phoenician Incantations on a Plaque of the Seventh Century BCE from Arslan Tash in Upper Syria," in *Leaves from an Epigrapher's Notebook: Collected Papers in Hebrew and West Semitic Palaeography and Epigraphy*, ed. F. M. Cross, 265–69 (Winona Lake, Ind.: Eisenbrauns, 2003), 269; Jacobus van Dijk, "The Authenticity of the Arslan Tash Amulets," *Iraq* 54 (1992): 65–68; Dennis Pardee, "Les documents d'Arslan Tash: authentique ou faux?" *Syria* 75 (1998): 15–54.

89. The translation is that of P. Kyle McCarter in *COS*, 2:222–23, text 2.86.

90. Lewis, "The Identity and Function of El/Baal Berith," 408. Alternatively, Meindert Dijkstra understands that "the Old Semitic deity Ilabrat is meant." See

Meindert Dijkstra, "The Ugaritic-Hurrian Sacrificial Hymn to El (RS 24.278 = KTU 1.128)," *UF* 25 (1993): 157–62, here 161.

91. Lewis, "The Identity and Function of El/Baal Berith," 401–23.

92. As implied by ʿammô, reading *milkōm* ("Milcom"), as reflected in the Septuagint, Syriac, and Vulgate instead of MT *malkām* ("their king").

93. Cross, "Kinship and Covenant," 12–13.

94. On this point, see Mark S. Smith, *The Memoirs of God: History, Memory, and the Experience of the Divine in Ancient Israel* (Minneapolis: Fortress Press, 2004), 38–39.

95. Regarding the Merneptah inscription, for an overview of scholarship and a cautious approach to connecting the "Israel" of this inscription with the Israel known from the Hebrew Bible and later inscriptions, see J. Maxwell Miller and John H. Hayes, *A History of Ancient Israel and Judah*, 2nd ed. (Louisville: Westminster John Knox, 2006), 39–42.

2. KNOWN BY GOD IN BIBLICAL PERSONAL NAMES

1. See the early studies by Eberhard Nestle, *Die israelitischen Eigennamen nach ihrer Religionsgeschichtlichen Bedeutung* (Haarlem: Bohn, 1876); George Buchanan Gray, *Studies in Hebrew Proper Names* (London: A&C Black, 1896); Martin Noth, *Die israelitischen Personennamen im Rahmen der gemeinsemitischen Namengebung* (Stuttgart: Kohlhammer, 1928); Rainer Albertz, *Persönliche Frömmigkeit und offizielle Religion: Religionsinterner Pluralismus in Israel und Babylon,* Calwer theologische Monographien 9 (Stuttgart: Calwer, 1978), 49–77; Jeffrey H. Tigay, *You Shall Have No Other Gods: Israelite Religion in the Light of Hebrew Inscriptions,* HSS 31 (Atlanta: Scholars, 1986); Jeaneane D. Fowler, *Theophoric Personal Names in Ancient Hebrew: A Comparative Study,* JSOTSup 49 (Sheffield: Sheffield Academic, 1988); Ran Zadok, *The Pre-Hellenistic Israelite Anthroponomy and Prosopography,* OLA 28 (Leuven: Peeters, 1988).

2. See Tigay, *You Shall Have No Other Gods,* 5–6.

3. See ibid., 5–7.

4. André Caquot, "Sur l'onomastique religieuse de Palmyre," *Syria* 39 (1962): 256. Compare Fowler's attempt to demonstrate that personal names express specific and distinctive ideas about different gods, particularly in the case of Israelite personal names. Fowler, *Theophoric Personal Names in Ancient Hebrew.* Though Fowler succeeded in demonstrating characterizations that might have been missing from the Israelite onomasticon, doing so only shows what might be expected in any case—namely, subtle differences from one language group to the next among various Semitic-speaking peoples.

5. See Daniel David Luckenbill, *The Annals of Sennacherib,* OIP 2 (Chicago: University of Chicago Press, 1924), 30, col. ii:56; and the translation by Mordechai Cogan in *COS* 2:302–303.

6. For this Edomite name, see John R. Bartlett, *Edom and the Edomites,* JSOTSup 77 (Sheffield: Sheffield Academic, 1989), 205.

7. See, e.g., Gen 4:1, 25; 5:29; 16:11; 21:3, 6; 25:25-26; 29:32-35; 30:6-24; 35:16-18; 41:50-52; Exod 2:22; Judg 13:24; 1 Sam 1:20; 2 Sam 12:24. For examples of children being named by someone other than the parents, see Ruth 4:17 and 2 Sam 12:25.

8. On the nature of biblical "folk etymologies" of personal names, see the discussion later in this chapter.

9. Joel S. Burnett, "Divine Absence in Biblical Personal Names," in *These Are the Names: Studies in Jewish Onomastics*, vol. 5, ed. Aaron Demsky (Ramat Gan, Israel: Bar-Ilan University Press, forthcoming).

10. Influential early studies of Hebrew personal names, especially those of George Buchanan Gray and Martin Noth, appeared before the relevant extra-biblical data had been brought into connection with the biblical names (see later in this chapter) and thus offer only ad hoc explanations for some of these names, and for others, no explanation at all. Gray, *Studies in Hebrew Proper Names*, 26 n. 4, 88, 102, 246 n. 1; Noth, *Die israelitischen Personennamen*, 11, 230, 235, 236. Though it was published much later, Jeaneane D. Fowler's study likewise fails to account for the possibility of "Where?" names in the Israelite onomasticon. Fowler, *Theophoric Personal Names in Ancient Hebrew*, 151, 155. But see more recent works including Ran Zadok, "Historical and Onomastic Notes," *WO* 9 (1977): 35–56; Zadok, *The Pre-Hellenistic Israelite Anthroponomy and Prosopography*, 58; Baruch Halpern, "Ehud," in *ABD*, 2:414.

11. William F. Albright, "The Egyptian Empire in Asia in the Twenty-First Century b.c.," *JPOS* 8 (1928): 239; "Northwest-Semitic Names in a List of Egyptian Slaves from the Eighteenth Century b.c.," *JAOS* 74 (1954): 225–27; "An Ostracon from Calah and the North-Israelite Diaspora," *BASOR* 149 (1958): 34 and n. 12. A number of these names from biblical and comparative sources were identified and grouped together earlier by Fritz Hommel, though he did not offer a viable explanation for the initial name element. See Fritz Hommel, *Ethnologie und Geographie des Alten Orients* (Munich: Beck, 1927), 95–96; cf. William F. Albright, "The Biblical Tribe of Massaʾ and Some Congeners," *Studi orientalistici in onore di Giorgio Levi Della Vida* (Rome: Istituto per l'Oriente, 1956), 5 n. 4. For the recognition of this name type in cuneiform sources by other scholars earlier in the twentieth century, see the comments of Albrecht Goetze cited by Elizabeth Douglas van Buren, "A Cylinder Seal with a History," *JCS* 5 (1951): 133–34, and see Benno Landsberger, "Assyrische Königsliste und 'Dunkles Zeitalter'," *JCS* 8 (1954): 47–73, here 60 and n. 126.

12. On this interrogative adjective/adverb and its grammatical use, see, for example, Edward Lipiński, *Semitic Languages: Outline of a Comparative Grammar*, OLA 80 (Leuven: Peeters, 2001) 336–37, 463.

13. For the names summarized here, see Landsberger, "Assyrische Königsliste," 60 and n. 126; Albright, "Northwest-Semitic Names," 225–27; Albright, "An Ostracon from Calah," 34 and n. 12; Herbert B. Huffmon, *Amorite Personal Names in the Mari Texts: A Structural and Lexical Study* (Baltimore: Johns Hopkins Press, 1965), 21, 101–102, 161; Frauke Gröndahl, *Die Personennamen der Texte aus Ugarit*, Studia Pohl 1 (Rome: Pontifical Biblical Institute, 1967), 48, 93–94; *CAD* A I 220, 224, 226–27, 231–38; Ignace J. Gelb, *Computer-Aided Analysis of Amorite*, AS 21 (Chicago: Oriental Institute of the University of Chicago, 1980), 13, 208–209; Gregorio del Olmo Lete and Joaquín Sanmartín, *A Dictionary of the Ugaritic Language in the Alphabetic Tradition*, trans. Wilfred G. E. Watson, HO 1.67 (Leiden: Brill, 2003), 1:133–36; Michael P. Streck, *Das amurritische Onomastikon der altbabylonischen Zeit*, vol. 1, *Die Amurriter, Die onomastische Forschung, Orthographie, und Phonologie, Nominalmorphologie* (Münster: Ugarit-Verlag, 2000), 154, 183, 233, 244, 248, and esp. 232;

Ran Zadok, "On the Amorite Material from Mesopotamia," in *The Tablet and the Scroll: Near Eastern Studies in Honor of William W. Hallo,* ed. Mark E. Cohen et al., 315–33 (Bethesda, Md.: CDL, 1993), 320; Regine Pruzsinszky, *Die Personennamen der Texte aus Emar,* ed. D. I. Owen and G. Wilhelm, Studies on the Civilization and Culture of Nuzi and the Hurrians 13 (Bethesda, Md.: CDL, 2003), 217 and n. 635. For even earlier names of this type from Ebla, see Manfred Krebernik, *Die Personennamen der Ebla-Texte: Eine Zwischenbilanz,* Berliner Beiträge zum vorderen Orient 7 (Berlin: Dietrich Reimer, 1988), 115.

14. On the use of kinship terms as divine elements in second-millennium personal names, see H. B. Huffmon, "Brother אח," in *DDD* 178–79; Huffmon, *Amorite Personal Names,* 101.

15. On *šm/sm* ("name") as a theophorous element in West Semitic personal names, see Huffmon, *Amorite Personal Names,* 100–101, 104–117; Frank L. Benz, *Personal Names in the Phoenician and Punic Inscriptions: A Catalog, Grammatical Study and Glossary of Elements,* Studia Pohl 8 (Rome: Biblical Institute Press, 1972), 419; Mark S. Smith, "Remembering God: Collective Memory in Israelite Religion," *CBQ* 62 (2002): 641–43; Frank M. Cross, "Newly Found Inscriptions in Old Canaanite and Early Phoenician Scripts," *BASOR* 238 (1980): 1–20; repr. in Frank M. Cross, "Newly Found Inscriptions in Old Canaanite and Early Phoenician Scripts," in *Leaves from an Epigrapher's Notebook: Collected Papers in Hebrew and West Semitic Paleography and Epigraphy* (Winona Lake, Ind.: Eisenbrauns, 2003), 216.

16. Gröndahl, in *Die Personennamen der Texte aus Ugarit,* 94, suggests that *tlm* is either the Hurrian *talami* ("to be great") or the name of a deity.

17. For *tr* ("bull") as an epithet of the god El at Ugarit, see *KTU²* 1.1 V 22; 1.2 I 16, 33, 36; 1.3 IV 54; 1.3 V 35; 1.4 I 4; 1.14 I 41.

18. Cross, "Newly Found Inscriptions," 213–30.

19. Johann Jakob Stamm, *Die Akkadische Namengebung* (Darmstadt: Wissenschaftliche Buchgesellschaft, 1968), 90–91, 165, 284–87; *CAD* A I 339.

20. For *y bʿlym,* see the vocalization *ī Baʿalīm by Krahmalkov, who understands it to contain a plural form with singular meaning and who invokes in this connection BH *bʿlym* in Judg 2:11; 3:7; 8:33; 1 Sam 7:4, etc. Charles R. Krahmalkov, *A Phoenician-Punic Grammar,* HO 1.54 (Leiden: Brill, 2001), 136.

21. Charles R. Krahmalkov, *A Phoenician-Punic Dictionary,* OLA 90 (Leuven: Uitgeverij Peeters en Department Oosterse Studies, 2000), 46; compare Benz, *Personal Names in the Phoenician and Punic Inscriptions,* 419.

22. The writing of the personal name element Zaphon (properly spelled *ṣpn*) in the Punic name *ʾyspn* (KAI 159:5) is consistent both with the Latin transcription of Punic *ṣ* by *s* and by the merging of *ṣ* with simple *s* in Late Punic. See Krahmalkov, *A Phoenician-Punic Grammar,* 24–25. Though neither commenting on this matter nor translating the name, Wolfgang Röllig draws the comparison with the name *ʾybʿl* (*KAI* 2:149). For the other Phoenician and Punic names, see Benz, *Personal Names in the Phoenician and Punic Inscriptions,* 55, 61, 223, 265; Krahmalkov, *A Phoenician-Punic Grammar,* 260; Krahmalkov, *A Phoenician-Punic Dictionary,* 46.

23. This name first appeared in an ostracon inscription in Aramaic, in a list of West Semitic names whose nationality is hard to pinpoint. J. B. Segal, "An Aramaic Ostracon from Nimrud," *Iraq* 19 (1957): 139–45; Albright, "An Ostracon from Calah," 34 and n. 12; Mohammed Maraqten, *Die semitischen*

Personennamen in den alt- und reichsaramäischen Inschriften aus Vorderasien, Texte und Studien zur Orientalistik 5 (Hildesheim: Olms, 1988), 68, 124–25. It subsequently appeared on an Ammonite seal excavated at Tall Jalul. Randall W. Younker, "An Ammonite Seal from Tall Jalul, Jordan: The Seal of ʾAynadab son of Zedekʾil," in *Frank Moore Cross Volume,* ed. Baruch Levine et al., 221*–24* (Jerusalem: Israel Exploration Society, 1999).

24. From an unprovenanced stamp seal purchased in Jerusalem during the first half of the twentieth century. A. Reifenberg, "Some Ancient Hebrew Seals," *PEQ* 70 (1938): 114; Nahman Avigad and Benjamin Sass, *Corpus of West Semitic Stamp Seals* (Jerusalem: Israel Academy of Sciences and Humanities, 1997), 71.62. For ʿdh as the "divine assembly," see ʿēdāt-ʾēl in Ps 82:1 and Ugaritic ʿdt ʾilm (*KTU*² 1.15 II 7, 11). Compare, based on the biblical names ʾlʿdh (1 Chr 7:20) and yhwʿdh (1 Chr 8:36), the interpretation of this name to mean "God [literally, 'the father'] has adorned," by Ruth Hestrin and Michal Dayagi-Mendels in *Inscribed Seals: First Temple Period, Hebrew, Ammonite, Moabite, Phoenician and Aramaic from the Collections of the Israel Museum and the Israel Department of Antiquities and Museums,* trans. Inna Pommerantz (Jerusalem: Israel Museum, 1979), 76. Based on the relationship between Iezer (Num 26:30) and Abiezer (Josh 17:2), Hestrin and Dayagi-Mendels understand the initial name element of ʾyʿdh to be a contracted spelling of ʾby. This type of explanation for these and other biblical names will be addressed later in this chapter.

25. See Ran Zadok, "Historical and Onomastic Notes," 50–53; Simo Parpola and Karen Radner, eds., *The Prosopography of the Neo-Assyrian Empire,* part 1.A, Neo-Assyrian Text Corpus Project (Helsinki: University of Helsinki, 1998), 89–94; Knut L. Tallqvist, *Assyrian Personal Names* (Helsinki: Societas Scientiarum Fennica, 1914), 2.

26. See Zadok, "Historical and Onomastic Notes," 51 and n. 115; Parpola, *The Prosopography of the Neo-Assyrian Empire,* 90.

27. See Parpola, *The Prosopography of the Neo-Assyrian Empire,* 91.

28. See ibid., 92.

29. See Zadok, "Historical and Onomastic Notes," 50 and n. 108. On the deity Mer/Wer in Bronze Age, see Huffmon, *Amorite Personal Names,* 272; E. Lipiński, "Light rwʾ," in *DDD,* 518.

30. See Zadok, "Historical and Onomastic Notes," 51 and n. 109. For the deity Gaš, see Gröndahl, *Die Personennamen der Texte aus Ugarit,* 130–31.

31. See Zadok, "Historical and Onomastic Notes," 51 and n. 111.

32. Ibid., 44–50; Parpola, *The Prosopography of the Neo-Assyrian Empire,* xxiv–xxvii, 89–94.

33. For these and many other such names, see Zadok, "Historical and Onomastic Notes," 46–50; Parpola, *The Prosopography of the Neo-Assyrian Empire,* 89–94.

34. See Zadok, "Historical and Onomastic Notes," 44–46.

35. Parpola, *The Prosopography of the Neo-Assyrian Empire,* xxiv–xxvii. On the writing and vocalization of Ea's name from pre-Sargonic times, see J. J. M. Roberts, *The Earliest Semitic Pantheon: A Study of the Semitic Deities Attested in Mesopotamia Before Ur III,* JHNES (Baltimore: Johns Hopkins University Press, 1972), 19–21. In a trilingual god list at Ugarit, Ea is assimilated to Aya based on the similarity of their names and the need for a masculine counterpart to the goddess as spouse of the feminine Ugaritic sun deity Shapshu. See Roberts,

Pantheon, 79 n. 115; H. D. Galter, "Aya," in *DDD*, 125–27. For Late Bronze Age West Semitic names showing a correspondence between $^dÉ.A$ and ^dA-a as elements in otherwise identical names, see Pruzsinszky, *Personennamen der Texte aus Emar*, 49 and nn. 2–4.

36. Mentioned in Sennarcherib's Annals; the reading of the name is clearly indicated in cuneiform and in transcription in Riekele Borger, *Babylonisch-assyrische Lesestücke*, 3 volumes (Rome: Pontificium Institutum Biblicum, 1963), 2:67 ii 57; 3:Tafel 45 ii 57; cf. the reading $^{md}Malik$-ram-mu in Luckenbill, *The Annals of Sennacherib*, 30 ii 57.

37. Robert H. Pfeiffer, *State Letters of Assyria: A Transliteration and Translation of 355 Official Assyrian Letters Dating from the Sargonid Period (722–625 B.C.)* (New Haven: American Oriental Society, 1935), 77; W. F. Albright, "The Biblical Tribe of Massaʾ," 4–5 and 5 n. 4.

38. The latter name appears in an eighth-century Assyrian letter found at Nimrud. See H. W. F. Saggs, "The Nimrud Letters, 1952: Part II," *Iraq* 17 (1955): 131–33 and pl. XXXII; W. F. Albright, "The Son of Tabeel (Isaiah 7:6)," *BASOR* 140 (1955): 34–35. For the interpretation of these three names as "Where?" names, see Albright, "Northwest-Semitic Names," 226; idem, "An Ostracon from Calah," 34 and n. 12; idem, "The Biblical Tribe of Massaʾ," 4–5 and n. 4.

39. This last suggestion was made by Albright in "The Biblical Tribe of Massaʾ," 4–5 and n. 4. Zadok also lists a number of names that are ambiguous in this regard. Zadok, "Historical and Onomastic Notes," 52–53; see also Parpola, *The Prosopography of the Neo-Assyrian Empire*, 89–94.

40. Stamm, *Die Akkadische Namengebung*, 278–87; Johann Jakob Stamm, "Hebräische Ersatznamen," in *Studies in Honor of Benno Landsberger on His Seventy-Fifth Birthday, April 21, 1965*, ed. Benno Landsberger, AS (Chicago: University of Chicago Press, 1965), 416, 423.

41. Karel van der Toorn, "Ancestors and Anthroponyms: Kinship Terms as Theophoric Elements in Hebrew Names," *ZAW* 108 (1996): 1–11.

42. On the West Semitic cult of the dead, see Theodore J. Lewis, *Cults of the Dead in Ancient Israel and Ugarit*, HSM 39 (Atlanta: Scholars, 1989); idem, "How Far Can Texts Take Us? Evaluating Textual Sources for Reconstructing Ancient Israelite Beliefs about the Dead," in *Sacred Time, Sacred Place: Archaeology and the Religion of Israel*, ed. B. M. Gittlen, 169–217 (Winona Lake, Ind.: Eisenbrauns, 2002).

43. Gray, *Studies in Hebrew Proper Names*, 254–55; Noth, *Die israelitischen Personennamen*, 66–75.

44. Van der Toorn, "Ancestors and Anthroponyms," 4.

45. For the general view presented here, see the comments and bibliography offered by Michael O'Connor, "The Onomastic Evidence for Bronze-Age West Semitic," *JAOS* 124 (2004): 439–70, here 445 and n. 21; see also Tigay, *You Shall Have No Other Gods*, 5–6. On the typical literary—as opposed to a historical-philological—interest of biblical popular etymologies, see, e.g., Manfred Görg, "Der Name im Kontext: Zur Deutung männlicher Personennamen auf -*at* im Alten Testament," in *Text, Methode und Grammatik: Wolfgang Richter zum 65. Geburtstag*, ed. Walter Gross et al. (St. Ottilien: EOS, 1991), 82–83. Compare the view of James Barr that "folk etymologies" not only may but typically do represent genuine (though often mistaken) efforts to explain the philological

meanings of older name types that had become obscure. James Barr, "The Symbolism of Names in the Old Testament," *BJRL* 52 (1969–70): 11–29.

46. For the discussion of this evidence, see P. Kyle McCarter Jr., *I Samuel: A New Translation with Introduction, Notes and Commentary,* AB 8 (New York: Doubleday, 1980), 115–16.

47. See O'Connor, "The Onomastic Evidence for Bronze-Age West Semitic," 459 and n. 104. The only exception O'Connor points to is Bronze Age West Semitic names formed with *balti*, which resemble Akkadian names with *balu*: e.g., *mannu-balti-ʾilu* ("Who is without *ʾIlu*?"). Cf. Akk. *mannum-balu-Šamaš* ("Who is without Shamash?"). Also in Akkadian are other names with negative particles, including *ailē* negating verbs or alone as a negative plea addressed to a deity, e.g., *ai abāš, ē nibāš* ("Let me/us not be ashamed"); *Ē-ᵈIštar* ("No, O Ishtar!"). See Stamm, *Die Akkadische Namengebung,* 174–75.

48. See, e.g., McCarter, *I Samuel,* 115–16.

49. See the usage of *zebel* with the meaning "manure" or "dung" in post-biblical Hebrew. Marcus Jastrow, *A Dictionary of the Targumim, the Talmud Babli and Yerushalmi, and the Midrashic Literature* (New York: Judaica, 1971), 379. Also cf. Arabic *zibl* ("dung, manure"). Corresponding to the scatological distortion of Jezebel's name is the elaboration on Elijah's fulfilled prediction of her violent death: "The corpse of Jezebel shall be as manure (*kĕdōmen*) on the field" (2 Kings 9:37; cf. 1 Kings 21:23). See, occurring formulaically in Jeremiah and Psalms, a very similar expression describing those who die a violent death and remain unburied and unmourned (Jer 8:2; 9:21; 16:4; 25:33; Ps 83:11). Furthermore, the pun on the hated queen's name continues in the final clause of this verse: "so that they may not say, 'This is Jezebel (*zōʾt ʾîzābel*)'"—a statement suggesting not only the small amount of her remains left by the scavenging dogs but also an answer to the question posed in the distorted meaning of the name, "Where is the dung?" I thank my colleague James M. Kennedy for bringing to my attention the full ironic significance of this part of the verse. On Ugaritic *zbl* as an epithet for Baal-Haddu (and for other gods), see William F. Albright, "Zabûl Yam and Thâpiṭ Nahar in the Combat between Baal and the Sea," *JPOS* 16 (1936): 17–20.

50. See, elsewhere in the Baal cycle, the mourning of this deity by the question, *ʾi ʾap bʿ[l . . .] ʾi hd* ("Where then is Baa[l]? . . . Where is Haddu?"). *KTU²* 1.5 IV: 6–7.

51. The correspondence was recognized early on by Charles Virolleaud, "Sur quatre fragments alphabétiques trouvés à Ras Shamra en 1934," *Syria* 16 (1935): 181–87, here 185 n. 1.

52. James A. Montgomery, *A Critical and Exegetical Commentary on the Books of Kings,* ed. Henry Snyder Gehman, ICC 10 (New York: Scribners, 1951), 291.

53. Cited in disagreement by Virolleaud, "Sur quatre fragments alphabétiques," 185 n. 1.

54. A point made by Felice Israel, review of R. Hestrin and M. Dayagi-Mendeles, *Ḥotamot miyamey Bet Rišon ʿivriyim, ʿammoniyim, moʾaviyim, finiqiyim, weʾaramaiyim* (Jerusalem, 1978), in *AION* 39 (1979): 516.

55. "The Seal of Jezebel," *IEJ* 14 (1964): 274–76.

56. Compare Phoenician-Punic *yš bšt* ("Bast [Baal] exists/lives/is there"; Pu EH 224.3; 2 Sam 2:8-4:12); *ʾš bʿl* ("Baal is alive!"; Puu *CIS* I 159.3; = *yš bʿl*; cf. 1

Chr 8:33, 9:39). Cited and thus translated by Krahmalkov, *A Phoenician-Punic Grammar*, 277.

57. Frank M. Cross, "An Aramaic Inscription from Daskyleion," *BASOR* 184 (1966): 7–10; repr. Cross, *Leaves from an Epigrapher's Notebook*, 181–83, here 182 n. 17.

58. This interpretation of the biblical name is found in Krahmalkov, *A Phoenician-Punic Grammar*, 260.

59. See, e.g., BDB, 4b; *Eerdmans Dictionary of the Bible*, 627 s.v. "Iezer."

60. See P. Bordreuil and A. Lemaire, "Nouveau groupe de sceaux hébreux, araméens et ammonites," *Semitica* 29 (1979): 71–84, here 76–78. See also Maraqten, *Die semitischen Personennamen in den alt- und reichsaramäischen Inschriften*, 68, 125. The scholars in both of these sources oppose understanding the element *ʾy* in this name and in others as a contracted form of *ʾby*, *ʾhy*, or *ʾly*.

61. See Fowler, *Theophoric Personal Names in Ancient Hebrew*, 355.

62. Benjamin Mazar, "On the Study of the Personal Names in the Bible," *Lešonénu* 15 (1947): 39–40.

63. Commenting on this pattern is P. Kyle McCarter Jr., *II Samuel: A New Translation with Introduction, Notes and Commentary*, AB 9 (New York: Doubleday, 1984), 169.

64. See also *hwdwh* and epigraphic Hebrew *hwdwyhw* and *hwdyh* in three seals—all from the antiquities market—cited in Avigad and Sass, *Corpus of West Semitic Stamp Seals*, 91–92, 160.

65. As implied in Fowler, *Theophoric Personal Names in Ancient Hebrew*, 342.

66. Of course, such Phoenician names are written in accordance with the lack of *matres lectiones* that is standard for Phoenician orthography. See Krahmalkov, *A Phoenician-Punic Grammar*, 260.

67. Halpern, "Ehud," 414.

68. For Albright, biblical *ʾiyyôb* would have derived from **ʾAyyâbu(m)*, "the dissimilated and contracted form" of the well-attested Bronze Age name. "The Egyptian Empire in Asia," 239 and n. 2.

69. From the root *ʾyb* ("to be hostile to"). See BDB, 33b.

70. This was noted, for example, in connection with Job 12:34 by Edward L. Greenstein, "Kirta," in *Ugaritic Narrative Poetry*, ed. S. B. Parker, SBLWAW 9 (Atlanta: Scholars, 1997), 10.

71. See, e.g., Cyrus H. Gordon, *Ugaritic Textbook: Grammar, Texts in Transliteration, Cuneiform Selections, Glossary, Indices*, AnOr 38 (Rome: Pontifical Biblical Institute, 1965), 356; McCarter, *I Samuel*, 116; Zadok, *The Pre-Hellenistic Israelite Anthroponomy and Prosopography*, 58; Halpern, "Ehud," 414.

72. For illustrations and discussions of the iconographic evidence, see Othmar Keel, *Goddesses and Trees, New Moon and Yahweh: Ancient Near Eastern Art and the Hebrew Bible*, JSOTSup 261 (Sheffield: Sheffield Academic, 1998); Othmar Keel and Christoph Uehlinger, *Gods, Goddesses, and Images of God in Ancient Israel*, trans. Thomas H. Trapp (Minneapolis: Fortress Press, 1998), especially with respect to the Jerusalem temple (pp. 169–72 in the latter). On the tree as a divine symbol in Solomon's temple and elsewhere, see Elizabeth Bloch-Smith, "'Who Is the King of Glory?' Solomon's Temple and Its Symbolism," in *Scripture and Other Artifacts: Essays on the Bible and Archaeology in Honor of Philip J. King*, ed. J. C. Exum, M. D. Coogan, and L. E. Stager, 18–31 (Louisville: Westminster John Knox, 1994), 24–25.

73. See BDB, 16a.

74. See, with noted reservation, Noth, *Die israelitischen Personennamen*, 236.

75. "Ithamar," in *ABD*, 3:579.

76. Albright made this explanation "feeling that the Y is in error." "An Ostracon from Calah," 34 n. 12. Compare also Zadok, "Historical and Onomastic Notes," 45 and n. 70.

77. For the suggestion that *'ayyah* is possibly a "Where?" name, see Halpern, "Ehud," 414.

78. BDB, 17a.

79. *'iy 'al'iyn b'l 'iy zbl b'l 'arṣ* ("Where is Mighty Baal, Where is the Prince, the Lord of the Earth?"; *KTU²* 1.6 IV:4–5, 15–16) and *'i 'ap b'[l . . .] 'i hd* ("Where then is Baa[l]? . . . Where is Haddu?"; *KTU²* 1.5 IV: 6–7); see discussion above, the discussion of Jezebel (*'izebel*).

80. This was suggested in connection with *'yzbl* by John Gray in *I and II Kings: A Commentary,* OTL (Philadelphia: Westminster, 1963), 333, and more recently by Phyllis Trible in "Exegesis for Storytellers and Other Strangers," *JBL* 114 (1995): 3–19, here 4, 16–17.

81. For both a critique and a reprise of this category, see, respectively, Mark S. Smith, *The Origins of Biblical Monotheism: Israel's Polytheistic Background and the Ugaritic Texts* (New York: Oxford University Press, 2001), 104–31; and Tryggve N. D. Mettinger, *The Riddle of the Resurrection: 'Dying and Rising Gods' in the Ancient Near East,* ConBOT 50 (Stockholm: Almqvist & Wiksell, 2001).

82. See Baruch A. Levine and Jean-Michel de Tarragon, "Dead Kings and Rephaim: The Patrons of the Ugaritic Dynasty," *JAOS* 104 (1984): 649–59, esp. 656–58.

83. See Karel van der Toorn, *From Her Cradle to Her Grave: The Role of Religion in the Life of the Israelite and the Babylonian Woman,* trans. Sara J. Denning-Bolle, Biblical Seminar 23 (Sheffield: Sheffield Academic, 1994), 77–84.

3. God and Israel in the Hebrew Bible

1. An excellent illustration of this point is Othmar Keel's discussion of ancient cosmologies in *The Symbolism of the Biblical World: Ancient Near Eastern Iconography and the Book of Psalms* (New York: Seabury, 1978), 15–60.

2. See E. E. Elnes and P. D. Miller, "Elyon עֶלְיוֹן," in *DDD*, 293–99.

3. This translation of the verse follows the reading *bny 'lwhym* (literarally, "children of the gods/of God") attested in 4QDeut^j and implied by *aggelōn theou* ("messengers of God") in the LXX. This expression, which corresponds well with *běnê 'ādām* ("children of humankind") in the parallelism of the verse, nonetheless would eventually have become theologically problematic for later scribes, hence the MT's *běnê yiśrā'ēl* ("children of Israel"), to which the former would be the preferable reading according to the principle of *lectio difficilior* ("the more difficult reading" being preferred; see P. Kyle McCarter Jr., *Textual Criticism: Recovering the Text of the Hebrew Bible,* Old Testament Guides [Philadelphia: Fortress, 1986], 72–73). See Julie A. Duncan, *Qumran Cave 4. IX: Deuteronomy, Joshua, Judges, Kings,* ed. E. Ulrich and F. M. Cross, DJD 14 (Oxford: Clarendon, 1995), 90. See the bibliography cited in Mark S. Smith, *God in Translation: Deities in Cross-Cultural Discourse in the Biblical World,* FAT 57 (Tübingen: Mohr

Siebeck, 2008), 195 n. 26; and the listing of variants among the witnesses by Smith in *God in Translation*, 139–40, 195–96), along with Smith's extensive discussion of this passage (pp. 139–43, 195–212). Based on the larger context of Deuteronomy 32 (especially vv. 12, 17, 21, 31, and 39), Smith concludes that "the composer presupposed the monotheistic identification of Yahweh in verse 9 with Elyon in verse 8" (p. 211). Notwithstanding the sentiments expressed in those other verses and Smith's demonstration of a similar understanding in the later additions to Deuteronomy in 4:19 and 29:25, the poem in chapter 32 seems not so much an expression of monotheism as the kind of rhetoric of Yahweh's incomparability that Smith discusses in his earlier book, *The Origins of Biblical Monotheism: Israel's Polytheistic Background and the Ugaritic Texts* (New York: Oxford University Press, 2001), 149–66. The difference between El Elyon and Yahweh denoted in 32:8-9 is one between authority and power, respectively. The present reality of Yahweh's incomparability as an active, dynamic god, as celebrated in the poem, is in no way compromised by the memory of his subordination to the senior god of the pantheon in the primordial past. The distinction is similar to that between El and Baal-Haddu in the Ugaritic Baal Cycle.

4. For similar language describing the land of the kingdom of Mari as a divine patrimonial holding, see Mari text A. 1121 + A. 2731 and the translation and discussion in Martti Nissinen, *Prophets and Prophecy in the Ancient Near East*, with contributions by C. L. Seow and Robert K. Ritner, ed. Peter Machinist, SBLWAW 12 (Atlanta: Society of Biblical Literature, 2003), 17–21. See chapter 1 for more discussion and bibliography on this text.

5. Friedrich Horst, "Zwei Begriffe für Eigentum (Besitz): נַחֲלָה und אֲחֻזָּה," in *Verbannung und Heimkehr: Beiträge zur Geschichte und Theologie Israels im 6. und 5. Jahrhundert v. Chr*, ed. Arnulf Kuschke, 135–56 (Tübingen: Mohr, 1961), 152; Abraham Malamat, "Pre-Monarchical Social Institutions in Israel in the Light of Mari," in *History of Biblical Israel: Major Problems and Minor Issues* (Leiden: Brill, 2001), 36–40; Harold D. Forshey, "The Construct Chain *naḥᵃlat YHWH/ᵉelōhîm*," *BASOR* 220 (1975): 51–53; Bernard F. Batto, "Land Tenure and Women at Mari," *JESHO* 23 (1983): 209–39, esp. 227–29; Joel S. Burnett, "The Pride of Jacob," in *David and Zion: Biblical Studies in Honor of J. J. M. Roberts,* ed. Bernard F. Batto and Kathryn L. Roberts, 319–50 (Winona Lake, Ind.: Eisenbrauns, 2004), esp. 328–38.

6. See the discussions by Gerhard von Rad, "Verheissenes Land und Jahwes Land im Hexateuch," *ZDPV* 66 (1943): 191–204; Horst, "Zwei Begriffe," 135–56; H. C. Brichto, "Kin, Cult, Land and Afterlife: A Biblical Complex," *HUCA* 44 (1973): 1–50; Samuel E. Loewenstamm, "*nḥlt yhwh*," in *Studies in Bible, 1986,* ed. Sara Japhet, 155–92, Scripta Hierosolymitana 3 (Jerusalem: Magnes, 1986); E. Lipiński, "נָחַל *nāḥal*; נַחֲלָה *naḥălâ*," in *TDOT*, 9:330–33.

7. See the discussion of the divine-warrior tradition, later in this chapter.

8. Smith, *God in Translation*, 142, citing Harold W. Attridge and Robert A. Oden Jr., *Philo of Byblos, The Phoenician History: Introduction, Critical Text, Translation, Notes*, CBQMS 9 (Washington, D.C.: Catholic Biblical Association of America, 1981), 56–57, 58–59.

9. *AEL*, 2:227 and *COS*, 1:89–93, cited by Smith, *God in Translation*, 142. As Smith notes, this parallel was adduced by Othmar L. Keel and Christoph Uehlinger, *Gods, Goddesses, and Images of God in Ancient Israel*, trans. Thomas H. Trapp (Minneapolis: Fortress Press, 1998), 116.

10. Smith, *The Origins of Biblical Monotheism*, 48–49.

11. However, as Smith advises, caution is warranted in proposing a direct relationship between these passages. *God in Translation*, 210–11.

12. Smith, *The Origins of Biblical Monotheism*, 48–49.

13. See the following essays by J. J. M. Roberts, all reprinted in *The Bible and the Ancient Near East: Collected Essays* (Winona Lake, Ind.: Eisenbrauns, 2002): "Zion in the Theology of the Davidic-Solomonic Empire," in *Studies in the Period of David and Solomon and Other Essays*, ed. Tomoo Ishida, 93–108 (Winona Lake, Ind.: Eisenbrauns, 1982); "The Davidic Origin of the Zion Tradition," *JBL* 92 (1973): 329–44; "The Religio-Political Setting of Psalm 47," *BASOR* 221 (1976): 129–32; "Zion Tradition," in *IDBSup*, 985–87; "In Defense of the Monarchy: The Contribution of Israelite Kingship to Biblical Theology," in *Ancient Israelite Religion: Essays in Honor of Frank Moore Cross*, ed. Patrick D. Miller, Paul D. Hanson, and S. Dean McBride, 377–96 (Philadelphia: Fortress Press, 1987), esp. 378, 386–87. For a review of scholarship on the Zion tradition, see Ben C. Ollenburger, *Zion the City of the Great King: A Theological Symbol of the Jerusalem Cult*, JSOT 41 (Sheffield: JSOT Press, 1987), 15–19. Ollenburger describes the tradition as "a coherent 'theological conception' which underlies most of the Psalms and is articulated above all in [the] Songs of Zion as well as in the creation Psalms, the Psalms of Yahweh's kingship and the royal Psalms" (p. 16). As Ollenburger recognizes, the Zion tradition finds expression in other portions of the Hebrew Bible as well, mainly among the prophets.

14. Form-critical analysis of the Psalter, beginning with Gunkel, has classified these texts as Psalms of Yahweh's Enthronement. See Herman Gunkel and Joachim Begrich, *Introduction to Psalms: The Genres of the Religious Lyric of Israel*, trans. James D. Nogalski, Mercer Library of Biblical Studies (Macon: Mercer University Press, 1998), 66–81. Following Gunkel, Mowinckel proposed that these and other psalms had their institutional setting in an annual enthronement festival, a hypothesis that other scholars developed in various forms. Sigmund Mowinckel, *The Psalms in Israel's Worship*, trans. D. R. Ap-Thomas (New York: Abingdon, 1962), 69–81; Aubrey R. Johnson, *Sacral Kingship in Ancient Israel*, 2nd ed. (Cardiff: University of Wales Press, 1967); Artur Weiser, *The Psalms: A Commentary*, trans. H. Hartwell, OTL (Philadelphia: Westminster, 1962); Hans-Joachim Kraus, *Worship in Israel: A Cult History of the Old Testament*, trans. G. Buswell (Richmond: John Knox, 1966). The thesis of a specific royal cultic festival lying behind these psalms is now generally considered to be defunct due to a lack of clear biblical evidence. See J. Clinton McCann, "The Book of Psalms: Introduction, Commentary, and Reflections," in *NIDB*, 4:639–1280, here 648–49. Nonetheless, the recognition of these psalms' shared correspondences of content and phraseology still stands. In addition to the basic thematic unity of these psalms as described, one might note that, with the exceptions of Psalms 95 and 98, which refer to Yahweh as *melek gādôl* ("great king," 95:3) and *hammelek* ("the king," 98:6), all of these psalms contain the assertion *mlk yhwh* ("Yahweh is/has become king," as in 47:9, accounting for the preference for *ʾĕlōhîm* over *yhwh* as the favored divine designation in Psalms 42–83, the Elohistic Psalter).

15. For the understanding of Elyon and its importance within the Zion tradition, see Roberts, "Davidic Origin of the Zion Tradition," 331–42; idem, "The

Religio-Political Setting of Psalm 47," 129–32; idem, "Zion in the Theology of the Davidic-Solomonic Empire," 94 and n. 3.

16. Such connections among these psalms (along with Psalm 45) are recognized by Jerome Creach as being at the basis of the shaping of this portion of the Psalter. Jerome F. D. Creach, *Yahweh as Refuge and the Editing of the Hebrew Psalter,* JSOTSup 217 (Sheffield: Sheffield Academic, 1996), 87. Psalms 46, 47, and 76 were associated with one another in Gunkel's form critical categories as Zion Psalms. See Gunkel, *Introduction to the Psalms,* 258.

17. Psalms 120–134, which in their superscriptions are labeled as songs "of ascents," are conventionally understood to reflect a pilgrimage tradition. See McCann, "The Book of Psalms," 1176–1217, esp. 1176, 1180.

18. Roberts, "Zion in the Theology of the Davidic-Solomonic Empire," 332–37.

19. J. J. M. Roberts, "The Old Testament's Contribution to Messianic Expectations," in Roberts, *The Bible and the Ancient Near East,* 376–89, here 380. Roberts understands this passage, along with Psalm 2, to indicate the divine birth, as opposed to divine adoption, of the human king.

20. See Joel S. Burnett, *A Reassessment of Biblical Elohim,* SBLDS 183 (Atlanta: Society of Biblical Literature, 2001), 67–68.

21. Albrecht Alt, "The God of the Fathers," in *Essays on Old Testament History and Religion,* trans. Robert A. Wilson, 1–77 (Oxford: Basil Blackwell, 1966; orig. pub. [as *Der Gott der Väter*] Stuttgart: Kohlhammer, 1929).

22. See, for example, the criticisms of Cross, *Canaanite Myth and Hebrew Epic,* 3–12.

23. See the discussions of Karel van der Toorn, who nonetheless understands the "god of the fathers" traditions to reflect a phase of Israelite religion before the monarchy, and alternatively Rainer Albertz, who sees the ancestral narratives as portraying the national god in terms of a mode of family religious practice that persisted during the monarchy, as Albertz describes it, "a substratum of Yahweh religion." As Albertz explains, "This religious stratum of the family is very much older than the specific history of Israelite religion; it is the basis on which Yahweh religion was built up." Karel van der Toorn, *Family Religion in Babylonia, Syria, and Israel: Continuity and Change in the Forms of Religious Life,* SHCANE 7 (Leiden: Brill, 1996), 236–65; Rainer Albertz, *A History of Israelite Religion in the Old Testament Period,* trans. John Bowden, 2 vols., OTL (Philadelphia: Westminster John Knox, 1994), 1:23–39, esp. 29.

24. Van der Toorn, *Family Religion,* 255–57.

25. The abrupt shift to third person singular marks the following parenthetical comment, "the gods of their fathers" (*ʾĕlōhê ʾăbîhem*; v. 53), as a redactional gloss. See Ephraim A. Speiser, *Genesis: Introduction, Translation, and Notes,* AB 1 (Garden City, N.Y.: Doubleday, 1964), 243, 248. Nonetheless, as verse 29 (quoted earlier in this paragraph) indicates, verse 53 denotes different ancestral gods for Laban and Jacob, even if the accompanying verb form was originally singular, hence *yišpōt,* as reflected in the Septuagint and Samaritan Pentateuch. Masculine singular verbs preceding compound subjects of more than one masculine singular noun occur frequently in Biblical Hebrew; see GKC 146 f. Whether original to the context or a later addition, this verse reflects the longstanding practice of the deities of two parties serving as treaty guarantors, as noted by Mark S. Smith, who points to similar phraseology in the conclusion of a letter from Late Bronze Age

Hazor: "The gods have decided between me and them / judged (*špṭ) me." Smith, God in Translation, 104 n. 41. For the letter and the translation of these lines, see Wayne Horowitz and Takayoshi Oshima with Seth Sanders, Cuneiform in Canaan: Cuneiform Sources from the Land of Israel in Ancient Times (Jerusalem: Israel Exploration Society and Hebrew University of Jerusalem, 2006), 80–81.

26. As Smith explains, even though Jacob and Laban are kindred, there is a definite "cross-cultural representation" between Israelite and Aramean in this chapter. God in Translation, 104–107. As in the case of Abraham's descendants, Nahor's family line is traced through twelve sons (Gen 22:20-24), indicating among the biblical traditions a regard for these two brothers as the progenitors of separate nations. See Edwin L. Hostetter, "Nahor," in EDB, 942.

27. Van der Toorn, Family Religion, 257.

28. For the importance of kinship (and other) settings to blessing in the Hebrew Bible, see the following discussions: Raymond Westbrook, Property and the Family in Biblical Law, JSOTSup 113 (Sheffield: JSOT, 1991), 137; C. W. Mitchell, The Meaning of BRK "To Bless" in the Old Testament, SBLDS 95 (Atlanta: Scholars, 1987), 26–52, 67–72, 79–90, 126–31, 165–71; Josef Scharbert, "ברך brk; בְּרָכָה; bᵉrākhāh," in TDOT, 2:279–308, esp. 304–307; Timothy G. Crawford, Blessing and Curse in Syro-Palestinian Inscriptions of the Iron Age, American University Studies, Theology and Religion Series 7, vol. 120 (New York: Lang, 1992). For a recent study of blessing and curse in the Hebrew Bible and an overview of scholarship on its cultural background, see J. K. Aitken, The Semantics of Blessing and Cursing in Ancient Hebrew, Ancient Near Eastern Studies Supplement 23 (Louvain: Peeters, 2007), esp. 3–22.

29. Cross, "Kinship and Covenant," 13–14.

30. The definitive study is Patrick D. Miller Jr., The Divine Warrior in Early Israel, HSM 5 (Cambridge, Mass.: Harvard University Press, 1973).

31. Frank Moore Cross Jr., Canaanite Myth and Hebrew Epic: Essays in the History of the Religion of Israel (Cambridge, Mass.: Harvard University Press, 1973), 142, quoted in the following sentence.

32. See Ronald E. Clements, God and Temple (Philadelphia: Fortress Press, 1965); Richard J. Clifford, The Cosmic Mountain in Canaan and the Old Testament, HSM 4 (Cambridge: Harvard University Press, 1972); Cross, Canaanite Myth and Hebrew Epic, 141–43; Levenson, Sinai and Zion.

33. For the recognition that both the sanctuary site and the broader land are in view in this text, see Abraham Malamat, "Pre-Monarchical Social Institutions in Israel in the Light of Mari," in History of Biblical Israel: Major Problems and Minor Issues, 36–40 (Leiden: Brill, 2001); Cross, Canaanite Myth and Hebrew Epic, 142. For further discussion and bibliography, see Burnett, "The Pride of Jacob," 332–33 and n. 41.

34. ANEP, 246.

35. Norbert Lohfink, Das Hauptgebot: Eine Untersuchung literarischer Einleitungsfragen zu Dtn 5–11, AnBib 20 (Rome: Pontificio Instituto Biblico, 1963), 164, cited in Smith, God in Translation, 143 and n. 143.

36. Smith, God in Translation, 143–47.

37. Ibid., 145.

38. For the recognition of separate cultic origins for the exodus-conquest and Sinai covenant traditions, see Gerhard von Rad, "The Form-Critical Problem of the Hexateuch," in From Genesis to Chronicles: Explorations in Old Testament

Theology, ed. K. C. Hanson, 1–58 (Minneapolis: Fortress Press, 2005; orig. pub. [as *Das formgeschichtliche Problem des Hexateuchs,* BWANT 78] Stuttgart: Kohlhammer, 1938).

39. Cross, *Canaanite Myth and Hebrew Epic,* 58–59.

40. For the lexical data, see Frank M. Cross, "אל *ʾēl,*" in *TDOT,* 1:242–61. For discussion of Yahweh's identification with El and relevant textual evidence, see Mark S. Smith, *The Early History of God: Yahweh and the Other Deities in Ancient Israel,* 2nd ed., Biblical Resource Series (Grand Rapids: Eeerdmans; Dearborn, Mich.: Dove, 2002), 32–43.

41. Patrick D. Miller, "El, The Creator of Earth," *BASOR* 239 (1980): 43–46, repr. in *Israelite Religion and Biblical Theology* (Sheffield: Sheffield Academic, 2000).

42. Also, Cross understands the epithets Elyon and Shadday to relate to El's role as divine warrior. *Canaanite Myth and Hebrew Epic,* 50–51, 59–60. See also Miller, *The Divine Warrior,* 48–58. As Mark S. Smith points out, the explicit West Semitic evidence is admittedly sparse for El as divine warrior and completely lacking for Baal as creator. Smith, *Early History of God,* 153–58; idem, *The Ugaritic Baal Cycle,* vol. 1, *Introduction with Text, Translation and Commentary of KTU 1.1–1.2,* VTSup 55 (Leiden: Brill, 1994), 75–87. For Smith, as the Ugaritic evidence suggests, in West Semitic tradition these were originally separate mythic roles belonging to different deities of the pantheon. Their combination in Israelite tradition results from the consolidation of divine power in a single deity, namely, Yahweh, and something similar happens in the case of the Babylonian state god Marduk as reflected in *Enuma Elish.* For further discussion of dynamics involved in consolidation of divine roles in state gods, see Smith, *God in Translation,* esp. 91–185. Though Smith's point about the scarcity of the West Semitic evidence is well taken, the totality of all the evidence (including the significant evidence of *Enuma Elish*) favors an integral connection between these roles (see the discussion in the following paragraphs).

43. *ANET,* 60–72; *COS,* 1:390–402; and the convenient translation by Stephanie Dalley, *Myths from Mesopotamia* (Oxford: Oxford University Press, 1989), 228–77. This motif apparently made its way into Mesopotamian theology from West Semitic origins; see, for example, Thorkild Jacobsen, *Toward the Image of Tammuz and Other Essays on Mesopotamian History and Culture,* ed. William L. Moran (Cambridge, Mass.: Harvard University Press, 1970; repr. Eugene, Ore.: Wipf & Stock, 2008), 36.

44. Cross, *Canaanite Myth and Hebrew Epic,* 57–58. The classic study drawing these comparisons is Hermann Gunkel, *Creation and Chaos in the Primeval Era and the Eschaton: A Religio-Historical Study of Genesis 1 and Revelation 12,* ed. Peter Machinist, trans. K. William Whitney Jr., Biblical Resource Series (Grand Rapids: Eerdmans, 2006), esp. 21–77, originally published as *Schöpfung und Chaos in Urzeit und Endzeit: Eine religionsgeschichtliche Untersuchung über Gen. 1 und Ap. Jon. 12* (Göttingen: Vandenhoeck & Ruprecht, 1895 [1921]). See other biblical references to Yahweh's defeat of Leviathan (Isa 27:1) and Yahweh's subordination of "Sea" (BH *yām*) as an element of creation (Pss 93:3-4; 96:11; 98:7; compare 95:5). The warrior god's defeat of the sea in combat also appears in the Ugaritic myth of Baal and Yamm, though without explicitly being tied to cosmogony (*KTU*[2] 1.2 IV).

45. *ANET*, 60–72; *COS*, 1:401; Dalley, *Myths from Mesopotamia*, 262–63.

46. For a convenient introduction and English translation, see Mark S. Smith, "The Baal Cycle," in *Ugaritic Narrative Poetry*, ed. Simon B. Parker, 81–180, SBLWAW 9 (Atlanta: Society of Biblical Literature, 1997), esp. 81–105. See also the definitive critical edition, Smith, *The Ugaritic Baal Cycle*, vol. 1 and Mark S. Smith and Wayne T. Pitard, *The Ugaritic Baal Cycle*, vol. 2, *Introduction with Text, Translation and Commentary of KTU/CAT 1.3-1.4*. VTSup 114 (Leiden: Brill, 2009).

47. See Raymond C. Van Leeuwen, "Cosmos, Temple, House: Building and Wisdom in Mesopotamia and Israel," in *Wisdom Literature in Mesopotamia and Israel*, ed. Richard J. Clifford, 67–90, Society of Biblical Literature Symposium Series 36 (Leiden: Brill, 2007).

48. See W. Herrmann, "El אֵל," in *DDD*, 274–80, esp. 275–76. Noting Ugaritic references to El as a progenitor of the gods and the evidence for El as creator of the world in first-millennium West Semitic texts, Hermann concludes, "As regards the creative activity of El the Ugaritic conception differed from that in the remaining Syrian-Palestinian area" (p. 276).

49. Just as Marduk's abode is built by the Annuna gods in *Enuma Elish*, so is Baal's house built by another god, Kothar wa-Hasis, at Ugarit (*KTU*² 1.4 V–VI). In the Ugaritic myth, it is Kothar who comes closest to the role of creator as encountered in the Hebrew Bible. See chapter 1 of Mark S. Smith, *The Priestly Vision of Genesis 1* (Minneapolis: Fortress Press, 2010).

50. Whether the equation of exodus and divine battle against chaos in Isa 51:9-11 represents "the historicizing of a mythical motif" that had occurred through the Jerusalem cult (Bernhard W. Anderson, *Creation versus Chaos: The Reinterpretation of Mythical Symbolism in the Bible* [Philadelphia: Fortress Press, 1987], 108–109) or "the secondary mythologizing of historical experiences to point to their cosmic or transcendent meaning" (Cross, *Canaanite Myth and Hebrew Epic*, 87–88, 144), the element allowing these two traditions to be joined in Isaiah 51 is Yahweh's role in both as divine warrior.

51. See chapter 4, on the "garden of God" tradition in Genesis 2–3 and elsewhere.

52. For a comprehensive study of the Priestly creation account, see Smith, *The Priestly Vision of Genesis 1*.

53. See also Job 26:12-13; Ps 74:12-17; Isa 27:1.

4. Cosmic and Terrestrial Realms of Divine Presence and Absence

1. Deut 32:37; 2 Kings 2:14; Isa 63:11, 15; Jer 2:6, 8; Joel 2:17; Pss 42:4, 11; 79:10; 115:2; Job 35:10; consider also Judg 6:13.

2. For questions formed with the locative interrogative adverb in Biblical Hebrew, see GKC, 296–97 sec. 100 o 5, 475–76 sec. 150 l; Bruce Waltke and Michael O'Connor, *An Introduction to Biblical Hebrew Syntax* (Winona Lake, Ind.: Eisenbrauns, 1990), 318 par. 18.1f; Edward Lipiński, *Semitic Languages: Outline of a Comparative Grammar*, 2nd ed., OLA 80 (Leuven: Peeters, 2001), 336–37, 463.

3. Terence E. Fretheim, *The Suffering of God: An Old Testament Perspective,* OBT (Philadelphia: Fortress Press, 1984), 60–78; and idem, *God and World in the Old Testament: A Relational Theology of Creation* (Nashville: Abingdon, 2005), esp. 22–27.

4. Fretheim, *God and World,* 25.

5. Ibid., 25.

6. For further discussion of this passage in light of the ancient Near Eastern understanding of divine abandonment, see chapter 7.

7. Fretheim, *God and World,* 25.

8. See Samuel E. Balentine, *The Hidden God: The Hiding of the Face of God in the Old Testament,* Oxford Theological Monographs (Oxford: Oxford University Press, 1983).

9. Othmar L. Keel, *The Symbolism of the Biblical World: Ancient Near Eastern Iconography and the Book of Psalms* (New York: Seabury, 1978), 26–35.

10. James P. Allen, *Genesis in Egypt: The Philosophy of Ancient Egyptian Creation Accounts,* Yale Egyptological Studies 2 (San Antonio: Van Siclen Books for the Yale Egyptological Seminar, Yale University, 1995), 5–7.

11. Ibid., 6.

12. Leonard H. Lesko, "Death and the Afterlife in Ancient Egyptian Thought," in *CANE,* 3:1763–74, here 1767.

13. Ibid., 1767.

14. Stephen Quirke, *Ancient Egyptian Religion* (London: British Museum Press, 1992), 67.

15. Lesko, "Death and the Afterlife in Ancient Egyptian Thought," 1767.

16. Joel S. Burnett, "Forty-Two Songs for Elohim: An Ancient Near Eastern Organizing Principle in the Shaping of the Elohistic Psalter," *JSOT* 31 (2006): 81–102, esp. 95–99; Joel S. Burnett, "A Plea for David and Zion: The Elohistic Psalter as a Psalm Collection for the Temple's Restoration," in *Diachronic and Synchronic—Reading the Psalms in Real Time: Proceedings of the Baylor Symposium on the Book of Psalms,* ed. Joel S. Burnett, W. H. Bellinger Jr., and W. Dennis Tucker Jr., LHBOTS 488 (New York: T&T Clark, 2007), 95–113, esp. 105–111.

17. See, e.g., James Henry Breasted, *Development of Religion and Thought in Ancient Egypt* (New York: Harper & Row, 1959), 301–2; Barbara Watterson, *The Gods of Ancient Egypt* (New York: Facts on File, 1984), 34, 86.

18. Lesko, "Death and the Afterlife in Ancient Egyptian Thought," 1763–74.

19. Jean Bottéro, *Religion in Ancient Mesopotamia,* trans. Teresa Lavender Fagan (Chicago: University of Chicago Press, 2001), 77–81.

20. W. G. Lambert, A. R. Millard, and M. Civil, *Atra-Ḫasīs: The Babylonian Story of the Flood* (Oxford: Clarendon, 1969; repr. Winona Lake, Ind.: Eisenbrauns, 1999), 8.

21. See, e.g., Jo Ann Scurlock, "Death and the Afterlife in Ancient Mesopotamian Thought," in *CANE,* 3:1883–93, here 1887.

22. Quite curiously, the Annunaki eventually come to be thus located in the infernal region after having ranked as the high council of deities in earlier Mesopotamian myth. See Bottéro, *Religion in Ancient Mesopotamia,* 55, 80, 99, 109.

23. Ibid., 226 n. 6.

24. Scurlock, "Death and the Afterlife in Ancient Mesopotamian Thought," 1888–89.

25. Paolo Xella, "Death and the Afterlife in Canaanite and Hebrew Thought," in *CANE*, 3:2059–70.

26. For an English translation, see Baruch A. Levine, Jean-Michel de Tarragon, and Anne Robertson, "The Patrons of the Ugaritic Dynasty (*KTU* 1.161)," in *COS*, 1:357–58, text 1.105. In the Hebrew Bible, the term *rĕpāʾîm* occurs in reference to the dead and also to legendary kings and heroes from the remote past. See Deut 2:20; 3:11; Isa 14:9; 26:14; Ps 88:11; Job 26:5; and H. Rouillard, "Rephaim רְפָאִים," in *DDD*, 692–700. As Theodore J. Lewis has aptly summarized, scholars have variously understood the Rephaim to be "(a) minor deities, (b) heroic warriors, (c) a tribal group, (d) the shades of the dead, or (e) some combination of (a)–(d)." Theodore J. Lewis, "The Rapiuma: 20–22. CAT 1.20–22," in *Ugaritic Narrative Poetry*, ed. Simon B. Parker, 196–205, SBLWAW 9 (Atlanta: Scholars, 1997), 196.

27. As persuasively reaffirmed by Tryggve N. D. Mettinger, *The Riddle of the Resurrection: "Dying and Rising Gods" in the Ancient Near East*, 55–81, ConBOT 50 (Stockholm: Almqvist & Wiksell, 2001). See also Johannes C. de Moor, *The Seasonal Pattern in the Ugaritic Myth of Baʿlu, according to the Version of Ilimilku*, AOAT 16 (Kevelaer: Butzon & Bercker, 1971). In response to Mark S. Smith's contention that Baal might be compared to Anatolian disappearing deities, Mettinger identifies significant differences between Baal and the latter, including what seems to be an actual death for Baal. See Mark S. Smith, "The Death of 'Dying and Rising Gods' in the Biblical World: An Update, with Special References to Baal in the Baal Cycle," *SJOT* 12 (1998): 257–313; Mark S. Smith, *The Origins of Biblical Monotheism: Israel's Polytheistic Background and the Ugaritic Texts* (New York: Oxford University Press, 2001), 104–31.

28. For biblical and archaeological evidence for an Israelite mortuary cult and for worship practices associated with the dead, see Theodore J. Lewis, *Cults of the Dead in Ancient Israel and Ugarit*, HSM 39 (Atlanta: Scholars, 1989); Karel van der Toorn, *Family Religion in Babylonia, Syria and Israel: Continuity and Change in the Forms of Religious Life*, SHCANE 7 (Leiden: Brill, 1996), 206–35; Mark S. Smith, *The Early History of God: Yahweh and the Other Deities in Ancient Israel*, 2nd ed., Biblical Resource Series (Grand Rapids: Eeerdmans; Dearborn, Mich.: Dove, 2002), 162–71. Arguing against an indigenous Israelite or more broadly West Semitic cult of the dead is Brian B. Schmidt, *Israel's Beneficent Dead: Ancestor Cult and Necromancy in Ancient Israelite Religion and Tradition* (Winona Lake, Ind.: Eisenbrauns, 1994), but see Lewis's thorough and persuasive refutation of Schmidt's position in "How Far Can Texts Take Us? Evaluating Textual Sources for Reconstructing Ancient Israelite Beliefs about the Dead," in *Sacred Time, Sacred Place: Archaeology and the Religion of Israel*, ed. B. M. Gittlen, 169–217 (Winona Lake, Ind.: Eisenbrauns, 2002).

29. The expression "Living God" (*ʾēl ḥay* Josh 3:10; Hos 2:1; Pss 42:3; 84:3; *ʾĕlōhîm ḥay* 2 Kings 19:4, 16 = Isa 37:4, 17; *ʾĕlōhîm ḥayyîm* Deut 5:23; 1 Sam 17:26, 36; Jer 10:10; 23:36) typically connotes a recognition of God's activity on behalf of God's people. See Helmer Ringgren, "חָיָה *chāyāh*; חַי *chai*; חַיִּים *chaiyîm*; חַיָּה *chaiyāh*; מִחְיָה *michyāh*," in *TDOT*, 4:324–44, esp. 338–40. The basic connotation of the expression's usage is recognized in the study by Kreuzer, but Kreuzer's claim that the term originally denoted a notion of the deity as ruler is not convincing. Siegfried Kreuzer, *Der lebendige Gott: Bedeutung, Herkunft*

und Entwicklung einer alttestamentlichen Gottesbezeichnung, BWANT Series 6, vol. 16 (Stuttgart: Kohlhammer, 1983).

30. See various discussions of this phenomenon in the following: Lowell K. Handy, *Among the Host of Heaven: The Syro-Palestinian Pantheon as Bureaucracy* (Winona Lake, Ind.: Eisenbrauns, 1994); Smith, *The Early History of God*, 9–12; Øystein LaBianca and Randall W. Younker, "The Kingdoms of Ammon, Moab and Edom: The Archaeology of Society in Late Bronze/Iron Age Transjordan (ca. 1400–500 BCE)," in *Archaeology of Society in the Holy Land,* ed. Thomas E. Levy, 399–415 (London: Leicester University Press, 1995); Daniel I. Block, *The Gods of the Nations: Studies in Ancient Near Eastern National Theology,* 2nd ed. (Grand Rapids: Baker Academic, 2000).

31. For a brief summary of this central point elaborated throughout the rest of his book, see Smith, *The Early History of God*, 7–9. See also the further development of Smith's ideas on dynamics involved in Bronze Age and Iron Age national religion in the ancient Near East, in *God in Translation: Deities in Cross-Cultural Discourse in the Biblical World,* FAT 57 (Tübingen: Mohr Siebeck, 2008), esp. 37–185.

32. Smith, *The Early History of God*, 19–147, 200–207.

33. See the literature cited in Smith, *The Origins of Biblical Monotheism*, 208 nn. 1–3.

34. Ibid., 27; J. David Schloen, *The House of the Father as Fact and Symbol: Patrimonialism in Ugarit and the Ancient Near East,* Studies in the Archaeology and History of the Levant 2 (Winona Lake, Ind.: Eisenbrauns, 2001), esp. 51–52, 65, 69–70, 198, 317–18, 359.

35. Schloen, *The House of the Father as Fact and Symbol*, 315 n. 1.

36. Smith, *The Origins of Biblical Monotheism*, 27.

37. Ibid., 27.

38. As Smith notes, the "outback" (Ugaritic ʾarṣ [m]dbr) is the setting for Baal's battle with Mot (*KTU²* 1.5 VI 6, 29; 1.6 II 20) and is where Baal confronts other enemies (1.12 I 19–22). Smith, *The Origins of Biblical Monotheism*, 29.

39. As Smith explains, "the center" includes civilized foreignness as represented by Egypt, Crete, and Cyprus. Smith, *The Origins of Biblical Monotheism*, 28–31.

40. See Shemaryahu Talmon, "Wilderness," in *IDBSup*, 946–49.

41. Shemaryahu Talmon, "The 'Desert Motif' in the Bible and in Qumran Literature," in *Biblical Motifs: Origins and Transformations,* ed. A. Altmann, 31–63 (Cambridge, Mass.: Harvard University Press, 1966).

42. On this point, see Smith, *The Origins of Biblical Monotheism*, 33–40.

43. For discussion of the early dating of these texts, see Frank Moore Cross and David Noel Freedman, *Studies in Ancient Yahwistic Poetry* (Grand Rapids: Eerdmans, 1997; orig. pub. Society of Biblical Literature, 1975), esp. 1–30, 64–81; David A. Robertson, *Linguistic Evidence in Dating Early Hebrew Poetry,* SBLDS 3 (Missoula, Mont.: Society of Biblical Literature, 1972).

44. See, for example, Carol Meyers, "Temple, Jerusalem," in *ABD,* 6:350–69.

45. Lawrence Stager, "Jerusalem and the Garden of Eden," *ErIsr* 26 (Frank Moore Cross Volume, 1999): 183–94; Mark S. Smith, "Like Deities, Like Temples (Like People)," in *Temple and Worship in Biblical Israel: Proceedings of the Oxford Old Testament Seminar,* ed. John Day, 3–27 (London: T&T Clark, 2007), 7–10.

46. P. Kyle McCarter Jr., "The Garden of Eden: Geographical and Etymological Ruminations on the Garden of God in the Bible and the Ancient Near East" (unpublished paper presented to the Colloquium for Biblical Research, Duke University, 19 August 2001), cited and discussed by Smith, "Like Deities, Like Temples," 8–10.

47. See Elizabeth Bloch-Smith, "'Who Is the King of Glory?' Solomon's Temple and Its Symbolism," in *Scripture and Other Artifacts: Essays on the Bible and Archaeology in Honor of Philip J. King*, ed. J. C. Exum, M. D. Coogan, and L. E. Stager, 18–31 (Louisville: Westminster John Knox, 1994), esp. 23–25; Smith, "Like Deities, Like Temples," 7–10.

48. See S. Dean McBride, "The Deuteronomic Name Theology" (Ph.D. diss., Harvard University, 1969). For more discussion of the theology of Deuteronomy and the books that follow it, see chapter 7.

49. See Antti Laato and Johannes C. de Moor, eds., *Theodicy in the Biblical World* (Leiden: Brill, 2003); James L. Crenshaw, *Defending God: Biblical Responses to the Problem of Evil* (Oxford: Oxford University Press, 2005).

50. Lothar Perlitt, "Die Verborgenheit Gottes," in *Probleme biblischer Theologie,* ed. Hans Walter Wolff, 373–75 (Munich: Kaiser, 1971).

51. Fretheim, *The Suffering of God*, 67–70.

52. See, e.g., Robert K. Gnuse, *The Old Testament and Process Theology* (St. Louis: Chalice, 2000). For the basic criticism against applying the categories of process thought to the Hebrew Bible, see David Penchansky's review of Gnuse's book in *CBQ* 64 (2002): 348–49. Though not from the perspective of process theology, other studies recognize how classic categories for considering divine power are similarly incongruous with the biblical portrayal of the divine. See, e.g., Michael Carasik, "The Limits of Omniscience," *JBL* 119 (2000): 221–32.

53. For an overview, see Richard J. Clifford and John J. Collins, "Introduction: The Theology of Creation Traditions," in *Creation in Biblical Traditions*, ed. Richard J. Clifford and John J. Collins, 1–15, CBQMS 24 (Washington, D.C.: Catholic Biblical Association of America, 1992).

54. Ibid., 8–9.

55. The parade example is G. Ernest Wright, *The Old Testament against Its Environment* (Chicago: Regnery, 1950). For a discussion from the perspectives of both history of religion and biblical theology, see Rainer Albertz, *A History of Israelite Religion in the Old Testament Period*, trans. J. Bowden, 2 vols., Old Testament Library (Philadelphia: Westminster John Knox, 1994), 1:20–21; Leo G. Perdue, *Reconstructing Old Testament Theology: After the Collapse of History,* OBT (Minneapolis: Fortress, 2005), 32–33.

56. The view that the Genesis 1 creation account is rooted in Mesopotamian myth and symbolism received powerful expression from Hermann Gunkel, *Creation and Chaos in the Primeval Era and the Eschaton: A Religio-Historical Study of Genesis 1 and Revelation 12*, ed. Peter Machinist, trans. K. William Whitney Jr., Biblical Resource Series (Grand Rapids: Eerdmans, 2006). See, more recently, Bernard F. Batto, *Slaying the Dragon: Mythmaking in the Biblical Tradition* (Louisville: Westminster John Knox, 1992); Bernard F. Batto, "Creation Theology in Genesis," in *Creation in the Biblical Traditions,* ed. Richard J. Clifford and John J. Collins, CBQMS (Washington, D.C.: Catholic Biblical Association of America, 1992), 16–38.

57. On this Iron Age dynamic, see Smith, *The Early History of God*, 185–91; *The Origins of Biblical Monotheism*, 142–45, 157–66. For dynamics common to the theology of national deities in Bronze Age and Iron Age contexts, see Smith, *God in Translation*, 91–184. On Assur as national god, see Bottéro, *Religion in Ancient Mesopotamia*, 57–58 and n. 14.

58. For recent surveys of scholarship, see John J. Collins, *Introduction to the Hebrew Bible* (Minneapolis: Fortress Press, 2004), 47–82; Michael D. Coogan, *The Old Testament: A Historical and Literary Introduction to the Hebrew Scriptures* (New York: Oxford University Press, 2006), 3–42.

59. Alternatives to the documentary hypothesis still within a largely source critical framework include, most prominently, those of John Van Seters and Erhard Blum. Erhard Blum, *Die Komposition der Vätergeschichte,* WMANT 57 (Neukirchen: Neukirchener, 1984); John Van Seters, *Prologue to History: The Yahwist as Historian in Genesis* (Louisville: Westminster, 1992). An approach that blurs the lines between source and redactional formation for the Pentateuch is that of David McLain Carr, *Reading the Fractures of Genesis: Historical and Literary Approaches* (Louisville: Westminster John Knox, 1996). The rejection of extended written sources across the Pentateuch in favor of a primarily redactional explanation as proposed by Rolf Rendtorff continues to be worked out in European scholarship. See the essays in Thomas B. Dozeman and Konrad Schmid, eds., *A Farewell to the Yahwist? The Composition of the Pentateuch in Recent European Interpretation*, Society of Biblical Literature Symposium Series 34 (Atlanta: Society of Biblical Literature, 2006).

60. See, for example, the bibliography listed in the previous two notes. Both P and J material in PH bear evidence of having been composed or edited during or after the exile. That evidence in J includes its resemblance to aspects of Mesopotamian myth, especially the prominence of a wisdom tree and the Babel story. While it is possible that such influences might have been apparent in Israelite literature before the Babylonian exile, the latter would seem to be the most likely time for their occurrence. Collins, *Introduction*, 75. Such would be in keeping with the late dating of J, as advocated by John Van Seters and Erhard Blum (cited in the previous note). At the same time, there are good reasons for dating J to the monarchic period—especially, its validation of various cult sites outside of Jerusalem, in contradiction to the idea of worship centralization that comes to prevail in Deuteronomic literature, P, Ezekiel, and the postexilic narrative of Chronicles and Ezra-Nehemiah. Accordingly, it is possible that the Yahwistic material in PH did not originally belong to J and was added during or after the exile, or alternatively that seemingly late elements were added to PH material original to J. See Collins, *Introduction*, 75.

61. Ibid., 77. Similarly and also in keeping with the classic source critical framework, Batto sees the J creation account as preexilic and P's account as a revision composed during or after the exile and prompted by the theological challenges of that experience. Batto, "Creation Theology in Genesis," esp. 17, 31–38. For a thorough treatment of the Priestly creation account, see Mark S. Smith, *The Priestly Vision of Genesis 1* (Minneapolis: Fortress Press, 2010).

62. Batto, "Creation Theology in Genesis," 31–38.

63. See Bernard F. Batto, "The Sleeping God: An Ancient Near Eastern Motif of Divine Sovereignty," *Bib* 68 (1987): 153–77.

64. See, for example, Batto, "Creation Theology in Genesis," 32.

65. Jeremiah 4:23 describes disruptions to the created order as a return to chaos, using the same expression from Genesis 1, *tōhû wābōhû.*

66. Jon D. Levenson, *Creation and the Persistence of Evil: The Jewish Drama of Divine Omnipotence* (San Francisco: Harper & Row, 1988).

67. Delbert R. Hillers, "Palmyrene Aramaic Inscriptions and the Bible (II)," *ZAH* 11 (1998): 32–49.

68. Collins, *Introduction*, 77. Based on affinities between the Priestly theology and Ezekiel and on the understanding of humankind as the true "image of God" in Genesis 1, John Kutsko argues that the book of Ezekiel implies God's presence among the exiles to be the true counterpart to false representations of the divine in cult statues as found in temples. See John F. Kutsko, *Between Heaven and Earth: Divine Presence and Absence in the Book of Ezekiel,* Biblical and Judaic Studies from the University of California, San Diego, vol. 7 (Winona Lake, Ind.: Eisenbrauns, 2000), esp. 66–76, 94–100.

69. Lambert and Millard, *Atra-Ḥasīs*, 88–97.

70. *Enuma Elish* I 32–33; *Atrahasis* I i 41–ii 62, 146–65, 176–77, etc.

71. See also Isa 6:1, 6. First Kings 22 contains descriptions of both human (vv. 1-18, 24-28) and divine (vv. 19-23) court scenes. The former case involves deliberation in the form of first-person-plural speech: "The king of Israel said to his servants, 'Do you know that Ramoth-gilead belongs to us, yet we are doing nothing to take it . . . ?'" (v. 3). Micaiah's prophetic vision of the divine court centers around Yahweh "sitting on his throne, with all the host of heaven standing beside him to the right and to the left of him" and soliciting a messenger to deceive the Israelite king (vv. 19-23).

5. Wisdom Literature

1. The trajectory of wisdom in the Hebrew Bible is represented by the deuterocanonical books of Ben Sira and the Wisdom of Solomon. The recognition of wisdom psalms has included all or parts of the following: Pss 1, 8, 14, 19 (esp. vv. 7-14), 25, 32, 34, 37, 39, 49, 53, 73, 78, 90, 91, 104, 105, 106, 111–112, 119, 127, 128, 131, 133, and 139. While the literary classification of "wisdom psalms," as first suggested by Hermann Gunkel, may be debatable, these psalms share in various degrees the language, devices, and themes that characteristically appear in the books of Proverbs, Job, and Qoheleth. See Herman Gunkel and Joachim Begrich, *Introduction to Psalms: The Genres of the Religious Lyric of Israel,* trans. James D. Nogalski, Mercer Library of Biblical Studies (Macon: Mercer University Press, 1998), 293–305. Based on a lack of agreement among scholars in criteria for defining the category, James Crenshaw denies its usefulness. James L. Crenshaw, "Wisdom Psalms?" *CurBS* 8 (2000): 9–17; idem, *The Psalms: An Introduction* (Grand Rapids: Eerdmans, 2001), 87–95; see the rejoinder by J. Kenneth Kuntz, "Reclaiming Biblical Wisdom Psalms: A Response to Crenshaw," *CurBS* (2003): 145–54. In some ways illustrating Crenshaw's objections but also elaborating on Kuntz's major point of response, Leo G. Perdue's recent discussion substantiates the existence of characteristic vocabulary and themes that allow for identifying a distinct wisdom emphasis in certain psalms, even if not allowing for clear-cut delineation of "wisdom psalms" from "Torah psalms" or "creation psalms." See

Leo G. Perdue, *The Sword and the Stylus: An Introduction to Wisdom in the Age of Empires* (Grand Rapids: Eerdmans, 2008), 152–97.

2. For discussion of wisdom thought's integral relationship to creation theology, see Walther Zimmerli, *Old Testament Theology in Outline* (Atlanta: John Knox, 1978), 39–40, 155–66; Roland E. Murphy, "Wisdom and Creation," *JBL* 104 (1985): 3–11; Leo G. Perdue, "Cosmology and the Social Order in the Wisdom Tradition," in *The Sage in Israel and the Ancient Near East*, ed. John G. Gammie and Leo G. Perdue, 457–78 (Winona Lake, Ind.: Eisenbrauns, 1990); Leo G. Perdue, *Wisdom and Creation: The Theology of Wisdom Literature* (Nashville: Abingdon, 1994); Terence E. Fretheim, *God and World in the Old Testament: A Relational Theology of Creation* (Nashville: Abingdon, 2005), 199–247.

3. Michael V. Fox, *The JPS Bible Commentary: Ecclesiastes* קהלת (Philadelphia: Jewish Publication Society, 2004), x–xi.

4. Michael V. Fox, *Proverbs 1–9: A New Translation with Introduction and Commentary*, AB 18A (New York: Doubleday, 2000), 17. As Fox points out, Qoheleth "contains much critical or reflective material, but as a whole it presents itself as a teaching about how to live one's life and is to be classed as didactic," as indicated by the epilogue in Qoh 12:9-14 (pp. 17–18). Though identifying Qoheleth as reflective and even "pessimistic" wisdom literature, C. L. Seow similarly notes the book's continuity with didactic wisdom and stresses that it is equally representative of the wisdom enterprise. Seow, *Ecclesiastes: A New Translation with Introduction and Commentary*, AB 18C (New York: Doubleday, 1997), 65–69.

5. James L. Crenshaw, "In Search of Divine Presence (Some Remarks Preliminary to a Theology of Wisdom)," *RevExp* 74 (1977): 353–69.

6. Lawrence E. Toombs, "Old Testament Theology and the Wisdom Literature," *JBR* 23 (1955): 193–96; Walther Zimmerli, "The Place and the Limit of the Wisdom in the Framework of the Old Testament Theology," in *Studies in Ancient Israelite Wisdom*, ed. James L. Crenshaw, 314–26 (New York: KTAV, 1976), 316, reprinted from *SJT* 17 (1964): 146–58; Robert Davidson, "Some Aspects of the Theological Significance of Doubt in the Old Testament," *ASTI* 7 (1970): 41–52, esp. 41–43; James Barr, *The Concept of Biblical Theology: An Old Testament Perspective* (Minneapolis: Fortress Press, 1999), 314–15, 323–25, 330–44, 380–81, 464–65, esp. 476–78, 541–42; Crenshaw, "In Search of Divine Presence," 362; Seow, *Ecclesiastes*, 65–66; Leo G. Perdue, *Wisdom Literature: A Theological History* (Louisville: Westminster John Knox, 2007), 15–36.

7. Zimmerli, *Old Testament Theology*, 155–56; Richard J. Clifford, *The Wisdom Literature*, Interpreting Biblical Texts (Nashville: Abingdon, 1998), 23–41; James Crenshaw, *Old Testament Wisdom: An Introduction*, rev. ed. (Louisville: Westminster John Knox, 1998), 205–226; Seow, *Ecclesiastes*, 60–66; Fox, *Proverbs 1–9*, 17–23. One of the most impressive and frequently invoked instances involves the extensive parallels between Prov 22:17—24:22 and the Egyptian Instruction of Amenemope (ca. 1100 B.C.E.). See *ANET*, 421–25; *AEL*, 2:146–63.

8. Gerhard von Rad, *Wisdom in Israel*, trans. James D. Martin (Harrisburg, Pa.: Trinity, 1972), 97–110 (discussed later in this chapter).

9. See the thorough discussion of this point by Antti Laato and Johannes C. de Moor, "Introduction," in *Theodicy in the Biblical World*, ed. Antti Laato and Johannes C. de Moor, vii–liv (Leiden: Brill, 2003); and Marcel Sarot, "Theodicy

and Modernity: An Inquiry into the Historicity of Theodicy," in Laato and de Moor, *Theodicy in the Biblical World*, 1–26.

10. *ANET*, 596–600; *COS*, 1:486–92, text 1.153.

11. Crenshaw, "In Search of Divine Presence," 367 n. 21. See William P. Brown's discussion of character formation in the three Wisdom books of the Hebrew Bible as a journey involving "The Self Moving Outward" and "The Self Returning." Brown, *Character in Crisis: A Fresh Approach to the Wisdom Literature of the Old Testament* (Grand Rapids: Eerdmans, 1996), 151–64.

12. Clifford, *The Wisdom Literature*, 34.

13. *Theology of the Old Testament*, vol. 2, trans. J. A. Baker, OTL (Philadelphia: Westminster, 1967), 87.

14. Michael V. Fox, "The Social Location of the Book of Proverbs," in *Texts, Temples, and Traditions: A Tribute to Menahem Haran*, ed. M. V. Fox et al., 227–39 (Winona Lake, Ind.: Eisenbrauns, 1996).

15. André Lemaire, "The Sage in School and Temple," in Gammie and Perdue, *The Sage in Israel and the Ancient Near East*, 165–81.

16. James L. Crenshaw, *Education in Ancient Israel: Across the Deadening Silence* (New York: Doubleday, 1998), 85–113; Christopher A. Rollston, "Scribal Education in Ancient Israel: The Old Hebrew Epigraphic Evidence," *BASOR* 344 (2006): 47–74.

17. Clifford, *The Wisdom Literature*, 26–27, 29; Fox, *Proverbs 1–9*, 8–9; Leo G. Perdue, "Sages, Scribes, and Seers in Israel and the Ancient Near East: An Introduction," in *Scribes, Sages, and Seers: The Sage in the Eastern Mediterranean World*, ed. Leo G. Perdue, 1–34 (Göttingen: Vandenhoeck & Ruprecht, 2008), esp. 17–31; Bendt Alster, "Scribes, Sages, and Seers in Ancient Mesopotamia," in Perdue, *Scribes, Sages, and Seers*, 47–63, esp. 48–52.

18. *ANET*, 421–25; *COS*, 1:115–22, text 1.47.

19. Clifford, *The Wisdom Literature*, 23–41; Perdue, "Sages, Scribes, and Seers in Israel and the Ancient Near East," 1–34.

20. See, for example, David W. Jamieson-Drake, for whom the correlation implies a negative argument from silence for a centralized state in Judah prior to the eighth century. Jamieson-Drake, *Scribes and Schools in Monarchic Judah: A Socio-Archaeological Approach*, JSOTSup 109 (Sheffield: Sheffield Academic, 1991), esp. 147–49, 154–57. Nevertheless, the Iron Age state most likely did not found scribal culture but rather co-opted and proliferated it. For the latter point, see Ryan Byrne, "The Refuge of Scribalism in Iron I Palestine," *BASOR* 345 (2007): 1–31; Seth L. Sanders, "Writing and Early Iron Age Israel: Before National Scripts, beyond Nations and States," in *Literate Culture and Tenth-Century Canaan: The Tel Zayit Abecedary in Context*, ed. Ron E. Tappy and P. Kyle McCarter, 97–112 (Winona Lake, Ind.: Eisenbrauns, 2008).

21. Fox, "Social Location," 227–39; Clifford, *The Wisdom Literature*, 49, 73, 99–101. This viewpoint provides the framework for Perdue, *The Sword and the Stylus* (see esp. pp. 70–80).

22. Fox, "Social Location," 239.

23. Crenshaw, *Old Testament Wisdom*, 45.

24. Clifford, *The Wisdom Literature*, 51, 56–68. For an outline of Proverbs, see Fox, *Proverbs*, 5; or Richard Clifford, "Proverbs, Book of," in *NIDB*, 4:656.

25. Raymond C. Van Leeuwen, "Cosmos, Temple, House: Building and Wisdom in Mesopotamia and Israel," in *Wisdom Literature in Mesopotamia and*

Israel, ed. Richard J. Clifford, 67–90, SBL Symposium Series 36 (Leiden: Brill, 2007).

26. Ibid., 67.

27. Thorkild Jacobsen, *The Treasures of Darkness: A History of Mesopotamian Religion* (New Haven: Yale University Press, 1976), 81.

28. Van Leeuwen, "Cosmos, Temple, House," 81. As Van Leeuwen points out based on his overview of related Mesopotamian texts, the pairing of these two verses from Proverbs represents a common cultural ideal that reaches far beyond the different genres, collections, and social contexts that the two passages represent. Nonetheless, Van Leeuwen offers a thorough review of the scholarly discussion of those differences (pp. 78–80 nn. 54–62).

29. Clifford, "Proverbs," 657.

30. Although the failure of Job's physical health seems to be the last straw in the prologue (2:4-13), it is not mentioned in the epilogue.

31. The opening verses introduce the book's principle speaker as Qoheleth (BH *qōhelet*), a term with the form of a verbal noun in BH (G active participle; though feminine in form, in contrast with the description of Qoheleth as male in 1:1 and elsewhere in the book) and with the ostensible meaning "one who gathers an assembly," hence the Latin translation *ecclesiastes* and the traditional English translations "The Preacher" (KJV) and "The Teacher" (NRSV). Qoheleth's royal identity fades as the book progresses. See Choon Leong Seow, "Qohelet's Autobiography," in *Fortunate the Eyes That See: Essays in Honor of David Noel Freedman in Celebration of His Seventieth Birthday,* ed. Astrid B. Beck et al., 275–87 (Grand Rapids: Eerdmans, 1995); Seow, *Ecclesiastes,* 36–37, 48, 65.

32. Clifford, *The Wisdom Literature,* 51.

33. Ibid., 54.

34. See Lawrence E. Stager, "The Archaeology of the Family in Ancient Israel," *BASOR* 260 (1985): 1–35, here 25–27.

35. Fox, *Proverbs 1–9,* 8–9.

36. For information on the text and dating, see the discussions of Bendt Alster, "Shuruppak," in *COS,* 1:569; Clifford, *The Wisdom Literature,* 28–29. For the text in English translation, see Wilfred Lambert, *Babylonian Wisdom Literature* (Winona Lake, Ind.: Einsenbrauns, 1996; repr. Oxford: Clarendon, 1960), 92–95; and excerpts in *ANET,* 594–95; *COS,* 1:569–70.

37. The English translation in these three quotations from Shuruppak is my rendering of Willem H. Ph. Römer's German translation of the Old Babylonian Sumerian texts in *TUAT,* 3, part 1:48–67, the three quotes here being from p. 50 lines 6–13, pp. 60–61 lines 173–75, and p. 66 lines 258–61. The first two of these texts are referenced and similarly translated into English by Clifford in *The Wisdom Literature,* 27–28 and 170 n. 7.

38. James M. Lindenberger, "Ahiqar (Seventh to Sixth Century B.C.): A New Translation and Introduction," in *The Old Testament Pseudepigrapha,* ed. J. H. Charlesworth, 2:479–507, Anchor Bible Reference Library (New York: Doubleday, 1985), 482. As Lindenberger explains, the Aramaic text is known from a late-fifth-century B.C.E. manuscript from Elephantine in Egypt, but the proverbs could reasonably date from the eighth century, and the lack of Persian loanwords indicates a date of composition before the mid-sixth century. The quotations that follow are from Lindenberger's English translation and are cited according to his numbering of the "sayings." For the Aramaic text and more discussion of

textual and linguistic issues, see James M. Lindenberger, *The Aramaic Proverbs of Ahiqar,* JHNES (Baltimore: Johns Hopkins University Press, 1983).

39. The missing words in Lindenberger's English translation results from a damaged portion of the text. See Lindenberger, "Ahiqar," 498.

40. Clifford, *The Wisdom Literature,* 65.

41. As this statement shows, Woman Wisdom can hardly be considered a substitute for royal authority after the exile, as argued by Claudia Camp, but rather throughout Proverbs, Wisdom represents the channel of divine authority and order through which kings rule. Compare Claudia Camp, *Wisdom and the Feminine in the Book of Proverbs,* Bible and Literature Series 11 (Decatur, Ga.: Almond, 1985), 278–80, 290–91. On the importance of the Great King to everyday life during the Persian period, see Choon-Leong Seow, "The Social World of Ecclesiastes," in Perdue, *Scribes, Sages, and Seers,* 189–217, esp. 199–215.

42. Clifford, *The Wisdom Literature,* 99; Seow, *Ecclesiastes,* 36–37.

43. Ronald F. G. Sweet, "The Sage in Akkadian Literature: A Philological Study," in Gammie and Perdue, *The Sage in Israel and the Ancient Near East,* 45–65, esp. 51–57; Clifford, *The Wisdom Literature,* 25–26.

44. Seow, *Ecclesiastes,* 36–37, 48.

45. Clifford, *The Wisdom Literature,* 99 (italics in original).

46. Seow, "The Social World," 190.

47. Seow, *Ecclesiastes,* 33–36; Seow, "The Social World," 199–215. See also Choon Leong Seow, "Linguistic Evidence and the Dating of Qoheleth," *JBL* 115 (1996): 645–66.

48. Clifford, *The Wisdom Literature,* 101.

49. See, for example, Erik Hornung, *Conceptions of God in Ancient Egypt: The One and the Many,* trans. John Baines (Ithaca, N.Y.: Cornell University Press, 1982), 43; Lambert, *Babylonian Wisdom Literature,* 34–35, 40–41, 46, and so forth; compare Lambert's suggestion that "god" (or its substitution by the plural form in reference to a single deity) refers to "the personal god" (p. 67). More likely, it simply refers to the god in question more generally. See Joel S. Burnett, *A Reassessment of Biblical Elohim,* SBLDS 183 (Atlanta: Society of Biblical Literature, 2001), 43–46. See also discussion of this generic usage for "god" in Egyptian wisdom texts by Mark S. Smith, *God in Translation: Deities in Cross-Cultural Discourse in the Biblical World,* FAT 57 (Tübingen: Mohr Siebeck, 2008), 54 n. 78.

50. Seow, *Ecclesiastes,* 66.

51. In these instances in Job, *šadday* ("the Almighty") appears most frequently, always in parallelism with either *ʾĕlôah* or *(ha)ʾēl* (both, "God"); *ʾĕlōhîm* ("God") occurs in the speeches only in 5:8; 28:23; and 34:9. See Marvin H. Pope, *Job: Introduction, Translation, and Notes,* 3rd ed., AB 15 (Garden City, N.Y.: Doubleday, 1979), 43.

52. Compare Carol Newsom's assessment that "Whatever the origins of the figure of Job, his story has been naturalized into Israelite religious culture, so that Job is presented unself-consciously as a worshiper of Yahweh (1:21)." Carol A. Newsom, "The Book of Job: Introduction, Commentary, and Reflections," in *NIB,* 4:317–637, here 345.

Noteworthy in the prophetic threat of Ezek 14:14, 20 is the individualism that breaks down traditional patrimonial solidarity in the face of divine judgment: "Even if Noah, Daniel, and Job were in [a land under Yahweh's condemnation], as I live, says the Lord GOD, they would save neither son nor daughter; they would save only their own lives by their righteousness" (v. 20). For Daniel, the protagonist known at Ugarit, see J. J. Collins, "Daniel דנ׳אל," in *DDD*, 219–20.

53. In contrast to the usual downplaying of specific divine identity in wisdom literature, the emphasis on national god as creator god belongs to what Mark Smith discusses as the nontranslatability of deities in Mesopotamian empire theology and in Israelite responses. Smith, *God in Translation*, 37–76, 131–85, 321–27. At the same time and against the suggestion of a kind of tolerant plural-ism in the explicit cross-cultural equation of deities in international texts during the Late Bronze Age—as suggested by Jan Assmann in *Die Mosaische Untersc-heidung: Oder der Preis des Monotheismus* (Munich: Hanser, 2003) and, more recently, *Of God and Gods: Egypt, Israel, and the Rise of Monotheism* (Madi-son: University of Wisconsin Press, 2008)—Smith points out that such equations occur in the context of projections of national power. The generic designation of the divine in traditional Mesopotamian and Egyptian wisdom thinking is some-thing different: an attempt at a universalizing viewpoint that, nonetheless, rests on the assumption of an Egyptian or Mesopotamian pantheon with no need for translation into the language of another theological system. As Smith explains, divine translatability in Late Bronze texts was a by-product of engagement among the elite of different kingdoms and cultures in the Near East within a setting of relative political parity. By contrast, the theological rhetoric of imperial domina-tion under the Neo-Assyrian and Neo-Babylonian empires brought about a cor-responding rejection of divine translatability in favor of "one-god" theism (or, to use Smith's term, *summodeism*, "the idea of one deity as the sum and summit of other deities who remain deities in their own right"; Smith, *God in Translation*, 168), as embodied by Assur and Marduk. Mesopotamian summodeism resulted in, among other things, Israelite responses like the explicitly Yahwistic creation theology of Proverbs. Insofar as biblical language reflects a limited pantheon in comparison with the elaborate polytheism of older textual traditions of Egypt and Mesopotamia, it expresses all the more a self-conscious nationalistic response to the theology of empire faced by the kingdoms of Israel and Judah beginning with the Neo-Assyrian period. Smith, *God in Translation*, 131–85.

54. Clifford, *The Wisdom Literature*, 50–51.

55. Clifford, "Proverbs," 657.

56. Von Rad, *Wisdom in Israel*, 97–110, discussed later in this chapter.

57. Ibid., 65–66.

58. See Michael Barré, "'Fear of God' and the World View of Wisdom," *BTB* 11 (1981): 41–43.

59. Seow, *Ecclesiastes*, 69.

60. Fox, *Proverbs 1–9*, 69–71.

61. Ibid., 69.

62. Ibid., 72.

63. Von Rad, *Wisdom in Israel*, 108.

64. Ibid., 108–9.

65. Crenshaw "In Search of Divine Presence," 355.

66. Ibid., 354–55.

67. Von Rad, *Wisdom in Israel*, 92.

68. Van Leeuwen, "Cosmos, Temple, House," 77–87, discussed earlier in this chapter.

69. The translation is from Lindenberger, "Ahiqar," 499; see also, with the Aramaic text and textual notes and discussion, Lindenberger, *The Aramaic Proverbs of Ahiqar*, 68–70.

70. Notwithstanding personified Wisdom's development from Proverbs to later wisdom texts Ben Sira and Wisdom of Solomon, Alan Lenzi's arguments for Prov 8:22-31's dependence on Prov 3:19-21, while valid, are not conclusive. Alan Lenzi, *Secrecy and the Gods: Secret Knowledge in Ancient Mesopotamia and Biblical Israel*, State Archives of Assyria Studies 19 (Helsinki: Neo-Assyrian Text Corpus Project, University of Helsinki, 2008), 338–62. Alternatively, the two might represent images with different nuance or even varying degrees of personification by the same author or different ones. See the comments of Fox, *Proverbs 1–9*, 331–32.

71. Van Leeuwen, "Cosmos, Temple, House," 67–90.

72. For secondary literature on this and other interpretations, see Gerlinde Baumann, *Die Weisheitsgestalt in Proverbien 1–9: Traditionsgeschichtliche und theologische Studien*, FAT 16 (Tübingen: Mohr [Siebeck], 1996), 202–9.

73. Camp, *Wisdom and the Feminine*, 23–147; Baumann, *Die Weisheitsgestalt in Proverbien 1–9*, esp. 56–57; Fox, *Proverbs 1–9*, 331–41; Perdue, *Wisdom Literature: A Theological History*, 338–40; Lenzi, *Secrecy and the Gods*, 339–62.

74. See especially Christa Bauer-Kayatz, *Studien zu Proverbien 1–9*, WMANT 22 (Neukirchen-Vluyn: Neukirchener, 1966), 13–14, 17; idem, *Einführung in die alttestamentliche Weisheit*, Biblische Studien 55 (Neukirchen-Vluyn: Neukirchener, 1969), 45–51; and the reviews of scholarship in Camp, *Wisdom and the Feminine*, 23–68 and Baumann, *Die Weisheitsgestalt in Proverbien 1–9*, 13–27. Many scholars point to the parallel imagery in Prov 3:16, which describes Wisdom offering "long life" in her right hand and "riches and honor" in her left, and the frequent Egyptian depiction of Maat holding the ankh (the Egyptian symbol of life) in one hand and a scepter (representing wealth and dignity) in the other. See, for example, Bauer-Kayatz, *Studien zu Proverbien 1–9*, 157; *Einführung in die alttestamentliche Weisheit*, 50–51. In addition, Victor Avigdor Hurowitz notes Mesopotamian parallels in inscriptions offering similar descriptions of the goddess Ishtar, with the conclusion, "Thus, the picture of personified wisdom extending her blessings to the wise need not be indications of particularly Egyptian background but can equally well be of Mesopotamian provenance or simply indicative of the common cultural heritage of the ancient Near East." Victor Avigdor Hurowitz, "Paradise Regained: Proverbs 3:13-20 Reconsidered," in *Sefer Moshe, The Moshe Weinfeld Jubilee Volume: Studies in the Bible and the Ancient Near East, Qumran, and Post-Biblical Judaism*, ed. Chaim Cohen, Avi Hurvitz, and Shalom M. Paul, 49–62 (Winona Lake, Ind.: Eisenbrauns, 2004), esp. 53–55 and quoting from 55. Based on the first-person rhetoric of self-exaltation, Wisdom's association with kings and royal patron goddesses like Egyptian Hathor, Isis, and Neith and Mesopotamian Ishtar, and her role as witness to creation, Bernhard Lang understands Proverbs 8 to depict Wisdom as a goddess, the daughter of the creator god Yahweh, comparable in some respects to Maat but more likely a "school goddess" like Egyptian Seshat or Sumerian Nisaba. Bernhard Lang, *Wisdom and the Book of Proverbs: A Hebrew Goddess Redefined* (New York: Pilgrim, 1986), 53–70, 129–31. As Lang understands, the goddess depiction is present in the text of Proverbs 8 but, within the framework

of developing monotheism in postexilic Judaism, was redefined as a poetic personification of wisdom teaching.

75. This explanation occurs as early as Wilhelm Schencke, *Die Chokma
(Sophia) in der jüdischen Hypostasenspekulation,* Videnskapsselskapets Skrifter
II. Hist.-filos. klasse 1912, no. 6 (Kristiania: Dybwad, 1913); and Wilhelm Bous-
set and Hugo Gressmann, *Die Religion des Judentums im späthellenistischen
Zeitalter* (Tübingen: Mohr, 1926), 342–54; both cited with quotations in Lang,
Wisdom and the Book of Proverbs, 174 n. 6. The trajectory of this explanation
in more recent scholarship begins with Helmer Ringgren, *Word and Wisdom*
(Lund: Haken Ohlssons Boktryckeri, 1947), 8, 95–106. For more detailed history
of scholarship, see Lang, *Wisdom and the Book of Proverbs,* 137–40; Baumann,
Die Weisheitsgestalt in Proverbien 1–9, 4–13.

76. See Sigmund Mowinckel, "Hypostasen," in *Die Religion in Geschichte
und Gegenwart: Handwörterbuch für Theologie und Religionswissenschaft,*
ed. Herman Gunkel et al., 2nd ed., 5 vols. (Tübingen: Mohr, 1928), 2065–68;
Aubrey R. Johnson, *The One and the Many in the Israelite Conception of
God,* 2nd ed. (Cardiff: University of Wales Press, 1961), 13–22, 28–37; S. Dean
McBride, "The Deuteronomic Name Theology" (Ph.D. diss., Harvard University,
1969); P. Kyle McCarter Jr., "Aspects of the Religion of the Israelite Monarchy:
Biblical and Epigraphic Data," in *Ancient Israelite Religion,* ed. P. D. Miller, P.
D. Hanson, and S. D. McBride, 137–55 (Philadelphia: Fortress Press, 1987); and
very early on, Ferdinand Weber, *Jüdische Theologie auf Grund des Talmud und
verwandter Schriften* (Leipzig: Dörfflin & Franke, 1897), 177, cited in Lang,
Wisdom and the Book of Proverbs, 138–39, 174 n. 5.

77. Thus, on analogy to the Phoenician-Punic goddess Tanit's identity as "the
face of Baal" (*pn b'l*), P. Kyle McCarter suggests that the goddess Asherah originated as the "trace" or "footprint" of the leading male deity. McCarter, "Aspects
of the Religion of the Israelite Monarchy," 148. See also Burnett, *A Reassessment
of Biblical Elohim,* 91 n. 36. Indirect support for McCarter's philological explanation now comes from increased attention to the divine footprints featured in
the paving stones of the temple at Ain Dara. John Monson, "The New Ain Dara
Temple: Closest Solomonic Parallel," *BA* 26 no.3 (2000): 20–35, 67.

78. See Fox, *Proverbs 1–9,* 285–87; Clifford, "Proverbs," 658; Lenzi, *Secrecy
and the Gods,* 354–57.

79. Camp, *Wisdom and the Feminine;* Baumann, *Die Weisheitsgestalt in Proverbien 1–9,* 280–82; Fox, *Proverbs 1–9,* 331–59.

80. Murphy, "Wisdom and Creation," 9–10.

81. Crenshaw, "In Search of Divine Presence," 359.

82. Fox, *Proverbs 1–9,* 334.

83. This usual aspect of the wisdom viewpoint makes Yahweh's appearance
and speeches to Job all the more remarkable (Job 38–42; see discussion later in
this chapter).

84. Crenshaw, "In Search of Divine Presence," 359.

85. Cited by ibid., 356.

86. Ibid., 359. Crenshaw, like other scholars, warns against "a chronological
fallacy: the belief that the wise underwent three distinct eras corresponding to the
understandings of God." As Crenshaw points out, "A single generation, indeed a
lone individual, may have experienced all three phenomena" (p. 362). Despite the
appearance of such an approach, Perdue's historical schema is nuanced around

the discussion of complexities and uncertainties relating to the literary histories of the books. See Perdue, *The Sword and the Stylus*, 86–89, 118–23, 200–202.

87. Sarot, "Theodicy and Modernity," 1–26. See also above, chapter 4.

88. Laato and De Moor, "Introduction," vii–liv; Sarot, "Theodicy and Modernity," 1–26.

89. The following overview of ancient Near Eastern wisdom texts is informed by the summaries of Crenshaw, *Old Testament Wisdom*, 205–226; and Clifford, *The Wisdom Literature*, 23–41.

90. As translated and edited by Dalley, *Myths from Mesopotamia*, 150.

91. *ANET*, 467; *AEL*, 1:194–97.

92. *ANET*, 407–10; *AEL*, 1:169–84.

93. *ANET*, 405–407; *AEL*, 1:163–69.

94. *ANET*, 441–44; *AEL*, 1:159–63. This characterization of the text follows Clifford, *The Wisdom Literature*, 37.

95. *ANET*, 589–91.

96. *ANET*, 601–604; *BWL*, 63–91, both relating the translation of W. G. Lambert, which is the source of the following quotations of the text. For Lambert's dating, see *BWL*, 67.

97. Citing Lambert's edition and translation in *ANET*, 596–600; *BWL*, 21–62.

98. Clifford, *The Wisdom Literature*, 70.

99. The move from suffering to exaltation of the divine is similar to the progression that characterizes individual lament in the book of Psalms. See the discussion in the following chapter.

100. Chrysostome Larcher, "Divine Transcendence as Another Reason for God's Absence," in *Scripture: The Presence of God,* ed. Roland Murphy Pierre Benoit and Bastiaan van Iersel, 49–64, Concilium: Theology in the Age of Renewal (New York: Paulist, 1969), 49.

101. Crenshaw, "In Search of Divine Presence," 360–61.

102. Newsom, "The Book of Job," 595. On this point, Newsom refers to Job 9:14-20, 32-35; 13:3, 15-24; 23:3-7, 15-17; 31:35-37.

103. Clifford, *The Wisdom Literature*, 77.

104. But compare Raymond C. Van Leeuwen, "Psalm 8.5 and Job 7.17-18: A Mistaken Scholarly Commonplace?" in *The World of the Aramaeans I: Biblical Studies in Honour of Paul-Eugène Dion,* ed. P. M. Michèle Daviau, John W. Wevers, and Michael Weigl, 205–215, JSOTSup 324 (Sheffield: Sheffield Academic, 2001).

105. Newsom, "The Book of Job," 595–96.

106. Mark S. Smith, *The Origins of Biblical Monotheism: Israel's Polytheistic Background and the Ugaritic Texts* (New York: Oxford University Press, 2001), 33–35.

107. Clifford, *The Wisdom Literature*, 94.

108. Samuel E. Balentine, "Job, Book of," in *NIDB*, 3:319–36, here 334.

109. Clifford, *The Wisdom Literature*, 77.

110. Larcher, "Divine Transcendence as Another Reason for God's Absence," 52–56.

111. Clifford, *The Wisdom Literature*, 73.

112. Crenshaw, "In Search of Divine Presence," 357.

113. Ibid., 358–59.

114. Ibid., 359.
115. Newsom, "The Book of Job," 326.
116. Seow, *Ecclesiastes*, 59.
117. Clifford, *The Wisdom Literature*, 103.
118. Crenshaw, "In Search of Divine Presence," 358.
119. Clifford, *The Wisdom Literature*, 105.
120. James L. Crenshaw, *Ecclesiastes: A Commentary*, OTL (Philadelphia: Westminster, 1987), 25.
121. Crenshaw, "In Search of Divine Presence," 361.
122. Seow, *Ecclesiastes*, 54–60.
123. Agustinus Gianto, "Ecclesiastes, Book of," in *NIDB*, 2:178–85, here 184.
124. See ibid., 184.
125. Ibid.
126. Ibid., 183.
127. Ibid., 183–84.

6. Seeking Divine Presence in Worship

1. Underscoring the vital interrelationship of these two sides of ancient Israel's cultic life and of the corresponding texts is Gary A. Anderson, "The Praise of God as a Cultic Event," in *Priesthood and Cult in Ancient Israel,* ed. Gary A. Anderson and Saul M. Olyan, 15–33 (Sheffield: Sheffield Academic, 1991), esp. 15.

2. This understanding of worship in the Hebrew Bible follows the explanatory rubric of Frank H. Gorman Jr., *The Ideology of Ritual: Space, Time and Status in the Priestly Theology,* JSOTSup 91 (Sheffield: Sheffield Academic, 1990), esp. 7–11, 27–38.

3. Baruch J. Schwartz reminds readers that ritual and legal texts, like other biblical texts, are works of literary artistry. Schwartz, "The Prohibitions Concerning the 'Eating' of Blood in Leviticus 17," in *Priesthood and Cult in Ancient Israel,* ed. Gary A. Anderson and Saul M. Olyan, 34–66, JSOTSup 125 (Sheffield: Sheffield Academic, 1991), 34–35. Seizing on this frequently overlooked notion is the idiosyncratic literary and theological treatment of Leviticus by the brilliant anthropologist Mary Douglas in *Leviticus as Literature* (Oxford: Oxford University Press, 1999). Though disavowing her own earlier treatment of ritual thinking in Leviticus, Douglas's tremendous contribution to the field remains elucidating the worldview of Priestly ritual through anthropological perspective. Mary Douglas, *Purity and Danger: An Analysis of the Concepts of Pollution and Taboo* (London: Routledge, 1966). Indeed, the literary nature of Priestly texts has merited long-overdue attention. Still, the textual mediation of the Priestly ritual hardly diminishes its status as a legitimate witness to general ritual thinking as attested in broader anthropological perspective. Saul Olyan advises caution in distinguishing "utopian" textual representations of ritual from historical practices and their historical contexts. Saul M. Olyan, *Rites and Rank: Hierarchy in Biblical Representations of Cult* (Princeton: Princeton University Press, 2000), 13. James W. Watts points out the difficulty in treating diachronic historical development of ancient Israel's ritual using biblical texts. Watts, *Ritual and Rhetoric in Leviticus: From Sacrifice to Scripture* (Cambridge: Cambridge University Press,

2007), esp. 1–36. Given the prescriptive nature of biblical ritual texts in attempt-ing to represent a given ideal of worship, Watts's emphasis on their rhetorical (persuasive) dimension is well placed. Another recent study that engages the liter-ary nature of ritual texts is Bryan D. Bibb, *Ritual Words and Narrative Worlds in the Book of Leviticus*, LHBOTS 480 (New York: T&T Clark, 2009), esp. 7–33.

4. Erhard Gerstenberger, *Der bittende Mensch: Bittritual und Klagelied des Einzelnen im Alten Testament* (Neukirchen-Vluyn: Neukirchener, 1980), 1–169; Thomas Podella, *Şôm-Fasten: Kollektive Trauer um den verborgenen Gott im Alten Testament*, AOAT 224 (Kevelaer: Butzon & Bercker, 1989), esp. 1–32, 117–289.

5. Gary A. Anderson, *A Time to Mourn, a Time to Dance: The Expression of Grief and Joy in Israelite Religion* (University Park: Pennsylvania State University Press, 1991), 96.

6. Ibid., 97.

7. Ibid., 88–91, 93.

8. Ibid., 59–97, esp. 82–97.

9. Saul M. Olyan, *Biblical Mourning: Ritual and Social Dimensions* (New York: Oxford University Press, 2004), p. 13 and n. 32, p. 139.

10. Ibid., 25–27, 137–39.

11. For the following points, see ibid., 137–53.

12. Ibid., 24.

13. "The end of the year" falls during autumn in the Canaanite agricultural cal-endar (Exod 23:17), as compared with the postexilic worship calendar, which has the year begin in the spring with Nisan (March–April; Exod 12:2; Lev 23:23-25).

14. For brief discussion of the festal calendar, see Philip J. King and Lawrence E. Stager, *Life in Biblical Israel*, Library of Ancient Israel (Louisville: Westmin-ster John Knox, 2001), 353–54.

15. Gary A. Anderson, "Introduction to Israelite Religion," in *NIB*, 1:272–83.

16. Theodore H. Gaster, *Thespis: Ritual, Myth, and Drama in the Ancient Near East*, with foreword by Gilbert Murray, Anchor Books A230 (Garden City, N.Y.: Doubleday, 1961), 128–29, 238; Johannes C. de Moor, *The Seasonal Pat-tern in the Ugaritic Myth of Baʿlu, According to the Version of Ilimilku*, AOAT 16 (Kevelaer: Butzon & Bercker, 1971); Mark S. Smith, *The Ugaritic Baal Cycle*, vol. 1, *Introduction with Text, Translation and Commentary of KTU 1.1–1.2*, VTSup 55 (Leiden: Brill, 1994), 60–75; W. Herrmann, "Baal בעל," in *DDD*, 132–39, here 134. Mettinger makes the best possible case for the cultic obser-vance of Baal's death and resurrection according to a vegetational cycle at Ugarit, but the evidence for the cultic observance of Baal's return to life is inconclusive. See Tryggve N. D. Mettinger, *The Riddle of the Resurrection: "Dying and Rising Gods" in the Ancient Near East*, ConBOT 50 (Stockholm: Almqvist & Wiksell, 2001); compare Smith, *The Ugaritic Baal Cycle*, 60–75.

17. See the introduction and chapter 2 of this book for discussion of these verses' resemblance to Jezebel and similar names in Ugaritic, Phoenician, and Punic. As discussed in chapter 2, personal names are not usually expected to refer to ritual or myth.

18. See Smith, *The Ugaritic Baal Cycle*, 69–75; Joel Burnett, "Tammuz," in *ABD*, 1274.

19. Ronald Simkins, *Yahweh's Activity in History and Nature in the Book of Joel*, Ancient Near Eastern Texts and Studies 10 (Lewiston, N.Y.: Mellen, 1991).

20. This point is noted by King and Stager, *Life in Biblical Israel*, 354.

21. Anderson, "Introduction to Israelite Religion," 275.

22. Frank H. Gorman, "Ritual," in *EDB*, 1131. On the exodus and other biblical traditions as products of collective memory as first identified by the French *Annales* school, see Ronald Hendel, "The Exodus in Biblical Memory," *JBL* 120 (2001): 601–622; Mark S. Smith, *The Memoirs of God: History, Memory, and the Experience of the Divine in Ancient Israel* (Minneapolis: Fortress Press, 2004).

23. Menahem Haran, *Temple and Temple-Service in Ancient Israel: An Inquiry into the Character of Cult Phenomena and the Historical Setting of the Priestly School* (Oxford: Clarendon, 1978; repr. with slight changes Winona Lake, Ind.: Eisenbrauns, 1985, 1995), esp. 149–229.

24. Baruch A. Levine, "Ritual as Symbol: Modes of Sacrifice in Israelite Religion," in *Sacred Time, Sacred Place: Archaeology and the Religion of Israel*, ed. Barry M. Gittlen, 125–35 (Winona Lake, Ind.: Eisenbrauns, 2002), 126.

25. Haran, *Temple and Temple-Service*, 13–57. See also Ziony Zevit, *The Religions of Ancient Israel: A Synthesis of Parallactic Approaches* (London: Continuum, 2001), 81–438.

26. Thorkild Jacobsen, *The Treasures of Darkness: A History of Mesopotamian Religion* (New Haven: Yale University Press, 1976), 81.

27. Levine, "Ritual as Symbol," 126.

28. Douglas, *Purity and Danger*, esp. 52–58. Douglas's discussion of Leviticus includes a portion of the book that scholars call the Holiness Code (H; Leviticus 17–26), a distinct block of material within the Priestly corpus that is set apart by its distinct style, vocabulary, and specific instructions on some points. For different views of H's relationship to the rest of Leviticus and P, see Israel Knohl, *The Sanctuary of Silence: The Priestly Torah and the Holiness School* (Minneapolis: Fortress Press, 1995); Baruch A. Levine, *Leviticus: The Traditional Hebrew Text with the New JPS Translation*, JPS Torah Commentary (Philadelphia: Jewish Publication Society, 1989); Jacob Milgrom, *Leviticus 1–16: A New Translation with Introduction and Commentary*, AB 3 (New York: Doubleday, 1991).

29. Mary Douglas, *Purity and Danger*, 52–53, 123–25.

30. In her more recent interpretation of Leviticus, Douglas understands the structure of the book to follow that of the physical worship place. Douglas, *Leviticus as Literature*. For a critique, see Watts, *Ritual and Rhetoric*, 15–26.

31. Milgrom, *Leviticus 1–16*, 711–12.

32. Zvi Abusch, "Blood in Israel and Mesopotamia," in *Emanuel: Studies in Hebrew Bible, Septuagint and Dead Sea Scrolls in Honor of Emanuel Tov*, ed. Shalom M. Paul et al. (Leiden: Brill, 2003), 675–84; Theodore J. Lewis, "Covenant and Blood Rituals: Understanding Exodus 24:3-8 in Its Ancient Near Eastern Context," in *Confronting the Past: Archaeological and Historical Essays on Ancient Israel in Honor of William G. Dever*, ed. Seymour Gitin, J. Edward Wright, and J. P. Dessel, 341–50 (Winona Lake, Ind.: Eisenbrauns, 2006), esp. 348.

33. Gorman, *The Ideology of Ritual*, 43.

34. *COS*, 1:390–402; and the discussion by Bernard F. Batto, "Creation Theology in Genesis," in *Creation in the Biblical Traditions*, ed. Richard J. Clifford and John J. Collins, 16–38, CBQMS (Washington, D.C.: Catholic Biblical Association of America, 1992).

35. Gorman, *The Ideology of Ritual*, 45.

36. See, for example, Baruch A. Levine, "Ritual as Symbol: Modes of Sacrifice in Israelite Religion," in *Sacred Time, Sacred Place: Archaeology and the Religion of Israel,* ed. Barry M. Gittlen, 125–35 (Winona Lake, Ind.: Eisenbrauns, 2002), esp. 125–26.

37. Baruch A. Levine, "*Lpny YHWH*—Phenomenology of the Open-Air-Altar in Biblical Israel," in *Biblical Archaeology Today: Proceedings of the Second International Congress on Biblical Archaeology, Jerusalem, June 1990*, 196–205 (Jerusalem: Israel Exploration Society, 1993). Levine points to the work of Manahem Haran in elucidating this basic aspect of worship in relationship to the textual description in P of the Tabernacle. Haran, *Temple and Temple Service in Ancient Israel.*

38. Levine, *In the Presence of the Lord*, 22–26.

39. Levine, "*Lpny YHWH*—Phenomenology of the Open-Air-Altar," 202; see also Levine, *In the Presence of the Lord*, 42–52, esp. 45–52; Levine, "Ritual as Symbol," 135. In elucidating the role and location of the Israelite *šĕlāmîm* (NRSV: "sacrifice of well-being") by comparison with the Mesopotamian *šulmānu* offering, Levine cites an important study by Thorkild Jacobsen, which examines corresponding textual and archaeological evidence for worship at Mesopotamian temples. Thorkild Jacobsen, "The Mesopotamian Temple Plan and the Kititum Temple," *ErIsr* 20 (Yigael Yadin Volume, 1989): 79–91. This illustration of a correspondence between textual description and architectural remains from different parts of the ancient Near East indicates that biblical ritual texts were in fact written with reference to known ritual tradition and practice, a fact on which their effectiveness for rhetorical or other literary purposes would have depended. In light of such affinities between textual and material evidence for ritual, James Watts's blanket criticism of other scholars of biblical ritual for "equating" ritual texts with historical ritual practice might be overstated. See Watts, *Ritual and Rhetoric*, 1–62.

40. Levine, *In the Presence of the Lord*, 23–26.

41. See this interpretation of the passage by Levine, *In the Presence of the Lord*, 25 and n. 62.

42. Interpreters have identified this passage as an example of a characteristically prophetic literary form called the covenant lawsuit (BH *rîb*). See William L. Holladay, *Jeremiah 1: A Commentary on the Book of the Prophet Jeremiah, Chapters 1–25*, Hermeneia (Philadelphia: Fortress Press, 1986), 47–112; Patrick D. Miller, "The Book of Jeremiah: Introduction, Commentary, and Reflections," in *NIB*, 6:553–926, here 596, 598. On the nature of the covenant lawsuit, see Herbert B. Huffmon, "The Covenant Lawsuit in the Prophets," *JBL* 78 (1959): 285–95; G. Ernest Wright, "The Lawsuit of God: A Form-Critical Study of Deuteronomy 32," in *Israel's Prophetic Heritage: Essays in Honor of James Muilenburg*, ed. Bernhard W. Anderson and Walter Harrelson, 26–67 (New York: Harper & Brothers, 1962); and more extensive bibliography listed in Holladay, *Jeremiah 1*, 47–48. Some scholars have called into question a strict form-critical identification of the *rîb* ("lawsuit"). See, for example, Dwight R. Daniels, "Is There a 'Prophetic Lawsuit' Genre?" *ZAW* 99 (1987): 339–60.

43. For possible cultic associations relating to the question "Where is God?" in its variants forms in Judges 6, 2 Kings 2, and Isaiah 63, see Joel S. Burnett, "The Question of Divine Absence in Israelite and West Semitic Religion," *CBQ* 67 (2005): 215–35.

44. Claus Westermann, *Praise and Lament in the Psalms*, trans. Keith R. Crim and Richard N. Soulen (Atlanta: John Knox, 1981; orig. pub. in German, 1961), 15–35, 52–90, 102–112. See further discussion of divine absence in worship as reflected in the book of Psalms, later in this chapter.

45. This progression is comparable to the abrupt shift from complaint to celebration that characterizes individual laments and, to a lesser extent, some communal laments. See Westermann, *Praise and Lament in the Psalms*, 59–70. For more discussion, see the discussion of the book of Psalms, later in this chapter.

46. Based on the alternating pattern in this "liturgy," Gunkel recognized an antiphonal exchange of individual complaint and priestly response. Hermann Gunkel and Joachim Begrich, *Introduction to Psalms: The Genres of the Religious Lyric of Israel*, trans. James D. Nogalski, Mercer Library of Biblical Studies (Macon: Mercer University Press, 1998), 125 n. 22, 192, 314–15, 347. Similarly, Mowinckel discussed this psalm among other "complex liturgies" (including Psalm 24) composed of "various voices" representing the congregation or its spokesman and the priests. Sigmund Mowinckel, *The Psalms in Israel's Worship*, trans. D. R. Ap-Thomas, 2 vols. (Nashville: Abingdon, 1962), 2:50, 76, 129–30. More recent discussion of the cultic nature of this psalm has tended to cast the matter in terms of pilgrimage, as reflected in the remarks of J. Clinton McCann, who observes, "The dialogical character of Psalm 121 would have made it suitable for an exchange between priest and pilgrim upon arrival at Jerusalem or perhaps in preparation for departure home." J. Clinton McCann Jr., "The Book of Psalms: Introduction, Commentary, and Reflections," in *NIB* 4:639–1280, here 1180.

47. See also Gen 22:7-8; 38:21; Exod 2:20; 2 Sam 17:20; Lam 2:12; and with the answer *hinnē(h)* ("Here"), 2 Sam 16:3.

48. For discussion of this formulaic recitation of the exodus tradition, see Joel S. Burnett, *A Reassessment of Biblical Elohim*, SBLDS 183 (Atlanta: Society of Biblical Literature, 2001), 79–105.

49. On alternate formulas for referencing the exodus tradition, see J. Wijngaards, "הוֹצִיא and הֶעֱלָה: A Twofold Approach to the Exodus," *VT* 15 (1965): 91–102.

50. Compare the singularized version of the formula in Neh 9:18, *ze(h)* *ʾĕlōhêkā* ("This is your God"), along with the understanding of a single calf image, *ʿēgel massēkâ* (NJPS: "molten calf") in the passage. For discussion and bibliography on the bull image in these passages, see Burnett, *Reassessment of Biblical Elohim*, 79–105; Mark S. Smith, "Counting Calves at Bethel," in *"Up to the Gates of Ekron": Essays on the Archaeology and History of the Eastern Mediterranean in Honor of Seymour Gitin*, ed. Seymour Gitin, Sidnie White Crawford, and Amnon Ben-Tor, 382–94 (Jerusalem: W. F. Albright Institute of Archaeological Research, 2007).

51. For fuller discussion of this passage and its relationship to Exod 32:4, 8 and 1 Kings 12:28, see Burnett, *Reassessment of Biblical Elohim*, 82–86.

52. For the reconstruction of this reading of the end of the verse as reflected indirectly in the LXX, see P. Kyle McCarter Jr., *I Samuel: A New Translation with Introduction and Commentary*, AB 8 (New York: Doubleday, 1980), 104 and the following note.

53. The formula in Jer 2:6 actually includes reference not only to the exodus tradition but also to the wilderness tradition. Thus, read superficially, the

occurrence there of the expression "in the wilderness" (*bammidbār*) would seem to match the MT reading of 1 Sam 4:8b. But this detail in the latter passage, which otherwise alludes to the exodus tradition itself and not that of the wilderness, is out of place. Preferable to the MT reading is the consonantal reading *wbmdbr* reflected in the LXX, which the latter renders "and in the wilderness" but which could also be read "and with pestilence." See McCarter, *I Samuel*, 104; compare Julius Wellhausen, *Der Text der Bücher Samuelis* (Göttingen: Vandenhoeck & Ruprecht, 1871), 55. It is possible that the MT reading was influenced by the cultic and literary joining of the exodus and wilderness traditions, as represented by Jer 2:6.

54. Though the syntax of this clause follows the formulaic structure of the other passages, the content—in keeping with Jeremiah's polemic—obviously represents a parody of a genuine worship formula.

55. See, for example, McCann, "The Book of Psalms," 639–1280; and various essays in Peter W. Flint and Patrick D. Miller, eds., *The Book of Psalms: Composition and Reception*, VTSup 99 (Leiden: Brill, 2005); and in Joel S. Burnett, W. H. Bellinger Jr., and W. Dennis Tucker Jr., eds., *Diachronic and Synchronic—Reading the Psalms in Real Time: Proceedings of the Baylor Symposium on the Book of Psalms*, LHBOTS 488 (New York: T&T Clark, 2007).

56. Those contending for the northern origins of some psalms (such as Psalms 77; 80; 81) include Martin J. Buss, "The Psalms of Asaph and Korah," *JBL* 82 (1963): 382–92; Michael Goulder, *The Psalms of the Sons of Korah*, JSOTSup 20 (Sheffield: Sheffield Academic, 1982); idem, *The Psalms of Asaph and the Pentateuch: Studies in the Psalter, III*, JSOTSup (Sheffield: Sheffield Academic, 1996); Gary Rendsburg, *Linguistic Evidence for the Northern Origin of Selected Psalms*, SBLMS 4 (Atlanta: Scholars, 1990).

The setting of the regional sanctuary or family-based place of worship has been considered most often for the individual laments, which present a worshiper's petition to God from the viewpoint of the individual (see more discussion below). According to Gunkel and Begrich, while some of these psalms "found their way into the worship service of the royal temple in Jerusalem (Psalms 28; 61; 63)," the general nature of their content reflects worship at the sanctuary more broadly considered (see, for example, Pss 5:8; 28:2). Furthermore for Gunkel, while not every psalm of this type may have actually been used in worship, the genre of the individual lament derived from certain worship activities, and "the poetry derives from cultic formulas." Hermann Gunkel and Joachim Begrich, *Introduction to Psalms: The Genres of the Religious Lyric of Israel*, trans. James D. Nogalski, Mercer Library of Biblical Studies (Macon: Mercer University Press, 1998), 122–24.

Building on Gunkel's form-critical approach, Sigmund Mowinckel posited as the cultic life setting (*Sitz im Leben*) of much of the Psalter an annual national festival of Yahweh's enthronement. Sigmund Mowinckel, *The Psalms in Israel's Worship*, trans. D. R. Ap-Thomas (New York: Abingdon, 1962), 69–81. Other scholars developed this hypothesis in various forms. Aubrey R. Johnson, *Sacral Kingship in Ancient Israel*, 2nd ed. (Cardiff: University of Wales Press, 1967); Artur Weiser, *The Psalms: A Commentary*, trans. H. Hartwell, OTL (Philadelphia: Westminster, 1962); Hans-Joachim Kraus, *Worship in Israel: A Cult History of the Old Testament*, trans. G. Buswell (Richmond: John Knox, 1966). The thesis of a specific royal cultic festival lying behind these psalms is now generally considered to be defunct due to a lack of clear biblical evidence. See McCann, "The Book of Psalms," 648–49.

Representing more recent form-critical effort to locate the psalms' original institutional setting in worship, Erhard Gerstenberger proposes that individual laments were associated with rituals for healing or for determining individual guilt or innocence, like those described as being performed by priests in Leviticus 13–14; Num 5:11-31; and Deut 17:8-13, but in a "small-group" kin-based setting, "independent of local shrines." Erhard S. Gerstenberger, *Psalms, Part I: With an Introduction to Cultic Poetry,* FOTL 14 (Grand Rapids: Eerdmans, 1988), 13–14; Erhard Gerstenberger, *Der bittende Mensch: Bittritual und Klagelied des Einzelnen im Alten Testament* (Neukirchen-Vluyn: Neukirchener, 1980), 134–60. Gerstenberger's attention both to social realities reflected in the individual laments and to the desired outcome of restoring the individual to life within the community represents an important advance in the understanding of these psalms. However, the sociological model of Israelite society assumed in Gerstenberger's work—positing as it does, on the one hand, a "primary" level of family and community and, on the other, a "secondary" level of tribal and national superstructure—does not adequately distinguish among the truly basic level of the patrimonial household (that is, the *bêt 'āb* "house of the father") and the more public levels of kinship and communal life involving clan, tribe, and nation as recognized in more recent scholarship. See King and Stager, *Life in Biblical Israel,* 4, 36–40; J. David Schloen, *The House of the Father as Fact and Symbol: Patrimonialism in Ugarit and the Ancient Near East,* Studies in the Archaeology and History of the Levant 2 (Winona Lake, Ind.: Eisenbrauns, 2001); see the discussion above, in chapter 1. Thus, Gerstenberger's scenario of a small group "ritual expert" or kinship setting distinct from local sanctuaries has little basis either in theory or in biblical or extrabiblical texts and would seem to have little to do with the laments themselves, which after all make explicit mention of sanctuaries and public acts of worship. For example, Pss 22:26; 26:6-8; 27:4-6; 35:18; 40:10; and reference to the national sanctuary of "Zion," as in Ps 9:12, 15).

57. Westermann, *Praise and Lament in the Psalms,* 15–35; Gunkel and Begrich, *Introduction to Psalms,* 1–21. For an accessible overview of form-critical scholarship on the book of Psalms, see W. H. Bellinger Jr., *Psalms: Reading and Studying the Book of Praises* (Peabody, Mass.: Hendrickson, 1990), esp. 15–26.

58. Westermann, *Praise and Lament in the Psalms,* 15–35, 52–90, 102–12.

59. Fredrik Lindström, "Theodicy in the Psalms," in *Theodicy in the World of the Bible,* ed. Antti Laato and Johannes C. de Moor, 256–303 (Leiden: Brill, 2003), 256.

60. For an overview with examples and a summary of scholarship on suggested causes behind the affliction mentioned in these psalms, see Bellinger, *Psalms: Reading and Studying the Book of Praises,* 48–55.

61. Psalm 22:1 is quoted by Jesus at his death in the crucifixion narratives of the New Testament Gospels (Matt 27:46; Mark 15:34).

62. Hermann Spieckermann, *Heilsgegenwart: Eine Theologie der Psalmen,* FRLANT 148 (Göttingen: Vandenhoeck & Ruprecht, 1989), 246–53.

63. Based on explicit references to the temple or temple mount elsewhere in the Psalter (for example, in Psalms 3; 5; 6; 13; 26; 27; 28; 35; 41; 42–43; 54; 57; 59; 61; 63; 69; 70), Spieckermann understands the spatial language of divine absence in Psalm 22 to relate explicitly to temple theology (*Heilsgegenwart,* 246–53, esp.

252). However, such an emphasis might be discerned only in verse 25, and there without necessary connection to the spatial language of divine absence.

64. Lindström, "Theodicy in the Psalms," 266.

65 Ibid.

66. Ibid., 258.

67. Gunkel and Begrich, *Introduction to Psalms*, 121–98, esp. 122. Though now divided and numbered as two separate psalms, Psalms 42 and 43 originally made up a single composition as indicated by the shared refrain (42:5, 11; 43:5) and other refrain-like sections (42:3, 10; 42:9; 43:20). The present discussion uses the numbering of the Psalms in the Masoretic Text (MT), the dominant Hebrew textual tradition and the tradition on which English translations of the book of Psalms are based. In the Septuagint (LXX), the most influential tradition of the Hebrew Bible's ancient translation into Greek, MT Psalms 42 and 43 are numbered Psalms 41 and 42.

68. Gunkel and Begrich, *Introduction to Psalms*, 121–98.

69. Westermann, *Praise and Lament in the Psalms*, 59–70. For a review of those proposals, see W. H. Bellinger Jr., *Psalmody and Prophecy*, JSOTSup 27 (Sheffield: JSOT, 1984), 78–82.

70. Joachim Begrich, "Die Vertrauensäusserungen im israelitischen Klagelied des Einzelnen und in seinem babylonischen Gegenstück," *ZAW* 34 (1928): 6–19. See also the discussion by W. H. Bellinger Jr., who essentially follows Begrich's hypothesis while cautioning that the cultic oracle could have been delivered by either a prophet or priest. Bellinger, *Psalmody and Prophecy*, 78–82. See also Patrick D. Miller's discussion of the salvation oracle and other divine responses to prayer in biblical and ancient Near Eastern texts in *They Cried to the Lord: The Form and Theology of Biblical Prayer* (Minneapolis: Fortress Press, 1994), 135–77.

71. Anderson, *A Time to Mourn, a Time to Dance*; see the discussion earlier in this chapter.

72. For discussion of the "honest spirituality" of the lament psalms, see Bellinger, *Psalms: Reading and Studying the Book of Praises*, 71–73.

73. Philip J. King and Lawrence E. Stager, *Life in Biblical Israel* (Louisville: Westminster John Knox, 2001), 39–40. See discussion in chapter 1 of this volume.

74. For the Zion tradition's distribution throughout the book of Psalms, see Susan Gillingham, "The Zion Tradition and the Editing of the Hebrew Psalter," in *Temple and Worship in Biblical Israel: Proceedings of the Oxford Old Testament Seminar,* ed. John Day (London: T&T Clark, 2007), 308–341.

75. See the following essays by J. J. M. Roberts, all reprinted in *The Bible and the Ancient Near East: Collected Essays* (Winona Lake, Ind.: Eisenbrauns, 2002): "Zion in the Theology of the Davidic-Solomonic Empire," in *Studies in the Period of David and Solomon and Other Essays,* ed. Tomoo Ishida, 93–108 (Winona Lake, Ind.: Eisenbrauns, 1982); "The Davidic Origin of the Zion Tradition," *JBL* 92 (1973): 329–44; "The Religio-Political Setting of Psalm 47," *BASOR* 221 (1976): 129–32; "Zion Tradition," in *IDBSup*, 985–87; "In Defense of the Monarchy: The Contribution of Israelite Kingship to Biblical Theology," in *Ancient Israelite Religion: Essays in Honor of Frank Moore Cross*, ed. Patrick D. Miller, Paul D. Hanson, and S. Dean McBride, 377–96 (Philadelphia: Fortress Press, 1987), esp. 378, 386–87. For a review of scholarship on the Zion tradition,

see Ben C. Ollenburger, *Zion the City of the Great King: A Theological Symbol of the Jerusalem Cult*, JSOT 41 (Sheffield: JSOT, 1987), 15–19, describing the tradition as "a coherent 'theological conception' which underlies most of the Psalms and is articulated above all in [the] Songs of Zion as well as in the creation Psalms, the Psalms of Yahweh's kingship and the royal Psalms" (p. 16). As Ollenburger recognizes, the Zion tradition finds expression in other portions of the Hebrew Bible as well, especially Isaiah.

76. See chapter 3 for more discussion of these psalms, known collectively as Psalms of Yahweh's Enthronement.

77. See the discussion by McCarter, *I Samuel*, 102–3, 105; P. Kyle McCarter Jr., *II Samuel: A New Translation with Introduction and Commentary*, AB 9 (New York: Doubleday, 1984), 163, 168–69. Compare the treatment of the full formula as a genuine cult epithet from the Shiloh sanctuary by Otto Eissfeldt, "Jahwe Zebaoth," in *Miscellanea Academica Berolinensia*, 128–50 (Berlin: Akademie-Verlag, 1950), esp. 139–46.

In the Hebrew Bible, cherubim are supernatural creatures combining the physical features of humans and animals. Their composite character symbolizes their role as liminal figures guarding the thresholds to forbidden (Gen 3:24) and divine realms (Ezek 28:14). They appear in royal iconography from ancient Syria-Palestine and as composite creatures guarding the divine throne in Ezek 1:5-14; 10:15, 20. See McCarter, *I Samuel*, 105–6; Dale Launderville, "Ezekiel's Throne-Chariot Vision: Spiritualizing the Model of Divine-Royal Rule," *CBQ* 66 (2004): 361–77. The association of cherubim with the ark of Yahweh is reinforced in the description of crafted cherubim figures that adorn the covering of the ark in Exod 25:17-22.

78. To use Mark Smith's language, temples as described in the Hebrew Bible and in other ancient Near Eastern texts are the ultimate places of divine–human "intersection." See Mark S. Smith, "Like Deities, Like Temples (Like People)," in *Temple and Worship in Biblical Israel: Proceedings of the Oxford Old Testament Seminar,* ed. John Day, 3–27 (London: T&T Clark, 2007), esp. 3–6.

79. See the discussion of the wilderness tradition earlier in this chapter and in chapter 4.

80. See Gillingham, "The Zion Tradition and the Editing of the Hebrew Psalter," 308–341.

81. See Bertil Albrektson, *History and the Gods: An Essay on the Idea of Historical Events as Divine Manifestations in the Ancient Near East and in Israel*, ConBOT 1 (Lund: Gleerup, 1967), 24–34; Jerrold S. Cooper, *The Curse of Agade*, JHNES (Baltimore, Md.: Johns Hopkins University Press, 1983). See also the discussion of various ancient Near Eastern texts dealing with divine abandonment by Daniel I. Block, "Divine Abandonment: Ezekiel's Adaptation of an Ancient near Eastern Motif," in *The Book of Ezekiel: Theological and Anthropological Perspectives*, 15–42, edited by Margaret S. Odell and John T. Strong (Atlanta: Society of Biblical Literature, 2000); and the convenient summary of the relevant primary sources in the table provided by John F. Kutsko, "Removal, Repair, and Return of Divine Images," app. in *Between Heaven and Earth: Divine Presence and Absence in the Book of Ezekiel*, 157–69, Biblical and Judaic Studies from the University of California, San Diego 7 (Winona Lake, Ind.: Eisenbrauns, 2000).

82. *ANET*, 455–63, 611–19; *COS*, 1:535–39; Thorkild Jacobsen, *The Harps That Once . . . : Sumerian Poetry in Translation* (New Haven: Yale University

Press, 1987), 447–74; Piotr Michalowski, *The Lamentation over the Destruction of Sumer and Ur,* Mesopotamian Civilizations 1 (Winona Lake, Ind.: Eisenbrauns, 1989).

83. From the translation by Jacob Klein in *COS,* 1:535–39, here 535–36.

84. Laura Joffe, "The Elohistic Psalter: What, How and Why?" *SJOT* 15 (2001): 142–66; Laura Joffe, "The Answer to the Meaning of Life, the Universe and the Elohistic Psalter," *JSOT* 27 (2002): 223–35. These aspects of 42's role apply to the Masoretic Text (MT) of Psalms, the standard Hebrew textual tradition. In the Septuagint tradition, MT Psalms 9 and 10 are treated as one psalm, so the numbering of subsequent psalms is affected, one result being that the Elohistic Psalter begins with Psalm 41 instead of 42. In addition to these two aspects of the Elohistic Psalter's ordering, Joffe also contends that it originally contained forty-two instances of the divine name Yahweh. As Joffe notes, though, the difficulty in determining "original" readings of divine names among the textual witnesses in many instances makes this last point of her thesis unverifiable. For discussion of all of these points and others, see Joel S. Burnett, "Forty-Two Songs for Elohim: An Ancient Near Eastern Organizing Principle in the Shaping of the Elohistic Psalter," *JSOT* 31 (2006): 81–102.

85. The text is preserved in copies from as early as the Eighteenth Dynasty (ca. 1550–1300 B.C.E.); see Stephen G. J. Quirke, "Judgment of the Dead," in *The Oxford Encyclopedia of Ancient Egypt,* ed. D. B. Redford, 2:212–13 (Oxford: Oxford University Press, 2001); Raymond O. Faulkner, *The Ancient Egyptian Book of the Dead,* ed. and trans. C. Andrews (Austin: University of Texas Press, 1985), 28–34.

86. See the "Protestation of Guiltlessness," trans. John A. Wilson, in *ANET,* 34–36.

87. For more thorough discussion of the biblical examples named in this paragraph, see Burnett, "A Plea for David and Zion," esp. 105–8.

88. For more discussion, including the meaning of the phrase "little boys" in this passage, see my article "'Going Down' to Bethel: Elijah and Elisha in the Theological Geography of the Deuteronomistic History," *JBL* (forthcoming).

89. For more extensive discussion relating to 42 in Mesopotamian hymn collection and the Elohistic Psalter, see Burnett, "A Plea for David and Zion," 108–113. This evidence was discussed by Gerald Wilson in connection with the editing of the Psalter but without attention to its relevance to the Elohistic Psalter. See Gerald H. Wilson, *The Editing of the Hebrew Psalter,* SBLDS 76 (Chico, Calif.: Scholars, 1985), 6–7, 13–61.

90. See the edition by Åke W. Sjöberg and E. Bergmann, *The Collection of the Sumerian Temple Hymns,* ed. A. L. Oppenheim, TCS 3 (Locust Valley, N.Y.: Augustin, 1969), as well as Claus Wilcke, "Der aktuelle Bezug der Sammlung der sumerischen Tempelhymnen und ein Fragment eines Klagelieds," *ZA* 62 (1972): 35–61.

91. Quoting William W. Hallo, who follows Wilcke ("Der aktuelle Bezug der Sammlung der sumerischen Tempelhymnen," 35–61). See William H. Hallo, "Toward a History of Sumerian Literature," in *Sumerological Studies in Honor of Thorkild Jacobsen on His Seventieth Birthday, June 7, 1974,* ed. Thorkild Jacobsen, 181–203 (Chicago: University of Chicago Press, 1976), 186–87.

92. For more discussion of the Elohistic Psalter's role in the early formation of the book of Psalms, see the following paragraphs in this section and, with more detail, Burnett, "A Plea for David and Zion," 108–113.

93. The communal lament psalms typically regarded as most analogous to the Sumerian laments are all located in the Elohistic Psalter: Psalms 44; 74; 79; 80; 83. See William W. Hallo, "Lamentations and Prayers in Sumer and Akkad," in *CANE*, 3:1871–81, esp. 1879.

94. Sumerologists identify the primary occasion of such laments to be rituals accompanying the razing of temple ruins preliminary to their rebuilding. See Hallo, "Lamentations and Prayers in Sumer and Akkad," 1872; William W. Hallo, "The Cultic Setting of Sumerian Poetry," in *Actes de la XVIIe Rencontre Assyriologique Internationale*, ed. A. Finet, 119–20 (Ham-sur-Heure [Belgium]: Comité belge de recherches en Mésopotamie, 1970); Mark E. Cohen, *Balag-Compositions: Sumerian Lamentation Liturgies of the Second and First Millennium B.C.*, Sources and Monographs on the Ancient Near East (Malibu: Undena, 1974), 11; idem, *The Canonical Lamentations of Ancient Mesopotamia*, 2 vols. (Potomac, Md.: Capital Decisions, 1988), 2:11–44. Jacobsen, in contrast, suggests a setting of ritual lamentation amid temple ruins with less apparent hope for restoration. See Jacobsen, *The Harps That Once . . .*, 447–48; though compare Jacobsen, review of S. N. Kramer, *Lamentation over the Destruction of Ur*, *AJSL* 58 (1941): 219–24, esp. 223; Jacob Klein, introduction to "Lamentation over the Destruction of Sumer and Ur," in *COS*, 1:535. In any case, current scholarship on genre-based comparative study recognizes that similar literary forms may result from more than one particular setting, so similar texts from different contexts need not be identified with one and only one *Sitz im Leben* ("setting in life"). See Kenton L. Sparks, *Ancient Texts for the Study of the Hebrew Bible: A Guide to the Background Literature* (Peabody, Mass.: Hendrickson, 2005), 14. That is to say, regardless of the specific *Sitz im Leben* reputed for the Sumerian laments, a collection of biblical lament psalms reflecting a similar concern need not be tied to the same institutional setting and may have been formed and recited at any time between the destruction and restoration of the temple.

95. Joffe, "The Elohistic Psalter," 146–49.

96. Ibid., 149.

97. The Dead Sea manuscripts of the book of Psalms show remarkable textual stability for manuscripts corresponding to Psalter books 1–3 and fluidity for books 4–5. See Peter W. Flint, *The Dead Sea Scrolls and the Book of Psalms*, Studies on the Texts of the Desert of Judah 17 (Leiden: Brill, 1997), esp. 148–49; Peter W. Flint, "Psalms, Book of," in *Encyclopedia of the Dead Sea Scrolls*, ed. Lawrence H. Schiffman and James C. VanderKam, 702–710 (Oxford: Oxford University Press, 2000), esp. 704. For more discussion of this evidence's implications for the Elohistic Psalter, see Burnett, "A Plea for David and Zion," 97–101.

98. Gerald H. Wilson, "The Shape of the Book of Psalms," *Int* 46 (1992): 129–42; Nancy L. deClaissé-Walford, *Reading from the Beginning: The Shaping of the Hebrew Psalter* (Macon: Mercer University Press, 1997); Gerald H. Wilson, "King, Messiah, and the Reign of God: Revisiting the Royal Psalms and the Shape of the Psalter," in *The Book of Psalms: Composition and Reception*, ed. Peter W. Flint and Patrick D. Miller, 391–406, VTSup 99 (Leiden: Brill, 2005).

7. JERUSALEM BEFORE AND AFTER THE EXILE

1. See Bertil Albrektson, *History and the Gods: An Essay on the Idea of Historical Events as Divine Manifestations in the Ancient Near East and in Israel,* ConBOT 1 (Lund: Gleerup, 1967), 24–34.

2. *ANET,* 455–63, 611–19; *COS,* 1:535–39; Thorkild Jacobsen, *The Harps That Once . . . : Sumerian Poetry in Translation* (New Haven: Yale University Press, 1987), 447–74; Jerrold S. Cooper, *The Curse of Agade,* JHNES (Baltimore, Md.: Johns Hopkins University Press, 1983); Piotr Michalowski, *The Lamentation over the Destruction of Sumer and Ur,* Mesopotamian Civilizations 1 (Winona Lake, Ind.: Eisenbrauns, 1989). See the discussion of various ancient Near Eastern texts dealing with divine abandonment by Daniel I. Block, "Divine Abandonment: Ezekiel's Adaptation of an Ancient near Eastern Motif," in *The Book of Ezekiel: Theological and Anthropological Perspectives,* 15–42, edited by Margaret S. Odell and John T. Strong (Atlanta: Society of Biblical Literature, 2000).

3. *ANET,* 320–21; *COS,* 2:137–38; Andrew Dearman, ed., *Studies in the Mesha Inscription and Moab,* Archaeology and Biblical Studies 2 (Atlanta: Scholars, 1989).

4. See the useful gathering of examples with bibliography of primary sources in John F. Kutsko, "Removal, Repair, and Return of Divine Images," app. in *Between Heaven and Earth: Divine Presence and Absence in the Book of Ezekiel,* 157–69, Biblical and Judaic Studies from the University of California, San Diego 7 (Winona Lake, Ind.: Eisenbrauns, 2000).

5. See Kutsko, *Between Heaven and Earth,* 104–9. In connection with the motif of divine abandonment, see the debate over related Assyrian practice and their religious ramifications in John W. McKay, *Religion in Judah under the Assyrians, 732–609 B.C.,* Studies in Biblical Theology 26 (London: SCM, 1973); Mordechai Cogan, *Imperialism and Religion: Assyria, Judah and Israel in the Eighth and Seventh Centuries B.C.E.,* SBLMS 19 (Missoula, Mont.: Scholars, 1974); Hermann Spieckermann, *Juda unter Assur in der Sargonidenzeit,* FRLANT 129 (Göttingen: Vandenhoeck & Ruprecht, 1982); Mordechai Cogan, "Judah under Assyrian Hegemony: A Reexamination of Imperialism and Religion," *JBL* 112 (1993): 403–414; Kutsko, *Between Heaven and Earth,* 109–122; and Steven W. Holloway, *Assur Is King! Assur Is King! Religion in the Exercise of Power in the Neo-Assyrian Empire,* CHANE 10 (Leiden: Brill, 2002), esp. 53–58.

6. According to Leonhard Rost, the Ark Narrative, an originally independent literary account, comprised 1 Sam 4:1b—7:1 and 2 Samuel 6. Rost, "Die Überlieferung von der Thronnachfolge Davids," in *Das kleine Credo und andere Studien zum Alten Testament,* 119–253 (Heidelberg: Quelle & Meyer, 1965), esp. 148–59, repr. of *Die Überlieferung von der Thronnachfolge Davids,* BWANT 3rd Series vol. 6 (Stuttgart: Kohlhammer, 1926). On the basis of ancient Near Eastern parallels describing the spoliation and return of cult images, Patrick D. Miller Jr. and J. J. M. Roberts demonstrated that 2 Samuel 6, which relates David's relocation of the ark to Jerusalem, would lie outside the thematic scope and compositional time frame of the original Ark Narrative and that portions of 1 Samuel 2, which present Eli's wicked sons as the reasons for the ark's capture, belonged to

the original literary work. Miller and Roberts, *The Hand of the Lord: A Reassessment of the "Ark Narrative" of 1 Samuel*, Johns Hopkins Near Eastern Studies (Baltimore: Johns Hopkins University Press, 1977), esp. 61–75. Accordingly, Miller and Roberts redefine the extent of the Ark Narrative to 1 Sam 2:12-17, 22-25, 27-36; 4:1b—7:1. Compare P. Kyle McCarter Jr., who excludes 1 Sam 2:27-36 as being Deuteronomistic and thus later. McCarter, *I Samuel: A New Translation with Introduction and Commentary*, AB 8 (New York: Doubleday, 1980), 26, 89–93. For discussion of the Deuteronomistic History, see the discussion in the next section.

7. Menahem Haran, *Temple and Temple-Service in Ancient Israel: An Inquiry into the Character of Cult Phenomena and the Historical Setting of the Priestly School* (Oxford: Clarendon, 1978; repr. with slight changes, Winona Lake, Ind.: Eisenbrauns, 1985, 1995), 45–46; Kutsko, *Between Heaven and Earth*, 11–13, 79–93.

8. See Ronald E. Clements, *God and Temple* (Philadelphia: Fortress Press, 1965); Richard J. Clifford, *The Cosmic Mountain in Canaan and the Old Testament*, HSM 4 (Cambridge: Harvard University Press, 1972); Jon D. Levenson, *Sinai and Zion: An Entry into the Jewish Bible* (Minneapolis: Winston, 1985); Lawrence Stager, "Jerusalem and the Garden of Eden," *ErIsr* 26 (Frank Moore Cross Volume, 1999): 183–94.

9. For discussion of divine hypostasis, see chapters 4 and 5. For a discussion of Yahweh's *kābôd* ("glory") in Ezekiel as an instance of divine hypostasis, see John T. Strong, "God's *Kābôd*: The Presence of Yahweh in the Book of Ezekiel," in *The Book of Ezekiel: Theological and Anthropological Perspectives*, edited by Margaret S. Odell and John T. Strong, 69–95 (Atlanta: Society of Biblical Literature, 2000).

10. Kutsko, *Between Heaven and Earth*, 150–56. With an eye on Gen 1:26-27, Kutsko presents a complex argument for Ezekiel's intimation that the people of Israel, rather than a cult statue, are the authentic earthly representation of divine presence (*selem ʾĕlōhîm*, "the image of God"), a conclusion supported by Ezekiel's affinities with Priestly theology (as noted earlier in this section).

11. As a number of interpreters have concluded, these passages represent editorial additions to an earlier form of the book. See, e.g., Walther Eichrodt, *Ezekiel: A Commentary*, OTL, translated by Cosslett Quin (Philadelphia: Westminster, 1970), 511–12; Walther Zimmerli, *Ezekiel: A Commentary on the Book of the Prophet Ezekiel*, 2 vols., Hermeneia (Philadelphia: Fortress, 1979, 1983), 2:418; and more recently Steven S. Tuell, "Divine Presence and Absence in Ezekiel's Prophecy," in *The Book of Ezekiel: Theological and Anthropological Perspectives*, 97–116, edited by Margaret S. Odell and John T. Strong (Atlanta: Society of Biblical Literature, 2000), 104, 116. Though appearing in continuity with the pro-Davidic sentiment of postexilic biblical texts like Hag 2:20-23 and Zech 3:8, as Daniel I. Block points out, the shepherd imagery of Ezek 34:23-25 and 37:22-24 also belongs to an ancient tradition of royal symbolism and is invoked in connection with divine abandonment and restoration in Mesopotamian texts like the Nippur Lament (ca. 1900 B.C.E.), which calls King Ishme-Dagan the "beloved shepherd" of the god Enlil, and the "Esarhaddon Account" (670 B.C.E.), which reports (for a Babylonian audience) that the Babylonian god Marduk bestowed the Assyrian king Esarhaddon with "shepherdship" over his realm (see Block, "Divine Abandonment," 40 and n. 60).

12. The book of Ruth, which appears between Judges and 1 Samuel in the Christian canon, was not originally part of this sequence of books, as indicated by its presence not in the Former Prophets but in the Writings of the Hebrew canon.

13. Noth's hypothesis was that Deuteronomy through 2 Kings was created by a single author during the exile as a unified editorial and compositional work, which Noth called the Deuteronomistic History (henceforth DH). See Martin Noth, *The Deuteronomistic History*, JSOTSup 15 (Sheffield: JSOT, 1981; orig. pub. [in German], Halle: Niemeyer, 1943). Major developments of the hypothesis were advanced by Frank Moore Cross, who argued that the principal edition of DH was composed during the time of Josiah and was then completed during the exile, and by Rudolph Smend, who posited more than one exilic stage of editing. Frank M. Cross, *Canaanite Myth and Hebrew Epic: Essays in the History of the Religion of Israel* (Cambridge, Mass.: Harvard University Press, 1973), 274–89; Rudolph Smend, "The Law and the Nations: A Contribution to Deuteronomistic Tradition History," in *Reconsidering Israel and Judah: Recent Studies on the Deuteronomistic History*, ed. G. N. Knoppers and J. G. McConville, trans. P. T. Daniels, 95–110 (Winona Lake, Ind.: Eisenbrauns, 2000; orig. pub. [in German], 1971). Subsequent variations on the hypothesis follow either Cross or Smend in positing successive editions, with at least one occurring each during preexilic and exilic periods. See William Schniedewind, "The Problem with Kings: Recent Study of the Deuteronomistic History," *Religious Studies Review* 22, no. 1 (January 1996): 22–27.

During the last ten years, further elaboration of editorial explanations has led to a renewal of debate regarding the extent of original literary and theological unity among these books. In a return to some of the alternative models in place before the establishment of Noth's hypothesis, recent challenges have proposed the Former Prophets' emergence from distinct redactional layers and editorial additions or from individual books joined by light editing or none at all. See Gary N. Knoppers, "Is There a Future for the Deuteronomistic History?" in *The Future of the Deuteronomistic History*, ed. Thomas Römer, 119–34, Bibliotheca Ephemeridum Theologicarum Lovaniensium 147 (Leuven: University Press, 2000); Thomas Römer and Albert de Pury, "Deuteronomistic Historiography (DH): History of Research and Debated Issues," in *Israel Constructs Its History: Deuteronomistic Historiography in Recent Research*, ed. Albert de Pury, Thomas Römer, and Jean-Daniel Macchi, 24–141, JSOTSup 306 (Sheffield: Sheffield Academic, 2000). In an attempt to reconcile the approaches of Cross and Smend, Thomas Römer posits successive editions in Neo-Babylonian, exilic, and Persian periods. Römer, *The So-Called Deuteronomistic History: A Sociological, Historical and Literary Introduction* (New York: T&T Clark, 2007; orig. pub. 2005). In a recent case for DH as a unified work mainly from the late seventh century b.c.e., Jeffrey C. Geoghegan shows that editorial tendencies of language, style, viewpoint, and purpose cut across the distinct literary units from which Römer and others would see DH emerging in different stages. Geoghegan, *The Time, Place, and Purpose of the Deuteronomistic History: The Evidence of "Until This Day,"* BJS 347 (Providence: Brown University Press, 2006); see also Richard Nelson, "The Double Redaction of the Deuteronomistic History: The Case Is Still Compelling," *JSOT* 29 (2005): 319–37. This debate on literary origins notwithstanding, the resulting form of the biblical text presents a cohesive narrative with certain recurring and overarching themes and theological emphases as discussed in the paragraphs that follow.

14. George E. Mendenhall, "Covenant Forms in Israelite Tradition," *BA* 17 (1954): 50–76; Moshe Weinfeld, "Traces of Treaty Formulae in Deuteronomy," *Bib* 41 (1965): 417–27; idem, *Deuteronomy and the Deuteronomic School* (Oxford: Oxford University Press, 1972; repr. Winona Lake, Ind.: Eisenbrauns, 1992), 59–157; Dennis J. McCarthy, *Treaty and Covenant: A Study in Form in the Ancient Oriental Documents and in the Old Testament*, 2nd ed., AnBib 21A (Rome: Pontifical Biblical Institute, 1981); Paul Kalluveettil, *Declaration and Covenant: A Comprehensive Review of Covenant Formulae from the Old Testament and the Ancient Near East*, AnBib 88 (Rome: Pontifical Biblical Institute, 1982).

15. *ANET*, 534–41. The pronouncement of blessings and curses in Deuteronomy 28 is modeled after ancient Near Eastern vassal treaties—for example, the Neo-Assyrian Vassal Treaty of Esarhaddon (672 B.C.E.). See Weinfeld, *Deuteronomy and the Deuteronomic School*, 116–29; Hans Ulrich Steymans, *Deuteronomium 28 und die adê zur Thronfolgerung Asarhaddons: Segen und Fluch im Alten Orient und in Israel,* Orbis biblicus et orientalis 145 (Göttingen: Vandenhoeck & Ruprecht, 1995).

16. See chapter 3 for more discussion of this passage.

17. As used here, the word *Deuteronomic* means having to do with the book of Deuteronomy itself, as distinct from *Deuteronomistic,* which pertains to the larger historical work based on that Deuteronomic viewpoint.

18. See P. Kyle McCarter, "Aspects of the Religion of the Israelite Monarchy: Biblical and Epigraphic Data," in *Ancient Israelite Religions,* ed. Patrick D. Miller, Paul D. Hanson, and S. Dean McBride, 137–55 (Philadelphia: Fortress Press, 1987), 148–49, 155, nn. 64, 69. For mention of the deity's "name" in human personal names, see Cross, *Canaanite Myth and Hebrew Epic,* 11–12; and chapter 2 of this book. For more discussion and bibliography on the name theology in Deuteronomy and in the Deuteronomistic History and on divine hypostases see chapters 4 and 5.

19. For bibliography and arguments against a distributive, rather than exclusive, understanding of Deuteronomy 12, see Bernard M. Levinson, *Deuteronomy and the Hermeneutics of Legal Innovation* (Oxford: Oxford University Press, 2002), 23–24 n. 1. Levinson argues that the Deuteronomic law collection, and the centralization law specifically, were created as an editing of "the Book of the Covenant" and its altar law in Exod 20:24.

20. See especially S. Dean McBride, "The Deuteronomic Name Theology" (Ph.D. diss., Harvard University, 1969). Disputing the notion of a Deuteronomic name theology, Sandra L. Richter argues that the relevant language in Biblical Hebrew originated in an Akkadian idiom from building inscriptions that has to do with establishing a king's fame. Thus, Deuteronomy would represent the temple not as a place of divine presence on earth but more like a physical monument to Israel's God as divine warrior and ruler of the land. Sandra L. Richter, *The Deuteronomistic History and the Name Theology: lĕšakkēn šĕmô šam in the Bible and the Ancient Near East,* BZAW 318 (Berlin: de Gruyter, 2002). Despite solid comparative philological analysis and rigorous interaction with previous scholarship, Richter's larger arguments are not persuasive in accounting for the biblical language associating Yahweh's "name" with worship places.

21. This extensive focus on Josiah suggests a Josianic preexilic edition of DH, to which subsequent editorial changes and additions were made. See Cross, *Canaanite Myth and Hebrew Epic*, 274–89.

22. Gary N. Knoppers shows that DH presents the temple's destruction not, as some scholars have understood, as a rejection of the temple and monarchy but rather as a punishment for the cultic offenses against Israel's God and his elect sanctuary in Jerusalem, thus underscoring the centrality of the temple for DH. Knoppers, "Yhwh's Rejection of the House Built for His Name: On the Significance of Anti-Temple Rhetoric in the Deuteronomistic History," in *Essays on Ancient Israel in Its Near Eastern Context: A Tribute to Nadav Naaman*, ed. Yaira Amit and Nadav Naaman, 221–38 (Winona Lake, Ind.: Eisenbrauns, 2006), esp. 234–35.

23. Ibid., 224–26.

24. Similarly, ibid., 234–35.

25. Like 1 and 2 Samuel and 1 and 2 Kings, 1 and 2 Chronicles originally formed a single book now divided into two parts, likewise Ezra and Nehemiah (discussed later in this chapter).

26. Interpreters of the past fifty years who argue for Ezra-Nehemiah's place within the Chronicler's history include David Noel Freedman, "The Chronicler's Purpose," *CBQ* 23 (1961): 436–42; Peter Ackroyd, "The Jewish Community in Palestine in the Persian Period," in *The Cambridge History of Judaism*, ed. W. D. Davies and Louis Finkelstein, 4 vols., 1:130–61 (Cambridge: Cambridge University Press, 1984–2006), esp. 1:133–34; though later with less certainty, Peter R. Ackroyd, *The Chronicler in His Age*, JSOTSup 101 (Sheffield: Sheffield Academic, 1991), 7. Even if now linked in some way, Ezra-Nehemiah is distinguished from Chronicles by conspicuous differences of language and style and on certain points by very different emphases, themes, and attitudes, as pointed out most forcefully by Sara Japhet in "The Supposed Common Authorship of Chronicles and Ezra-Nehemiah Investigated Anew," *VT* 18 (1968): 330–71; and *The Ideology of the Book of Chronicles and Its Place in Biblical Thought*, trans. Anna Barber, BEATAJ (Frankfurt: Lang, 1989). For the position that the differences of style result from different sources and style employed by the same author in creating two separate books, see Thomas Willi, *Die Chronik als Auslegung: Untersuchungen zur literarischen Gestaltung der historischen Überlieferung Israels*, FRLANT 106 (Göttingen: Vandenhoeck & Ruprecht, 1972), esp. 176–84.

27. See Steven L. McKenzie, *The Chronicler's Use of the Deuteronomistic History*, Harvard Semitic Monographs 33 (Atlanta: Scholars, 1985); M. Patrick Graham and Steven L. McKenzie, eds., *The Chronicler as Author: Studies in Text and Texture*, JSOTSup 263 (Sheffield: Sheffield Academic, 1999); and M. Patrick Graham, Kenneth G. Hoglund, and Steven L. McKenzie, eds., *The Chronicler as Historian*, JSOTSup 238 (Sheffield: Sheffield Academic, 1997). A noteworthy exception is Graham Auld's thesis that both DH and Chronicles derive from the same postexilic source, a hypothesis that, while plausible, has yet to persuade many (A. Graeme Auld, *Kings without Privilege: David and Moses in the Story of the Bible's Kings* [Edinburgh: T&T Clark, 1994]).

28. Japhet, *The Ideology of the Book of Chronicles*, 11.

29. Ralph W. Klein, "Chronicles, Book of 1–2," in *ABD*, 1:992–1002, here 1000.

30. Japhet, *The Ideology of the Book of Chronicles*, 229–32, 485–89.

31. Mark A. Throntveit, *When Kings Speak: Royal Speech and Royal Prayer in Chronicles*, SBLDS 93 (Atlanta: Scholars, 1987), esp. 114–15.

32. Julius Wellhausen, *Prolegomena to the History of Ancient Israel (with a reprint of the article* Israel *from the Encyclopedia Britannica* (New York: Meridian, 1957), 182; citation provided by Klein, "Chronicles," 997.

33. The interpretation offered here and in the rest of this paragraph follows Gary N. Knoppers, *I Chronicles 10–29: A New Translation with Introduction and Commentary*, AB 12A (New York: Doubleday, 2004), 651–54, 659–61.

34. See the discussion of these two major aspects of worship in chapter 6.

35. Throntveit, *When Kings Speak*, 115.

36. Klein, "Chronicles," 1000.

37. Mark A. Throntveit, "The Relationship of Hezekiah to David and Solomon in the Books of Chronicles," in *The Chronicler as Theologian: Essays in Honor of Ralph W. Klein*, ed. M. Patrick Graham, Steven L. McKenzie, and Gary N. Knoppers, 105–21, JSOTSup 371 (London: T&T Clark, 2003), 105–106. See also H. G. M. Williamson, *1 and 2 Chronicles*, New Century Bible Commentary (Grand Rapids: Eerdmans, 1982), 350–88; McKenzie, *The Chronicler's Use of the Deuteronomistic History*, 159–68; Sara Japhet, *I & II Chronicles: A Commentary*, OTL (Louisville: Westminster John Knox, 1993), 910–98.

38. Japhet, *I & II Chronicles*, 912.

39. Williamson, *1 and 2 Chronicles*, 360–88, esp. 361. As Mark Throntveit suggests, based not only on the structure of the book and its treatment of David and Solomon's reigns as a unity but also on specific parallels that apply to David and Hezekiah specifically, Chronicles in fact treats Hezekiah as "a Second David and a Second Solomon." See Throntveit, "The Relationship of Hezekiah to David and Solomon," esp. 117–21.

40. Williamson, *1 and 2 Chronicles*, 350–88, esp. 371.

41. Japhet, *The Ideology of the Book of Chronicles*, 515–16; idem, *I & II Chronicles*, 46–47, 49; Klein, "Chronicles," 1000.

42. Japhet, *I & II Chronicles*, 45.

43. For an incisive study of both biblical and archaeological evidence for activities of worship relating to postexilic Jerusalem, see Melody D. Knowles, *Centrality Practiced: Jerusalem in the Religious Practice of Yehud and the Diaspora during the Persian Period*, Archaeology and Biblical Studies 16 (Atlanta: Society of Biblical Literature, 2006).

44. See Japhet, *The Ideology of the Book of Chronicles*, 44–45, 125–98.

45. Japhet's insistence that Neco's words refer to the Pharaoh's own god, as opposed to the one, true God of the Bible, involves more nuance than is apparent in the text itself, notwithstanding the phrase "God who is with me." See Japhet, *I & II Chronicles*, 1056–57.

46. Compare Japhet's emphasis on the prophets as direct mediators between the people and God. Ibid., 45–46.

47. Ibid., 43–44.

48. Ibid., 45; Knoppers, *I Chronicles 10–29*, 659–61.

49. Japhet, *I & II Chronicles*, 43–49.

50. Though separated into two books in Jerome's Latin Vulgate translation, the Hebrew textual tradition treats Ezra-Nehemiah as a single book. Ralph W. Klein, "Ezra-Nememiah, Books of," in *ABD* 2:731–42, here 731–32. Based

on differences of viewpoint and linguistic style, some scholars argue that Ezra and Nehemiah were created as separate books. James C. VanderKam, "Ezra-Nehemiah or Ezra and Nehemiah?" in *Priests, Prophets and Scribes: Essays on the Formation and Heritage of Second Temple Judaism in Honour of Joseph Blenkinsopp*, ed. Eugene Ulrich et al., 55–75, JSOTSup 149 (Sheffield: Sheffield Academic, 1992); David Kraemer, "On the Relationship of the Books of Ezra and Nehemiah," *JSOT* 59 (1993): 73–92. In the case of Ezra-Nehemiah, these differences could be attributed to the author's own variations or to different sources for the successive periods treated. Sara Japhet, "Composition and Chronology in the Book of Ezra-Nehemiah," in *Second Temple Studies 2: Temple Community in the Persian Period*, ed. Tamara Cohn Eskenazi and Kent H. Richards, 189–216, JSOTSup 175 (Sheffield: Sheffield Academic, 1994), esp. 192–201; Ralph W. Klein, "The Books of Ezra and Nehemiah: Introduction, Commentary, and Reflections," in *NIB*, 3:661–851, here 664. Sara Japhet's proposed structure for Ezra-Nehemiah makes a convincing case for its genuine unity (Japhet, "Composition and Chronology," 208–216).

51. Japhet, "Composition and Chronology," 208–216.

52. For discussion of issues relating to the date of Ezra-Nehemiah, see Klein, "Ezra-Nehemiah," 735–37; Japhet, "Composition and Chronology," 201–6.

53. Japhet, "Composition and Chronology," 216.

54. The Davidic ancestry of Sheshbazzar and Zerubbabel is found in the genealogy of David and Solomon in 1 Chr 3:18-19, with the understanding that "Shenazzar" (v. 18) and "Sheshbazzar" in Ezra 1 are variant representations of the same Babylonian name. Also, Ezra 1 calls Sheshbazzar "the prince of Judah" (v. 8). See Carol L. Meyers and Eric M. Meyers, *Haggai, Zechariah 1–8: A New Translation with Introduction and Commentary*, AB 25B (Garden City, N.Y.: 1987), 11.

55. Japhet, "Composition and Chronology," 209–210. As reflected in the NRSV, Ezra-Nehemiah employs Jeshua (*yēšûaʿ*; Ezra 2:2; 3:2, 8, 9; 4:3; 5:2; Neh 7:7; 12:1), the Aramaic form of the name Joshua (BH *yĕhôšuaʿ*), in reference to the same priestly "son of Jozadak" called Joshua in Hag 1:1, 12; 2:2, 4; Zech 3:1, 8; 6:11. To avoid confusion, the present discussion will use only the name-form Jeshua in reference to this individual.

56. Compare the view of Carol and Eric Meyers, who understand the eschatological and theocratic elements of the vision to rule out a corresponding royal-politcal status for Zerubbabel as vice regent to Yahweh. Meyers and Meyers, *Haggai, Zechariah 1–8*, 82–84. This relationship between Yahweh and the Davidic ruler is the same in the classic Zion tradition. Even if eschatological in nature, the depiction of Yahweh's overthrow of the Persian Empire to the benefit of Zerubbabel would be perceived as nothing less than a challenge to Persian rule.

57. Both are dated 520–518 B.C.E. On grounds of form and content, the collection of visions making up Zechariah 1–8 is typically treated separately from the sayings that follow in chapters 9–14 but shows close links with the preceding book of Haggai by its date formulas (Zech 1:1, 7; 7:1; compare Hag 1:1; 2:1) and by its attention to Zerubbabel and Joshua (= Jeshua in Ezra-Nehemiah). See Meyers and Meyers, *Haggai, Zechariah 1–8*, xliv–xlviii.

58. The term *messianic* derives from a term in Biblical Hebrew, *māšî(a)ḥ* (literally, "anointed"), used principally in reference to kings, whose installation

to office included ritual anointing (1 Sam 10:1; 16:13). In the context of second-temple Judaism, the term *messiah* refers to a leader or leaders specially designated by God to exercise leadership in a coming age of God's rule. See Adela Yarbro Collins and John J. Collins, *King and Messiah as Son of God: Divine, Human, and Angelic Messianic Figures in Biblical and Related Literature* (Grand Rapids: Eerdmans, 2008).

59. Meyers and Meyers, *Haggai, Zechariah 1–8*, 266–67.

60. An article by Amélie Kuhrt emphasizes that the rebuilding of the Jerusalem temple represents not so much a general Persian policy of resettling populations and restoring temples throughout the empire, as sometimes concluded on the basis of the Cyrus Cylinder (*ANET* 315–16; *COS* 314–16), but rather a circumstantial measure showing Achaemenid Persian imperial policy to follow that of its Assyrian and Babylonian predecessors (Amélie Kuhrt, "The Cyrus Cylinder and Achaemenid Imperial Policy" *JSOT* 25 [1983]: 83-97). Yet the strategic and situational nature of Persian restoration of Jerusalem and its temple was recognized long ago, for example by A. T. Olmstead, *History of the Persian Empire* (Chicago: University of Chicago Press, 1948), 57–58.

61. See Japhet's discussion on the interrelationship between these two factors in narratives such as Ezra-Nehemiah and Chronicles. Japhet, "Composition and Chronology," 215–16; Sara Japhet, "The Historical Reliability of Chronicles: The History of the Problem and Its Place in Biblical Research," *JSOT* 33 (1985): 83–107.

62. Japhet, "Composition and Chronology," 210.

63. Ibid., 211.

64. Lester L. Grabbe, *A History of the Jews and Judaism in the Second Temple Period*, vol. 1, *Yehud: A History of the Persian Province of Judah* (London: T & T Clark International, 2004), 337, 342. The closest approximation to a verbal parallel or quotation between EN and the Pentateuch relates to the ban on marrying outside of the community of returning exiles (Ezra 9–10; Neh 9:1-2; 10:31; 13:1-2; and esp. 13:25; cf. Deut 7:1-5; 23:3-8). See Grabbe, *A History of the Jews*, 336–37 for a chart summarizing EN's possible connections with passages from the Pentateuch. As Grabbe points out, most of the EN passages that seem closest to the Pentateuch are more closely associated with the persona of Nehemiah than that of Ezra (Ibid., 331–37).

65. Though scholars have recently qualified the earlier view of general Persian interest in imperial rule of law beginning with Darius I (522–486 B.C.E.; as espoused, e.g., by Olmstead, *History of the Persian Empire*, 119–34; cf. Donald B. Redford, "The So-Called 'Codification' of the Egyptian Law under Darius I," in *Persia and Torah: The Theory of Imperial Authorization of the Pentateuch*, SBL Symposium Series 17, pp. 135–59, edited by James W. Watts, [Atlanta: Society of Biblical Literature, 2001]), the Persian sources nonetheless show an interest in local legal tradition, if only for exploitive purposes (see the review of the evidence, though with different assumptions, by Grabbe, *A History of the Jews*, 209–16).

66. Ibid., 210–12.

67. Sara Japhet, "The Walls of Jerusalem from a Double Perspective: Kings versus Chronicles," in Amit and Naaman, *Essays on Ancient Israel*, 205–219.

68. Ibid., 205–211.

69. Ibid., 206–216, esp. 213–14.
70. Ibid., 217.
71. Ibid., 215; Japhet, "Composition and Chronology," 215–16.
72. Japhet, "Composition and Chronology," 216.
73. Japhet, "The Walls of Jerusalem," 212.

Conclusion

1. This point was explained by Lawrence E. Stager and his students. See Lawrence E. Stager, "The Patrimonial Kingdom of Solomon," in *Symbiosis, Symbolism, and the Power of the Past: Canaan, Ancient Israel, and Their Neighbors from the Late Bronze Age through Roman Palaestina,* ed. William G. Dever and Seymour Gitin, 63–74 (Winona Lake, Ind.: Eisenbrauns, 2003); and the discussion in chapter 1.

BIBLIOGRAPHY

Abusch, Zvi. "Blood in Israel and Mesopotamia." In *Emanuel: Studies in Hebrew Bible, Septuagint and Dead Sea Scrolls in Honor of Emanuel Tov*, edited by Shalom M. Paul et al., 675–94. Leiden: Brill, 2003.

Ackroyd, Peter. *The Chronicler in His Age*. Journal for the Study of the Old Testament Supplement Series 101. Sheffield: Sheffield Academic, 1991.

———. "The Jewish Community in Palestine in the Persian Period." In *The Cambridge History of Judaism*, edited by W. D. Davies and Louis Finkelstein, 1:130–61. Cambridge: Cambridge University Press, 1984–2006.

Aitken, J. K. *The Semantics of Blessing and Cursing in Ancient Hebrew*. Ancient Near Eastern Studies Supplement 23. Louvain: Peeters, 2007.

Albertz, Rainer. *A History of Israelite Religion in the Old Testament Period*. Translated by John Bowden. 2 vols. Old Testament Library. Philadelphia: Westminster John Knox, 1994.

———. *Persönliche Frömmigkeit Und Offizielle Religion: Religionsinterner Pluralismus in Israel Und Babylon*. Calwer Theologische Monographien 9. Stuttgart: Calwer, 1978.

Albrektson, Bertil. *History and the Gods: An Essay on the Idea of Historical Events as Divine Manifestations in the Ancient Near East and in Israel*. Coniectanea Biblica: Old Testament Series 1. Lund: Gleerup, 1967.

Albright, William Foxwell. "The Biblical Tribe of Massaʾ and Some Congeners." In *Studi orientalistici in onore di Giorgio Levi Della Vida*, 4–14. Rome: Istituto per l'Oriente, 1956.

———. "The Egyptian Empire in Asia in the Twenty-First Century B.C." *Journal of the Palestine Oriental Society* 8 (1928): 223–56.

———. "Northwest-Semitic Names in a List of Egyptian Slaves from the Eighteenth Century B.C." *Journal of the American Oriental Society* 74 (1954): 222–33.

———. "An Ostracon from Calah and the North-Israelite Diaspora." *Bulletin of the American Schools of Oriental Research* 149 (1958): 33–36.

———. "The Son of Tabeel (Isaiah 7:6)." *Bulletin of the American Schools of Oriental Research* 140 (1955): 34–35.

———. "Zabûl Yam and Thâpiṭ Nahar in the Combat between Baal and the Sea." *Journal of the Palestine Oriental Society* 16 (1936): 17–20.

Allen, James P. *Genesis in Egypt: The Philosophy of Ancient Egyptian Creation Accounts.* Yale Egyptological Studies 2. San Antonio: Van Siclen Books for the Yale Egyptological Seminar, Yale University, 1995.

Alster, Bendt. "Scribes, Sages, and Seers in Ancient Mesopotamia." In *Scribes, Sages, and Seers: The Sage in the Eastern Mediterranean World*, edited by Leo G. Perdue, 47–63. Göttingen: Vandenhoeck & Ruprecht, 2008.

———. "Shuruppak." In *The Context of Scripture*, edited by W. W. Hallo and K. L. Younger, 1:569. 3 vols. Leiden, 1997–2002.

Alt, Albrecht. "The God of the Fathers." In *Essays on Old Testament History and Religion*, 1–77. Translated by Robert A. Wilson. Oxford: Basil Blackwell, 1966. Originally published as *Der Gott der Väter* (Stuttgart: Kohlhammer, 1929).

Anderson, Bernhard W. *Creation versus Chaos: The Reinterpretation of Mythical Symbolism in the Bible.* Philadelphia: Fortress Press, 1987.

Anderson, Gary A. "The Praise of God as a Cultic Event." In *Priesthood and Cult in Ancient Israel*, edited by Gary A. Anderson and Saul M. Olyan, 15–33. Sheffield: Sheffield Academic, 1991.

———. *A Time to Mourn, a Time to Dance: The Expression of Grief and Joy in Israelite Religion.* University Park: Pennsylvania State University Press, 1991.

Assmann, Jan. *Die Mosaische Unterscheidung: Oder der Preis des Monotheismus.* Munich: Carl Hanser, 2003.

———. *Of God and Gods: Egypt, Israel, and the Rise of Monotheism.* Madison: University of Wisconsin Press, 2008.

Attridge, Harold W., and Robert A. Oden Jr. *Philo of Byblos, The Phoenician History: Introduction, Critical Text, Translation, Notes.* Catholic Biblical Quarterly Monograph Series 9. Washington, D.C.: Catholic Biblical Association of America, 1981.

Aufrecht, Walter E. *A Corpus of Ammonite Inscriptions.* Lewiston, N.Y.: Edwin Mellen, 1989.

Auld, A. Graeme. *Kings without Privilege: David and Moses in the Story of the Bible's Kings.* Edinburgh: T&T Clark, 1994.

Avigad, Nahman. "The Seal of Jezebel." *Israel Exploration Journal* 14 (1964): 274–76.

Avigad, Nahman, and Benjamin Sass. *Corpus of West Semitic Stamp Seals.* Jerusalem: Israel Academy of Sciences and Humanities, 1997.

Balentine, Samuel E. *The Hidden God: The Hiding of the Face of God in the Old Testament.* Oxford: Oxford University Press, 1983.

———. "Job, Book of." In *The New Interpreters Dictionary of the Bible*, edited by K. D. Sakenfeld, 3:319–36. Nashville: Abingdon, 1996–.

Baltzer, Klaus. *The Covenant Formulary in Old Testament, Jewish, and Early Christian Writings.* Philadelphia: Fortress Press, 1971.

Barfield, Thomas. "Tribe and State Relations: The Inner Asian Perspective." In *Tribes and State Formation in the Middle East*, edited by Philip S. Khoury and Joseph Kostiner, 153–82. Berkeley: University of California Press, 1990.

Barr, James. *The Concept of Biblical Theology: An Old Testament Perspective.* Minneapolis: Fortress Press, 1999.

―――. "Some Semantic Notes on the Covenant." In *Beiträge zur alttestamentlichen Theologie: Festschrift für Walther Zimmerli zum 70. Geburtstag,* edited by Herbert Donner, Robert Hanhart, and Rudolf Smend, 23–38. Göttingen: Vandenhoeck & Ruprecht, 1977.

―――. "The Symbolism of Names in the Old Testament." *Bulletin of the John Rylands Library* 52 (1969–70): 11–29.

Barré, Michael. "'Fear of God' and the World View of Wisdom." *Biblical Theology Bulletin* 11 (1981): 41–43.

Bartlett, John R. *Edom and the Edomites.* Journal for the Study of the Old Testament, Supplement Series 77. Sheffield: Sheffield Academic, 1989.

Batto, Bernard F. "Creation Theology in Genesis." In *Creation in the Biblical Traditions,* edited by Richard J. Clifford and John J. Collins, 16–38. Catholic Biblical Quarterly Monograph Series. Washington, D.C.: Catholic Biblical Association of America, 1992.

―――. "Land Tenure and Women at Mari." *Journal of the Economic and Social History of the Orient* 23 (1983): 209–239.

―――. *Slaying the Dragon: Mythmaking in the Biblical Tradition.* Louisville: Westminster John Knox, 1992.

―――. "The Sleeping God: An Ancient Near Eastern Motif of Divine Sovereignty." *Biblica* 68 (1987): 153–77.

Bauer-Kayatz, Christa. *Einführung in die alttestamentliche Weisheit.* Biblische Studien 55. Neukirchen-Vluyn: Neukirchener, 1969.

―――. *Studien zu Proverbien 1–9.* Wissenschaftliche Monographien zum alten und neuen Testament 22. Neukirchen-Vluyn: Neukirchener, 1966.

Baumann, Gerlinde. *Die Weisheitsgestalt in Proverbien 1–9: Traditionsgeschichtliche und theologische Studien.* Forschungen zum Alten Testament 16. Tübingen: Mohr, 1996.

Begrich, Joachim. "Die Vertrauensäusserungen im israelitischen Klagelied des Einzelnen und in seinem babylonischen Gegenstück." *Zeitschrift für die alttestamentliche Wissenschaft* 34 (1928): 6–19.

Bellinger, W. H., Jr. *Psalmody and Prophecy.* Journal for the Study of the Old Testament, Supplement Series 27. Sheffield: JSOT, 1984.

―――. *Psalms: Reading and Studying the Book of Praises.* Peabody, Mass.: Hendrickson, 1990.

Bendor, S. *The Social Structure of Ancient Israel: The Institution of the Family (beit ʾab) from the Settlement to the End of the Monarchy.* Jerusalem: Simor, 1996.

Benz, Frank L. *Personal Names in the Phoenician and Punic Inscriptions: A Catalog, Grammatical Study and Glossary of Elements.* Studia Pohl 8. Rome: Biblical Institute, 1972.

Berthier, André, and René Charlier. *Le sanctuaire punique d'El-Hofra à Constantine.* Paris: Arts et métiers graphiques, 1955.

Bibb, Bryan D. *Ritual Words and Narrative Worlds in the Book of Leviticus.* Library of Hebrew Bible/Old Testament Studies 480. New York: T&T Clark, 2009.

Bienkowski, Piotr, and Eveline van der Steen. "Tribes, Trade, and Towns: A New Framework for the Late Iron Age in Southern Jordan and the Negev." *Bulletin of the American Schools of Oriental Research* 323 (2001): 21–47.

Black, Jeremy, and Anthony Green, eds. *Gods, Demons and Symbols of Ancient Mesopotamia: An Illustrated Dictionary.* Illustrations by Tessa Rickards. Austin: University of Texas Press, 1992.

Blenkinsopp, Joseph. "The Family in First Temple Israel." In *The Family, Religion, and Culture,* edited by Leo G. Perdue, Joseph Blenkinsopp, John J. Collins, and Carol Meyers, 48–103. Louisville: Westminster John Knox, 1997.

Bloch-Smith, Elizabeth. "'Who Is the King of Glory?' Solomon's Temple and Its Symbolism." In *Scripture and Other Artifacts: Essays on the Bible and Archaeology in Honor of Philip J. King,* edited by J. C. Exum, M. D. Coogan, and L. E. Stager, 18–31. Louisville: Westminster John Knox, 1994.

Block, Daniel I. "Divine Abandonment: Ezekiel's Adaptation of an Ancient Near Eastern Motif." In *The Book of Ezekiel: Theological and Anthropological Perspectives,* edited by Margaret S. Odell and John T. Strong, 15–42. Atlanta: Society of Biblical Literature, 2000.

————. *The Gods of the Nations: Studies in Ancient Near Eastern National Theology.* 2nd ed. Grand Rapids: Baker Academic, 2000.

Blum, Erhard. *Die Komposition der Vätergeschichte.* Wissentschaftliche Monographien zum Alten und Neuen Testament 57. Neukirchen: Neukirchener, 1984.

Bordreuil, Pierre, and André Lemaire. "Nouveau groupe de sceaux hébreux, araméens et ammonites." *Semitica* 29 (1979): 71–84.

Borger, Riekele. *Babylonisch-assyrische Lesestücke.* 3 volumes. Rome: Pontificium Institutum Biblicum, 1963.

Bottéro, Jean. *Religion in Ancient Mesopotamia.* Chicago: University of Chicago Press, 2001.

Bousset, Wilhelm, and Hugo Gressmann. *Die Religion des Judentums im späthellenistischen Zeitalter.* Tübingen: Mohr, 1926.

Breasted, James Henry. *Development of Religion and Thought in Ancient Egypt.* New York: Harper & Row, 1959.

Brichto, H. C. "Kin, Cult, Land and Afterlife: A Biblical Complex." *Hebrew Union College Annual* 44 (1973): 1–50.

Brown, William P. *Character in Crisis: A Fresh Approach to the Wisdom Literature of the Old Testament.* Grand Rapids: Eerdmans, 1996.

Burnett, Joel S. "Divine Absence in Biblical Personal Names." In *These Are the Names: Studies in Jewish Onomastics.* Vol. 5, edited by Aaron Demsky. Ramat Gan, Israel: Bar-Ilan University Press, forthcoming.

————. "Forty-Two Songs for Elohim: An Ancient Near Eastern Organizing Principle in the Shaping of the Elohistic Psalter." *Journal for the Study of the Old Testament* 31 (2006): 81–102.

————. "'Going Down' to Bethel: Elijah and Elisha in the Theological Geography of the Deuteronomistic History," *Journal of Biblical Literature* (forthcoming).

————. "A Plea for David and Zion: The Elohistic Psalter as a Psalm Collection for the Temple's Restoration." In *Diachronic and Synchronic—Reading the Psalms in Real Time: Proceedings of the Baylor Symposium on the Book of Psalms,* edited by Joel S. Burnett, W. H. Bellinger Jr., and W. Dennis Tucker Jr., 95–113. Library of Hebrew Bible/Old Testament Studies 488. New York: T&T Clark, 2007.

————. "The Pride of Jacob." In *David and Zion: Biblical Studies in Honor of J. J. M. Roberts,* edited by Bernard F. Batto and Kathryn L. Roberts, 319–50. Winona Lake, Ind.: Eisenbrauns, 2004.

————. "The Question of Divine Absence in Israelite and West Semitic Religion." *Catholic Biblical Quarterly* 67 (2005): 215–35.

————. *A Reassessment of Biblical Elohim.* Society of Biblical Literature Dissertation Series 183. Atlanta: Society of Biblical Literature, 2001.

Burnett, Joel S., W. H. Bellinger Jr., and W. Dennis Tucker Jr., eds. *Diachronic and Synchronic—Reading the Psalms in Real Time: Proceedings of the Baylor Symposium on the Book of Psalms.* Library of Hebrew Bible/Old Testament Studies 488. New York: T&T Clark, 2007.

Buss, Martin J. "The Psalms of Asaph and Korah." *Journal of Biblical Literature* 82 (1963): 382–92.

Byrne, Ryan. "The Refuge of Scribalism in Iron I Palestine." *Bulletin of the American Schools of Oriental Research* 345 (2007): 1–31.

Camp, Claudia. *Wisdom and the Feminine in the Book of Proverbs.* Bible and Literature Series 11. Decatur, Ga.: Almond, 1985.

Caquot, André. "Sur l'onomastique religieuse de Palmyre." *Syria* 39 (1962): 231–56.

Carasik, Michael. "The Limits of Omniscience." *Journal of Biblical Literature* 119 (2000): 221–32.

Carr, David McLain. *Reading the Fractures of Genesis: Historical and Literary Approaches.* Louisville: Westminster John Knox, 1996.

Cazelles, Henri. "Der persönliche Gott Abrahams und der Gott des Volkes Israel." In *Der Weg zum Menschen: Zur philologischen und theologischen Anthropologie für Alfons Deissler,* edited by R. Mosis and L. Ruppert, 46–61. Freiburg: Herder, 1988.

Clements, Ronald E. *God and Temple.* Philadelphia: Fortress Press, 1965.

Clifford, Richard J. *The Cosmic Mountain in Canaan and the Old Testament.* Harvard Semitic Monographs 4. Cambridge: Harvard University Press, 1972.

————. *The Wisdom Literature.* Interpreting Biblical Texts. Nashville: Abingdon, 1998.

Clifford, Richard J., and John J. Collins. "Introduction: The Theology of Creation Traditions." In *Creation in Biblical Traditions,* edited by Richard J. Clifford and John J. Collins, 1–15. Catholic Biblical Quarterly Monograph Series 24. Washington, D.C.: Catholic Biblical Association of America, 1992.

Cogan, Mordechai. *Imperialism and Religion: Assyria, Judah and Israel in the Eighth and Seventh Centuries B.C.E.* Society of Biblical Literature Monograph Series 19. Missoula, Mont.: Scholars, 1974.

———. "Judah under Assyrian Hegemony: A Reexamination of Imperialism and Religion." *Journal of Biblical Literature* 112 (1993): 403–414.

Cohen, Mark E. *Balag-Compositions: Sumerian Lamentation Liturgies of the Second and First Millennium B.C.* Sources and Monographs on the Ancient Near East. Malibu: Undena, 1974.

———. *The Canonical Lamentations of Ancient Mesopotamia.* 2 vols. Potomac, Md.: Capital Decisions, 1988.

Collins, Adela Yarbro, and John J. Collins. *King and Messiah as Son of God: Divine, Human, and Angelic Messianic Figures in Biblical and Related Literature.* Grand Rapids: Eerdmans, 2008.

Collins, John J. "Daniel דניאל." In *Dictionary of Deities and Demons in the Bible,* edited by Karel van der Toorn, Bob Becking, and Pieter W. van der Horst, 219–20. 2nd ed. Leiden: Brill, 1999.

———. *Daniel: A Commentary on the Book of Daniel.* Hermeneia. Minneapolis: Fortress Press, 1993.

———. *Introduction to the Hebrew Bible.* Minneapolis: Fortress Press, 2004.

Coogan, Michael D. *The Old Testament: A Historical and Literary Introduction to the Hebrew Scriptures.* New York: Oxford University Press, 2006.

Cooper, Jerrold S. *The Curse of Agade.* Johns Hopkins Near Eastern Studies. Baltimore, Md.: Johns Hopkins University Press, 1983.

Crawford, Sidnie White. "The Book of Esther: Introduction, Commentary, and Reflections." In *The New Interpreter's Bible,* edited by Leander Keck et al., 3:853–941. Nashville: Abingdon, 1999.

Crawford, Timothy G. *Blessing and Curse in Syro-Palestinian Inscriptions of the Iron Age.* American University Studies, Theology and Religion Series 7 vol. 120. New York: Peter Lang, 1992.

Creach, Jerome F. D. *Yahweh as Refuge and the Editing of the Hebrew Psalter.* Journal for the Study of the Old Testament, Supplement Series 217. Sheffield: Sheffield: Academic, 1996.

Crenshaw, James L. *Defending God: Biblical Responses to the Problem of Evil.* Oxford: Oxford University Press, 2005.

———. *Ecclesiastes: A Commentary.* Old Testament Library. Philadelphia: Westminster, 1987.

———. *Education in Ancient Israel: Across the Deadening Silence.* New York: Doubleday, 1998.

———. "In Search of Divine Presence (Some Remarks Preliminary to a Theology of Wisdom)." *Review and Expositor* 74 (1977): 353–69.

———. *Old Testament Wisdom: An Introduction.* 2nd ed. Louisville: Westminster John Knox, 1998.

———. *The Psalms: An Introduction.* Grand Rapids: Eerdmans, 2001.

———. "Wisdom Psalms?" *Currents in Research: Biblical Studies* 8 (2000): 9–17.

Cross, Frank Moore. *Canaanite Myth and Hebrew Epic: Essays in the History of the Religion of Israel.* Cambridge, Mass.: Harvard University Press, 1973.

———. "לא *'ēl.*" In *Theological Dictionary of the Old Testament,* edited by G. J. Botterweck, H. Ringgren, and H.J. Fabry, 1:242–61. Grand Rapids: Eerdmans, 1974–.

———. "Kinship and Covenant in Ancient Israel." In *From Epic to Canon: History and Literature in Ancient Israel,* 3–21. Baltimore: Johns Hopkins University Press, 1998.

———. *Leaves from an Epigrapher's Notebook: Collected Papers in Hebrew and West Semitic Paleography and Epigraphy.* Winona Lake, Ind.: Eisenbrauns, 2003.

Cross, Frank Moore, and David Noel Freedman. *Studies in Ancient Yahwistic Poetry.* Grand Rapids: Eerdmans, 1997. First published in 1975 by Society of Biblical Literature.

Cross, Frank Moore, and Richard J. Saley. "Phoenician Incantations on a Plaque of the Seventh Century BCE from Arslan Tash in Upper Syria." In *Leaves from an Epigrapher's Notebook: Collected Papers in Hebrew and West Semitic Palaeography and Epigraphy,* edited by Frank Moore Cross, 265–69. Winona Lake, Ind.: Eisenbrauns, 2003.

Dalley, Stephanie. *Myths from Mesopotamia.* Oxford: Oxford University Press, 1989.

Daniels, Dwight R. "Is There a 'Prophetic Lawsuit' Genre?" *Zeitschrift für die alttestamentliche Wissenschaft* 99 (1987): 339–60.

Davidson, Robert. "Some Aspects of the Theological Significance of Doubt in the Old Testament." *Annual of the Swedish Theological Institute* 7 (1970): 41–52.

Dearman, Andrew, ed. *Studies in the Mesha Inscription and Moab.* Archaeology and Biblical Studies 2. Atlanta: Scholars, 1989.

deClaissé-Walford, Nancy L. *Reading from the Beginning: The Shaping of the Hebrew Psalter.* Macon: Mercer University Press, 1997.

de Moor, Johannes C. *The Seasonal Pattern in the Ugaritic Myth of Baʿlu, According to the Version of Ilimilku.* Alter Orient und Altes Testament 16. Kevelaer: Butzon & Bercker, 1971.

de Vaux, Roland. *Ancient Israel.* New York: McGraw-Hill, 1961.

Dijkstra, Meindert. "The Ugaritic-Hurrian Sacrificial Hymn to El (RS 24.278=KTU 1.128)." *Ugarit-Forschungen* 25 (1993): 157–62.

Dion, Paul E. "The Ammonites: A Historical Sketch." In *Excavations at Tall Jawa, Jordan.* Vol. 1, *The Iron Age Town,* edited by P. M. Michèle Daviau, 481–518. Culture and History of the Ancient Near East 11 part 1. Leiden: Brill, 2003.

———. "Aramaean Tribes and Nations of First-Millennium Western Asia." In *Civilizations of the Ancient Near East,* edited by Jack M. Sasson, 2:1281–94. New York: Scribners, 1995.

Dossin, Georges. "Une lettre de Iarîm-Lim, roi d'Alep, à Iašûb-iaḫ ad, roi de Dîr." *Syria* 33 (1956): 63–69.

Douglas, Mary. *Leviticus as Literature.* Oxford: Oxford University Press, 1999.

———. *Purity and Danger: An Analysis of the Concepts of Pollution and Taboo.* London: Routledge, 1966.

Dozeman, Thomas B., and Konrad Schmid, eds. *A Farewell to the Yahwist? The Composition of the Pentateuch in Recent European Interpretation.* Society of Biblical Literature Symposium Series 34. Atlanta: Society of Biblical Literature, 2006.

Duncan, Julie A. *Qumran Cave 4. IX: Deuteronomy, Joshua, Judges, Kings.* Edited by E. Ulrich and F. M. Cross. Discoveries in the Judaean Desert 14. Oxford: Clarendon, 1995.

Eichrodt, Walther. *Ezekiel: A Commentary.* Translated by Cosslett Quin. Old Testament Library. Philadelphia: Westminster, 1970.

———. *Theology of the Old Testament.* Translated by J. A. Baker. 2 vols. Philadelphia: Westminster, 1961–67. Originally published as *Theologie des Alten Testaments,* 6th German ed. (Stuttgart: Ehrenfried Klotz, 1959), first published in 1933–39 by Hinrichs.

Eissfeldt, Otto. "Jahwe Zebaoth." In *Miscellanea Academica Berolinensia,* 128–50. Berlin: Akademie-Verlag, 1950.

Elnes, Eric E., and Patrick D. Miller. "Elyon עליון." In *Dictionary of Deities and Demons in the Bible,* edited by Karel van der Toorn, Bob Becking, and Pieter W. van der Horst, 293–99. 2nd ed. Leiden: Brill, 1999.

Exum, J. Cheryl. *Song of Songs: A Commentary.* Old Testament Library. Louisville: Westminster John Knox, 2005.

Faulkner, Raymond O. *The Ancient Egyptian Book of the Dead.* Edited and translated by C. Andrews. Austin: University of Texas Press, 1985.

Feeley-Harnick, Gillian. "Is Historical Anthropology Possible? The Case of the Runaway Slave." In *Humanizing America's Iconic Book,* edited by Gene M. Tucker and Douglas A. Knight, 95–126. Chico, Calif.: Scholars, 1982.

Finkelstein, Israel. "The Emergence of the Monarchy: The Environmental and Socio-Economic Aspects." In *Community, Identity, and Ideology: Social Science Approaches to the Hebrew Bible,* edited by Charles E. Carter and Carol L. Meyers, 377–403. Winona Lake, Ind.: Eisenbrauns, 1996.

Fleming, Daniel E. "Schloen's Patrimonial Pyramid: Explaining Bronze Age Society." *Bulletin of the American Schools of Oriental Research* 328 (2002): 73–80.

Flint, Peter W. *The Dead Sea Scrolls and the Book of Psalms.* Studies on the Texts of the Desert of Judah 17. Leiden: Brill, 1997.

———. "Psalms, Book of." In *Encyclopedia of the Dead Sea Scrolls,* edited by Lawrence H. Schiffman and James C. VanderKam, 702–710. Oxford: Oxford University Press, 2000.

Flint, Peter W., and Patrick D. Miller, eds. *The Book of Psalms: Composition and Reception.* Supplements to Vetus Testamentum 99. Leiden: Brill, 2005.

Forshey, Harold D. "The Construct Chain *naḥ⁰lat YHWH/ ⁰lōhîm.*" *Bulletin of the American Schools of Oriental Research* 220 (1975): 51–53.

Foster, Benjamin. *Before the Muses: An Anthology of Akkadian Literature.* 3rd ed. Bethesda, Md.: CDL, 2005.

Fowler, Jeaneane D. *Theophoric Personal Names in Ancient Hebrew: A Comparative Study.* Journal for the Study of the Old Testament, Supplement Series 49. Sheffield: Sheffield Academic, 1988.

Fox, Michael V. *The JPS Bible Commentary: Ecclesiastes* קהלת: *The Traditional Hebrew Text with the New JPS Translation.* Philadelphia: Jewish Publication Society, 2004.

———. *Proverbs 1–9: A New Translation with Introduction and Commentary.* Anchor Bible 18A. New York: Doubleday, 2000.

———. "The Social Location of the Book of Proverbs." In *Texts, Temples, and Traditions: A Tribute to Menahem Haran,* edited by M. V. Fox et al., 227–39. Winona Lake, Ind.: Eisenbrauns, 1996.

Foxvog, D., W. Heimpel, and A. D. Kilmer. "Lamma/Lammassu." In *Reallexikon der Assyriologie,* edited by Erich Ebeling et al., 6:446–53. Berlin: Walter De Gruyter Inc., 1928–.

Freedman, Amelia Devin. *God as an Absent Character in Biblical Hebrew Narrative: A Literary-Theoretical Study.* Studies in Biblical Literature 82. New York: Peter Lang, 2005.

Freedman, David Noel. "The Chronicler's Purpose." *Catholic Biblical Quarterly* 23 (1961): 436–42.

Fretheim, Terence E. "The Book of Genesis: Introduction, Commentary, and Reflections." In *The New Interpreter's Bible,* edited by L. Keck, 1:320–674. Nashville: Abingdon, 1994–.

———. *God and World in the Old Testament: A Relational Theology of Creation.* Nashville: Abingdon, 2005.

———. *The Suffering of God: An Old Testament Perspective.* Overtures to Biblical Theology 14. Philadelphia: Fortress Press, 1984.

Friedman, Richard E. *The Disappearance of God: A Divine Mystery.* Boston: Little, Brown, 1995. Also published as *The Hidden Face of God.* San Francisco: Harper, 1995, 1997.

Gammie, John G., and Leo G. Perdue, eds. *The Sage in Israel and the Ancient Near East.* Winona Lake, Ind.: Eisenbrauns, 1990.

Gaster, Theodore H. *Thespis: Ritual, Myth, and Drama in the Ancient Near East.* Foreword by Gilbert Murray. Anchor Books A230. Garden City, N.Y.: Doubleday, 1961.

Gelb, Ignace J. *Computer-Aided Analysis of Amorite.* Assyriological Studies 21. Chicago: Oriental Institute of the University of Chicago, 1980.

Geoghegan, Jeffrey C. *The Time, Place, and Purpose of the Deuteronomistic History: The Evidence of "Until This Day."* Brandeis Judaic Studies 347. Providence: Brown University Press, 2006.

Gerstenberger, Erhard S. *Der bittende Mensch: Bittritual und Klagelied des Einzelnen im Alten Testament.* Neukirchen-Vluyn: Neukirchener, 1980.

————. *Psalms, Part I: With an Introduction to Cultic Poetry.* Forms of the Old Testament Literature 14. Grand Rapids: Eerdmans, 1988.

————. "'Where Is God?' The Cry of the Psalmists." In *Where Is God? A Cry of Human Distress*, edited by C. Duquoc and C. Floristan, 11–22. London: SCM, 1992.

Gianto, Agustinus. "Ecclesiastes, Book of." In *The New Interpreters Dictionary of the Bible*, edited by K. D. Sakenfeld, 2:178–85. Nashville: Abingdon, 1996–.

Gibson, John C. L. *Textbook of Syrian Semitic Inscriptions.* 3 vols. Oxford: Clarendon, 1971–82.

Gillingham, Susan. "The Zion Tradition and the Editing of the Hebrew Psalter." In *Temple and Worship in Biblical Israel: Proceedings of the Oxford Old Testament Seminar,* edited by John Day, 308–341. London: T&T Clark, 2007.

Gnuse, Robert K. *The Old Testament and Process Theology.* St. Louis: Chalice, 2000.

Gordon, Cyrus H. *Ugaritic Textbook: Grammar, Texts in Transliteration, Cuneiform Selections, Glossary, Indices.* Analecta Orientalia 38. Rome: Pontifical Biblical Institute, 1965.

Görg, Manfred. "Der Name im Kontext: Zur Deutung männlicher Personennamen auf *-at* im Alten Testament." In *Text, Methode und Grammatik: Wolfgang Richter zum 65. Geburtstag,* edited by Walter Gross et al., 82–83. St. Ottilien: EOS, 1991.

Gorman, Frank H., Jr. *The Ideology of Ritual: Space, Time and Status in the Priestly Theology.* Journal for the Study of the Old Testament, Supplement Series 91. Sheffield: Sheffield Academic, 1990.

————. "Ritual." In *Eerdmans Dictionary of the Bible,* edited by D. N. Freedman, 1131. Grand Rapids: Eerdmans, 2000.

Goulder, Michael. *The Psalms of Asaph and the Pentateuch: Studies in the Psalter, III.* Journal for the Study of the Old Testament, Supplement Series 233. Sheffield: Sheffield Academic, 1996.

————. *The Psalms of the Sons of Korah.* Journal for the Study of the Old Testament, Supplement Series 20. Sheffield: Sheffield Academic, 1982.

Grabbe, Lester L. *Ancient Israel: What Do We Know and How Do We Know It?* London: T&T Clark, 2007.

————. *A History of the Jews and Judaism in the Second Temple Period, Volume 1, Yehud: A History of the Persian Province of Judah.* London: T & T Clark, 2004.

Graham, M. Patrick, Kenneth G. Hoglund, and Steven L. McKenzie, eds. *The Chronicler as Historian.* Journal for the Study of the Old Testament, Supplement Series 238. Sheffield: Sheffield Academic, 1997.

Graham, M. Patrick, and Steven L. McKenzie, eds. *The Chronicler as Author: Studies in Text and Texture.* Journal for the Study of the Old Testament, Supplement Series 263. Sheffield: Sheffield Academic, 1999.

Gray, George Buchanan. *Studies in Hebrew Proper Names.* London: A&C Black, 1896.

Gray, John. *I and II Kings: A Commentary*. Old Testament Library. Philadelphia: Westminster, 1963.

Greenfield, Jonas C. "The Aramean God Rammān/Rimmōn." *Israel Exploration Journal* 26 (1976): 195–98.

———. "Hadad הדד," In *Dictionary of Deities and Demons in the Bible*, edited by Karel van der Toorn, Bob Becking, and Pieter W. van der Horst, 377–82. 2nd ed. Leiden: Brill, 1999.

Gröndahl, Frauke. *Die Personennamen Der Texte Aus Ugarit*. Studia Pohl 1. Rome: Pontifical Biblical Institute, 1967.

Gunkel, Hermann. *Creation and Chaos in the Primeval Era and the Eschaton: A Religio-Historical Study of Genesis 1 and Revelation 12*. Foreword by Peter Machinist. Edited and translated by K. William Whitney Jr. Biblical Resource Series. Grand Rapids: Eerdmans, 2006. Originally published as *Schöpfung und Chaos in Urzeit und Endzeit: Eine religionsgeschichtliche Untersuchung über Gen. 1 und Ap. Jon. 12* (Göttingen: Vandenhoeck & Ruprecht, 1895).

Gunkel, Hermann, and Joachim Begrich. *Introduction to Psalms: The Genres of the Religious Lyric of Israel*. Translated by James D. Nogalski. Mercer Library of Biblical Studies. Macon: Mercer University Press, 1998.

Gurney, Oliver R. *The Hittites*. London: Penguin, 1952. Reprint, London: Penguin, 1990.

———. *Some Aspects of Hittite Religion*. Oxford: Oxford University Press, 1977.

Haas, Volkert. *Geschichte der hethitischen Religion*. Handbuch der Orientalistik, Erste Abteilung 15. Leiden: Brill, 1994.

Hallo, William H. "The Cultic Setting of Sumerian Poetry." In *Actes de la XVIIe Rencontre Assyriologique Internationale*, edited by A. Finet, 119–20. Ham-sur-Heure [Belgium]: Comité belge de recherches en Mésopotamie, 1970.

———. "Lamentations and Prayers in Sumer and Akkad." In *Civilizations of the Ancient Near East*, edited by Jack M. Sasson, 3:1871–81. New York: Scribners, 1995.

———. "Toward a History of Sumerian Literature." In *Sumerological Studies in Honor of Thorkild Jacobsen on His Seventieth Birthday, June 7, 1974*, edited by Thorkild Jacobsen, 181–203. Chicago: University of Chicago Press, 1976.

Hallo, William H., and K. Lawson Younger Jr., eds. *The Context of Scripture*. 3 vols. Leiden: Brill, 1997–2002.

Halpern, Baruch. "Ehud." In *The Anchor Bible Dictionary*, edited by D. N. Freedman, 2:414. New York: Doubleday, 1992.

———. "Sectionalism and the Schism." *Journal of Biblical Literature* 93 (1974): 519–32.

Handy, Lowell K. *Among the Host of Heaven: The Syro-Palestinian Pantheon as Bureaucracy*. Winona Lake, Ind.: Eisenbrauns, 1994.

Haran, Menahem. *Temple and Temple-Service in Ancient Israel: An Inquiry into the Character of Cult Phenomena and the Historical Setting of the Priestly*

School. Oxford: Clarendon, 1978. Reprinted with slight changes, Winona
Lake, Ind.: Eisenbrauns, 1985, 1995.

Hendel, Ronald. "The Exodus in Biblical Memory." *Journal of Biblical Literature*
120 (2001): 601–622.

Herrmann, Wolfgang. "El אֵל." In *Dictionary of Deities and Demons in the
Bible,* edited by Karel van der Toorn, Bob Becking, and Pieter W. van der
Horst, 274–80. 2nd ed. Leiden: Brill, 1999.

Hestrin, Ruth, and Michal Dayagi-Mendeles, *Inscribed Seals: First Temple
Period, Hebrew, Ammonite, Moabite, Phoenician and Aramaic from the Col-
lections of the Israel Museum and the Israel Department of Antiquities and
Museums.* Translated by Inna Pommerantz. Jerusalem: Israel Museum, 1979.

Hillers, Delbert R. *Covenant: The History of a Biblical Idea.* Seminars in the
History of Ideas. Baltimore: Johns Hopkins University Press, 1969.

———. "Palmyrene Aramaic Inscriptions and the Bible (II)." *Zeitschrift für Alt-
hebräistik* 11 (1998): 32–49.

Holladay, William L. *Jeremiah 1: A Commentary on the Book of the Prophet
Jeremiah, Chapters 1–25.* Hermeneia. Philadelphia: Fortress Press, 1986.

Holloway, Steven W. *Assur Is King! Assur Is King! Religion in the Exercise of
Power in the Neo-Assyrian Empire.* Culture and History of the Ancient Near
East 10. Leiden: Brill, 2002.

Hornung, Erik. *Conceptions of God in Ancient Egypt: The One and the Many.*
Ithaca: Cornell University Press, 1982.

Horowitz, Wayne, and Takayoshi Oshima. *Cuneiform in Canaan: Cuneiform
Sources from the Land of Israel in Ancient Times.* With Seth Sanders. Jerusalem: Israel Exploration Society and Hebrew University of Jerusalem, 2006.

Horst, Friedrich. "Zwei Begriffe für Eigentum (Besitz): נַחֲלָה und אֲחֻזָּה." In
*Verbannung und Heimkehr: Beiträge zur Geschichte und Theologie Israels im
6. und 5. Jahrhundert v. Chr.,* edited by Arnulf Kuschke, 135–56. Tübingen:
Mohr, 1961.

Hostetter, Edwin L. "Nahor." In *Eerdmans Dictionary of the Bible,* edited by D.
N. Freedman, 942. Grand Rapids: Eerdmans, 2000.

Huffmon, Herbert B. *Amorite Personal Names in the Mari Texts: A Structural
and Lexical Study.* Baltimore: Johns Hopkins Press, 1965.

———. "The Covenant Lawsuit in the Prophets." *Journal of Biblical Literature*
78 (1959): 285–95.

Hurowitz, Victor Avigdor. "Paradise Regained: Proverbs 3:13-20 Reconsidered."
In *Sefer Moshe: The Moshe Weinfeld Jubilee Volume; Studies in the Bible and
the Ancient Near East, Qumran, and Post-Biblical Judaism,* edited by Chaim
Cohen, Avi Hurvitz, and Shalom M. Paul, 49–62. Winona Lake, Ind.: Eisenbrauns, 2004.

Jackson, Kent P., and J. Andrew Dearman. "The Text of the Mesha᾽ Inscription."
In *Studies in the Mesha Inscription and Moab,* edited by J. Andrew Dearman,
93–95. Atlanta: Scholars, 1989.

Jacobsen, Thorkild. *The Harps That Once . . . : Sumerian Poetry in Translation.*
New Haven: Yale University Press, 1987.

———. "The Mesopotamian Temple Plan and the Kititum Temple." *Eretz-Israel* 20 (Yigael Yadin Volume, 1989): 79–91.

———. Review of S. N. Kramer, *Lamentation over the Destruction of Ur. American Journal of Semitic Languages and Literature* 58 (1941): 219–24.

———. *Toward the Image of Tammuz and Other Essays on Mesopotamian History and Culture.* Edited by William L. Moran. Cambridge, Mass.: Harvard University Press, 1970. Reprint, Eugene, Ore.: Wipf & Stock, 2008.

———. *The Treasures of Darkness: A History of Mesopotamian Religion.* New Haven: Yale University Press, 1976.

Jamieson-Drake, David W. *Scribes and Schools in Monarchic Judah: A Socio-Archaeological Approach.* Journal for the Study of the Old Testament, Supplement Series 109. Sheffield: Sheffield Academic, 1991.

Japhet, Sara. "Composition and Chronology in the Book of Ezra-Nehemiah." In *Second Temple Studies 2: Temple Community in the Persian Period,* edited by Tamara Cohn Eskenazi and Kent H. Richards, 189–216. Journal for the Study of the Old Testament, Supplement Series 175. Sheffield: Sheffield Academic, 1994.

———. *I & II Chronicles: A Commentary.* Old Testament Library. Louisville: Westminster John Knox, 1993.

———. "The Historical Reliability of Chronicles: The History of the Problem and Its Place in Biblical Research." *Journal for the Study of the Old Testament* 33 (1985): 83–107.

———. *The Ideology of the Book of Chronicles and Its Place in Biblical Thought.* Translated by Anna Barber. Beiträge zur Erforschung des Alten Testaments und des Antiken Judentums. Frankfurt: Peter Lang, 1989.

———. "The Supposed Common Authorship of Chronicles and Ezra-Nehemiah Investigated Anew." *Vetus Testamentum* 18 (1968): 330–71.

———. "The Walls of Jerusalem from a Double Perspective: Kings versus Chronicles." In *Essays on Ancient Israel in Its Near Eastern Context: A Tribute to Nadav Naaman,* edited by Yaira Amit and Nadav Naaman, 205–219. Winona Lake, Ind.: Eisenbrauns, 2006.

Jastrow, Marcus. *A Dictionary of the Targumim, the Talmud Babli and Yerushalmi, and the Midrashic Literature.* New York: Judaica, 1971.

Joffe, Alexander H. "The Rise of Secondary States in the Iron Age Levant." *Journal of the Economic and Social History of the Orient* 45 (2002): 425–67.

Joffe, Laura. "The Answer to the Meaning of Life, the Universe and the Elohistic Psalter." *Journal for the Study of the Old Testament* 27 (2002): 223–35.

———. "The Elohistic Psalter: What, How and Why?" *Scandinavian Journal of the Old Testament* 15 (2001): 142–66.

Johnson, Aubrey R. *The One and the Many in the Israelite Conception of God.* 2nd ed. Cardiff: University of Wales Press, 1961.

———. *Sacral Kingship in Ancient Israel.* 2nd ed. Cardiff: University of Wales Press, 1967.

Kallai, Zecharia. "A Note on the Twelve-Tribe Systems of Israel." *Vetus Testamentum* 49 (1999): 125–27.

———. "The Twelve-Tribe Systems of Israel." *Vetus Testamentum* 47 (1997): 53–90.

Kalluveettil, Paul. *Declaration and Covenant: A Comprehensive Review of Covenant Formulae from the Old Testament and the Ancient Near East*. Analecta biblica 88. Rome: Pontifical Biblical Institute, 1982.

Keel, Othmar. *Goddesses and Trees, New Moon and Yahweh: Ancient Near Eastern Art and the Hebrew Bible*. Journal for the Study of the Old Testament, Supplement Series 261. Sheffield: Sheffield Academic, 1998.

———. *The Symbolism of the Biblical World: Ancient Near Eastern Iconography and the Book of Psalms*. New York: Seabury, 1978.

Keel, Othmar, and Christoph Uehlinger. *Gods, Goddesses, and Images of God in Ancient Israel*. Translated by Thomas H. Trapp. Minneapolis: Fortress Press, 1998.

Khoury, Philip S., and Joseph Kostiner. "Introduction: Tribes and the Complexities of State Formation in the Middle East." In *Tribes and State Formation in the Middle East*, edited by Philip S. Khoury and Joseph Kostiner, 1–22. Berkeley: University of California Press, 1990.

Khoury, Philip S., and Joseph Kostiner, eds. *Tribes and State Formation in the Middle East*. Berkeley: University of California Press, 1990.

King, Philip J., and Lawrence E. Stager, *Life in Biblical Israel*. Library of Ancient Israel. Louisville: Westminster John Knox, 2001.

Klein, Jacob. "Lamentation over the Destruction of Sumer and Ur." In *The Context of Scripture*, edited by W. W. Hallo and K. L. Younger, 1:535. Leiden: Brill, 1997–.

Klein, Ralph W. "The Books of Ezra and Nehemiah: Introduction, Commentary, and Reflections." In *The New Interpreter's Bible*, edited by Leander E. Keck, 3:661–851. Nashville: Abingdon, 1999.

———. "Chronicles, Book of 1–2." In *The Anchor Bible Dictionary*, edited by David Noel Freedman, 1:992–1002. New York: Doubleday, 1992.

Knauf, E. A. "Qôs קוֹשׁ." In *Dictionary of Deities and Demons*, edited by Karel van der Toorn, Bob Becking, and Pieter W. van der Horst, 674–77. 2nd ed. Leiden: Brill, 1999.

Knohl, Israel. *The Sanctuary of Silence: The Priestly Torah and the Holiness School*. Minneapolis: Fortress Press, 1995.

Knoppers, Gary N. "Ancient Near Eastern Royal Grants and the Davidic Covenant: A Parallel?" *Journal of the American Oriental Society* 116 (1996): 670–97.

———. *I Chronicles 10–29: A New Translation with Introduction and Commentary*. Anchor Bible 12A. New York: Doubleday, 2004.

———. "Is There a Future for the Deuteronomistic History?" In *The Future of the Deuteronomistic History*, edited by Thomas Römer, 119–34. Bibliotheca Ephemeridum Theologicarum Lovaniensium 147. Leuven: University Press, 2000.

———. "Yhwh's Rejection of the House Built for His Name: On the Significance of Anti-Temple Rhetoric in the Deuteronomistic History." In *Essays on Ancient Israel in Its Near Eastern Context: A Tribute to Nadav Naaman,* edited by Yaira Amit and Nadav Naaman, 221–38. Winona Lake, Ind.: Eisenbrauns, 2006.

Knowles, Melody D. *Centrality Practiced: Jerusalem in the Religious Practice of Yehud and the Diaspora during the Persian Period.* Archaeology and Biblical Studies 16. Atlanta: Society of Biblical Literature, 2006.

Kraemer, David. "On the Relationship of the Books of Ezra and Nehemiah." *Journal for the Study of the Old Testament* 59 (1993): 73–92.

Kraetzschmar, Richard. *Die Bundesvorstellung im Alten Testament in ihrer geschichtlichen Entwickelung.* Marburg: Elwert, 1896.

Krahmalkov, Charles R. *A Phoenician-Punic Dictionary.* Orientalia Lovaniensia Analecta. Leuven: Uitgeverij Peeters en Department Oosterse Studies, 2000.

———. *A Phoenician-Punic Grammar.* Handbuch Der Orientalistik. Leiden: Brill, 2001.

Kraus, Hans-Joachim. *Worship in Israel: A Cult History of the Old Testament.* Translated by G. Buswell. Richmond: John Knox, 1966.

Krebernik, Manfred. *Die Personennamen der Ebla-Texte: Eine Zwischenbilanz.* Berliner Beiträge zum vorderen Orient 7. Berlin: Dietrich Reimer, 1988.

Kreuzer, Siegfried. *Der lebendige Gott: Bedeutung, Herkunft und Entwicklung einer alttestamentlichen Gottesbezeichnung.* Beiträge zur Wissenschaft vom Alten und Neuen Testament Series 6, volume 16. Stuttgart: Kohlhammer, 1983.

Kuhrt, Amélie. "The Cyrus Cylinder and Achaemenid Imperial Policy." *Journal for the Study of the Old Testament* 25 (1983): 83-97.

Kuntz, J. Kenneth. "Reclaiming Biblical Wisdom Psalms: A Response to Crenshaw." *Currents in Biblical Research* (2003): 145–54.

Kutsko, John F. *Between Heaven and Earth: Divine Presence and Absence in the Book of Ezekiel.* Biblical and Judaic Studies 6. Winona Lake, Ind.: Eisenbrauns, 2000.

Laato, Antti, and Johannes C. de Moor, eds. *Theodicy in the Biblical World.* Leiden: Brill, 2003.

LaBianca, Øystein. "Salient Features of Iron Age Tribal Kingdoms." In *Ancient Ammon,* edited by Burton Macdonald and Randall W. Younker, 19–29. Leiden: Brill, 1999.

LaBianca, Øystein, and Randall W. Younker. "The Kingdoms of Ammon, Moab and Edom: The Archaeology of Society in Late Bronze/Iron Age Transjordan (ca. 1400–500 BCE)." In *Archaeology of Society in the Holy Land,* edited by Thomas E. Levy, 399–415. London: Leicester University Press, 1995.

Lafont, Bertrand. "Le roi de Mari et les prophètes du dieu Adad." *Revue d'assyriologie et d'archéologie orientale* 78 (1984): 7–18.

Lambert, Wilfred G. *Babylonian Wisdom Literature.* Oxford: Clarendon, 1960. Reprint, Winona Lake, Ind.: Eisenbrauns, 1996.

———. "The Historical Development of the Mesopotamian Pantheon: A Study in Sophisticated Polytheism." In *Unity and Diversity: Essays in the History, Literature, and Religion of the Ancient Near East,* edited by Hans Goedicke and J. J. M. Roberts, 191–200. Baltimore: Johns Hopkins University Press, 1975.

Lambert, Wilfred G., and Alan R. Millard. *Atra-Ḥasis: The Babylonian Story of the Flood.* With Miguel Civil. Oxford: Clarendon, 1969. Reprinted, Winona Lake, Ind.: Eisenbrauns, 1999.

Landsberger, Benno. "Assyrische Königsliste Und 'Dunkles Zeitalter.'" *Journal of Cuneiform Studies* 8 (1954): 47–73.

Lang, Bernhard. *Wisdom and the Book of Proverbs: A Hebrew Goddess Redefined.* New York: Pilgrim, 1986.

Larcher, Chrysostome. "Divine Transcendence as Another Reason for God's Absence." In *Scripture: The Presence of God,* edited by Roland Murphy, Pierre Benoit, and Bastiaan van Iersel, 49–64. Concilium: Theology in the Age of Renewal. New York: Paulist, 1969.

Launderville, Dale. "Ezekiel's Throne-Chariot Vision: Spiritualizing the Model of Divine-Royal Rule." *Catholic Biblical Quarterly* 66 (2004): 361–77.

Lemaire, André. "The Sage in School and Temple." In *The Sage in Israel and the Ancient Near East,* edited by John G. Gammie and John G. Perdue, 165–81. Winona Lake, Ind.: Eisenbrauns, 1990.

Lemche, Niels Peter. "From Patronage Society to Patronage Society." In *Origins of the Ancient Israelite States,* edited by Vokmar Fritz and Philip R. Davies, 106–120. Sheffield: Sheffield Academic, 1996.

Lenzi, Alan. *Secrecy and the Gods: Secret Knowledge in Ancient Mesopotamia and Biblical Israel.* State Archives of Assyria Studies 19. Helsinki: Neo-Assyrian Text Corpus Project, University of Helsinki, 2008.

Lesko, Leonard H. "Death and the Afterlife in Ancient Egyptian Thought." In *Civilizations of the Ancient Near East,* edited by J. M. Sasson, 3:1763–74. New York: Scribners, 1995.

Levenson, John D. *Creation and the Persistence of Evil: The Jewish Drama of Divine Omnipotence.* San Francisco: Harper & Row, 1988.

———. *Esther: A Commentary.* Old Testament Library. Louisville: Westminster John Knox, 1997.

———. *Sinai and Zion: An Entry into the Jewish Bible.* Minneapolis: Winston, 1985.

Levine, Baruch A. *Leviticus: The Traditional Hebrew Text with the New JPS Translation.* JPS Torah Commentary. Philadelphia: Jewish Publication Society, 1989.

———. "*Lpny YHWH*: Phenomenology of the Open-Air-Altar in Biblical Israel." In *Biblical Archaeology Today: Proceedings of the Second International Congress on Biblical Archaeology, Jerusalem, June 1990,* 196–205. Jerusalem: Israel Exploration Society, 1993.

———. "Ritual as Symbol: Modes of Sacrifice in Israelite Religion." In *Sacred Time, Sacred Place: Archaeology and the Religion of Israel,* edited by Barry M. Gittlen, 125–35. Winona Lake, Ind.: Eisenbrauns, 2002.

Levine, Baruch A., and Jean-Michel de Tarragon. "Dead Kings and Rephaim: The Patrons of the Ugaritic Dynasty." *Journal of the American Oriental Society* 104 (1984): 649–59.

Levine, Baruch A., Jean-Michel de Tarragon, and Anne Robertson. "The Patrons of the Ugaritic Dynasty (*KTU* 1.161)." In *The Context of Scripture*, edited by W. W. Hallo and K. L. Younger, 1:357–58. Leiden: Brill, 1997–2002.

Levinson, Bernard M. *Deuteronomy and the Hermeneutics of Legal Innovation.* Oxford: Oxford University Press, 2002.

Lewis, Theodore J. "Covenant and Blood Rituals: Understanding Exodus 24:3-8 in Its Ancient Near Eastern Context." In *Confronting the Past: Archaeological and Historical Essays on Ancient Israel in Honor of William G. Dever*, edited by Seymour Gitin, J. Edward Wright, and J. P. Dessel, 341–50. Winona Lake, Ind.: Eisenbrauns, 2006.

———. *Cults of the Dead in Ancient Israel and Ugarit.* Harvard Semitic Monographs 39. Atlanta: Scholars, 1989.

———. "How Far Can Texts Take Us? Evaluating Textual Sources for Reconstructing Ancient Israelite Beliefs about the Dead." In *Sacred Time, Sacred Place: Archaeology and the Religion of Israel*, edited by B. M. Gittlen, 169–217. Winona Lake, Ind.: Eisenbrauns, 2002.

———. "The Identity and Function of El/Baal Berith." *Journal of Biblical Literature* 115 (1996): 401–23.

———. "The Rapiuma: 20–22. CAT 1.20–22." In *Ugaritic Narrative Poetry*, edited by Simon B. Parker, 196–205. Society of Biblical Literature Writings from the Ancient World 9. Atlanta: Scholars, 1997.

Lichtheim, Miriam. *Ancient Egyptian Literature.* 3 vols. Berkeley: University of California Press, 1975–80.

Lindenberger, James M. "Ahiqar (Seventh to Sixth Century B.C.): A New Translation and Introduction." In *The Old Testament Pseudepigrapha*, edited by J. H. Charlesworth, 2:479–507. Anchor Bible Reference Library. New York: Doubleday, 1985.

———. *The Aramaic Proverbs of Ahiqar.* Johns Hopkins Near Eastern Studies. Baltimore: Johns Hopkins University Press, 1983.

Lindström, Fredrik. "Theodicy in the Psalms." In *Theodicy in the World of the Bible*, edited by Antti Laato and Johannes C. de Moor, 256–303. Leiden: Brill, 2003.

Lipiński, Edward. "נָחַל *nāḥal*; נַחֲלָה *naḥălâ*." In *Theological Dictionary of the Old Testament*, edited by G. J. Botterweck, H. Ringgren, and H.J. Fabry, 9:319–35. Grand Rapids: Eerdmans, 1974–.

———. *Semitic Languages: Outline of a Comparative Grammar.* Orientalia lovaniensia analecta 80. Leuven: Peeters, 2001.

Liverani, Mario. "The Great Powers' Club." In *Amarna Diplomacy: The Beginnings of International Relations*, edited by Raymond Cohen and Raymond Westbrook, 15–27. Baltimore: Johns Hopkins University Press, 2000.

Lods, A., and G. Dossin. "Une tablette inédite de Mari, intéressante pour l'histoire ancienne du prophétisme sémitique." In *Studies in Old Testament Prophecy Presented to Professor Theodore H. Robinson*, edited by H. H. Rowley, 103–110. Edinburgh: T&T Clark, 1957.

Loewenstamm, Samuel E. "*nḥlt yhwh*." In *Studies in Bible, 1986,* edited by Sara Japhet, 155–92. Scripta Hierosolymitana 31. Jerusalem: Magnes, 1986.

Lohfink, Norbert. *Das Hauptgebot: Eine Untersuchung literarischer Einleitungsfragen zu Dtn 5–11.* Analecta biblica 20. Rome: Pontificio Instituto Biblico, 1963.

Luckenbill, Daniel David. *The Annals of Sennacherib.* University of Chicago Oriental Institute Publications 2. Chicago: University of Chicago Press, 1924.

Malamat, Abraham. "Pre-Monarchical Social Institutions in Israel in the Light of Mari." In *History of Biblical Israel: Major Problems and Minor Issues,* 36–40. Leiden: Brill, 2001.

Maraqten, Mohammed. *Die semitischen Personennamen in den alt- und reichsaramäischen Inschriften aus Vorderasien.* Texte und Studien zur Orientalistik 5. Hildesheim: Olms, 1988.

Master, Daniel. "State Formation Theory and the Kingdom of Israel." *Journal of Near Eastern Studies* 60 (2001): 117–31.

Mattingly, Gerald L. "Moabite Religion." In *Studies in the Mesha Inscription and Moab,* edited by Andrew Dearman, 213–38. Archaeology and Biblical Studies 2. Atlanta: Scholars, 1989.

Mazar, Benjamin. "On the Study of the Personal Names in the Bible." *Lešonénu* 15 (1947): 37–44.

McBride, S. Dean. "The Deuteronomic Name Theology." Ph.D. diss., Harvard University, 1969.

McCann, J. Clinton. "The Book of Psalms: Introduction, Commentary, and Reflections." In *The New Interpreters Dictionary of the Bible,* edited by K. D. Sakenfeld, 4:639–1280. Nashville: Abingdon, 1996–.

McCarter, P. Kyle, Jr. "Aspects of the Religion of the Israelite Monarchy: Biblical and Epigraphic Data." In *Ancient Israelite Religions,* edited by Patrick D. Miller, Paul D. Hanson, and S. Dean McBride, 137–55. Philadelphia: Fortress Press, 1987.

———. *I Samuel: A New Translation with Introduction and Commentary.* Anchor Bible 8. New York: Doubleday, 1980.

———. *II Samuel: A New Translation with Introduction, Notes and Commentary.* Anchor Bible 9. New York: Doubleday, 1984.

———. *Textual Criticism: Recovering the Text of the Hebrew Bible.* Old Testament Guides. Philadelphia: Fortress, 1986.

McCarthy, Dennis J. *Treaty and Covenant: A Study in Form in the Ancient Oriental Documents and in the Old Testament.* 2nd ed. Analecta biblica 21a. Rome: Pontifical Biblical Institute, 1981.

McKay, John W. *Religion in Judah under the Assyrians, 732–609 B.C.* Studies in Biblical Theology 26. London: SCM, 1973.

McKenzie, Steven L. *The Chronicler's Use of the Deuteronomistic History.* Harvard Semitic Monographs 33. Atlanta: Scholars, 1985.

———. "The Typology of the Davidic Covenant." In *The Land that I Will Show You: Essays on the History and Archaeology of the Ancient Near East in Honour of J. Maxwell Miller,* edited by J. Andrew Dearman and M. Patrick

Graham, 152–78. Journal for the Study of the Old Testament, Supplement Series 343. Sheffield: Sheffield Academic, 2001.

McMahon, Gregory. *The Hittite State Cult of the Tutelary Deities.* Assyriological Studies 25. Chicago: Oriental Institute of the University of Chicago, 1991.

Meier, Samuel A. "Diplomacy and International Marriages." In *Amarna Diplomacy: The Beginnings of International Relations,* edited by Raymond Cohen and Raymond Westbrook, 165–73. Baltimore: Johns Hopkins University Press, 2000.

Mendenhall, George E. "Covenant." In *The Interpreter's Dictionary of the Bible,* edited by G. A. Buttrick, 1:714–23. Nashville: Abingdon, 1962.

———. "Covenant Forms in Israelite Tradition." *Biblical Archaeologist* 17 (1954): 50–76.

Mendenhall, George E., and Gary A. Herion. "Covenant." In *The Anchor Bible Dictionary,* edited by D. N. Freedman, 1:1179–1202. New York: Doubleday, 1992.

Mettinger, Tryggve N. D. *The Riddle of the Resurrection: 'Dying and Rising Gods' in the Ancient Near East.* Coniectanea Biblica Old Testament Series. Stockholm: Almqvist & Wiksell, 2001.

Meyers, Carol. "Contesting the Notion of Patriarchy: Anthropology and the Theorizing of Gender in Ancient Israel." In *The Question of Sex? Gender and Difference in the Hebrew Bible and Beyond,* edited by Deborah W. Rooke, 83–105. Hebrew Bible Monographs 14. Sheffield: Sheffield Phoenix, 2007.

———. "Families in Ancient Israel." In *Families in Ancient Israel,* edited by Leo G. Perdue, Joseph Blenkinsopp, John J. Collins, and Carol Meyers, 1–47. The Family, Religion, and Culture. Louisville: Westminster John Knox, 1997.

———. "Hierarchy or Heterarchy? Archaeology and the Theorizing of Israelite Society." In *Confronting the Past: Archaeological and Historical Essays on Ancient Israel in Honor of William G. Dever,* edited by William G. Dever, Seymour Gitin, J. Edward Wright, and J. P. Dessel, 245–54. Winona Lake, Ind.: Eisenbrauns, 2006.

———. "Temple, Jerusalem." In *The Anchor Bible Dictionary,* edited by D. N. Freedman, 6:350–69. New York: Doubleday, 1992.

Meyers, Carol L., and Eric M. Meyers. *Haggai, Zechariah 1–8: A New Translation with Introduction and Commentary.* Anchor Bible 25B. Garden City, N.Y.: Doubleday, 1987.

Michalowski, Piotr. *The Lamentation over the Destruction of Sumer and Ur.* Mesopotamian Civilizations 1. Winona Lake, Ind.: Eisenbrauns, 1989.

Milgrom, Jacob. *Leviticus 1–16: A New Translation with Introduction and Commentary.* Anchor Bible 3. New York: Doubleday, 1991.

Miller, J. Maxwell, and John H. Hayes. *A History of Ancient Israel and Judah.* 2nd ed. Louisville: Westminster John Knox, 2006.

Miller, Patrick D. "The Book of Jeremiah: Introduction, Commentary, and Reflections." In *The New Interpreter's Bible,* edited by Leander Keck et al., 6:553–926. Nashville: Abingdon, 1999.

———. *The Divine Warrior in Early Israel.* Harvard Semitic Monographs 5. Cambridge, Mass.: Harvard University Press, 1973.

———. "El, the Creator of Earth," *Bulletin of the American Schools of Oriental Research* 239 (1980): 43–46. Reprinted in *Israelite Religion and Biblical Theology.* Sheffield: Sheffield Academic, 2000.

———. *They Cried to the Lord: The Form and Theology of Biblical Prayer.* Minneapolis: Fortress Press, 1994.

Miller, Patrick D., Jr., and J. J. M. Roberts. *The Hand of the Lord: A Reassessment of the "Ark Narrative" of 1 Samuel.* Johns Hopkins Near Eastern Studies. Baltimore: Johns Hopkins University Press, 1977.

Mitchell, C. W. *The Meaning of BRK "To Bless" in the Old Testament.* Society of Biblical Literature Dissertation Series 95. Atlanta: Scholars, 1987.

Monson, John. "The New Ain Dara Temple: Closest Solomonic Parallel." *Biblical Archaeologist* 26, no. 3 (2000): 20–35, 67.

Montgomery, James A. *A Critical and Exegetical Commentary on the Books of Kings.* Edited by Henry Snyder Gehman. International Critical Commentary 10. New York: Scribners, 1951.

Moran, William L. *The Amarna Letters.* Baltimore: Johns Hopkins University Press, 1992.

———. "The Ancient Near Eastern Background of the Love of God in Deuteronomy." *Catholic Biblical Quarterly* 25 (1963): 77–87.

Moscati, Sabatino. *The World of the Phoenicians.* Translated by Alastair Hamilton. Praeger History of Civilizations. New York: Praeger, 1968.

Mowinckel, Sigmund. "Hypostasen." In *Die Religion in Geschichte und Gegenwart: Handwörterbuch für Theologie und Religionswissenschaft,* edited by Herman Gunkel and et al., 2:2065–68. 2nd ed. 5 vols. Tübingen: Mohr, 1928.

———. *The Psalms in Israel's Worship.* Translated by D. R. Ap-Thomas. New York: Abingdon, 1962.

Munn-Rankin, J. M. "Diplomacy in Western Asia in the Early Second Millennium." *Iraq* 18 (1956): 68–110.

Murphy, Roland E. "Wisdom and Creation." *Journal of Biblical Literature* 104 (1985): 3–11.

Mykytiuk, Lawrence J. *Identifying Biblical Persons in Northwest Semitic Inscriptions of 1200–539 B.C.E.* Academia biblica 12. Atlanta: Society of Biblical Literature, 2004.

Nelson, Richard. "The Double Redaction of the Deuteronomistic History: The Case Is Still Compelling." *Journal for the Study of the Old Testament* 29 (2005): 319–37.

Nestle, Eberhard. *Die Israelitischen Eigennamen nach ihrer Religionsgeschichtlichen Bedeutung.* Haarlem: Bohn, 1876.

Newsom, Carol A. "The Book of Job: Introduction, Commentary, and Reflections." In *The New Interpreter's Bible,* edited by Leander Keck et al., 4:317–637. Nashville: Abingdon, 1999.

Nicholson, Ernest W. *God and His People: Covenant and Theology in the Old Testament.* New York: Oxford University Press, 1986.

Nissinen, Martti. *Prophets and Prophecy in the Ancient Near East.* With contributions by C. L. Seow and Robert K. Ritner. Edited by Peter Machinist. Society of Biblical Literature Writings from the Ancient World 12. Atlanta: Society of Biblical Literature, 2003.

Noth, Martin. *The Deuteronomistic History.* Journal for the Study of the Old Testament, Supplement Series 15. Sheffield: JSOT, 1981. First published 1943 by Niemeyer (in German).

———. *Die Israelitischen Personennamen Im Rahmen Der Gemeinsemitischen Namengebung.* Stuttgart: Kohlhammer, 1928.

O'Connor, Michael. "The Onomastic Evidence for Bronze-Age West Semitic." *Journal of the American Oriental Society* 124 (2004): 439–70.

Oden, Robert A., Jr. "The Place of Covenant in the Religion of Israel." In *Ancient Israelite Religion,* edited by Patrick D. Miller, Paul D. Hanson, and S. Dean McBride, 429–49. Philadelphia: Fortress Press, 1987.

Ollenburger, Ben C. *Zion the City of the Great King: A Theological Symbol of the Jerusalem Cult.* Journal for the Study of the Old Testament, Supplement Series 41. Sheffield: JSOT, 1987.

Olmo Lete, Gregorio del, and Joaquín Sanmartín. *A Dictionary of the Ugaritic Language in the Alphabetic Tradition.* 2nd ed. Translated by Wilfred G. E. Watson. Handbuch Der Orientalistik, Section 1, vol. 67. Leiden: Brill, 2003.

Olmstead, A. T. *History of the Persian Empire.* Chicago: University of Chicago Press, 1948.

Olyan, Saul M. *Biblical Mourning: Ritual and Social Dimensions.* New York: Oxford University Press, 2004.

———. *Rites and Rank: Hierarchy in Biblical Representations of Cult.* Princeton: Princeton University Press, 2000.

Oppenheim, A. Leo, and Erica Reiner, *Ancient Mesopotamia: Portrait of a Dead Civilization.* Chicago: University of Chicago Press, 1977.

Ornan, Tallay. *The Triumph of the Symbol: Pictorial Representation of Deities in Mesopotamia and the Biblical Image Ban.* Fribourg: Academic Free Press, 2005.

Pardee, Dennis. "Les documents d'Arslan Tash: Authentique ou faux?" *Syria* 75 (1998): 15–54.

———. "Koshar כשׁר." In *Dictionary of Deities and Demons,* edited by Karel van der Toorn, Bob Becking, and Pieter W. van der Horst, 490–91. 2nd ed. Leiden: Brill, 1999.

Parker, Simon B., ed. *Ugaritic Narrative Poetry.* Society of Biblical Literature Writings from the Ancient World 9. Atlanta: Scholars, 1997.

Parpola, Simo, ed. *The Prosopography of the Neo-Assyrian Empire.* Neo-Assyrian Text Corpus Project. Edited by Simo Parpola. Helsinki: University of Helsinki, 1998–.

————. *The Standard Babylonian Epic of Gilgamesh: Cuneiform Text, Transliteration, Glossary, Indices and Sign List*. State Archives of Assyria Cuneiform Texts 1. Helsinki: Neo-Assyrian Text Corpus Project, 1997.

Parpola, Simo, and Karen Radner, eds. *The Prosopography of the Neo-Assyrian Empire. Part 1.A*. Neo-Assyrian Text Corpus Project. Helsinki: University of Helsinki, 1998.

Perdue, Leo G. "Cosmology and the Social Order in the Wisdom Tradition." In *The Sage in Israel and the Ancient Near East,* edited by John G. Gammie and Leo G. Perdue, 457–78. Winona Lake, Ind.: Eisenbrauns, 1990.

————. *Reconstructing Old Testament Theology: After the Collapse of History*. Overtures to Biblical Theology. Minneapolis: Fortress Press, 2005.

————. "Sages, Scribes, and Seers in Israel and the Ancient Near East: An Introduction." In *Scribes, Sages, and Seers: The Sage in the Eastern Mediterranean World,* edited by Leo G. Perdue, 1–34. Göttingen: Vandenhoeck & Ruprecht, 2008.

————. *The Sword and the Stylus: An Introduction to Wisdom in the Age of Empires*. Grand Rapids: Eerdmans, 2008.

————. *Wisdom and Creation: The Theology of Wisdom Literature*. Nashville: Abingdon, 1994.

————. *Wisdom Literature: A Theological History*. Louisville: Westminster John Knox, 2007.

Perlitt, Lothar. *Bundestheologie im Alten Testament*. Wissenschaftliche Monographien zum Alten und Neuen Testament 36. Neukirchen-Vluyn: Neukirchener, 1969.

————. "Die Verborgenheit Gottes." In *Probleme Biblischer Theologie,* edited by H. W. Wolff, 367–82. Munich: Chr. Kaiser, 1971.

Peterson, David L. "Introduction to Prophetic Literature." In *The New Interpreter's Bible,* edited by Leander Keck et al., 6:1–23. Nashville: Abingdon, 1999.

Pfeiffer, Robert H. *State Letters of Assyria: A Transliteration and Translation of 355 Official Assyrian Letters Dating from the Sargonid Period (722–625 B.C.)*. New Haven: American Oriental Society, 1935.

Podella, Thomas. *Ṣôm-Fasten: Kollektive Trauer um den verborgenen Gott im Alten Testament*. Alter Orient und Altes Testament 224. Kevelaer: Butzon & Bercker, 1989.

Pope, Marvin H. *Job: Introduction, Translation, and Notes*. 3rd ed. Anchor Bible 15. Garden City, N.Y.: Doubleday, 1979.

Pritchard, James Bennett, ed. *Ancient Near Eastern Texts Relating to the Old Testament*. 3rd ed. Princeton: Princeton University Press, 1969.

————. *The Ancient Near East in Pictures Relating to the Old Testament*. 2nd ed. with supplement. Princeton: Princeton University Press, 1969.

Pruzsinszky, Regine. *Die Personennamen der Texte aus Emar*. Edited by D. I. Owen and G. Wilhelm. Studies on the Civilization and Culture of Nuzi and the Hurrians 13. Bethesda, Md.: CDL, 2003.

Puech, Emile. "Milcom מלכם." In *Dictionary of Deities and Demons in the Bible,* edited by Karel van der Toorn, Bob Becking, and Pieter W. van der Horst, 575–76. 2nd ed. Leiden: Brill, 1999.

Quirke, Stephen G. J. *Ancient Egyptian Religion*. London: British Museum Press, 1992.

———. "Judgment of the Dead." In *The Oxford Encyclopedia of Ancient Egypt*, edited by D. B. Redford, 2:212–13. Oxford: Oxford University Press, 2001.

Redford, Donald B. "The So-Called 'Codification' of the Egyptian Law under Darius I." Pages 135-59 in *Persia and Torah: The Theory of Imperial Authorization of the Pentateuch*. Edited by James W. Watts. Atlanta: Society of Biblical Literature, 2001.

Reifenberg, A. "Some Ancient Hebrew Seals." *Palestine Exploration Quarterly* 70 (1938): 113–16 and pl. VI.

Rendsburg, Gary. *Linguistic Evidence for the Northern Origin of Selected Psalms*. Society of Biblical Literature Monograph Series 4. Atlanta: Scholars, 1990.

Richter, Sandra L. *The Deuteronomistic History and the Name Theology:* lĕšakkēn šĕmô šam *in the Bible and the Ancient Near East*. Beihefte zur Zeitschrift für die alttestamentliche Wissenschaft 318. Berlin: de Gruyter, 2002.

Ringgren, Helmer. *Word and Wisdom*. Lund: Haken Ohlssons Boktryckeri, 1947.

Roberts, J. J. M. *The Bible and the Ancient Near East: Collected Essays*. Winona Lake, Ind.: Eisenbrauns, 2002.

———. *The Earliest Semitic Pantheon: A Study of the Semitic Deities Attested in Mesopotamia before Ur III*. Johns Hopkins Near Eastern Studies. Baltimore: Johns Hopkins University Press, 1972.

Robertson, David A. *Linguistic Evidence in Dating Early Hebrew Poetry*. Society of Biblical Literature Dissertation Series 3. Missoula, Mont.: Society of Biblical Literature, 1972.

Robins, Gay. "Cult Statues in Ancient Egypt." In *Cult Image and Divine Representation in the Ancient Near East*, edited by Neil H. Walls, 1–12. American Schools of Oriental Research Book Series 10. Boston: American Schools of Oriental Research, 2005.

Rollston, Christopher A. "Scribal Education in Ancient Israel: The Old Hebrew Epigraphic Evidence." *Bulletin of the American Schools of Oriental Research* 344 (2006): 47–74.

Römer, Thomas. *The So-Called Deuteronomistic History: A Sociological, Historical and Literary Introduction*. New York: T&T Clark, 2007. First published 2005.

Römer, Thomas, and Albert de Pury. "Deuteronomistic Historiography (DH): History of Research and Debated Issues." In *Israel Constructs Its History: Deuteronomistic Historiography in Recent Research*, edited by Albert de Pury, Thomas Römer, and Jean-Daniel Macchi, 24–141. Journal for the Study of the Old Testament, Supplement Series 306. Sheffield: Sheffield Academic, 2000.

Rost, Leonhard. "Die Überlieferung von der Thronnachfolge Davids." In *Das kleine Credo und andere Studien zum Alten Testament*, 119–253. Heidelberg: Quelle & Meyer, 1965. Reprint of *Die Überlieferung von der Thronnachfolge Davids*. Beiträge zur Wissenschaft vom Alten und Neuen Testament, Series 3, vol. 6. Stuttgart: Kohlhammer, 1926.

Rouillard, H. "Rephaim רְפָאִים." In *Dictionary of Deities and Demons in the Bible,* edited by Karel van der Toorn, Bob Becking, and Pieter W. van der Horst, 692–700. 2nd ed. Leiden: Brill, 1999.

Saggs, H. W. F. "The Nimrud Letters, 1952: Part II." *Iraq* 17 (1955): 131–33.

Sanders, Seth L. "Writing and Early Iron Age Israel: Before National Scripts, beyond Nations and States." In *Literate Culture and Tenth-Century Canaan: The Tel Zayit Abecedary in Context,* edited by Ron E. Tappy and P. Kyle McCarter, 97–112. Winona Lake, Ind.: Eisenbrauns, 2008.

Sarot, Marcel. "Theodicy and Modernity: An Inquiry into the Historicity of Theodicy." In *Theodicy in the Biblical World,* edited by Antti Laato and Johannes C. de Moor, 1–26. Leiden: Brill, 2003.

Sasson, Jack M., ed. *Civilizations of the Ancient Near East.* 4 vols. New York: Scribners, 1995.

Scharbert, Josef. "בָּרַךְ *brk;* בְּרָכָה; *berākhāh.*" In *Theological Dictionary of the Old Testament,* edited by G. J. Botterweck, H. Ringgren, and H.J. Fabry, 2:279–308. Grand Rapids: Eerdmans, 1974–.

Schencke, Wilhelm. *Die Chokma (Sophia) in der jüdischen Hypostasenspekulation.* Videnskapsselskapets Skrifter II. Hist.-filos. klasse 1912, no. 6. Kristiania: Dybwad, 1913.

Schloen, J. David. *The House of the Father as Fact and Symbol: Patrimonialism in Ugarit and the Ancient Near East.* Studies in the Archaeology and History of the Levant 2. Winona Lake, Ind.: Eisenbrauns, 2001.

Schmidt, Brian B. *Israel's Beneficent Dead: Ancestor Cult and Necromancy in Ancient Israelite Religion and Tradition.* Winona Lake, Ind.: Eisenbrauns, 1994.

Schniedewind, William. "The Problem with Kings: Recent Study of the Deuteronomistic History." *Religious Studies Review* 22, no. 1 (January 1996): 22–27.

Schrade, Hubert. *Der Verborgene Gott: Gottesbild und Gottesvorstellung in Israel und im Alten Orient.* Stuttgart: Kohlhammer, 1949.

Schroer, Silvia, and Othmar Keel. *Die Ikonographie Palästinas/Israels und der Alte Orient: Eine Religionsgeschichte in Bildern.* Vol. 1, *Vom Ausgehenden Mesolithikum bis zur Frühbronzezeit.* Fribourg: Academic Press Fribourg, 2005.

Schwartz, Baruch J. "The Prohibitions Concerning the 'Eating' of Blood in Leviticus 17." In *Priesthood and Cult in Ancient Israel,* edited by Gary A. Anderson and Saul M. Olyan, 34–66. Journal for the Study of the Old Testament, Supplement Series 125. Sheffield: Sheffield Academic, 1991.

Scurlock, Jo Ann. "Death and the Afterlife in Ancient Mesopotamian Thought." In *Civilizations of the Ancient Near East,* edited by Jack M. Sasson, 3:1883–93. New York: Scribners, 1995.

Segal, J. B. "An Aramaic Ostracon from Nimrud." *Iraq* 19 (1957): 139–45.

Seow, Choon Leong. *Ecclesiastes: A New Translation with Introduction and Commentary.* Anchor Bible 18C. New York: Doubleday, 1997.

———. "Linguistic Evidence and the Dating of Qoheleth." *Journal of Biblical Literature* 115 (1996): 645–66.

———. "Qohelet's Autobiography." In *Fortunate the Eyes That See: Essays in Honor of David Noel Freedman in Celebration of His Seventieth Birthday,* edited by Astrid B. Beck et al., 275–87. Grand Rapids: Eerdmans, 1995.

———. "The Social World of Ecclesiastes." In *Scribes, Sages, and Seers: The Sage in the Eastern Mediterranean World,* edited by Leo G. Perdue, 189–217. Göttingen: Vandenhoeck & Ruprecht, 2008.

Simkins, Ronald. *Yahweh's Activity in History and Nature in the Book of Joel.* Ancient Near Eastern Texts and Studies 10. Lewiston, N.Y.: Mellen, 1991.

Sjöberg, Åke W., and E. Bergmann. *The Collection of the Sumerian Temple Hymns.* Edited by A. L. Oppenheim. Texts from Cuneiform Sources 3. Locust Valley, N.Y.: Augustin, 1969.

Smend, Rudolph. "The Law and the Nations: A Contribution to Deuteronomistic Tradition History." In *Reconsidering Israel and Judah: Recent Studies on the Deuteronomistic History,* edited by G. N. Knoppers and J. G. McConville, 95–110. Translated by P. T. Daniels. Winona Lake, Ind.: Eisenbrauns, 2000. First published 1971 (in German).

Smith, Mark S. "The Baal Cycle." In *Ugaritic Narrative Poetry,* edited by Simon B. Parker, 81–180. Writings from the Ancient World 9. Atlanta: Society of Biblical Literature, 1997.

———. "Counting Calves at Bethel." In *"Up to the Gates of Ekron": Essays on the Archaeology and History of the Eastern Mediterranean in Honor of Seymour Gitin,* edited by Seymour Gitin, Sidnie White Crawford, and Amnon Ben-Tor, 382–94. Jerusalem: W. F. Albright Institute of Archaeological Research, 2007.

———. "The Death of 'Dying and Rising Gods' in the Biblical World: An Update, with Special References to Baal in the Baal Cycle." *Scandinavian Journal of the Old Testament* 12 (1998): 257–313.

———. *The Early History of God: Yahweh and the Other Deities in Ancient Israel.* 2nd ed. Biblical Resource Series. Grand Rapids: Eeerdmans; Dearborn, Mich.: Dove, 2002.

———. *God in Translation: Deities in Cross-Cultural Discourse in the Biblical World.* Forschungen zum Alten Testament 57. Tübingen: Mohr Siebeck, 2008.

———. "Like Deities, Like Temples (Like People)." In *Temple and Worship in Biblical Israel: Proceedings of the Oxford Old Testament Seminar,* edited by John Day, 3–27. London: T&T Clark, 2007.

———. *The Memoirs of God: History, Memory, and the Experience of the Divine in Ancient Israel.* Minneapolis: Fortress Press, 2004.

———. *The Origins of Biblical Monotheism: Israel's Polytheistic Background and the Ugaritic Texts.* New York: Oxford University Press, 2001.

———. *The Priestly Vision of Genesis 1.* Minneapolis: Fortress Press, forthcoming.

———. "Remembering God: Collective Memory in Israelite Religion." *Catholic Biblical Quarterly* 62 (2002): 631–51.

———. *The Origins of Biblical Monotheism: Israel's Polytheistic Background and the Ugaritic Texts.* New York: Oxford University Press, 2001.

————. *The Ugaritic Baal Cycle.* Volume 1, *Introduction with Text, Translation and Commentary of KTU 1.1–1.2.* Supplements to Vetus Testamentum 55. Leiden: Brill, 1994.

————. "'Your People Shall Be My People': Family and Covenant in Ruth 1:16-17." *Catholic Biblical Quarterly* 69 (2007): 242–58.

Smith, William Robertson. *Lectures on the Religion of the Semites: The Fundamental Institutions.* 3rd ed. with introduction by Stanley A. Cook. London: A&C Black, 1927.

Sparks, Kenton L. *Ancient Texts for the Study of the Hebrew Bible: A Guide to the Background Literature.* Peabody, Mass.: Hendrickson, 2005.

Speiser, Ephraim A. *Genesis: Introduction, Translation, and Notes.* Anchor Bible 1. Garden City, N.Y.: Doubleday, 1964.

Spieckermann, Hermann. *Heilsgegenwart: Eine Theologie der Psalmen.* Forschungen zur Religion und Literatur des Alten und Neuen Testaments 148. Göttingen: Vandenhoeck & Ruprecht, 1989.

————. *Juda unter Assur in der Sargonidenzeit.* Forschungen zur Religion und Literatur des Alten und Neuen Testaments 129. Göttingen: Vandenhoeck & Ruprecht, 1982.

Stager, Lawrence E. "The Archaeology of the Family in Ancient Israel." *Bulletin of the American Schools of Oriental Research* 260 (1985): 1–35.

————. "Jerusalem and the Garden of Eden." *Eretz-Israel* 26 (Frank Moore Cross Volume, 1999): 183–94.

————. "The Patrimonial Kingdom of Solomon." In *Symbiosis, Symbolism, and the Power of the Past: Canaan, Ancient Israel, and Their Neighbors from the Late Bronze Age through Roman Palaestina*, edited by William G. Dever and Seymour Gitin, 63–74. Winona Lake, Ind.: Eisenbrauns, 2003.

Stamm, Johann Jakob. *Die Akkadische Namengebung.* Darmstadt: Wissenschaftliche Buchgesellschaft, 1968.

————. "Hebräische Ersatznamen." In *Studies in Honor of Benno Landsberger on His Seventy-Fifth Birthday, April 21, 1965*, edited by Benno Landsberger, 16:413–24. Chicago: University of Chicago Press, 1965.

Steymans, Hans Ulrich. *Deuteronomium 28 und die adê zur Thronfolgerung Asarhaddons: Segen und Fluch im Alten Orient und in Israel.* Orbis biblicus et orientalis 145. Göttingen: Vandenhoeck & Ruprecht, 1995.

Streck, Michael P. *Das amurritische Onomastikon der altbabylonischen Zeit.* Vol. 1, *Die Amurriter, Die onomastische Forschung, Orthographie, und Phonologie, Nominalmorphologie.* Münster: Ugarit-Verlag, 2000.

Strong, John T. "God's *Kābôd*: The Presence of Yahweh in the Book of Ezekiel." In *The Book of Ezekiel: Theological and Anthropological Perspectives.* Edited by Margaret S. Odell and John T. Strong, 69–95. Atlanta: Society of Biblical Literature, 2000.

Sweet, Ronald F. G. "The Sage in Akkadian Literature: A Philological Study." In *The Sage in Israel and the Ancient Near East,* edited by John G. Gammie and John G. Perdue, 45–65. Winona Lake, Ind.: Eisenbrauns, 1990.

Tadmor, Hayim. "Treaty and Oath in the Ancient Near East: A Historian's Approach." In *Humanizing America's Iconic Book,* edited by Gene M. Tucker and Douglas A. Knight, 127–52. Chico, Calif.: Scholars, 1982.

Tallqvist, Knut L. *Assyrian Personal Names.* Helsinki: Societas Scientiarum Fennica, 1914.

Talmon, Shemaryahu. "The 'Desert Motif' in the Bible and in Qumran Literature." In *Biblical Motifs: Origins and Transformations,* edited by A. Altmann, 31–63. Cambridge, Mass.: Harvard University Press, 1966.

———. "Wilderness." In *Interpreter's Dictionary of the Bible: Supplementary Volume,* edited by K. Crim, 946–49. Nashville: Abingdon, 1976.

Tapper, Richard. "Anthropologists, Historians, and Tribespeople on Tribe and State Formation in the Middle East." In *Tribes and State Formation in the Middle East,* edited by Philip S. Khoury and Joseph Kostiner, 48–73. Berkeley: University of California Press, 1990.

Tarragon, Jean-Michel de, and Baruch A. Levine. "Dead Kings and Rephaim: The Patrons of the Ugaritic Dynasty." *Journal of the American Oriental Society* 104 (1984): 649–59.

Teixidor, Javier, and P. Amiet. "Les tablettes d'Arslan Tash au Musée d'Alep." *Aula orientalis* 1 (1983): 105–109.

Terrien, Samuel. *The Elusive Presence: Toward a New Biblical Theology.* San Francisco: Harper & Row, 1978.

Throntveit, Mark A. "The Relationship of Hezekiah to David and Solomon in the Books of Chronicles." In *The Chronicler as Theologian: Essays in Honor of Ralph W. Klein,* edited by M. Patrick Graham, Steven L. McKenzie, and Gary N. Knoppers, 105–121. Journal for the Study of the Old Testament, Supplement Series 371. London: T&T Clark, 2003.

———. *When Kings Speak: Royal Speech and Royal Prayer in Chronicles.* Society of Biblical Literature Dissertation Series 93. Atlanta: Scholars, 1987.

Tibi, Bassam. "Simultaneity of the Unsimultaneous: Old Tribes and Imposed Nation-States in the Modern Middle East." In *Tribes and State Formation in the Middle East,* edited by Philip S. Khoury and Joseph Kostiner, 127–52. Berkeley: University of California Press, 1990.

Tigay, Jeffrey H. *You Shall Have No Other Gods: Israelite Religion in the Light of Hebrew Inscriptions.* Harvard Semitic Studies 31. Atlanta: Scholars, 1986.

Toombs, Lawrence E. "Old Testament Theology and the Wisdom Literature." *Journal of Bible and Religion* 23 (1955): 193–96.

Trible, Phyllis. "Exegesis for Storytellers and Other Strangers." *Journal of Biblical Literature* 114 (1995): 3–19.

Tuell, Steven S. "Divine Presence and Absence in Ezekiel's Prophecy." In *The Book of Ezekiel: Theological and Anthropological Perspectives*, edited by Margaret S. Odell and John T. Strong, 97–116. SBL Symposium Series 9. Atlanta: Society of Biblical Literature, 2000.

Van Buren, Elizabeth Douglas. "A Cylinder Seal with a History." *Journal of Cuneiform Studies* 5 (1951): 133–34.

VanderKam, James C. "Ezra-Nehemiah or Ezra and Nehemiah?" In *Priests, Prophets and Scribes: Essays on the Formation an Heritage of Second Temple Judaism in Honour of Joseph Blenkinsopp,* edited by Eugene Ulrich et al., 55–75. Journal for the Study of the Old Testament, Supplement Series 149. Sheffield: Sheffield Academic, 1992.

van der Steen, Eveline J. "Tribes and Power Structures in Palestine and the Transjordan." *Near Eastern Archaeology* 69, no. 1 (2006): 27–47.

———. *Tribes and Territories in Transition.* Orientalia lovaniensia analecta 130. Leuven: Peeters, 2004.

van der Toorn, Karel. "Ancestors and Anthroponyms: Kinship Terms as Theophoric Elements in Hebrew Names." *Zeitschrift für die alttestamentliche Wissenschaft* 108 (1996): 1–11.

———. *Family Religion in Babylonia, Syria and Israel: Continuity and Change in the Forms of Religious Life.* Studies in the History and Culture of the Ancient Near East 7. Leiden: Brill, 1996.

———. *From Her Cradle to Her Grave: The Role of Religion in the Life of the Israelite and the Babylonian Woman.* Translated by Sara J. Denning-Bolle. Biblical Seminar. Sheffield: Sheffield Academic, 1994.

———. "God (I) אלהים." In *Dictionary of Deities and Demons in the Bible,* edited by Karel van der Toorn, Bob Becking, and Pieter W. van der Horst, 352–65. 2nd ed. Leiden: Brill, 1999.

———. "Rakib-El." In *Dictionary of Deities and Demons in the Bible,* edited by Karel van der Toorn, Bob Becking, and Pieter W. van der Horst, 686–87. 2nd ed. Leiden: Brill, 1999.

van der Toorn, Karel, Bob Becking, and Pieter W. van der Horst, eds. *Dictionary of Deities and Demons in the Bible.* 2nd ed. Leiden: Brill, 1999.

van Dijk, Jacobus. "The Authenticity of the Arslan Tash Amulets." *Iraq* 54 (1992): 65–68.

Van Leeuwen, Raymond C. "Cosmos, Temple, House: Building and Wisdom in Mesopotamia and Israel." In *Wisdom Literature in Mesopotamia and Israel,* edited by Richard J. Clifford, 67–90. Society of Biblical Literature Symposium Series 36. Leiden: Brill, 2007.

———. "Psalm 8.5 and Job 7.17-18: A Mistaken Scholarly Commonplace?" In *The World of the Aramaeans I: Biblical Studies in Honour of Paul-Eugène Dion,* edited by P. M. Michèle Daviau, John W. Wevers, and Michael Weigl, 205–215. Journal for the Study of the Old Testament, Supplement Series 324. Sheffield: Sheffield Academic, 2001.

Van Seters, John. *Prologue to History: The Yahwist as Historian in Genesis.* Louisville: Westminster, 1992.

van Voss, M. Heerma. "Ptah *פתוה / *פתה." In *Dictionary of Deities and Demons in the Bible,* edited by Karel van der Toorn, Bob Becking, and Pieter W. van der Horst, 668–69. 2nd ed. Leiden: Brill, 1999.

Virolleaud, Charles. "Sur quatre fragments alphabétiques trouvés à Ras Shamra en 1934." *Syria* 16 (1935): 181–87.

von Rad, Gerhard. "The Form-Critical Problem of the Hexateuch." In *From Genesis to Chronicles: Explorations in Old Testament Theology,* edited by K. C. Hanson, 1–58. Translated by E. W. Trueman Dicken. Minneapolis: Fortress Press, 2005.

———. "Verheissenes Land und Jahwes Land im Hexateuch." *Zeitschrift des deutschen Palästina-Vereins* 66 (1943): 191–204.

———. *Wisdom in Israel.* Translated by James D. Martin. Harrisburg, Pa.: Trinity, 1972.

Vorländer, Hermann. *Mein Gott: Die Vorstellungen vom persönlichen Gott im Alten Orient und im Alten Testament.* Alter Orient und Altes Testament 23. Kevelaer: Butzon & Bercker, 1975.

Walls, Neal H., ed. *Cult Image and Divine Representation in the Ancient Near East.* American Schools of Oriental Research Book Series 10. Boston: American Schools of Oriental Research, 2005.

Waltke, Bruce, and Michael O'Connor. *An Introduction to Biblical Hebrew Syntax.* Winona Lake, Ind.: Eisenbrauns, 1990.

Watts, James W. *Ritual and Rhetoric in Leviticus: From Sacrifice to Scripture.* Cambridge: Cambridge University Press, 2007.

Weber, Ferdinand. *Jüdische Theologie auf Grund des Talmud und verwandter Schriften.* Leipzig: Dörfflin & Franke, 1897.

Webster, Brian L. "Divine Abandonment in the Hebrew Bible." Ph.D. diss., Hebrew Union College–Jewish Institute of Religion, 2000.

Weinfeld, Moshe. "בְּרִית; bĕrīth." In *Theological Dictionary of the Old Testament,* edited by G. J. Botterweck, H. Ringgren, and H.J. Fabry, 2:253–79. Grand Rapids: Eerdmans, 1974–.

———. "The Covenant of Grant in the Old Testament and in the Ancient Near East." *Journal of the American Oriental Society* 90 (1970): 184–203.

———. *Deuteronomy and the Deuteronomic School.* Oxford: Oxford University Press, 1972. Reprint, Winona Lake, Ind.: Eisenbrauns, 1992.

———. "The Loyalty Oath in the Ancient Near East." *Ugarit-Forschungen* 8 (1976): 379–414.

———. "Traces of Treaty Formulae in Deuteronomy," *Biblica* 41 (1965): 417–27.

Weiser, Artur. *The Psalms: A Commentary.* Translated by H. Hartwell. Old Testament Library. Philadelphia: Westminster, 1962.

Wellhausen, Julius. *Prolegomena to the History of Ancient Israel.* New York: Meridian, 1957. Originally published as *Prolegomena zur Geschichte Israels* (Berlin: G. Reimer, 1883).

———. *Der Text der Bücher Samuelis.* Göttingen: Vandenhoeck & Ruprecht, 1871.

Wenham, Gordon. *Genesis 16–50.* Word Biblical Commentary 2. Dallas: Word, 1994.

Westbrook, Raymond. *Property and the Family in Biblical Law.* Journal for the Study of the Old Testament, Supplement Series 113. Sheffield: JSOT, 1991.

Westermann, Claus. *Praise and Lament in the Psalms.* Translated by Keith R. Crim and Richard N. Soulen. Atlanta: John Knox, 1981. First published 1961 (in German).

Wiggermann, F. A. M. "Theologies, Priests, and Worship in Ancient Mesopotamia." In *Civilizations of the Ancient Near East,* edited by Jack M. Sasson, 3:1857–70. New York: Scribners, 1995.

Wilcke, Claus. "Der aktuelle Bezug der Sammlung der sumerischen Tempelhymnen und ein Fragment eines Klagelieds." *Zeitschrift für Assyriologie* 62 (1972): 35–61.

Wilkinson, Richard H. *The Complete Gods and Goddesses of Ancient Egypt.* London: Thames & Hudson, 2003.

Willi, Thomas. *Die Chronik als Auslegung: Untersuchungen zur literarischen Gestaltung der historischen Überlieferung Israels.* Forschungen zur Religion und Literatur des Alten und Neuen Testaments 106. Göttingen: Vandenhoeck & Ruprecht, 1972.

Williamson, H. G. M. *1 and 2 Chronicles.* New Century Bible Commentary. Grand Rapids: Eerdmans, 1982.

Wills, Lawrence M. *The Jew in the Court of the Foreign King: Ancient Jewish Court Legends.* Harvard Dissertations in Religion 26. Minneapolis: Fortress Press, 1990.

Wilson, Gerald H. *The Editing of the Hebrew Psalter.* Society of Biblical Literature Dissertation Series 76. Chico, Calif.: Scholars, 1985.

———. "King, Messiah, and the Reign of God: Revisiting the Royal Psalms and the Shape of the Psalter." In *The Book of Psalms: Composition and Reception,* edited by Peter W. Flint and Patrick D. Miller, 391–406. Supplements to Vetus Testamentum 99. Leiden: Brill, 2005.

———. "The Shape of the Book of Psalms." *Interpretation* 46 (1992): 129–42.

Wright, G. Ernest. "The Lawsuit of God: A Form-Critical Study of Deuteronomy 32." In *Israel's Prophetic Heritage: Essays in Honor of James Muilenburg,* edited by Bernhard W. Anderson and Walter Harrelson, 26–67. New York: Harper & Brothers, 1962.

———. *The Old Testament against Its Environment.* Chicago: Regnery, 1950.

———. "The Provinces of Solomon." In *Eretz-Israel.* Vol. 8, E. L. Sukenik Volume, edited by N. Avigad et al., pp. 58*–68*. Jerusalem: Israel Exploration Society, 1967.

Xella, Paolo. "Death and the Afterlife in Canaanite and Hebrew Thought." In *Civilizations of the Ancient Near East,* edited by Jack M. Sasson, 3:2059–70. New York: Scribners, 1995.

Yee, Gale A. "Jezebel." In *The Anchor Bible Dictionary,* edited by David Noel Freedman, 3:848–49. New York: Doubleday, 1992.

Younker, Randall W. "An Ammonite Seal from Tall Jalul, Jordan: The Seal of ʾAynadab Son of Zedekʾil." In *Erets-Israel.* Vol. 26, Frank Moore Cross Volume, edited by Baruch Levine et al., pp. 221*–24*. Jerusalem: Israel Exploration Society, 1999.

Zadok, Ran. "Historical and Onomastic Notes." In *Die Welt Des Orients: Wissenschaftliche Beiträge Zur Kunde Des Morgenlandes,* edited by Wolfgang Röllig and Wolfram von Soden, 9:35–56. Göttingen: Vandenhoeck & Ruprecht, 1977.

———. "On the Amorite Material from Mesopotamia." In *The Tablet and the Scroll: Near Eastern Studies in Honor of William W. Hallo,* edited by Mark E. Cohen et al., 315–33. Bethesda, Md.: CDL, 1993.

———. *The Pre-Hellenistic Israelite Anthroponomy and Prosopography.* Orientalia lovaniensia analecta 28. Leuven: Peeters, 1988.

Zevit, Ziony. *The Religions of Ancient Israel: A Synthesis of Parallactic Approaches.* New York: Continuum, 2001.

Zimmerli, Walther. *Ezekiel: A Commentary on the Book of the Prophet Ezekiel.* 2 vols. Hermeneia. Philadelphia: Fortress, 1979, 1983.

———. *Old Testament Theology in Outline.* Atlanta: John Knox, 1978.

———. "The Place and the Limit of the Wisdom in the Framework of the Old Testament Theology." In *Studies in Ancient Israelite Wisdom,* edited by James L. Crenshaw, 314–26. New York: KTAV, 1976.

Scripture Index

Author Index

Subject Index

42, cultic significance, 145–46, 225n84

ʾay / ʾiy, 5, 30. *See also* Where?-names
Abel, 28, 81
Abraham, 16, 54
Abrahamic covenant, 50. *See also* covenant
Adad, 12, 20
adoption, 21
adulterous woman. *See* Woman Wisdom
afterlife, 64, 65
Ahiqar, 91–92, 101
Akkadian, 12, 31, 32, 40, 82, 91, 103, 194–95n47
alliances. *See* kinship
alternate names, 37
Ammon/Ammonites, 19, 186n58
Amun, 3, 45
ancestral god. *See* god of the fathers, household god
Annunaki. *See* Mesopotamian myths
anthropomorphism, 9-10, 11, 14, 110, 181n9. *See also* theophany
anthroponyms. *See* names; theophoric names
Anu. *See* Mesopotamian myths
Apsu. *See* Mesopotamian myths
Aramaic, 36–37, 91
ark of the covenant, 35, 40, 133, 141, 154–55, 160, 163, 225n77
Asherah/Athirat. *See* Ugaritic
Assur/Ashur. *See* national/state deities; Assyria
Assyria, 24, 32
Atrahasis, 10, 11, 65, 77, 82, 83

Aya, 32
Ayyah, 31, 39

Baal, 3, 4, 31, 36, 54, 66, 121
Babel, 82
Babylon, 10, 54, 82, 107
Babylonian Exile, 2, 78; and ritual, 126, 128; and Jerusalem, 144, 147, 161. *See also* hidden God; Jerusalem
behavior, right. *See* fear of God
blood, 125
boundary. *See* center-periphery opposition; chaos
Bronze Age, 18, 31, 68
Bundesformel. *See* covenant

Cain, 28, 81–82
calendar, Festal, 121
Canaanite, 49, 53, 121, 127
celebration, 116–17, 120
center-periphery opposition: and boundary, 116–17, 119–20, 124, 177; examples, 81, 82, 109; and temple theology, 123, 127, 148–49, 159, 161, 167
centralization (of worship), 140, 149, 159–161, 163–65, 173, 177. *See also* Jerusalem; temple
chaos, 109, 110, 137; and creation, 54, 80; worship as boundary, 116–17, 119
childbirth, 42
children of Ammon, 19
children of Israel, 15, 19
clans, 17, 18, 47
companions, with animals, 80. *See also* divine-human relationship

283

55 Deuz ?

176 The 3- tiered Universe
Universe

144 ISA - when that also offends the Syrian

con ISA 4   §ISA p.11, 74 -
47   147 The Land - 121
18a 9   46 Zion offered his place
47, 49   53 The Rich Man
148   you
154 -f
defeat taken as absence
The Ark narrative(?)
166   177

538 Deut 6:5 "ungrateful
Deut.   loyalty"

71 Gen 28:10-22
Jacob at the Jephel Site

157 Ezek: "Present - but h
what he wants

151-8 "On the" D' hosting X
(NOT)